THE PEOPLE'S HEALTH

States, People, and the History of Social Change

Series editors Rosalind Crone and Heather Shore

The States, People, and the History of Social Change series brings together cutting-edge books written by academic historians on criminal justice, welfare, education, health, and other areas of social change and social policy. The ways in which states, governments, and local communities have responded to 'social problems' can be seen across many different temporal and geographical contexts. From the early modern period to contemporary times, states have attempted to shape the lives of their inhabitants in important ways. Books in this series explore how groups and individuals have negotiated the use of state power and policy to regulate, change, control, or improve peoples' lives and the consequences of these processes. The series welcomes international scholars whose research explores social policy (and its earlier equivalents) as well as other responses to social need, in historical perspective.

The People's Health

Health Intervention and Delivery

in Mao's China, 1949–1983

ZHOU XUN

McGill-Queen's University Press

Montreal & Kingston • London • Chicago

ISBN 978-0-2280-0193-5 (cloth)
ISBN 978-0-2280-0194-2 (paper)
ISBN 978-0-2280-0327-4 (ePDF)

Legal deposit third quarter 2020
Bibliothèque nationale du Québec

Printed in Canada on acid-free paper that is 100% ancient forest free
(100% post-consumer recycled), processed chlorine free

Funded by the   Financé par le
Government   gouvernement
of Canada   du Canada

Canada Council   Conseil des arts
for the Arts   du Canada

We acknowledge the support of the Canada Council for the Arts.
Nous remercions le Conseil des arts du Canada de son soutien.

Library and Archives Canada Cataloguing in Publication

Title: The people's health : health intervention and delivery in Mao's China,
1949–1983 / Zhou Xun.
Names: Zhou, Xun, 1968– author.
Series: States, people, and the history of social change ; 2.
Description: Series statement: States, people and the history of social change ; 2
  | Includes bibliographical references and index.
Identifiers: Canadiana (print) 20200201689 | Canadiana (ebook) 20200201697
  | ISBN 9780228001935 (cloth) | ISBN 9780228001942 (paper) | ISBN
  9780228003274 (ePDF)
Subjects: LCSH: Medical policy—China—History—20th century. | LCSH: Medical
  care—China—History—20th century. | LCSH: Public health—China—History
  20th century. | LCSH: China—History—1949-1976.
Classification: LCC RA395.C6 Z46 2020 | DDC 362.10951/0904—dc23

This book was typeset in 10.5/13 Sabon.

I dedicate this book to my parents, who with many of their colleagues worked day and night for more than fifty years trying to bring parasitic diseases such as schistosomiasis under some degree of control.

Contents

Figures

Acknowledgments

This book is a part of bigger project funded by the European Commission Research Executive Agency (REA). Between September 2014 and December 2018, I was in receipt of the Marie Curie Career Integration Grants (CIG) PCIG14-GA-2013-631344 from the REA. This grant allowed me to carry out essential research for this book, which I acknowledge with gratitude. I also thank the Universities' China Committee in London (UCCL). In 2013, the UCCL gave me a travel grant that enabled me to fly to China to conduct preliminary research for this project. In May 2015, the International Centre for Studies of Chinese Civilization (ICSCC) at Fudan University in China provided generous financial support for the international workshop Old and New Paradigms of Public Health: Historical Perspectives and Global Challenges. I was the convenor for the workshop. This book has benefitted greatly from the conversations generated at that workshop.

During the course of my research, I benefitted greatly from conversations with Yuan Hongchang, formerly of the School of Public Health at Fudan University and a renowned expert in schistosomiasis control in China, and Gu Xueguang, formerly of the Sichuan Provincial Centre for Disease Control and Prevention. Professor Gu also helped me to arrange some of my research trips in southwestern China. I am grateful to my parents, in particular my mother for giving me much help and useful insights as well as constant support while I was researching for this book in China. I would also like to thank He Yongkang, the deputy director at the Hunan Provincial Schistosomiasis Control Institute, for assisting me with my research in Hunan. I am indebted to Zhang Lihua, the former director of the

Jiaxing City Library in Zhejiang province. She provided me with invaluable assistance during my many research trips to Jiaxing. Chen Ling at Hangzhou Dianzi University helped me to conduct archival research at the Zhejiang Provincial Archive. Long Haiying at the Kaili High School helped to arrange an oral history field trip in southeastern Guizhou. Socrates Litsios, the former senior scientist in the WHO's Division of the Control of Tropical Diseases, Iijima Wataru, a historian of medicine at Aoyama Gakuin University in Tokyo, Hilary Rose, visiting professor of sociology at the London School of Economics and emeritus professor of social policy at the University of Bradford, Li Yushang at Shanghai Jiaotong University, and the late Gao Wanglin, formerly of Renmin University of China and Qinghua University, were generous in sharing their works and insights. I wish to thank them. I also thank Dr Vivienne Lo, director of the UCL China Centre for Health and Humanities, for helping to shape my initial ideas about this project.

My heartfelt thanks go to Sander L. Gilman, distinguished professor of liberal arts and sciences as well as professor of psychiatry at Emory University, for his invaluable suggestions and encouragement throughout my research. Without his support, this book would not have been possible. I also wish to thank Sheila Hillier, visiting professor at the School of Public Health, the Chinese University of Hong Kong, and emeritus professor of medical sociology at Queen Mary University of London for the enthusiastic and steadfast support she has given me in the course of writing this book. She kindly read a draft version, and, as always, her useful comments are much appreciated.

I thank Nicola Gray for carefully reading the draft manuscript and her invaluable suggestions for improvement, in particularly with the English language.

During the course of composition, several people read portions of the manuscript, listened to my ideas, or made insightful suggestions. They are Paul Thompson, the British oral historian and emeritus professor of sociology at the University of Essex; Dušan Radunović, an expert in Soviet cinema at Durham University; Anne Summers, a historian of medicine at Birkbeck College, University of London; Tim H. Barrett, emeritus professor of East Asia history at the School of Orient and African Studies (SOAS); David Napier, a medical anthropologist at the University College London (UCL); and Mike Jay, an author and cultural historian who has written extensively on scientific and medical history. I am grateful to the History

Department at the University of Essex for providing me with the environment and essential support needed for me to continue my research and complete this book.

Finally, I wish to thank McGill-Queen's University Press for its commitment and enthusiasm and in particular my editor, Richard Baggaley, for his crucial assistance.

Zhou Xun
Essex, 2020

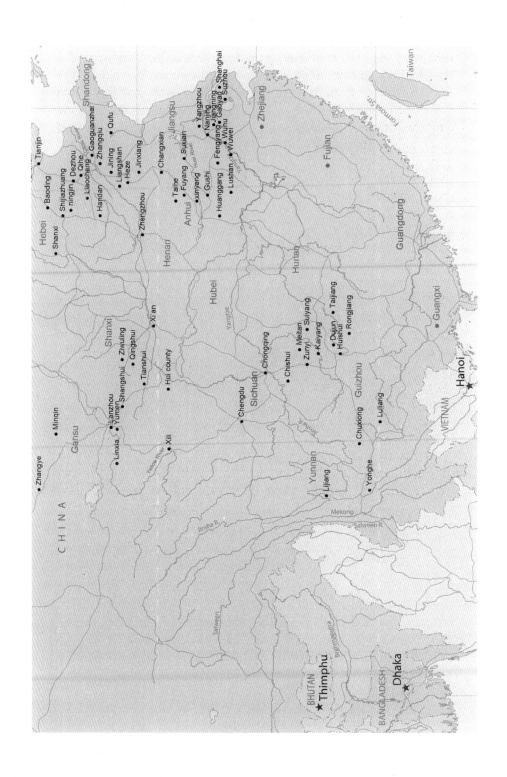

THE PEOPLE'S HEALTH

Introduction

WHAT IS THE PEOPLE'S HEALTH?

This is a book about the people's health in the modern age.[1] From the medieval practice of quarantining a ship to control the Black Death in 1377 in Dubrovnik to John Snow locking the water pumps in Victorian London in 1854 to prevent the spread of cholera, the idea of preventing the spread of disease demanded looking at social control as providing some sort of immediate intervention to preserve life. The goal was, and is, the gradual elimination of those factors that are seen as damaging to health, but the underlying idea is the creation of a world in which health is a right guaranteed by the state. The pursuit of this goal was to be accomplished through institutions such as public health authorities and via credentialed medical practitioners entrusted with improving the people's health. This book looks at the debates about and the practices that were introduced to improve the people's health in the People's Republic of China (the PRC) as a product of the politics of the Cold War, from the Communist Party's seizure and coalescing of power in 1949 to the period immediately after the death of Mao Zedong in 1976, in a global context. Health played an outsized role in the internal politics of the new Communist state and came in complex ways to define the PRC globally. My focus is on how the state imagines medicine being utilized as a tool of political action. This has been examined before, if not in the same detail. What lies at the core of my interest is to examine how the people who were impacted by the politics of health responded to control from 'above' and to examine the experts' views and their national and global reception, as well as looking at how such interventions were experienced from 'below' by listening to those impacted by disease and the policies developed to confront its causes and to cure those people who were/are impacted by the disease. Such a perspective is not an attempt merely to imagine a centre/periphery model of tension between the state and the individual but to outline how resistance or acquiescence among those impacted by state policies concerning health and illness continued to shape and reshape health policy in the PRC under Mao. Simultaneously, such varying levels of power reflected the use from 'above' and 'below' of both 'expert' and 'popular' medicine, of models of allopathic medicine that arose in the first great age of Western biology at the close of the nineteenth century, and systems of folk medicine (as defined from the perspective of allopathic medicine) that jumbled religious or ritual practices, systems of popular medicine, and folklore, as practised among the various population groups living in China. At the core are the shifting patterns of state power, of how health policy came to be one of the central means of impacting and influencing the 'masses' – and how both expert and popular medicine became tools of political power. The reality in the end is how those who were ill or at risk believed in the efficacy of such claims, for good or for ill.

This book is neither intended to be a comparative history of disease eradication across different countries nor 'merely' an internal history of the people's health in the PRC. Such a history, as I shall show in detail, reflects the shifts on the national level as a result of changes in the global understanding of the people's health and the role of the state as its provider and protector. Globally, such shifts occurred in the shadow of the nineteenth and early twentieth centuries. Claims about the role of the state as an active agent in intervening to control the spread of disease and the concomitant colonial medical practice were developed to improve the people's health in Asia and Africa as a means of improving productivity (in a new field labelled 'tropical medicine'). But after the collapse of both Imperial Japan and Nazi Germany in 1945 – states that used health as a rationale for the cruellest and most horrific experiments in promoting the people's health and for many of the same goals as the colonial powers as well as in the context of genocidal racial policies – such models of the 'white man's burden' in public health became untenable. Following the trials of the Nazi doctors at Nuremberg in 1947, there was a search globally for a positive model for what had become a discredited claim that the state needed to protect, preserve, and further the people's health, and this came to be found in Communist China under Mao.

The image of the PRC, the country most identified by many international health stakeholders as a 'positive deviant' in the 'Long 1970s' in achieving better health outcomes with limited resources, is a prime example of the search for answers to the people's health in the mid–twentieth century and beyond. My goal here is to illustrate how politics and health are inextricably linked in the PRC. Policy shifts were not merely internal debates about specific approaches to the people's health among specialists in public health in the PRC. They were at once responses to global attitudes toward health systems, in particular health care delivery and public health intervention but also, in turn, helped to shape them. While the PRC was a developing country during the Cold War, the claims about health and health care in China also reflected the concerns in many developing countries about the efficacy of their own health systems. Cold War politics impacted medical practice and public health initiatives, and China became the touchstone for such discussions.

HOW DO WE EXAMINE THE PEOPLE'S HEALTH?

What is different about what I am undertaking here is both the reach of the evidence and my methodology. Social scientists (specifically those working in anthropology, development studies, and policy design), as well as historians, deploy history in different ways to achieve different insights. In this book, I have tried to find a balance between the pragmatic needs of the social scientist and the demands of the historian that will contribute to a 'more rounded' history of health and medicine in the PRC. It begins with techniques familiar to social historians of medicine that describe the human stories behind the statistics. More specifically, it uses an integrated approach by analyzing the accounts of local implementation and individual testimonies about health care against the state-sanctioned statistical analyses and official party rhetoric. Local and personal stories, for example, shed crucial light on issues of access, inequalities, and so on, while statistics, as a larger evaluation of impact across populations, may point to a different assessment of individual opportunity and entitlement. Official rhetoric and reports from the archives provide the necessary background information, chronology, and statistics that are often missing in the oral interviews. The oral interviews, on the other hand, tell of individual experiences of and interactions with, as well as resistance to, such large-scale government health campaigns. Through the interviews,* we learn the particular way in which individuals remember these past events but not how they were actually implemented or intended to function. Juxtapose one to the other and there is a fuller sense of what was occurring at the time in different places, as well as of how historical memory shaped individual memories and how individuals' remembrances of what happened have continued to impact their lives up to the present day. Based on hundreds of files from rarely seen party archives in eight impacted provinces across China, and on freshly collected oral testimonies from experts, local cadres, and villagers in those provinces, we can now illustrate the huge diversity of everyday interactions and the diverse aspects of support, accommodation, and resistance.† By analyzing local implementations and personal testimonies against statistical analysis and political rhetoric, we can better understand the many complexities involved in the implementation of large-scale public health initiatives. While analysis of these cases provides immediate lessons for those seeking to strengthen health systems, it also generates background information for future research. Since health systems are, essentially, collections of people, this book is as much about the human story of innovations and responsiveness to changing politics and human needs as it is about the politics of health. The oral testimonies, as with my earlier work on the Great Leap famine as well as Gail Hershatter's work on the lives of rural women in the early PRC, open a unique window into what life was like for different individuals living under communism.[2]

---

* I have concealed the true identities of the people interviewed. This is to protect their privacy and for political considerations.

† I selected eight county and provincial archives where relatively rich documentation can be deemed representative of the many dimensions of state interaction in everyday life. All these provinces present a measure of geographical and political diversity, and they went through very different experiences under Mao. These provinces are also interesting because they contain areas where the Anti-Schistosomiasis Campaign or the Barefoot Doctor program were most vigorously carried out.

MY TWO CASE STUDIES

To illustrate the complexity of both the voices heard from 'below' and the political and expert culture from 'above', I focus on the two internationally acclaimed public health initiatives in the PRC under Mao Zedong's leadership – namely, the Anti-Schistosomiasis Campaign and the Barefoot Doctor program – as case studies to explore the complex and dynamic relationships between politics and health and, equally important, between individual lives and the political system as well as the health system. It is clear that public health objectives became an integral part of the Chinese revolution from its outset in 1911 through the 1920s. Medicine had been part of European 'soft power' in China from the time of Western missionaries such as Peter Parker in the early nineteenth century* to the various medical undertakings of the Rockefeller Foundation in the early twentieth century. The world of post–World War II China, which came under Mao's leadership after 1949, presented continuities as well as ruptures with this already revolutionary political and public health world. I do not assert that the contested claims of the success and failures of the PRC's health system as reflected by these two case studies are wholly accurate or inaccurate; rather, these claims must be understood through the political visions that formed the public health initiatives and shaped the accounts about them both within and beyond the PRC. We can develop a better and more nuanced understanding of the Chinese approach to health by exploring the processes through which the Maoist health system was conceived and the political context in which they were, and could be, evaluated. My perspective in evaluating the Maoist health system ranges from the political (and poetic) pronouncements attributed to Mao to the popular experience on the ground of the Anti-Schistosomiasis Campaign and the Barefoot Doctor programme.

The centrepiece of the PRC's public health campaign was the Anti-Schistosomiasis Campaign. This campaign began in 1955 when Mao was mounting the 'Socialist High Tide' to bring the socialist revolution to the Chinese countryside. The Communist state singled out schistosomiasis because it is a disease transmitted by working in the

---

* Peter Parker (1804–1888) was the first American Protestant medical missionary to China. In 1835, he opened Ophthalmic Hospital in Canton. This was the first Western-style hospital in China.

paddy fields and is aided in this by the traditional way of life of the farming communities living in rice-growing regions. It was decided that the national goal should be to eradicate it. Schistosomiasis is a disease that afflicted people in many parts of the underdeveloped world, and it was thought that it would bring prestige to the country if the PRC could be the first to eliminate it. The central party leadership declared that the goal of eradication would be achieved in seven years – although this obviously did not happen. In fact, toward the end of the Great Leap Forward in the early 1960s, the morbidity rate was sharply on the rise. By this time, the rural health system had essentially collapsed, and people had turned back to local traditional practitioners. From these localized initiatives emerged the 'Barefoot Doctors', and the Chinese Communist Party (CCP) more or less adopted a system that people had already shown that they wanted and rolled it out locally – all of which speaks to the legitimacy that the CCP lost in the aftermath of the famine that had resulted from the Great Leap Forward.

The PRC's public health initiatives in the Anti-Schistosomiasis Campaign and the Barefoot Doctor program are well known around the world because they became the touchstone for public health innovations during the Cold War. A historical account of how these campaigns were implemented and received at the local level throughout China on the political as well as on the experiential level that also addresses their impact on global health is long overdue. Until now there has been no systematic study of the health system in the PRC under Mao Zedong's leadership. The reason for this is simple: from 1949 to 1976, China was largely closed to the West. Needless to say, there were many difficulties in undertaking extensive, nationwide oral histories. Even after the country opened its doors following the death of Mao, access to party archives remained extremely difficult, forcing researchers to rely on published official and semi-official literature. Lack of access to primary data other than policy formulations and party propaganda meant that the earlier historical literature could do no more than provide a very general survey of the field, unable to offer any concrete evidence or critical insights regarding how health care was actually experienced by the population at large.[3] Social scientists have focused rather narrowly on state policy formulations alone, and therefore little is known about how these grand schemes were actually carried out on the ground and experienced by the communities involved.[4] Even the few detailed historical studies of traditional Chinese medicine, such as that by Kim Taylor, are based on published policy documents and propaganda material.[5] Furthermore, Taylor's analysis relied heavily on what is now agreed by historians of the PRC as an outdated historiography in which the CCP was credited with establishing a stable government after decades of war and political turmoil and with carrying out a successful social transformation program, including public health initiatives. To date, there are only a small handful of excellent ethnographically based case studies of the Barefoot Doctor program, but these studies are focused on specific villages.[6] There is one historical assessment of the Anti-Schistosomiasis Campaign in a particular region in eastern China.[7] All of these studies have a narrow geographic focus, yet it is all too apparent that no broad historical analysis can be based on a mere handful of archival files narrowly selected from one single holding or on interviews from a single village. This present book does not enter into the debate about whether the Chinese public health policy was a success or a failure. Instead, I focus on how people experienced these public health campaigns by ranging more widely across China and listening to the participants, as well as reading archival materials that only became available in the late 1990s. As a result of the new national regulations regarding archives, introduced in the 1990s, this book is able to offer a more nuanced account of the debates about the people's health in the PRC under Mao Zedong and how they were perceived on multiple levels in society. My intent is neither to praise nor to condemn the activities but to provide an account of the often-unintended consequences attendant to them.

THE COURSE OF THE PEOPLE'S HEALTH IN THE PRC

From the onset of the Chinese Communist revolution in the 1920s to the end of World War II in the mid-1940s, shortly before the CCP seized power, public health objectives were an integral part of the ideology of the revolution. The overwhelming poverty in the Chinese countryside, which signalled China's backwardness to the world, was linked to the poor hygiene and poor health of the rural population. China was the 'Sick Man of Asia' in more than one way. Leaders of the revolution, including Mao Zedong, who was to become the supreme head of the CCP and chairman of the PRC in 1949, believed that improving rural health and medical care would therefore open the door for modernization. Between the late 1920s and the 1940s, in the CCP-controlled Soviet bases, public health work became a priority for the party. The communist praxis was to change manners of living, moving toward the modernization of the collective. To reach such goals, including those of public health, it was inevitable that the whole population had to be involved as part of the transformative vision of the CCP.

After the CCP seized power in 1949, it quickly took on the challenge of eradicating the snail-borne parasite *Schistosomiasis japonica* (usually labelled simply as schistosomiasis). The national Anti-Schistosomiasis Campaign linked allopathic medicine and public health work with the ongoing legitimization of the new order. Interrelated with the predominant agricultural way of life, especially for rural, rice-growing farmers, schistosomiasis has been endemic in much of China's rice-growing regions along and south of the Yangtze River. Historically, the disease had evoked widespread fear in these regions. It was believed to have contributed to infertility and thus was perceived as the cause of under-population and poor productivity, the underlying causes of China's rural poverty. Immediately upon the founding of the PRC in 1949, schistosomiasis was elevated to one of the most serious diseases that needed to be combated. Fighting the disease was viewed as vital to national security, productivity, and the military manpower of the new state and came to stand for fighting for socialism.

Furthermore, the difficulty of controlling the disease, widely acknowledged internationally, proved a real test for the new Communist state. To eradicate something and succeed where others, especially 'Western' (which often stands for 'imperialist') experts, had failed was a prize worth trying for. Public health teams, trained and led by experts, took the first steps in the campaign to control the disease. Their job was to discover the extent of the problem, and for them this was a proper and necessary public health objective. At the same time, conquering an intractable medical and public health problem would also bring them global scientific prestige. In this respect, both the CCP and the experts potentially had a win/win situation – if they could succeed.

Central economic and political planning was extended helter-skelter across the country during the first decade of the PRC. Concurrent with this, the central government's sense of urgency with regard to schistosomiasis control, as with many other aspects involved in centralization, caused the local responses to the complexities of the hasty implementation of such a massive public health campaign to be fragmented and often contradictory. By bringing those directly impacted by the campaign (from the villagers involved to the cadres in charge of implementing the campaign) back into this history and seeing them as active participants in this state public health campaign, we can see how great plans on paper were transformed into makeshift solutions that bore little or no resemblance to the original political project as soon as they encountered the wide variety of human experiences of health, disease, and, indeed, changing politics. To overcome obstacles, in the early stage of the campaign, the frontline workers, or the CCP cadres managing the day-to-day control of the disease, understood the need to be persuasive rather than authoritarian in their approach. This was reflected in the extensive public health propaganda as well as in the more detailed and local organizational work during this period.

Beginning in 1956, as an integral part of the transformative project of the CCP to end rural poverty, the mass population in the Chinese countryside was mobilized in a nationwide eradication campaign aimed at the various vectors of disease, in particular the water-borne snails that transmitted the infectious agent that causes *Schistosomiasis japonica*. With the advent of the Great Leap Forward between 1957 and 1960, there was an even greater political demand to speed up the process of eliminating the snails. Land reclamation and irrigation schemes were methods used to bury and hence kill the snails. Not only did this prove extremely costly and wasteful, but these schemes also ran into conflict with the system for water conservation, contributing to severe flooding as well as causing alkalization of the soil. In the end, the reclamation initiatives had to be abandoned, and hence the snails returned. The subsequent switch to killing the snails using molluscicides further damaged the ecosystem, with long-lasting negative consequences on the environment.

This period of radical and rapid political change also saw intensification of direct treatment through the application of shorter courses of the highly toxic antimony tartrate (tartar emetic), an accepted intervention of the time known to control the infection. Such an approach was not only limited in its effectiveness, but many people died from exposure to the substance. At the same moment, the utopian project of the Great Leap Forward, aimed at transforming the Chinese countryside into a communist paradise, subsequently led to the worst famine in history, which lasted for four years between 1958 and 1962 and claimed tens of millions of lives as well as many animals. This, needless to say, also complicated the earlier eradication initiatives. At the height of the Great Leap Forward, and in the aftermath of the famine, millions of new agricultural migrants as well as farm animals were sent to the infected regions to help with agricultural production. A huge number of people and animals were infected by schistosomiasis, while many who had been cured of the disease became re-infected. In the meantime, famine-related oedema, gynaecological problems, and child malnutrition became even more widespread in the countryside. Unable to cope with the crisis, the PRC's rural health system literally collapsed. In the face of diminishing returns, in order to control the collapse of the public health system, ever more authoritarian and centralized methods came into play. With increasing desperation and despite the claims being made, officials saw the promised goal of schistosomiasis eradication and the rural utopia it was to help create slipping away from them.

Since it became clear that the centralized approach to people's health was neither politically effective nor even feasible, the result, whether intentional or not, was the decentralization of the PRC's health care delivery in response to the post-famine rural health crisis. From 1965 to 1977, the shift was away from expert, centralized programs that dealt with the people's health, such as the Anti-Schistosomiasis Campaign, to a focus on what would come to be called the 'Barefoot Doctor' program. With the collapse of the rural health system, villagers took their health and well-being into their own hands. From stories that emerged from previously unseen archive documents and from interviews with a wide swathe of those involved in the Barefoot Doctor program, as well as with the experts, some of whom continued to undertake their specialized research on schistosomiasis control during this period, we can learn much about a number of local health and medical innovations. Many of these local innovations involved the quiet acquiescence, if not active cooperation, of the local cadres. These initially quiet and local health initiatives in villages were accelerated by the post-famine decentralization of rural health care delivery in the PRC. They also coincided with a series of political campaigns during this period that tried to re-establish more centralized control in the wake of the chaos caused by the famine. The climax was the Great Proletarian Cultural Revolution, which began in 1966 and lasted until Mao's death in 1976. At this time, the Ministry of Health, as well as the 'expert' allopathic medicine and public health models, came under fire as part of Mao's effort to dismantle the technocratic and bureaucratic structure that had by then been firmly established in the PRC. The Barefoot Doctor program and other local innovations, including the training of village health workers and the revival of some local healing practices, came to represent those 'newly emerged revolutionary things' intended to replace the 'old bourgeois' expert- and hospital-centred health system.

In 1968, at the height of the Great Proletarian Cultural Revolution, the Barefoot Doctor program, coupled with the Rural Co-operative Medical System (RCMS), was officially launched. By 1976, as we are told, 90 per cent of China was covered by the RCMS, and Barefoot Doctors could be seen throughout rural China providing invaluable if often unequal care and aid to millions of villagers. The radical differences in training and resources, as recounted by the participants, often led to the provision of inefficient and insufficient health care, but this sometimes encouraged relatively untrained practitioners to acquire further knowledge, in the realms of both allopathic and alternative systems of medicine, from the codified 'Traditional Chinese Medicine' (TCM) to folk medicines.

What had begun as a hodgepodge of local initiatives, together with fragments of expert medicine that evolved in response to the collapse of the state health care system during the years of famine, came by the Long 1970s to be the public face of the PRC in its relationship with the 'First' and 'Third' Worlds. During this period of the Cold War, the 'Chinese approach to health' came to hold out the promise of a true alternative to the crumbling, single disease–centred 'vertical' health care program advocated by the United States or the centralized health care structure of the Soviet Union. Having seen that neither model was truly effective in improving the people's health, Western public health professionals and policy-makers sought a way out of the perceived Western post-war health crisis. The PRC's Barefoot Doctor program and the Anti-Schistosomiasis Campaign came to be seen as the 'best show in town'. They were widely cited by international public health experts as evidence of the PRC's purportedly superior primary health care system. This was simultaneously an implied critique of the earlier approaches taken by the British and the American health authorities and other international health organizations, which denied the participation of the impacted communities in health care delivery. Neither the post-war American public health system, exemplified by the creation of the Centers for Disease Control in 1946 (as the Communicable Disease Center) nor William Beveridge's model of the National Health Service (NHS), which was introduced in the UK by Aneurin Bevan in the same year, bore the same sort of utopian promise for the economically strapped 'Third' World. Halfdan Mahler, the new director general of the World Health Organization (WHO) at the time, and his colleague Kenneth Newell felt strongly that the Chinese approach to tackling health problems with limited financial, technological, and human resources should be promoted around the world. In 1975, Mahler proposed 'Health for All', and this was adopted by the Twenty-Ninth World Health Assembly in 1976 as its goal, to be achieved by the year 2000. Two years later, in 1978, it was formally included in the Declaration of Alma Ata.

In the meantime, the PRC leadership realized that health initiatives could be 'inexpensive but profitable' undertakings, which could boost its effort to promote a new international order: a 'people's revolutionary movement' against colonialism, imperialism, and hegemonism. Between 1963 and 1989, the PRC sent medical teams to more than forty countries in Africa. In addition, China gave medical and health training to a large number of students from Africa, Southeast Asia, and Latin America, competing with the extensive parallel programs for training physicians in the Soviet Union. With this expansion, the PRC's influence on health systems in Africa, Asia, and Latin America grew exponentially. But the reputation of the medical model evolved in the PRC turned out to be phantasmagoric. All of the praise by physicians and public health specialists who visited China in the Long 1970s was based, at best, on selective reporting and visits and, at worst, on a level of self-deception that was rooted in the desire for a utopian model that seamlessly integrated medical, social, and economic goals. Yet the PRC's model became the gold standard for global public health.

In 1977, Kenneth Warren was appointed director of health science at the Rockefeller Foundation. Warren and his colleague Julia Walsh argued that the goal set at Alma Ata was 'unattainable because of the cost and numbers of trained personnel required'. They proposed a Selective Primary Health Care model that introduced a package of low-cost technical interventions to tackle the main disease problems as an interim strategy for disease control in developing countries

(1979).[8] A number of United Nation agencies quickly adopted this selective approach, since it was less costly than the more integrated approached advocated by Mahler and Newell. Known to be obsessed with health quality and information, Warren advocated this model of 'good healthcare at low cost', with an emphasis on expert medicine. As an expert on schistosomiasis, he favoured controlling the disease with chemotherapy. According to him, using newer single-dose, oral, non-toxic chemotherapeutic agents in treating the disease simply cost less than attempts to eliminate snails. Warren used the PRC's Anti-Schistosomiasis Campaign as his counter-argument. He argued that the Chinese approach of involving the rural masses to kill the snails by burying old canals and digging new ones was too costly and ineffective in controlling the disease, at least for the interim period.[9] Warren's study also cast doubt on the earlier claim that the Chinese had successfully eradicated the disease. The subsequent re-evaluation in the West, as well as in China itself, of the PRC's health system of the Mao era (1949–76) suggested that the original claims for the superior health care system, and for the eradication of schistosomiasis, were, indeed, to a great extent invalid.

Coincidentally, the post-Mao PRC leadership under Deng Xiaoping after 1978 gradually embraced the neoliberal market economy and opted for a selective primary health care model, with an emphasis on specialized and hospital-centred health care as well as a focus on short-term economic gain. Health professionals in the PRC were prompted to 'put their shoes on' in order to catch up with developments in medicine and health care in the West. In 1983, the internationally acclaimed Barefoot Doctor program was officially abandoned, and millions of disadvantaged rural villagers, together with urban migrants, were deprived of access to any form of health care. My extensive interviews with experts, health officials, former Barefoot Doctors, and individuals who lived through this transition demonstrate that there has been a deepening inequality between urban and rural health care. These interviews also demonstrate that, once again, in some quiet corners of China, individuals and communities took health and well-being into their own hands. Yet, with little support and even disapproval from the authorities, many of the local health initiatives and health workers could not sustain either their efforts or their livelihood. The PRC may serve as a model for public health dysfunction as well as for successful adaptation, depending on the level of analysis and the historical context in which it is found.

In modern times, a well-functioning health system has been seen as intrinsic to the well-being of any society, but we know little about how to achieve such a system. Health systems, by definition, are complex and dynamic. In the end, they are the work of collections of people and are designed for the people. Inevitably, all health systems carry within them human strengths and weaknesses. While political vision and the leadership's ability to mobilize the masses may contribute to a better health system and ultimately better health, political factors can also have unintended yet real negative consequences. The story of the debates about improving the people's health in the first three decades of the People's Republic of China can serve as much a model for such complexity as it served as an ideal, if badly flawed, model for the improvement of people's health throughout the world during many decades of the twentieth century. Today, such problems continue to haunt developed as well as developing countries: no model has turned out to be sufficient to cover all of the problems confronting people's health. The utopian vision of Mao's programs have given way to the pragmatics of dealing with each social and medical problem in its existing context rather than applying a universal panacea that guarantees the people's health. The desire for such programs (the 'mirage of health', as Rene Dubois put it[10]) remains, and the notion that the goal of the public's health is static and that approaches need only be sharpened and improved, which haunted all of the attempts in the PRC, is still a dream being pursued, even if the history of such approaches is littered not only with half-successes but also with greater failures and unintended, often fatal, consequences.

I

Declaring War on Schistosomiasis

THE MILITARY ENCOUNTERS DISEASE

In the extremely cold winter of January 1949, the Communist Party's
Eastern China Field Army under the leadership of General Su Yu, in
collaboration with the Central Plain Field Army, successfully completed the third phase of the Huai River (military) Campaign. The
battle, which lasted sixty-six days during the winter of 1948 and
1949, has been widely regarded as the most decisive victory for the
Communist army during the Chinese Civil War. It resulted in the
Nationalists losing more than 550,000 soldiers, almost half of their
entire army. The end of the ten-year civil war brought hope to millions living on the war-torn northern and central China plain. In the
meantime, on 15 January 1949, the Communists' Northeastern and
Northern China Field Armies, led by Marshall Gao Gang, captured
Tianjin, one of the most important port cities in northern China.
Defenceless, Fu Zuoyi, the Nationalist general in charge of northern China, surrendered. On 31 January, the third day of the Year
of the Earth Ox in the Chinese calendar, the Communists' People's
Liberation Army (PLA) marched peacefully into Peking, the 'City of
Northern Peace' (today it is called Beijing, 'the Northern Capital').
As the early warm spring wind swept across the north China plain,
people in Peking and the surrounding regions danced to celebrate
the New Year as well as to welcome the Communist soldiers. Many
civilians saw the coming of the PLA soldiers as an auspicious sign –
the Earth Ox sent by heaven. In Chinese mythology, the arrival of
the Earth Ox represents heavenly promise. To realize this heavenly
promise, however, would involve paying a price in hard labour.[1]

For those who lived south of the Yangtze River, as well as in China's deep southwest, the conflict and its concomitant uncertainty dragged on. After the spectacular victory at the Huai River Campaign, the Chinese Communist Party (CCP) and the PLA leadership did not rest. The dream of unifying China entailed more difficult struggles. In February, the Eastern China Field Army underwent serious reorganization and changed its name to the Third Field Army. Once again, General Su Yu was put in charge of the critical military campaign to cross the Yangtze. In anticipation of the campaign, Su selected some of his finest young soldiers for preparatory training. To ford the river would entail fighting in the water, but the majority of Su's soldiers were from Shandong province and were not used to fighting on waterways. A major part of their training was therefore intensive swimming lessons in the labyrinth of creeks on the edge of the Yangtze near Anhui province. Yang Qiaoyun oversaw the army's health activities. Sixty years later, in a memoir, Qiaoyun recalled how General Su's soldiers were spirited and motivated and how they quickly immersed themselves in the aquatic training. Soon, however, many of them suffered from severe diarrhoea and high fever, making them unfit for action. Unprepared for this, Qiaoyun remembered, the army doctors, most of whom were also from northern China, misdiagnosed the problem as dysentery and malaria and treated it accordingly. Unable to see any improvement, the army's health unit engaged some medical experts from local hospitals and the Nationalist government's Central Health Station. After examining their faeces, the experts determined that the soldiers were infected with a locally endemic disease, schistosomiasis japonicum.[2]

Schistosomiasis japonicum (schistosomiasis, hereafter), also known as 'oriental bilharzia', was linked to the rural way of life and especially rice-growing farmers. It is caused by the blood fluke *Schistosomiasis japonica*. The larval form of this parasite lives in snails, but it can penetrate the human body via the skin when contacted in water. In the first instance, those infected would often experience minor symptoms of abdominal pain, diarrhoea, and blood in their stools. If left untreated, the disease can be debilitating as the trapped larvae or eggs increasingly introduce inflammatory reactions in various human organs. This can cause liver enlargement as well as, in more severe cases, enlargement of the spleen, nervous disorders, and potentially death. Historically, for the villagers who lived in affected regions, schistosomiasis, as well as other diseases such as malaria and otitis, were understood as divine retributions for misdeeds or were caused by bad *fengshui*. During the outbreak seasons, villagers would light incense at their associated temples and make offerings to the gods, asking for forgiveness and protection. The Confucian temple at Buyun Township in Zhejiang province's Jiaxing County was conveniently situated near a bridge. As one of the larger temples in the region and one of the busiest, it had more rooms, better facilities, and quite a few resident nuns. During the disease outbreak seasons, the temple served as a refuge for those local people who fell sick. After the Communist army takeover in Jiaxing, the temple, along with many other religious institutions, were converted into mass treatment centres for schistosomiasis victims, and in 1952 the temple was officially configured into Jiaxing region's schistosomiasis prevention centre.[3]

The Yangtze River delta and the outflow areas of the river (which are also known as 'the lake regions') are called 'China's rice basket'. The lush paddy fields, the large areas of wetland, and the humid climate conditions provide, in addition to rich crops, a fertile environment for the snails that are the carriers of schistosomiasis. When the PLA's Third Field Army was preparing for the river crossing, it was estimated that the disease was endemic in some 1,300 townships near the prospective battlefield and that there were more than 11 billion square metres of snail-infested areas.[4] The disease had already impacted more than 10 million of the local population.[5] Since spring was the outbreak season, it was not surprising that many of the soldiers, being from the north and with little or no resistance to the disease, became infected. The serious schistosomiasis outbreaks amongst the PLA soldiers as they were preparing for crossing the Yangtze also demonstrated how quickly the disease could become endemic. As mentioned, the blood fluke can penetrate the human body via the skin when contacted in water and cause infection immediately. The regions along the lower reaches of the Yangtze are covered with extensive networks of waterways. Traditionally, local populations built their houses along the water. Families used the same water for cooking and for washing vegetables and clothing as well as for cleaning their 'night stool' or chamber pots. Boat people who lived on their boats had no toilet facilities and they excreted directly into the river, as did their dogs. Such life habits meant that the water could easily become contaminated, and the disease could spread quickly through this contaminated water. In addition, local famers used a mixture of river mud, green manure, and human excrement as fertilizer in their paddy fields.[6] After the schistosoma eggs entered the paddy fields, when the weather turned warmer they would quickly hatch into snails and multiply in great numbers. Prior to the incident of outbreak amongst the PLA soldiers, there had been frequent reports of outbreaks in previous years that had wiped out some entire villages in the regions.[7]

Despite being severely weakened by the disease, this was no time for the army, including the sick soldiers, to retreat. After the Nationalists turned down the proposal from the United States to sign a peace agreement with its Communist rival, on 20 April 1949 the PLA Third Field Army fired at HMS *Amethyst*, the British Royal Navy frigate sailing down the Yangtze to the Nationalist capital Nanjing on a mission to protect British interests there.[8] This first gunfire marked the beginning of the PLA's Yangtze River-Crossing Campaign, also known as the Nanjing, Shanghai, and Hangzhou Military Campaign. The campaign signalled that the Communists were approaching the point where they would take over the rest of China. On 23 April, the PLA Third Field Army captured Nanjing, and in the next five weeks it rallied and successfully seized Hangzhou and Shanghai, two of the most important cities on the Yangtze River. The CCP's red flag with its five stars replaced the blue sky–white sun flag of Republican China. In the Yangtze River delta, people welcomed peace, but they did not see the Communist army as ful-filling any auspicious heavenly promise. Many of them were still tormented by the traumatic memory of being terrorized by the civil war that had waged between the Taiping heavenly army and the Qing imperial army some eighty years earlier and, more recently, by the Japanese occupation. Would these young peasant soldiers from northern China who spoke strange dialects be any different? The local populations observed them with fear and distrust that was mingled with a certain amount of curiosity. Some were impressed by how disciplined the PLA soldiers were. Others were intrigued to see female cadres walking on the street dressed in their grey uniforms.[9]

For the PLA as well as for the CCP's southbound officers, the relatively easy conquest was, however, followed by further compli-cations. Just as the local population found these northern peasant cadres and soldiers strange, the CCP officials and soldiers found the southern climate and culture challenging, as they did the incom-prehensible and varied dialects spoken in the region. Unable to tell the difference between green and black tea, some CCP officials dismissed the tea-drinking culture in the south as decadent and thus 'unhealthy'.[10] For the CCP, however, the more pressing issue was the military resistance of various local non-Communist groups, including the remnants of Nationalist loyalists. At the same time, although Chiang Kai-shek and the Nationalist army had been driven to the small island of Formosa (Taiwan, as it is known today), they continued to present a serious military threat. There was a constant fear that they would attack the mainland. In August 1949, less than three months after the Third Field Army entered Shanghai, the CCP Central Committee, led by Chairman Mao Zedong, gave an order to General Su Yu to train his men to be prepared to attack Taiwan as well as to guard the security of Shanghai and the surrounding regions. The Ninth Regiment's Third Field Army (the PLA Twentieth Group Army) was assigned to the task. To invade Taiwan would involve the soldiers being able to swim, since they would have to fight battles in waterways. This entailed at least an hour of intensive daily swimming lessons for the soldiers in the waterways in Zhejiang's Jiaxing and Pinghu and at Jinshan, a small port of great military importance just southwest of Shanghai. Since these were schistosomiasis-endemic regions, not surprisingly more than one-third of the soldiers from the three army units were quickly reported to have been infected with schistosomiasis japonicum. The news of yet another serious schistosomiasis outbreak shocked the CCP leadership. They began to see this strange southern disease as an additional threat to their newly gained victory. Could this shatter their mission to unify China?

Would the Battle of Red Cliff, recounted in the classics of Chinese history, be repeated? In one of China's most important history books, the *Comprehensive Mirror to Aid in Government* (资治通鉴), compiled by the northern Song scholar official Sima Guang (1019–1086), as well as in other works, there is the account of the famous Battle of Red Cliff (third century CE). The book tells how disease and poor health had contributed to General-in-Chief Cao Cao's defeat: in the winter of 208–09, Cao Cao moved to unify the Han Empire. While preparing for the Battle of Red Cliff at Dongting Lake on the Yangtze River in central China, his soldiers succumbed to a mysterious illness. Like the Third Field Army soldiers in the twentieth century, Cao Cao's men in the third century were also northerners from the region along the Yellow River delta. Unaccustomed to the strange environment and humid climate of the Yangtze region, they had become severely ill. Cao Cao and his remaining army were forced to flee.[11] Their defeat at the Battle of Red Cliff is widely acknowledged as one of the most catastrophic moments in Chinese history. Some recent studies by Chinese researchers have identified schistosomiasis as the 'mysterious' illness that caused the defeat of Cao Cao's army.[12] As result of Cao Cao's defeat at the Battle of Red Cliff, China was divided into three warring countries, known as the Three Kingdoms. The Three Kingdom Period (220–80), also known as the 'Period of Disunity', is remembered in China as one of the bloodiest periods in history.

The CCP and its PLA were determined that they would be immortalized in the history books not as failed rebels but as victorious conquerors. Proven unbeatable so far in their struggle against the Nationalist armies, they now embarked on a battle to defeat the 'enemy of the natural world'. The newly founded CCP Shanghai Municipal Government, led by Marshall Chen Yi, appointed Cui Yitian, a southern-bound CCP cadre and graduate of the Liaoning Medical University, to take charge of the battle against this strange southern parasitic disease: schistosomiasis japonicum. Cui was a native of Liaoning province in Manchuria. In September 1931, his home region was lost to the Japanese. Believing that wartime medical and health work was essential in saving his country and the Chinese people from becoming 'stateless slaves' (colonized by Japan), he joined the CCP and volunteered to go to the battlefield to treat sick and wounded soldiers. Before the PLA entered Shanghai, Cui, along with thousands of patriotic youth who supported the Communist revolution, underwent a month-long intensive cadre-training program. During this time, he worked closely with Marshall Chen Yi to plan future medical and health work in Shanghai and the surrounding regions. Schistosomiasis had not been on their agenda; as a northerner, Cui claimed little or no knowledge of it. Now, in his position as the new director of the Shanghai Municipal Health Bureau, Cui appealed to medical and health professionals in Shanghai and Zhejiang province, where the PLA soldiers were infected, for help.[13]

The local experts quickly joined forces with their new Communist patron. Linked to the rural way of life and particularly to rice-growing farmers, schistosomiasis was of political, economic, and cultural importance in this region. Local records tell us that from the fifteenth to the nineteenth century, several outbreaks along the Yangtze River delta had devastated the region. The dramatic increase in the number of people infected by the disease was linked to the agricultural expansion driven by the imperial government and backed by local elites, with the aim of relieving the chronic problem of famine. Large-scale irrigation projects and the newly opened paddy fields, as well as the increased amount of river mud being used as fertilizer, created an ideal environment for snails – the vector for schistosomiasis – to breed. At the same time, intense agricultural activities increased the chance of infection as more and more people were exposed to the vector. The steady population growth, on the one hand, as a result of agricultural migration and famine control, and the increase in agricultural livestock, on the other, speeded up transmission. In the second half of the seventeenth century, the disease was said to have become so prevalent that it was regarded by the local people as a real menace. While some died of the disease, even more fled in fear of being infected. The disease, coupled with the Taiping Rebellion in the 1860s – the worst civil war in Chinese history – resulted in large parts of the countryside being left uninhabited and agricultural fields abandoned.[14]

Social reformers and modernizers from the endemic regions linked the disease to infertility and thus to under-population and poor productivity. They viewed it as a serious handicap to rural development, contributing to the overwhelming rural poverty and more generally to the backwardness of China. Experts trained in Western allopathic 'tropical medicine' and public health were called in to begin a top-down attack on the spread of the infection. One of these was Chen Fangzhi, a graduate of the Imperial Tokyo University's Medical School created under the leadership of German physicians in the late nineteenth century. In 1928, Chen was appointed the first director of the Sanitary Department in the Nationalists' Ministry of Interior. When the Sanitary Department was incorporated into the newly established Ministry of Health later that year, Chen passed the directorship to his former student from the Zhejiang Public School of Medicine (founded by doctors trained under the German and Japanese system 德日系), Yao Yongzheng. Chen himself went to Shanghai to head the Ministry of Health's new agency, the Central Hygiene Laboratory (CHL). The task of the CHL was to conduct chemical and pharmaceutical analysis, bacteriological and pathological examinations, and laboratory research, as well as to exercise control over drugs and patent medicine.[15] During his tenure, Chen conducted extensive field research on the problem of schistosomiasis in the Shanghai and Zhejiang region, which made him one of the foremost Chinese experts on the subject. His research established the most authoritative data used by the new Communist authority as well as by the experts engaged by the CCP to tackle the disease in the initial stage of its anti-schistosomiasis crusade. A native of rural Zhejiang, Chen grew up witnessing the extensive damage caused by the disease. He called schistosomiasis 'the disease of national humiliation' (国耻病) because it injured China's national economy as well as people's livelihood – two keys to China's rejuvenation, according to Sun Yatsen, a trained physician who became the founder of modern China. For Chen, schistosomiasis control work had to be a responsibility shared by all Chinese persons.[16]

Chen's concern linked the disease to the survival of China as a country and a 'race'. This concern was also widely felt by other members of local medical communities, most of whom were Western-trained and who advocated modernizing China through bio-medicine. Xu Xifan, who also grew up in rural Zhejiang province, was a graduate of the Rockefeller Foundation's Peking Union Medical College (PUMC) and had a PhD in parasitology (financed by the Rockefeller Foundation International Health Commission) from the University of Neuchatel in Switzerland. Reinhard Hoeppli, a former doctor for the German navy during World War I who later became a distinguished parasitologist and headed the PUMC's Division of Parasitology, once remarked that Xu was 'one of the best qualified of the younger workers in the field of parasitology in China'.[17] In 1948 and 1949, Xu, by then a world-class helminthologist, was the head of the Parasitology Laboratory of the Nationalist government's National Institute of Health in Nanjing. In 1948, after he witnessed how a major schistosomiasis outbreak that year had wiped out the entire population of a village in Zhejiang province's Qu County and left lush agricultural land in waste, he compared schistosomiasis to the 'opium plague': 'If not treated and prevented, there will be no one left in the countryside to tend the farming fields.'[18] By linking the disease to people's livelihood, a key principle of the Chinese revolution, tackling the schistosomiasis problem was not only of military urgency for the CCP but a critical issue of national concern. Successful control of the disease and reducing the mortality from it was an effective way to consolidate the CCP's rule in this 'disease-swamped land' – which was the image of China that was depicted by many Western observers as well China's modernizers.

POLITICS OF THE DISEASE

After World War II, a global interest in fighting schistosomiasis emerged. This budding interest had more than just a purely scientific impetus. The increasing presence of the United States in the Pacific, as well as the British involvement in Egypt, meant that this previously little-known 'Oriental disease' and its 'African cousins' were now of geopolitical and global importance.

A decade earlier, in 1938, at the twenty-ninth session of the League of Nations' Health Committee (LNHC), Dr Hilmy Bey, then Egypt's under-secretary of state for public health (medical affairs) and the country's official delegate to the League of Nations Health Organization (LNHO), had warned the LNHC that the problem of schistosomiasis was becoming more prevalent in many parts of the world. He proposed that the LNHC undertake serious investigation of the disease 'on lines similar to those followed by the [League of Nations] Malaria Commission' and organize international collaborations to ensure its prevention.[19] Responding to the Egyptian proposal, the LNHC called upon a handful of Western experts, led by Robert Leiper, the director of the Department of Parasitology at the London School of Hygiene and Tropical Medicine.

At the start of his career, Leiper had spent 1906–07 in Cairo studying under Robert Looss, the celebrated German helminthologist. It was in Egypt, where a third of population was infected by schistosomiasis, that Leiper had developed a research interest in the disease. In November 1913, the British Colonial Office made a special grant to the relatively new London School of Tropical Medicine (which was founded in 1899 and later changed its name to the London School of Hygiene and Tropical Medicine following a Rockefeller grant to rebuild and fund a school of public health) to allow Leiper, the school's Wandsworth Scholar, to go to the Far East 'to study the mode of spread of bilharziasis [an alternative European name for schistosomiasis] and to obtain ... definite experimental evidence on the subject'. Leiper's 'Oriental' expedition also gained support from the British Royal Navy, since *Schistosomiasis japonica* was said to be a concern for the crews of British ships operating on the Yangtze River. It seconded the Navy Surgeon-Lieutenant Atkinson to assist Leiper's scientific expedition. Although the expedition was 'abruptly' interrupted by the outbreak of World War I, Leiper was reported to have obtained enough evidence to 'throw discredit' upon Looss's highly controversial hypothesis of human-to-human transmission and argued that the disease was not communicable directly from person to person.[20] In 1915, the British War Office sent Leiper and his two colleagues from the London School of Tropical Medicine to 'investigate bilharzia disease in that country [Egypt] and advise on the preventive measures to be adopted in connection with the troops'.[21] This Egyptian mission allowed Leiper to solve the main problems of the life cycles of the African species of human schistosomes, caused by blood flukes of either *Schistosoma haematobium* or *Schistosoma mansoni*. Leiper's study showed that the transmission of each species of schistosome was firmly tied to the distribution of their permissive snail hosts (freshwater *Biomphalaria* and *Bulinus* snails), which had been historically confined to the Nile delta region. It led Leiper to conclude that schistosomiasis could be eradicated by destroying its intermediate host, the snail. This was important from the War Office's perspective because Leiper's discovery showed that an infected solider could not be re-infected and could not spread the disease directly to other soldiers or to the home population in Britain where there were no local molluscs to act efficiently as carriers. In addition, according to Leiper, the disease could be effectively prevented by supplying British troops with filtered water: 'it is obvious ... [that] in large towns where filtered water is supplied for drinking and bathing, there is practically no risk to Europeans.' Leiper's findings had lifted the British Army's fear of schistosomiasis as a burden to colonial expansion.[22] More than twenty years later, with Leiper as their leading expert, the LNHC took the view that the disease was only a local condition and therefore not directly related to the health of a broader Western community.[23]

This attitude persisted until 1944. In late October 1944, the Allied forces entered the Leyte Gulf off the Philippines and fought what came to be the largest naval battle of World War II – perhaps the largest naval battle in history. Once the troops landed, they found themselves in one of the most endemic regions of *Schistosomiasis japonica* in Asia. Over the next few months, some 1,700 cases of *Schistosomiasis japonica* were reported amongst the US Army and the Royal Australian Air Force. It was also reported that 30 per cent of the US prisoners of war who survived internment at the Davao Penal Colony on Mindanao, Philippine Islands, were infected. Despite earlier warnings by the surgeon general, *Schistosomiasis japonica* was a disease relatively new to the US War Department. Fearing a major epidemic amongst its forces, in early 1945 the US Army Epidemiological Board in Washington, DC, appointed a Sub-commission on Schistosomiasis to go to Leyte to undertake further investigations. Ernest Carroll Faust, a parasitologist at the Department of Tropical Medicine at Tulane University in New Orleans, was appointed its director.[24]

Interestingly, in his earlier career Faust had spent several years in China teaching and researching. It was in China that he began to develop an interest in *Schistosomiasis japonica*. In 1924, twenty years after the Japanese pathologist Fujiro Katsurada discovered a trematode that was the etiological agent of a disease that had been a major health hazard in the Katayama region of Japan and named it 'schistosomia japonicum', Faust and his colleague Henry Meleney at the Rockefeller Foundation's China enterprise – the Peking Union Medical College – published a monograph, *Studies on Schistosomiasis Japonica*.[25] This work was based on their meticulous field research in the central Yangtze Valley. It remained the most important and comprehensive study on the disease for the subsequent two decades. It was through their work that the world learned that the disease was a major health risk for the entire Yangtze Valley's waterways, as well as for the coastal river valleys south of Shanghai. Faust and Meleney became widely acknowledged in the international and Chinese medical communities as the most authoritative voice on the disease, from the life cycle of the disease, to its distribution, to its treatment.

In 1945, as World War II was coming to an end, there was a strong possibility that an Allied force invading Japan would be launched from the coastal region of China, where schistosomia japonicum was endemic. Faust and Meleney's earlier work grew ever more important, even though the dropping of atomic bombs on Hiroshima and Nagaski made an invasion unnecessary. There remained, however, further urgent need for more epidemiological surveys, and for studies of prevention and treatment of the disease, because of the unstable political situation in China. It became necessary to disseminate such knowledge amongst the army and civilian health practitioners in a China racked by civil war. This made schistosomiasis and its control an urgent but also a fashionable field for study. In 1947, the renowned parasitologist and president of the American Society of Parasitology, Norman Stoll, another of the Rockefeller Foundation's 'old China hands', produced the first assessment of the total world distribution of schistosomiasis. In his seminal publication "This Wormy World" (1947), Stoll argued

that schistosomiasis, a complex and little-known disease affecting
114 million people across three different regions – Asia, Africa, and
Latin America – was 'a mountain worth conquering'. Quoting an
old Chinese saying, 'If you do not scale the mountain, you cannot
view the plain', Stoll urged the international scientific community
that there should be more professional engagement with the disease to 'help reduce the prospect of having the world forge ahead to
more than 3,000 million human helminthiases by the year 2000'.[26]
Stoll's article became a rallying call for an international effort to
tackle the disease.

Around the same time, Hilmy Bey's successor, Dr Aly Tewlik
Shousha of Egypt, who was also a member of the technical preparatory committee of the newly founded World Health Organization
(WHO), pushed hard for the WHO to include the issue of schistosomiasis as one of the items on the agenda for the First World Health
Assembly. On 8 July 1948 in Geneva, the question of schistosomiasis was discussed during the assembly's eleventh meeting under the
item titled 'Special Endemic Diseases'. During the meeting, Shousha
argued that after malaria, schistosomiasis was the most widespread
and destructive disease in the world.[27] His draft resolution to establish an expert committee on the disease was supported by India,
Iran, France, and Ireland, as well as the Food and Agricultural
Organization of the UN (FAO) – another newly created post-war
international agency. For the French and the FAO, schistosomiasis
was of economic importance because it would affect agricultural
production in the Mediterranean basin as well as in many other
colonial food-growing regions. The FAO had actively sought to col-
laborate with the WHO on its plan to develop irrigation projects in
the Near East (including the Middle East and parts of northern and
eastern Africa) – the 'desert belt lying along the Tropic of Cancer'.
This gave an immediate urgency to the control of schistosomiasis.[28]
But the representatives of the Eastern Bloc countries, including the
USSR, Romania, Poland, and Czechoslovakia, opposed the resolution by upholding the LNHC's earlier view that schistosomiasis was
only a local condition and of only regional concern and argued that
the WHO should not finance such an expert committee from its own
budget.[29] This reflected the USSR's overall foreign policy at the time,
since it took a rather negative view on social and economic development as advocated by the UN and the United States – hence, the
USSR never joined the FAO.[30]

Although the opposition to Shousha's draft resolution numbered only a small minority and the health of the world was fundamental to the WHO's claim, the opinion of the USSR and the Eastern Bloc nevertheless mattered politically. In 1947, prior to the WHO's formal inauguration, Rolf Struthers, associate director of the Rockefeller's Medical Sciences Division, had expressed deep anxiety that 'If ... Russia will not join ... it will not be a World Health Organization.'[31] Politics and economic interests have always played a crucial role in international health. From the outset – as Dr Sze Szeming, one of the WHO's founding fathers, remembered – the WHO really had more to do with politics than medicine.[32] Schistosomiasis, like malaria, had become as much a political phenomenon as a biological one. In the end, the First World Health Assembly Programme Committee compromised by agreeing to send observers to the Fourth International Congress of Tropical Medicine and to establish a study group to carry out further research and make recommendations on the control of the disease.[33]

Shousha did not give up, for in a post-war Egypt anxious about its national unity and stability and concerned with rejuvenation as well as international recognition, turning fighting schistosomiasis into a global undertaking was a battle worth winning. Shousha was a strong advocate for vector control, since his teams had succeeded in wiping out malarial mosquitos after seven months of the routine application of Paris Green, a powerful larvicide for anopheline larvae.[34] In 1921, following the French entomologist Emile Roubaud's success in using trioxymethylene to poison anopheline larvae, Marshall Barber, a specialist working for the United States Public Health Service as well as a former and future employee of IHB and subsequently the International Health Division (IHD),* along with his assistant Theodore Brevard Hayne and the entomologist William Komp, developed this powerful larvicide. They called it Paris Green because of its green colour. With the discovery of Paris Green, the vector control approach increasingly became a key component in malaria as well as other parasitic disease control projects around the world.[35] For Shousha, an international war on schistosomiasis

---

* The International Health Division of the Rockefeller Foundation was created in 1913 with the name International Health Commission (IHC). Throughout its history, it underwent several mandate and name changes, becoming the International Health Board (IHB) in 1916 and the International Health Division (IHD) in 1927.

would allow him to push his vector control program further forward and afield.[36] A few months later, under his chairmanship, the
Executive Board submitted a proposed program and budget for 1950
to be discussed at the Second World Health Assembly. Accentuating
the severity of schistosomiasis, which 'after malaria, is perhaps the
most widespread debilitating disease in many parts of the world'
and 'an international problem from the social and economic, as well
as from the health, point of view', the proposed program included
field action to control snails in endemic regions, therapeutic trials,
and engaging relevant stakeholders to get involved in controlling
the disease.[37] Two months later, in June 1949, the WHO Programme
Committee at the Second World Health Assembly adopted this proposed program for 1950.[38]

MEDICINE, HEALTH, AND NATION-BUILDING

Despite China's role in the creation of the WHO, the Chinese representatives kept their distance from the debate over the issue of a
schistosomiasis control program within the WHO. Remember that
China, where the disease was endemic, was regularly mentioned in
these very international discussions about schistosomiasis, but at this
point, the Nationalist government of China, which held the 'Chinese
seat' at the United Nations until 1971, had just been driven out of
the Chinese mainland by their Communist opposition and had no
immediate political interest in dealing with this matter on the mainland. Yet it would soon find schistosomiasis prevalent on the island
of Formosa (Taiwan). In comparison, the CCP and its new People's
Republic of China (PRC) government, which was not a member of
the UN until 1971, quickly became involved in schistosomiasis control. It would later use the struggle against the disease in a propaganda war against the Nationalist enemy.[39]

Adding to the military urgency that first sparked their engagement
in the issue, as was the case with the US Army in the Philippines;
schistosomiasis control was also a matter of national survival for
the new China.[40] Widely acknowledged as one of the worst health
risks to the 8 per cent of the population living in China's agricultural heartland, the disease was linked to a 'feudal' way life that
was seen by many of the modernizing elites to have contributed to
China's overwhelming poverty. Since the health of the nation was
labelled as intrinsic to China's national survival and thus high on

the CCP's revolutionary agenda, its pledge of a war against schistosomiasis was understood as integral to achieving the revolutionary
goal of transforming China into a 'new, independent, and prosperous society'.[41] Such a vow would help the CCP to legitimize its newly
acquired power in the affected regions along the Yangtze regions
and in southern China and in turn allow it to bring about political
changes. On the other hand, the difficulty of eradicating the disease
– now widely acknowledged internationally – proved a real test for
the CCP, which had just succeeded in achieving the 'unachievable' by
driving the Nationalists out of the Chinese mainland. This victory
had stunned the world. To eradicate a disease that the capitalist West
and the enemies of the world communist movement had failed to
accomplish would further allow the new government to win international recognition. Future success at disease control would be the
manifestation of the revolution's success on the world stage, so it
was therefore a worthy prize. Shanghai and the surrounding regions
near China's east coast were areas with a long history of health and
medical outreach work by missionary groups as well as a concentration of Western-trained parasitologists and epidemiologists from the
Nationalist era. For the public health campaigners and health officials from the Nationalist era, controlling schistosomiasis had been
an integral part of a modernizing project that sought to redeem their
diseased, backward country through bio-medicine and public health
activities. For the medical communities there, it was also in their
professional interest to support the CCP. To conquer the apparently
intractable medical problem of schistosomiasis would bring them
international scientific prestige and therefore status with the new
regime. This was potentially a win/win situation, and they quickly
began to work in concert against schistosomiasis in a political war
as well as a public health one.

In December 1949, leading public health figures and medical
experts in Shanghai worked alongside the new Communist authority
to set up a special schistosomiasis task force, the Shanghai Region
Schistosomiasis Prevention and Treatment Committee. This com
mittee of experts consisted of thirty-six members and twenty-nine
researchers. Some were specialists in the field, while others were
active members of the Shanghai medical and public health community. The committee's leadership was made up of a mixture of
party officials and renowned names in the public health and medical
world. Amongst them was Yan Fuqing, a graduate of Yale Medical

School and one of the most prominent educators and advocates of bio-medicine in China. Others included leading medical cadres of the PLA: Song Shilun, the former commander of the Ninth Regiment of the Third Field Army, and Cui Yitian and his colleague Gong Naiquan. Liu Shenwang, a veteran revolutionary from the Yangtze region, was appointed secretary, and Su Delong, an Oxford-trained epidemiologist, was the vice-secretary.[42] Su had first become involved in schistosomiasis control in the 1930s after graduating from the Shanghai Medical School. Inspired by Yan Fuqing, his former dean, he had worked in a rural health experimental program in Shanghai County that aimed to introduce modern health care to the Chinese countryside. During this period, he gained first-hand experience of treating patients with advanced-stage schistosomiasis. This kind of leadership structure – small numbers of senior party military officials mixed with a group of professional experts – served as an organizational template for all professional organizations in the early PRC. This was not only to ensure that the CCP's takeover of the existing professional bodies went as smoothly as possible, it was also a mirror of the idea of the 'United Front' that had begun some thirty years earlier during the New Cultural Movement – a movement aimed at the rejuvenation of China by breaking away from traditional ethics and culture, which were blamed for preventing China from developing into a modern industrial nation. Many of those who took part were young intellectuals – college and university students – who sought to save their troubled and backward country by introducing 'Western Democracy, Science and Culture' to China.[43] The battle against schistosomiasis allowed them to combine all of these disparate modernizing strands into a single, focused political undertaking.

As with Chen Fangzhi and Xu Xifan, whom we met earlier, Yan Fuqing and Su Delong, as well as the non-CCP committee members, shared with the Communist revolutionaries the same New Cultural spirit that was characterized by anti-imperialism, anti-feudalism, and the desire for China's rejuvenation (or the Dream of a Strong China 强国梦).[44] Their professional honour and self-respect derived from their sense of duty to the Chinese nation and the Chinese people and had little to do with governmental changes and class interests. Such individual professional integrity was embedded in the universal love for their 'sick' country and people; hence, their desire to modernize China through medical and health work made them loyal supporters of the CCP's revolutionary utopian claim to transform China into a new, independent, and prosperous modern nation, eventually free of all diseases.

Yan Fuqing's biographers also tell of an earlier encounter between Yan and the youthful Mao Zedong during the New Cultural period. At the time, Yan was the president of Hunan-Yale (Xiang-Ya 湘雅) Medical College and the vice-president of its associated hospital. Both the medical college and the hospital were a Yale missionary endeavour in Changsha (in Hunan province in central China), first set up by the medical missionary Dr Edward Hume in the early twentieth century. The aim was to 'save' China through bio-medicine and modern education. After World War I, the Treaty of Versailles (1919) granted the rights to German colonial properties in China to Japan. It sparked the May the Fourth Students Demonstration in Peking. This incident, known in Chinese historiography as the May Fourth Incident, marked the turning point of the New Cultural Movement from the movement of cultural renewal to an anti-imperialist one. Mao Zedong returned to his native Hunan province in September 1919 and took up the editorship of *New Hunan*, the journal of the Hunan-Yale Medical College that advocated the New Cultural Movement. Mao used it to propagate the spirit of New Culture as well as Bolshevism and anti-imperialism. Newly married, Mao sought help from Yan for his young wife's gynaecological problems. Yan not only treated her but treated her for free. This personal experience undoubtedly made a deep impression on Mao. Yet Yan's mass public health experiment a few years earlier in Pingxiang's Anyuan colliery in central China, bordering Hunan and Jiangxi, impressed Mao even more. From 1917 to 1919, the Rockefeller Foundation's International Health Board (IHB) sponsored a hookworm control and sanitary program in the Anyuan colliery, China's largest colliery, 'as a means of entering public health fieldwork in China'.[45] Here, they replicated their earlier successful work in hookworm control in the southern United States.[46] If it worked in the poverty-ridden areas of Jim Crow America, the assumption was that it would be successful in the poverty-stricken areas of China. The IHB appointed Yan Fuqing to take charge of the work. As with most of the IHB's public health campaigns, Yan's team began with mass treatment and health education, followed by the setting up of a permanent sanitary board to build latrines and enforce a strict discipline of hygiene.[47] In 1921, Mao, who had recently joined the CCP, and his comrades Li Lishan and Liu Shaoqi chose the same colliery for their mass mobilization work. Existing scholarship on Mao and Li's Anyuan activities in this period stresses their involvement in the mass education campaigns that were advocated by leading modernizers such as Liao Qichao, Hu Shi, and Jimmy Yen, but a closer reading of the two episodes also shows that Mao and his colleagues' field strategy bore a remarkable resemblance to that employed by Yan's team during the IHB's hookworm control campaign.[48] Along with public lectures, they made use of pamphlets, posters, and brochures to disseminate the message of revolutionary change (in place of the transmission of health and hygiene information during the IHB campaign). Although the miners at Anyuan colliery distrusted bio-medicine, the IHB campaign raised their awareness of how poor work and living conditions had contributed to their ill health and that by pushing the colliery authority to improve hygiene standards, along with their general material condition, they would, in turn, improve their own health and well-being. Mao and his colleagues capitalized on this.

The post–World War I period was an age of growing confidence in public health. In China, as well as in the Soviet Union and South America, the binary of healthy and diseased became an integral part of the revolutionary rhetoric. Hygiene rituals, on the other hand, were also a means of introducing revolutionary discipline. Mao was first introduced to the miners by a distant relative named Mao Ziyun, a folk healer who had won the miners' trust by healing their minor ailments such as sore throats. Mao, however, took it much further in showing the miners a more radical path: that they could achieve betterment as well as human dignity through revolutionary upheaval that was 'out of the barrel of gun'.

NEW STATE, OLD CHALLENGES

In 1949, the CCP took the world by surprise by driving the Nationalists out of the Chinese mainland in spite of the American support that the Nationalists had been given. Having achieved power 'out of the barrel of gun', the CCP leadership was presented with the challenge of continuing to fight disease and of improving the people's health, with both being part of its revolutionary goal from the outset. In the new China, disease and ill health, once seen as the enemy of the revolution, continued to threaten the security of this new and fragile nation-state as well as drain its limited resources.

Figure 1.1 On 18 July 1953, Pinghu County Patriotic Health Campaign Propaganda Team parade through Chengguan township while holding the banner 'To Eradicate Schistosomiasis Is to Support the War in Korea to Fight the Americans'.

Along with natural disasters and famine, poor health and disease presented a huge burden to an economically weakened state struggling to recover from the damage of war as well as guard its security against the ongoing Nationalist threat. Of equal importance, since revolutionaries viewed ill health and disease as expressions of socio-economic inequality, medical advancement, together with the improvement of material conditions and the environment, were linked to the legitimacy of the new order. Declaring a war against a disease such as schistosomiasis would open up a field for the CCP to work with the medical community and with public health and social hygiene campaigners, giving the new authorities access to the social capital associated with such earlier undertakings.

With the beginning of the Korean War in the latter half of 1950, the need for a healthy and efficient army added a further political and military urgency to the PRC's health work. An official estimate says that more than forty million people died of infectious diseases and other illnesses between 1949 and 1950 and that many more lives were permanently impacted.[49] Ill health was not only an enormous drain on social and human resources, it also seriously undermined military manpower and economic productivity. The crusade against schistosomiasis, together with other public health initiatives such as the Anti-Germ Warfare Campaign and the Patriotic Health Campaign during the Korean War (1952), became an integral part of national defence.[50]

Along the Yangtze regions, it was reported that 90 per cent of the local population was infected with schistosomiasis, leaving virtually no healthy young men to join the army or to engage in agricultural activities. Near Shanghai, in Jiangsu province's Qingpu County, for example, more than 90 per cent of young men were excluded from army service after testing positive for schistosomiasis.[51] Anhui province's She County was the birthplace of Ke Qingshi, another revolutionary of the New Cultural generation who would become the party boss overseeing the PRC's nationwide Anti-Schistosomiasis Campaign between 1955 and 1965. She County was at one time central China's most important cultural and trading centre and the birthplace of the Peking opera. Between 1522 and 1820, She County was reckoned to be one of China's most prosperous areas, and the local merchants were widely held in awe for their immense wealth.[52] Yet by the time the CCP took over the region, sixty-two villages, some of which had had more than a hundred families, were deserted and without any trace of human habitation. Many formerly grand and revered memorial halls were left in ruins, and cobbled stone streets were covered in moss. Investigations have shown that severe outbreaks of schistosomiasis in 1948 and in earlier years had killed and debilitated many of the local inhabitants. Those who managed to survive had abandoned their homes and run away, leaving more than 1,600 hectares of agricultural land laid to waste.[53] As in earlier times, schistosomiasis continued to contribute to wasted land and deserted villages. The successful political revolution still had to deal with precisely the same health quandaries as its predecessor.

At the same time, disease, in particular schistosomiasis, and poor health were understood to have contributed to high rates of infertility and infant mortality in China. Sharing the language of the social Darwinists in Europe, social reformers and cultural and revolutionary theorists, as well as public health campaigners in China, viewed maternal and child health as indexes to China's national reconstruction or the 'Dream of a Strong China'. In September 1949, on the eve of the founding of the People's Republic of China – the PRC – the top leadership of the CCP drafted their new country's provisional constitution entitled 'The Common Program of the Chinese People's Consultative Congress'. Presented by the new premier Zhou Enlai and approved by acclimation by the Chinese People's Consultative Congress, the Common Program listed child and maternal health as one of its sixty articles.[54] In this new China, children not only were seen as the building blocks of a strong China, as Yan Fuqing had once stated, but they had become 'The Future of China', 'the Little Masters', and 'the Heirs of Revolution'. To guard their health was thus to guard the fruit of the revolution and to build the future utopian state.

Because it is part of communist praxis to seek to move patterns of living toward the collective, it was inevitable that the war on disease as well as other public health initiatives in the PRC would involve the entire population. But how could the new political leadership motivate the 'masses' to take part in such a 'revolutionary' health endeavour? This conundrum would prove a real test for the CCP and its health officials. As observed at the turn of the century by the Scottish parasitologist Patrick Manson, widely acknowledged as one of the founders of 'tropical medicine' as a discipline and who had lived in the Far East for nearly twenty-five years, 'to give water taps, traps, drains, ventilator to the Chinaman ... [who were] unappreciative of their purpose and ignorant of their use ... was like giving a monkey a fiddle; they did not understand their purpose and they broke them.' In other words, these 'Chinamen' would never change their unsanitary habits.[55] For the next fifty years, despite concerted efforts by Western missionaries, the IHB, and China's modernizers, there was little improvement to be seen regarding changing the 'unclean habits' of the 'ignorant' and 'retarded' 'Chinaman'. The vast countryside continued to be rampant with disease, and the unclean habits of the Chinese peasantry were believed to have contributed to the high rate of morbidity and mortality. The need to refute imperialists, and to prove the CCP's own power, added a further urgency to involve the entire population in its heroic and historic project to transform China into a 'clean country' and to turn the 'Sick Man of Asia' into the new and healthy 'socialist man and woman'. To teach the Chinese peasants to live a clean life was to 'change the prevailing social customs' (移风易俗). Bio-medicine would serve as the pillar in this cultural revolution. The help would come from public health campaigners and members of the medical community.

CONTROLLING SCHISTOSOMIASIS AND
GUARDING CHINA'S NATIONAL SECURITY

On 19 December 1949, under the leadership of Cui Yitian, a team of thirty-three medical/health professionals from the Shanghai Medical School, the only state-run medical college in China until 1949, went to Zhejiang province's Jiading County to continue treating army casualties of schistosomiasis. For the previous decade, as part of their anti-Japanese and post-war reconstruction efforts, these health professionals had immersed themselves in treating ill and wounded soldiers and undertaking other medical humanitarian and public health work among the civilian population. Witnesses at the time stated how they saw treating the sick Communist soldiers as their irrefutable duty.[56]

In the meantime, in December 1949, Mao, the leader of the new China, went on a state mission to Moscow. Stalin showed reluctance to accede to Mao's request to 'send volunteer pilots or secret military detachments to speed up the conquest of Formosa [Taiwan]' and, rather, advised Mao to organize an uprising in Taiwan using propaganda and not to attack the island with military force.[57] In January 1950, the Central Committee of the Communist Party of China (CPCC) took the decision to launch military assaults on Taiwan and other Nationalist-controlled islands between Taiwan and Zhejiang province. In order to ensure success, General Su Yu proposed that soldiers resume intensive swimming lessons, which had been terminated in the aftermath of a schistosomiasis outbreak amongst thousands of PLA soldiers a few months earlier. The Central Committee approved Su's proposal, fully aware that there was a great risk of even more soldiers being infected. To mitigate casualties, schistosomiasis treatment and prevention work became a top priority on the PLA's health and medical work agenda. On 1 February 1950, the Military Schistosomiasis Prevention and Treatment Committee was set up to ensure correct leadership and strict discipline. Schistosomiasis control was geared to military action. Geng Xichen, a veteran revolutionary from Shandong who had built up extensive experience in managing the PLA medical and health work, took charge.[58]

On the ground, experts continued to provide technical assistance, but their number would increase dramatically and over a short period of time. By linking schistosomiasis control to the PLA's mission to liberate Taiwan and rid the country of Nationalist remnants, the political and military importance of schistosomiasis was ever increasing. More than 2,000 experts – technical staff as well as students from major medical universities in Shanghai, Nanjing, and nearby Hangzhou – were recruited to train the PLA health service personnel and assist them in carrying out extensive check-ups and treatment. They were also simultaneously to undertake thorough epidemiological investigations of the disease. To win over medical and health professionals, including medical students, in April 1950 the newly merged Shanghai Medical Workers' Union, a frontline organization assisting the CCP's takeover of Shanghai's existing medical and public health institutions, honoured 181 health and medical professionals for their 'heroic action' in supporting the PLA to guard the national security of the PRC by treating sick PLA soldiers and carrying out preventive work 'day and night', despite 'the spartan conditions and the lack of equipment'.[59] In Zhejiang province, the army officials praised students for showing 'unprecedented levels of political consciousness'. Jiang Minghua, a student nurse from the former Zhejiang Midwifery School (which merged into Zhejiang Medical University), and Wang Xiangyun, a medical student from Shanghai, were chosen as 'model workers' for demonstrating deep commitment to the work and for their caring attitudes toward these patients. As model workers, they set the example for others to follow, but more importantly they had become the exemplary 'masters of the new China'. Excited to take part in creating a new China through medical and health work, they and their colleagues were seen to be full of enthusiasm.[60] Many of the 'model workers' were given further training and went on to become frontline workers in public health and in women's work over the next decades. Whilst delivering health care and prevention, they were also the party's messengers and the bridge that linked the CCP to the people. Many more medical and public health students volunteered to serve in the Korean War to showcase the importance of medical and health work in guarding the new China's national security. The technical experts, too, were given special recognition. Mao Shoubai, for instance, who was internationally known for his research on the distribution of schistosomiasis in China's Yangtze region, was given the military award, 'second class', in addition to being honoured as Nanjing municipal's 'model worker' for supporting the PLA's schistosomiasis control work. From there he went on to lead the PRC's nationwide schistosomiasis control. He would also represent the new China on the international stage of parasitology. In the early years of the PRC, like many experts, Mao was relatively free of interference from the party. Thereafter, however, in 1957, with the advent of the Anti-Rightist Movement, he joined the CCP, persuaded to do so by both professional and political considerations.[61]

CIRCUMNAVIGATING SCIENCE

Having succeeded in co-opting young students as well as established experts into the system, disagreement amongst the experts on what approaches to take presented the Communist authorities with a serious challenge. Managing science was just as difficult as managing human resources, if not more so. One of the major obstacles in schistosomiasis control work was the unreliability of diagnosis results. Throughout the world, detection of the ova is the traditional method of schistosomiasis diagnosis. Before the two Japanese parasitologists Kan Kato and Momoshige Miura introduced the cellophane thick smear technique to the world in 1954, the standard method used for diagnosing schistosomiasis was the direct smear procedure. This was complicated and expensive and could be highly inaccurate, since it required a minute amount of faecal sample and used recyclable ordinary glass instead of disposable cellophane. The Kato method simplified such procedures. It was thought to be more accurate than the former methods, since it required a larger amount of the sample. The technique was refined in 1968, and from then on it became known as the Kato-Katz thick smear method. It is still the most widely used diagnosis technique for detecting both Asian and African schistosomiasis (*Schistosomiasis japonica* and *Schistosomiasis mansoni*). However, because of the everyday variations in the level of faecal egg excretion in individual patients, as well as its uneven distribution in excreta, both the direct smear technique, which used ordinary cover glass, and the Kato-Katz method thereafter lacked a high degree of accuracy and sensitivity.[62] In 1950 in China, the unreliability of diagnosis results led to expert disagreement on treatment methods. Su Delong, who had gained experience in treating schistosomiasis victims during the eight years of the Sino-Japanese war, favoured a mass therapy intervention and advocated setting up massive treatment centres. This was the method introduced by John Brian Christopherson, the British physician employed by the colonial office during World War I. Its success at the time led to him to conclude that 'It is mass treatment in schools and villages where the hope of eradicating the disease lies.' It was this method that was implemented by the Egyptian public health department.[63] Zhang Changshao, China's leading pharmacologist and a graduate of the School of Pharmacy at the University of London, had been involved in treating malaria victims at a cotton mill in southern China with a traditional local fever remedy made of hydrangea (*Dichroa febrifuga*; in Chinese 常山 Changshan).[64] Zhang vociferously argued against mass therapy, reasoning that it was both wasteful and impractical. His view was that unlike tuberculosis, it was not always possible to determine whether a person had been infected with schistosomiasis and that treating every villager in the affected regions was an enormous waste of limited resources on potentially healthy individuals.[65]

To accommodate the experts' disagreement would delay the treatment work, but to alienate them would jeopardize the party's goal of winning its war against the disease. In addition to the disagreement amongst the experts, the wide range of localities and conditions on the ground also meant that mass therapy was impractical. For instance, the simple lack of beds at local treatment centres (some were former missionary hospitals, others temporary centres converted from old temples) meant that most of them could only take a very limited number of patients. Furthermore, mass therapy needed enormous quantities of treatment drugs. At the time, *fouadin* or *stibophen*, first manufactured by Bayer in the late 1920s, had to be imported, but it was not an affordable commodity in the amounts required for the new post-war nation with very limited resources. An injection of sodium antimony tartrate (at half a grain per day for twenty-nine days) was the therapy of choice for mass treatment throughout much of the world until the 1980s.* In China at the time, the therapy with sodium antimony tartrate was reported to have produced fantastic results when used to treat sick PLA soldiers.[66] However, there were serious reservations about its wide use, since the drug is known to be highly toxic and can therefore be dangerous

---

* Praziquantel (PZQ) is now the drug of choice for schistosomiasis treatment throughout the world. The drug was first discovered in Germany in the 1970s, but it only became available to the international market in the 1980s through a public and private partnership of the WHO and Bayer. Before PZQ became commercially available in 1978, China began to introduce it for clinic use. Soon after that, China successfully obtained the technology of synthesizing PZQ.

if applied without the supervision of trained staff. Since the complete course of treatment took twenty-nine days, patients needed to be hospitalized for that length of time. Not only was there a shortage of beds and bedding, but most villagers refused to leave their homes for that length of time for complex cultural, social, and economic reasons (as will be discussed in chapters 2 and 5). Furthermore, the drug is not effective for patients in the advanced stages of schistosomiasis. Building on their previous experiences of controlling kala-azar, a parasitic disease prevalent in the Communist-controlled regions during the war, some army doctors experimented with using neostibosan (sodium stibogluconate), a comparatively non-toxic drug used to treat this sand fly–borne parasitic disease (visceral leishmaniasis). Because of high demand, China had been manufacturing its own neostibosan, so it would make good economic sense if it could also be used to treat schistosomiasis. However, experts in the south, such as Chen Fangzhi, felt less comfortable with this newer version of the tartar emetic. Unsure about neostibosan's efficacy, they argued that it should only be used as a temporary measure, not as a long-term solution for schistosomiasis.[67]

One month prior to the outbreak of schistosomiasis among the PLA soldiers, Chen had deemed that existing drug therapies were largely ineffective and that they were, in any case, too costly for a war-torn country. To control the disease more effectively, he advocated a more comprehensive rescue plan. Having devoted many years to epidemiological investigations in Zhejiang and the nearby regions, Chen argued strongly for a nationwide epidemiological survey. His reasoning was that more data would allow the government to allocate limited resources efficiently. He also favoured building a small number of flagship hospitals in cities and towns with more resources and easier access by modern transport (at the time, many villages were not accessible except by narrow, unpaved paths). If all resources were directed into these central hospitals, they would act as nodal points for research as well as being responsible for treatment and health education plus providing prevention training on the ground. This rescue plan also emphasized the importance of implementing grassroots prevention programs. Such programs ranged from sanitizing villages to vector control and introducing 'hygiene-disciplines' to the impacted population. For Chen, the integral part of public health education was the literacy campaign, so those 'retarded and ignorant' villagers, as he called them, would be equipped to comprehend the new bio-medical knowledge.[68] The Financial and Economic Committee of the CCP's East China Bureau, responsible for managing the economic matters of eastern regions of China, favoured Chen's rescue plan, since it resonated well with the CCP's goal of introducing a cultural revolution to transform rural China. Faced with the reality of a shortage of funding, drugs, and medical equipment as well as trained personnel, the small-scale local program, together with public exhortations to change people's 'unclean' practices, was something, perhaps the only thing, they could really deliver. This was in no way unique to the PRC, however, since public health attempts aimed at changing behaviour were usually more cost-effective than other public health interventions.[69]

Two months later, in April 1950, in consultation with leading experts, including Chen Fangzhi and Mao Shoubei, the newly formed PRC's Ministry of Health, an entity separate from but parallel to the Military Health Unit and which would oversee the nation's health work, issued a call for a nationwide schistosomiasis control program. While this program echoed Chen's rescue plan, there were also significant changes.[70] Instead of prioritizing epidemiological survey and research, the Ministry of Health's national schistosomiasis control program emphasized health education and the training of grassroots health workers, using them to spread health propaganda and introduce sanitation measures. This was not surprising. The PRC's new minister of health, Madame Li Dequan, was a former social activist and feminist who in the 1920s had sought refuge in the Soviet Union with her warlord husband Feng Yuxiang. Nicknamed the 'Christian General', Feng was an advocate for mass education, women's liberation, and the eradication of 'superstitions' and 'unclean' habits. He was also sympathetic to union activities and was said to have helped the CCP in developing its networks amongst students and workers. Li Dequan herself had been a strong advocate in promoting maternal and children's health. She also actively supported refugee children's relief work during the wartime, although she was not then directly involved in this or in any other aspects of public health work. The very existence of disease and ill health was a political question for her: they had resulted from 'unclean' habits that were directly linked to the 'feudal' way of life. Health education that promoted 'clean' habits, along with hygienic discipline, was therefore integral to disease prevention and the improvement of the population's health.[71] Li was not alone in this. The belief that clean living conditions and healthy behaviours, as well as ordered lives, would produce healthy bodies and a politically enlightened, productive, and happy population was widely shared by contemporary revolutionaries and Marxist cultural theorists in China. For them, disease control was not merely about science but a core part of the utopian project, although science would have an important role to play in hastening the coming of the socialist utopia. In this utopian future, they envisioned a virile and productive population. In order to create the utopian body of the future, Madame Li and the new Ministry of Health worked alongside medical and hygiene professionals in Shanghai and other large urban areas to introduce measures to change habits of body and life.[72] Schistosomiasis control thus presented a real opportunity to carry out their revolutionary experiments. It had to be framed into the PRC's overall public health agenda: to live a socialist life was to live a healthy life. Living such a healthy life would in turn bring forth the socialist utopia – or, to use the words of Lu Dingyi, the man in charge of the PRC's national political cultural work who would become the first minister of propaganda, schistosomiasis control work was a cultural revolution against 'old customs', 'superstitions', and 'unclean habits'.[73] Just as healthy behaviour was viewed as a signifier of politically correct behaviour, from its outset the PRC's crusade against schistosomiasis was a political project in which scientific expertise would play a vital but subordinate role.

As we have seen to this point, at the very moment that the PRC was established in 1949, there had been specific connections between health and politics as part of the foundational definition of the goals of the new state. The problem of schistosomiasis quickly became the poster child for public health in the new China because the disease was seen as deterring the progress of the revolution. This was true on both the level of medical professionals and the organizational level of the state. Pragmatically, the struggle against the disease reflected both internal divisions and Cold War politics but also the simple availability of current resources. Symbolically, it also reflected the function of such a public health undertaking as the fulcrum for the goals of a new, utopian society. The following chapters will show how early themes of disease intractability, the political desire for success, competing demands, and organizational and professional conflict play out in ways unsuspected by those involved at the outset of the building of a new communist society.

2

An Unfolding Drama

TO TAKE OVER SCHISTOSOMIASIS CONTROL
IS TO FIGHT 'FEUDAL SUPERSTITIONS'

On 30 May 1950, just a month after the Ministry of Health had issued the directive of a nationwide schistosomiasis control program, the Political Department of the People's Liberation Army (PLA)'s Twentieth Army announced that the mass treatment work amongst the infected PLA soldiers had been successfully completed. A large number of soldiers (13,294) were treated, had recovered, and had returned to their units, and the first battle was declared won.[1] Schistosomiasis control work soon shifted to civilian society. It would become the centrepiece for public health in the People's Republic of China (PRC).

For the new Communist state, schistosomiasis control provided a convenient model emphasizing the need for overall systematic state intervention. China's medical community and its many scientific-minded reformers also favoured state intervention. For them, the prevalence of schistosomiasis was but one example of the Nationalist government's failure to introduce a systematic disease control program. This view was also held by international public health advocates and parasitologists who sought to 'change' China through the benefit of concerted public health initiatives and a move to allopathic medicine.* In their 1924 landmark publication *Studies on Schistosomiasis Japonica*, Faust and Meleney drew the conclusion

---

* Modernizing elites in China usually also favoured allopathic medicine and advocated the need for making modern medicine widely available.

that schistosomiasis could not, under the present circumstances, be controlled in China, since 'neither the provincial nor the local authorities have any real interest in the welfare of the inhabitants' and 'it is not merely a public health problem; for within its scope are also included problems of economic and political life and general education.'[2] On another occasion, Meleney even went as far as to suggest it was the 'type of mind the Chinese have' that ruled out any possibility of controlling the disease.[3] Therefore, the new Communist government's promise to improve the people's health by controlling the disease offered a startling contrast to the perceived reluctance of the previous regime. It rekindled a diminishing hope for 'reforming and improving' China and, if Meleney was correct, the Chinese themselves.[4] With the Chinese Communist Party (CCP) and the state now backing them up, Chinese experts in parasitology (the majority of whom were at one point students of Faust and Meleney at the PUMC's Division of Parasitology), as well as social reformers, were determined to show the world that the Chinese were capable of rising to this public health challenge.

In its early stage, schistosomiasis control also gave the CCP legitimate reason to take over several existing medical and health institutions left by the Nationalists. After the establishment of the Shanghai Region Schistosomiasis Prevention and Treatment Committee, the Eastern China Military Committee gave the order to establish a parallel civilian schistosomiasis prevention committee in the former Nationalist capital Nanjing. Li Zhenxiang, a graduate of the Hunan-Yale Medical College, headed this new committee. Soon after the Japanese marched across the Yangtze, he joined the PLA to become an army doctor. Well trained and extremely efficient, Li successfully operated on thousands of wounded soldiers. He won himself the reputation of being the 'PLA's Hua Tuo'.* From being an army surgeon, Li quickly rose to lead the PLA's public health work, working alongside Cui Yitian during the Chinese civil war in the 1940s. Other committee members, who were all trained in the West (a few were Faust and Meleney's students from the PUMC), were prominent figures of the Nanjing medical community during the Nationalist era. The committee in Nanjing was the first provincial

---

* Hua Tuo was a physician and surgeon who lived in the second and third centuries in the Han Empire, celebrated for his superior surgical skills and for using a 'herbal anaesthetic' made from hemp.

authority other than the military to run a schistosomiasis control institution in the PRC. Its main function was not to carry out actual control work but to ensure the smooth integration of the existing Nationalist health and medical institutions into the new regime.[5]

In the next months, a huge number of local treatment centres and stations mushroomed in the endemic rural counties and towns around Nanjing and Shanghai, as well as in regions of Zhejiang province where the PLA's swimming training was taking place in preparation for invading Taiwan. Employees from the former Nationalist medical and health institutions were relocated to fill vacancies in these new centres. CCP military representatives took the leadership role at such centres to make sure they would not be simply replicas of former Nationalist institutions but would become socialist public health organizations for the new China. After carefully reviewing each employee's file, party officials at each of the centres would assign appropriate posts to them depending on their political reliability. Some of the posts were filled by recent graduates from the medical and nursing schools in the big cities. These newly minted physicians and nurses were among the most loyal supporters of the CCP and the new Communist state. The schistosomiasis control work imbued them with a specific sense of the inflection of the PRC's historical utopian mission: they were to use their bio-medical knowledge and skills to build a new and modern Chinese society that would lead to a world free of disease.[6]

Many new schistosomiasis treatment and control centres also served the function of co-opting existing local resources into the new state-run socialist health system. These centres held regular meetings for local private practitioners – some practised Chinese medicine – in the name of preparing them for the work of schistosomiasis control. Such meetings not only disseminated bio-medical knowledge but also doubled as political study meetings, spreading the message of the new state's commitment to an ideal future. Some of these practitioners welcomed the new authority's commitment to tackling this intrinsic public health problem. There were also those who had been unemployed or underemployed in the former private systems and who saw schistosomiasis control work as an opportunity for upward mobility. By taking part in this work, the latter (many of whom had been made redundant by their former employers) became state employees and thus earned a monthly salary. They also compensated for their lower-level skills by taking part in what was labelled a vital project to create the new socialist state. Many were greatly motivated by having a sense of higher purpose, and they subsequently became local activists in public health work in the ensuing years.[7] On the other hand, those who had come from a long tradition of family practice, who had been economically better off due to their professional skills and reputations, were being classified as 'landlords'. Their businesses were shut down, and their practices, along with their private possessions, were confiscated and redistributed as part of the Land Reform or forcibly converted to state ownership. Folk and spiritual practices, which had earlier played a central role in delivering health and well-being to rural villagers, were officially banned as 'feudal superstitions' and were eliminated from the new socialist health system. A few healers continued to practise in private, but in general, healing temples or shrines, including a number of those dedicated to Guandi or Lord Guan, and ancestral halls were converted to schistosomiasis treatment centres or local health stations.[8]

In Chinese popular belief, Lord Guan was the god of valour and loyalty. Throughout history, various social groups have assigned him different attributes. He was spontaneously the custodian of the empire, the protector of communities, and the provider of wealth and health for individuals. During the outbreak of bubonic plague in the late nineteenth century that ravaged southern China, the image of Lord Guan as a filial and righteous official in charge of the department of epidemics who intervened with Heaven on behalf of humans was deployed first by the Buddhist Society for the Performance of Good Deeds and then by the imperial authorities in order to mobilize the populace in efforts to control the crisis. In the process, unorthodox religious practices such as magical remedies, animal sacrifices, and the burning of paper-joss were disparaged. It was rumoured that in order to spare them misfortune, the voice of Lord Guan called the populace to repent of their misdeeds and to do good work. People were encouraged to attach an amulet with the ten characters of Lord Guan's name and title to their doors to ward off the infection. As important village institutions, Guandi temples would also provide free treatment as well as burial and crisis relief work in time of any major epidemics. In the Yangtze delta region, local popular beliefs often likened schistosomiasis to bad *fengshui* or misfortune. During the outbreak season, villagers regularly visited Guandi temples or other local village temples, praying to be spared the infection.[9]

However, the new socialist China needed new cultural symbols. There was no place for the cult of Lord Guan or any of the other popular superstitions that had served 'feudal' ideologies. In the official culture for the new China, the war on disease was simultaneously a cultural war attacking 'feudal superstitions'. According to Article 41 of the Common Program of the Chinese People's Political Consultative Conference (CPPCC), to create a 'socialist and democratic culture' that was 'Chinese, scientific and popular' was 'to raise the cultural level of the people', to eradicate 'feudal, comprador and fascist ideology', as well as to 'develop the ideology of service to the people'.[10] In the process of creating a new socialist democratic Chinese culture, schistosomiasis control became an arena in which to fight 'feudal superstitions' and at the same time to improve the people's health. Since the PRC's new socialist countryside would not be founded on ignorance and superstitions but rather on education and science, villagers were taught that the 'socialist bio-medical' interventions (socialist bio-medicine refers to Soviet medicine as opposed to the bio-medicine first introduced to China by Western 'imperialists') were the only means of relieving them of the sufferings caused by schistosomiasis, the 'disease of the feudal past'. They also learnt that Chairman Mao was more powerful than Lord Guan and any other healing gods.[*11] To overcome the scepticism and distrust shown by villagers, some officials of the new Communist authorities promised free treatment as well as painless injections by the best doctors from the big city of Shanghai.[12] When villagers lined up outside local prevention and treatment centres demanding free treatment and expecting a miracle cure, many local authorities found they had no means of delivering the new regime's promise of health.[13]

---

* The CCP's cultural war on 'feudal superstitions' shared some similarities with the modernist campaign during the early Republican period attacking popular religion Indeed, many of the voices that advocated the earlier campaign continued to serve as cultural theorists for the new Communist regime. However, the new Communist authorities were very conscious of marking its new cultural war as 'socialist', thus separating it from the earlier Nationalist campaign. For a study of the earlier Republican campaign, see Prasenjit Duara, 'Knowledge and Power in the Discourse of Modernity: The Campaigns against Popular Religion in Early Twentieth-Century China', *The Journal of Asian Studies* 50, no. 1 (1991): 67–83.

PREVENTION AND PUBLIC ENGAGEMENT
AS THE HEALTH BLUEPRINT

In the first two years following the Communist Liberation, shortages in funding, personnel, and goods were common problems faced by local authorities throughout the country. Even the large cities with more resources were not exempt. In newly liberated Nanjing and Shanghai, for instance, homeless refugees resulting from the revolution upheaval packed the streets, queuing for relief supplies. Food soon ran out. Malnutrition as well as unclean and crowded living conditions led to outbreaks of smallpox, tuberculosis, whooping cough, diphtheria, and measles. In the meantime, drought and floods wrecked large parts of the countryside. An influx of villagers had migrated to the cities for survival. Suffering severe malnutrition and exhaustion, many fell victim to the epidemics. This was exacerbated by the huge number of livestock that died of diseases that spread quickly.[14] The economically defunct state had no resources to cope with the escalating public health devastation that accompanied the regime change. With only one trained health professional (including doctors, nurses, and paramedics) for every 1,000 people and a total of 2,600 hospitals, with only 80,000 hospital beds in all of China (the situation was much worse in rural China where there was only one hospital bed for every 20,000 people), the new regime's promise of free medical care for all was quickly suspended.[15] It was replaced by the Labour Insurance Regulation in 1951 that guaranteed protection for a select few, namely workers in the larger state-owned factories as well as other government employees. At the time, China's population was 500 million, but only 12 million were industrial workers. The introduction of this Labour Insurance Regulation meant that unemployed urban residents, most of whom were poor, as well as rural villagers (the latter counted for more than 80 per cent of the total population) were left without health and medical care.[16] Following the new insurance regulation, some regional authorities, such as the Nanjing municipal authority, introduced a three-tiered referral system that aimed to distribute the restricted resources more efficiently to the poor and the needy. In practice, however, instead of delivering resources to the poor and those most in need, the referral system encouraged often unfair competition for the limited resources. This meant that only those with good connections and political power had access to quality medical and health care, and so cronyism prevailed. The situation was worse in regions where there were fewer resources. Often, the most vulnerable not only had very little or zero access to medical care but were also denied the basic minimum for their health and well-being. In the name of helping them to become 'self-reliant', different districts in Nanjing municipality were assigned quotas to take in the disabled and vagrants. Having no resources, districts pushed the responsibility for looking after these people back on their families and communities. Homeless vagrants who had no family or community to return to were detained and forced to do hard labour at the detention centres. Later, these detention centres were configured into 're-education through labour' camps. Between 1950 and 1952, more than 10,510 homeless vagrants in Nanjing municipality, from orphans to petty criminals, including the disabled and elderly, were sent to such camps. More than 97 per cent of those incarcerated suffered from lung diseases, gastric diseases, and other infectious diseases. Having little or no access to medicine and health care, some 200 people died in these camps; 456 were lucky enough to escape.[17]

In the meantime, to the dismay of the authorities, the 'old feudal' healing practices that the new regime had tried hard to eradicate continued to attract many followers who either had no access to or did not trust a new health system that was based on science and rationality as well as favouritism. In rural Zhejiang, for instance, villagers were reported lining up under a 100-year-old gingko tree, waiting for the spirit to be revealed at night and deliver them the healing water that would protect them from ill health.[18] In Sichuan's Luojiang County, historically a strategic crossroad linking the Chinese empire with the Himalayas, some 60,000 to 70,000 people of mixed cultural and ethnic backgrounds from the other side of Ngawa Prefecture on the Tibetan Plateau, as well as from Sichuan province, made annual pilgrimages here to pray to Guanyin (the Goddess of Mercy) for protection, wellness, and health. The pilgrims would bring with them a small empty container to draw the water from the river beneath the Guanyin rock, water that was said to possess healing power. Failing to understand the world view of the villagers who saw disease and ill health as a result of fate and divine retribution, the authorities viewed the claims of healing made by local cults as threatening to their newly gained political power. Presenting the pilgrims as seriously jeopardizing the necessary implementation of rural public health work, the local public security (police) blocked the road to the rock. In the meantime, local health officials tried to persuade these villagers to seek treatment for their ailments at local state-run treatment centres. Despite the repeated efforts of the authorities, however, more than 10,000 people continued to make pilgrimages to seek Guanyin's blessing and to draw the healing water.[19] Throughout the countryside, various local sects also navigated their way under socialism to find new social meanings for their continuing existence. In the agricultural heartland of Henan province, a certain local sect that practised healing with 'divine water' appropriated the new regime's propagandist messages and methods for its own use. In the Land Reform, they maintained that 'the heavenly god sent the divine water to save the poor. But if landlords drunk the water, they would die.' A few months later in 1951, the context of Anti-Germ Warfare Campaign and the Patriotic Health Campaign during the Korean War allowed the sect to make the claim that the 'divine water' would kill germs and prevent epidemics.[20]

Anxious that diseases were as much a destabilizing factor to its rule as 'the drought, flood, and locust' (the three natural phenomena traditionally seen as signs that predicted dynastic changes), the Central People's Government's State Administration Council (this would be replaced by the State Council in 1954) worked with its subsidiary, the Ministry of Health, as well as the PLA's Health Unit, to find solutions for the country's health crisis. The new state could barely provide the promised medicines and health care in major urban centres, let alone the impoverished countryside where 80 per cent of the population still lived. Prophylaxis, or preventive medicine, appeared the only affordable option.[21] This matter was discussed at the first National Health Conference in August 1950. One month later, the PRC's new minister of health, Madame Li Dequan, reported back to the State Administration Council. Her report highlighted the fact that 'feudal superstitions' continued to have a stranglehold on rural villages. According to her, these superstitions were a major obstacle to disseminating bio-medical knowledge and to delivering socialist medicine and health care in the Chinese countryside. Yearning for China to overcome its historical backwardness through science and mass education, Madame Li believed, as did many of her contemporary modernizers, that the entire Chinese nation must be taught the difference between superstition and modern science and that it was necessary for the state to introduce the benefits of bio-medical science in order to prevent the occurrence of disease and thus improve the people's health. She argued forcefully: 'Medicine is a scientific battle between the human and the disease ... Relying solely on health professionals to win such a battle would only cause alienation between them and the people ... Health professionals mustn't wait for people to get sick and turn up asking for treatment. Our job is to teach people how to fight diseases.'[22] Preventive medicine became the blueprint of a new national program to improve the people's health. Since the socialist state considered the people one of its most valuable assets – perhaps the only tangible asset in the case of the PRC in the 1950s – Madame Li and her supporters called for a public engagement in the field of disease prevention. A few months later, at the second National Health Conference in 1952, it was officially announced that socialist medicine was to serve the people and also involve the people. Public health work would become the work of the masses.[23]

In the PRC's socialist war against disease, the most celebrated showcase was schistosomiasis control. As discussed earlier, the crusade against schistosomiasis was the epitome of the new Communist state's political commitment to transform the backward (read: diseased) countryside through mass participation in disease prevention and science. Although it is classic communist praxis to move the focus from the individual to the collective, the PRC's view of bringing about advancement or modern transformation through community participation in the struggle to improve the people's health was, however, not new to the Chinese experience. For the first half of the twentieth century, Christian medical missionaries had been at the forefront of engaging local communities to 'improve' people's lives through changing attitudes and behaviours. Improving the health of 'the Sick Man of Asia' was central to the goal of reform of Western medical missionaries and the early twentieth-century political modernizers in China alike. It was backed by the financial commitment of the Rockefeller Foundation's International Health Board (IHB). The China Medical Board (CMB) was the second and perhaps largest-ever program of the IHB. The program included building a world-class medical school and hospital and facilitating the introduction of bio-medicine into post-Imperial China, Asia's first modern republic. In a CMB publication celebrating its 100th anniversary, the reader is informed that 'the knowledge generated through Peking Union Medical College (PUMC) helped usher in a revolution in the understanding and practice of medicine in China, which catalysed dramatic health progress over the course of a century ... It is an unprecedented human achievement.'[24]

Claude Barlow was a former Baptist medical missionary who first went to China in 1908. Famously known as a 'martyr to medicine', Barlow identified an internal parasite *fasciolopsis buski*, which claimed countless victims in Zhejiang province's Shaoxing County in eastern China. With a fellowship from the CMB, Barlow conducted field research on this human intestinal fluke. Toward the end of his study, in 1922, eager to save the suffering Chinese, he swallowed thirty-two flukes taken from the body of his Chinese patient so that he could bring them back to the United States for laboratory study. His act literally bore fruit. His subsequent study on the life cycle of *fasciolopsis buski* in humans established him as the world's leading authority on the topic. The study demonstrated that the main contributing factors for the prevalence of the disease amongst the local population in rural Zhejiang province was their practice of using night-soil for fertilizer, as well as their habit of eating land snails raw, just 'as we do oysters'. From this finding, he concluded that the disease was easily controllable. One preventive measure was to 'disinfect the night-soil in the jars and ripening tanks'. 'Addition of lime will accomplish this,' he assured. Another was killing the immediate snail hosts. As a medical missionary, Barlow was also a firm believer in community engagement through health education: 'All of these [preventive] measures require the voluntary support of the community and to gain this there needs to be a widespread propaganda of enlightenment.'[25] Although he did not have the privilege of trying out his plan for action in his beloved China, it did make him an ideal person to lead the IHB's sanitary campaign in Egypt to eradicate hookworm and schistosomiasis between 1929 and 1940.[26]

Barlow's initial finding in China would lead to ever more sophisticated public health interventions in the country. Undoubtedly, the increasing popularity of the vector control approach following the discovery of Paris Green in 1921 (see chapter 1) had an impact on Barlow's belief in the efficacy of killing snails in controlling *fasciolopsis buski* in humans as well as in controlling the snail vectors for schistosomiasis, although a large-scale public health intervention by controlling the vector was only made possible in China with the advent of the Communist Liberation after 1949 (as will be discussed in chapter 3).

For the first half of the twentieth century, the control of contaminated faeces, the elimination of reservoir hosts, and access to clean water supplies were the most common interventions for schistosomiasis and hookworm prevention. The IHB Egyptian campaign aimed at controlling schistosomiasis began with sanitizing targeted Egyptian villages by building latrines, but it ended with killing snails. The former proved to have no measurable effect on morbidity or any impact on the parasite; the latter, however, was too labour- and time-intensive. In the end, the IHB concluded that ridding the communities of schistosomiasis by clearing snails in Egyptian canals was too lengthy an undertaking, and, losing patience, they passed the responsibility to the Egyptian government. Barlow stayed in Egypt for another three years on a contract with the Egyptian government to head an independent Bilharzia Destruction Section. Yet by 1949, the Egyptians had lost any hope of eradicating bilharzia, 'the most important disease of Egypt'. A year later, Barlow returned to the United States.[27] Back home, he reminisced about his earlier time in disease eradication in China: 'it was futile, since it saved lives and gave relief, but it did nothing about the basic control of disease. At the age of 54 with a wife and four daughters I gave it all up, went back to college, got my doctorate in science and have been working ever since on Preventive Medicine.'[28]

At this exact moment, the Communist leadership in China waged their 'socialist' crusade against the 'oriental' schistosomiasis. Having drawn the conclusion that mass therapy was simply not affordable, following the advice of experts they turned to prevention through mass participation. This was not actually a surprising turn. As mentioned earlier, the majority of Chinese experts in public health were trained in the PUMC or other Rockefeller-funded institutions in the West, such as the Johns Hopkins School of Hygiene and Public Health. Many of them had received their modern education as children in missionary schools. Like Barlow, they, too, advocated engaging the public through a widespread 'propaganda of enlightenment'. The strategies employed for the new China's 'socialist' campaign resembled, in turn, those of the IHB's earlier sanitary campaign in Egypt, but this time around the CCP was determined that the outcome of its 'socialist' campaign would be different. It would show the world that what the Western 'imperialists' had failed to achieve in Egypt would succeed in the new China under its direction.

In the received historiography, the CCP has been credited for its success in mobilizing the Chinese peasantry during the Chinese revolution. Such a claim also resonates in the official publications about the PRC's public health campaigns during the Mao era. Amongst these campaigns, the mass campaign against schistosomiasis was a shining example. Internationally, the campaign was also received positively at the time. In the Long 1970s, too, vast numbers of international medical and public health experts agreed that the PRC was the most successful example globally in terms of combatting the disease. The CCP's purported heroic struggle against schistosomiasis through mass participation was widely cited as evidence of the PRC's superior health system by those in favour of a horizontal approach to health care delivery. In contrast, the Egyptians' long and failed battle against the disease was used to critique a colonial approach to public health that neglected the participation of the community.[29] However, evidence I have unearthed from archives and oral interviews shows that as soon as the PRC campaign was set in motion, the authorities quickly learned that they really had little control over it. People responded to the campaign in vastly different ways, ranging from enthusiastic participation and passive conformity, to supplication, manipulation, and stealthy resistance, or even to active opposition. Confronted with unforeseen contingencies as well as political uncertainties, the authorities constantly revised their strategies. This added further obstacles to implementation. Contrary to the aim of bringing 'cultural revolution' to modernize the countryside, thus raising the cultural level of the 'ignorant' peasantry by involving the masses in the campaign to fight the disease through 'ruralizing' medicine and science, the day-to-day reality was very different and much more varied. To an extent, the more nuanced process of 'acculturation' allowed parallel systems, including multitudes of folk practices, to exist alongside the state system, hence paving the way for the decentralization of health care delivery in the late 1960s and early 1970s. While the commonplace idea that increased centralization was a hallmark of the PRC's health care system during the Mao era – at least in the propaganda from Beijing and the international reception of such views – the reality on the ground remained a complex mix of local, regional, and national solutions to the ongoing public health dilemmas of the new state, some of which were more effective than others.

SCHISTOSOMIASIS CONTROL CADRES

To engage and educate the masses demanded many more frontline grassroots workers. In 1951, more than 400 young people were recruited for the twenty-two local schistosomiasis control institutions in the three provinces of Zhejiang, Jiangsu, and Anhui where the disease was endemic. In the meantime, thousands of medical and nursing students from surrounding large cities were mobilized to go to the countryside during their school vacations to assist local schistosomiasis prevention and treatment work, as well as helping to conduct epidemiological surveys and gathering data.[30] Some stayed on to lead local disease prevention work in the following years. These new recruits were officially named 'schistosomiasis control cadres' (血防干部). This was part of the nationwide drive to train 'personnel for national construction work, the eradicating of feudal, comprador and fascist ideology and the developing of the ideology of service to the people', as stated in the Common Program.[31] In 1950, the Ministry of Health and the Ministry of Education jointly issued an edict to train health cadres and health personnel at various levels for the 'urgent need' of building a health system for the new China.[32] In some areas, however, recruitment of schistosomiasis cadres did not go as smoothly as hoped. The Zhejiang provincial authority had planned to build up to 200 grassroots schistosomiasis prevention and treatment teams. This would have required a large number of trained personnel, including 200 doctors, 200 paramedics, 400 nurses, and 200 lab technicians. Failing to meet the recruitment target, the authority turned to local private practitioners who had lost their livelihood as a result of the revolutionary upheaval and to young people just out of school who were drifting about with no prospect of employment. The latter were recruited according to their class background. It was believed that consciousness or 'socialist attitudes' depended on class (family) background. Hence, those from poorer peasant and working-class families had a greater chance of being accepted into the new system. The irony was that the greater the level of education (and the higher the economic status), the less likelihood there was of being employed in this new undertaking. The selected youngsters were enrolled in short crash courses on schistosomiasis prevention, without any general training in public health goals.[33] In these crash courses, they learned how to give injections, take blood pressure and temperature, and collect faecal samples. Ren Jixian was only eighteen years old. He had already joined a mass organization, the Communist Youth League. After two months of training, he was seconded to villages to lead schistosomiasis control work on the ground. It did not matter that he had little knowledge of treatment and prevention. The key was that he had the 'correct socialist attitude': he did not mind that there was no bed to sleep on at night, nor did he complain that his salary was only a meagre 30 *yuan* (less than $10) per month. He was motivated by the idea of taking part in a greater historical mission that was for the good of his country, and he took pride in his ability to convey the message of the party concerning health and civic improvement to rural peasants. On the other hand, schistosomiasis control work, as part of the CCP's project of socialist transformation, offered young activists such as Jixian an opportunity for upward mobility. Three years on, the local authority awarded Jixian the position of deputy director of the Pinghu County epidemic prevention centre. He was to lead the county's schistosomiasis control work for the next three decades. Pinghu County in Zhejiang province was one of the places where Faust and Meleney conducted their field research back in the 1920s. In 1952, when Jixian first arrived at Pinghu, it was said that snails were so plentiful that one could easily grab a handful. As a model worker, Jixian was good with people as well as in organizing activities. He went out of his way to persuade villagers to hand over night-soil for disinfection, not to wash their night stool bucket in the canal, and to join him in burying snails. He tirelessly told stories of how schistosomiasis had claimed countless lives in the past and how in the new China, under the leadership of the CCP, victims of the disease were being restored to health.[34] After nearly thirty years of battling schistosomiasis, in 1978 the *People's Daily* declared that Pinghu County had succeeded in eradicating the disease. In 2014, at the advanced age of eighty-one, Jixian went to the local party archive to hand over his papers and his photos of local schistosomiasis control over the previous sixty years. When asked why, he answered that he wanted the history of schistosomiasis control in Pinghu to be remembered by future generations.[35] At Pinghu, the success story of schistosomiasis control did not arise automatically from the central policy, nor did it rely solely on the political commitment of the CCP. If China's schistosomiasis control was locally successful, it was because of the individual commitment of people such as Ren Jixian who participated in it and who, through the propaganda of the CCP, became emblematic of overall rather than local success.

Not everyone shared the same level of commitment and enthusiasm or indeed of success. Zhu Zhiwen was a near contemporary of Ren Jixian. She also enrolled in a short course on schistosomiasis prevention in 1952 and subsequently became a schistosomiasis control cadre in nearby Jiaxing County in Zhejiang province. Zhiwen, however, had a very different story to tell. She remembered how difficult it was to collect night-soil from the villagers. In China, chemical fertilizer only replaced bio-fertilizers in the 1980s. Until the 1970s, human and animal night-soil was the most important bio-fertilizer for farming. To villagers, night-soil was worth its weight in gold. To hand over night-soil simply meant to have less food on the table. Thus, for this reason alone villagers were hostile to schistosomiasis control cadres and sanitation work. Villagers mocked them as 'Mr Shit'(大便先生) or 'Shit Collector' (讨粪先生), comparing them to the despised tax collectors from the former Nationalist regime.[36] On one occasion, on Zhiwen's mission to collect night-soil, the villagers set their vicious guard dog to chase her away. She was so frightened that she began to cry. Zhiwen also remembered that many of her fellow grassroots health workers frequently vomited over the awful smell of the faeces. In the early days, her team consisted of only four to five people. Each day they had to examine between 100 and 200 packages of faeces. They were not supplied with rubber gloves, so their hands were in direct contact with the samples. After spending an entire day handling faeces, they could not abide their own smell. What troubled her even more was watching villagers die of the disease and being unable to help. On one occasion, a severely ill male patient went to her team begging for treatment after his local centre had refused him. Moved by his pleading, Zhiwen's team took him in, and after twenty courses of sodium antimony tartrate injections the patient was on his way to recovery. But three days after the treatment ended, he suffered withdrawal and died. Fearing the guard dog would devour the man's dead body, Zhiwen and another team member stayed up all night guarding it. She was so traumatized by this event that decades later she could still viscerally remember how cold and frightened she felt that night.[37]

CHAOS ON THE GROUND

In 1953, as the Land Reform was drawing to a close in many parts of rural China, the CCP's rural work entered its next phase: to consolidate state control over the management and distribution of agricultural resources. The party introduced an increasing number of such campaigns across the countryside, ranging from grain procurement (state monopoly over grain distribution) to developing agricultural co-operatives* and improving agricultural productivity. Grain procurement and the collectivization of agricultural production became the party's core rural policy. Over time, such policies trumped any public health catastrophes occasioned by agricultural expansion. The rural administrative machinery was constantly overburdened by these new programs. Because of the shortage of trained personnel, grassroots cadres often had to at least make attempts at multi-tasking. Many schistosomiasis control cadres were also assigned to implementing other public health programs. They had to enforce 'new-style' medicalized childbirth, engage villagers in the Patriotic Health Campaign (1952), help with mass immunization and combatting seasonal infectious diseases, as well as support army recruitment work and enforce the New Marriage law. In addition, they were dragged into implementing the party's core rural policy of supporting agricultural collectivization and grain procurement work. Ren Jixian remembered that after spending an entire day examining the faeces of schoolchildren, as well as treating those who tested positive, his team stayed up all night to help procure grain for the state.[38] Juggling their multiple tasks, besides having little experience in disease control and a limited amount of time and resources, the majority of grassroots cadres focused on completing each task quickly rather than implementing the policy systematically. Tasks were often measured in quantitative terms, with numbered targets set by their superiors, and in some cases when cadres resented what they were asked to do they came up with makeshift solutions. Planning was thrown out the window, and responsibility was pushed around as if in a ball game. In some villages, for instance, with no time to mobilize the villagers to catch snails, local cadres spent the government-allocated schistosomiasis prevention funds purchasing enough snails to meet the snail elimination quota.[39]

---

* In the early stage, collectivization of agricultural production took place in the form of co-operatives.

A lack of planning, the rush to meet quantitative goals, and eager-ness to outdo each other, in some cases with over-enthusiasm and an overt emphasis on mass involvement, led to carelessness that, in turn, caused the enormous waste of already scarce resources. An official evaluation in 1951–52 of disease prevention work in the country-side near Shanghai showed there was no system of managing and distributing the precariously scarce equipment and drugs. Damage to equipment was common. Fearing failure to meet the designated treatment targets, and without sufficient time to obtain the neces-sary data on patient numbers, some treatment centres overstocked massive amounts of drugs.[40] Many local cadres also resented or had no patience for the time-consuming sanitation work. Ignoring the government's policy of putting prevention first, they focused on treat-ment, since it was quicker to obtain quantifiable results that way. In terms of mass mobilization, it was also more visibly persuasive to use the testimonies of those being cured. Thus, public engagement became engagement in therapy only. In Zhejiang province's Shaoxing region, local authorities spent the entire prevention fund on mass therapy alone, and those cadres who were trained to carry out san-itation work were sent to do propaganda work instead. In nearly two years, no progress at all was made in prevention.[41] Further west, in Qu County, one township was reported to have spent more than 128 million *yuan* treating 128 sick patients. Most of that money was wasted because in a rush to reach the treatment target set by the higher-ups, the local authority had engaged a huge number of vol-unteers to give injections, but since the volunteers were not properly trained and lacked the necessary experience, they often botched the shots. Such incidents so angered villagers that they drove the schisto-somiasis prevention team out of the village and occupied their office for other, more pragmatic uses.[42] To meet the assigned prevention target quickly, local cadres spent a total of 18,686,200 *yuan* from the schistosomiasis prevention fund to build a brand new communal village lavatory. Built in haste, and badly, the lavatory was not rain-proof. The cadres had failed to consult or engage the villagers, and as a result no one would use it; in the end it had to be dismantled. In another village, after exhausting the schistosomiasis prevention fund in building a new village well, there was no money left for any new bricks. Instead, the construction team used old bricks from a ruined burial ground, but as a result the water became contaminated and the well was never used.[43] On the other hand, because of the lack of advance planning, the southern Jiangsu regional health bureau simply failed to allocate the necessary funding in time for schistoso-miasis control. The shortfall in the community jeopardized the entire preventive program for the region.[44]

There were also rampant problems that undermined safety, a muddled reporting structure, and regular overcharging of treat-ment fees. In racing to meet their treatment targets, for instance, some local treatment centres shortened the sodium antimony tar-trate treatment course from twenty days to fifteen days. However, this shortened treatment led to overdoses and subsequent deaths. After four patients died as result, the Eastern China Health author-ity gave the order to put safety first. Some local treatment centres then became overly cautious and reduced the treatment dosage. This weakened the effectiveness of the treatment, resulting in a high rate of re-infection and leading to the wastage of the limited number of drugs. Lacking enough personnel and equipment, many treatment centres also failed to carry out the necessary 'prep' work prior to the actual treatment. This often led to even greater waste. At one centre, for example, because of the lack of preparation, 6,000 faecal samples got muddled up. Mistakes such as this delayed treatment and caused unnecessary waste of human and material resources.[45] Because of the lack of funding and limited access to the necessary drugs to ensure the mandated rate of success, some centres refused to treat the newly infected or those who were severely ill. In some areas, only prime labourers received treatment, since agricultural production depended on them staying healthy, but villagers fought against such discrimination by raising their grievances with the local authorities.[46] In Kunshan County, outside of Shanghai, to make up for the shortfall in funding, the local authority overcharged patients for each treatment. The villagers rioted and demanded that the authority not only subsidize the treatment but reimburse them for the work time lost while they were receiving treatment. They also bargained for greater compensation for the cost of digging new wells.[47] The conflict between implementing schistosomiasis therapy and the villagers' desire to improve family income would be exacer-bated with the introduction of the work point distribution system as of 1955 and the commune system as of 1958.

Health education, and propaganda too, failed to convey the desired message around health. In 1951, the official estimate is that 6,560 schistosomiasis prevention educational posters were distributed in eastern and western Zhejiang's endemic villages; there was also the sponsoring of 403 public lectures, fifty-seven slide shows, and nine public health exhibitions. Songs and operas were composed to teach people about the danger of disease as well as methods of prevention. There were even short stories written on the theme. Aiming to educate the masses in order to change their behaviour, those involved in health education and propaganda failed to appreciate that schistosomiasis was closely bound up with the way of life of the rural population. Centuries-old habits would not change overnight, especially when people's living conditions stayed the same. Villagers enjoyed the entertainment, but they rejected the message: 'Our livelihood depended on water and night-soil. Keeping away from the water and centrally managing night-soil prevents us getting on with our farming work. It's wasting our time.'[48] Some authorities sought to use new technologies such as slide shows or short films to engage the public. Villagers were excited about the new media but, again, were unimpressed by the content. In Zhejiang province's Changshan County, for example, 300 villagers were invited to a slide show on schistosomiasis prevention, but they quickly got bored. Only nineteen of them stayed to watch the show to the end.[49] With the aim of engaging the masses with science, rural villagers in some endemic regions were invited to look at *cercariae* (the free-swimming larval stage of the parasite as it passed from the snail to humans and other animals) under the microscope. Unimpressed by the science, they thought schistosomiasis control cadres were playing magic tricks. In 1953, during a local snail elimination campaign in Zhejiang province's Qu County, where Xu Xifan had been deeply distraught by the damage caused by a major schistosomiasis outbreak in 1948, one villager crushed a snail with his hands and threw the dead snail on a fellow villager's leg: 'Let's see you get infected,' he mocked.[50]

MODELS OF SUCCESS

Official reports were biased toward the successes, however. San huanfan district in Zhuji County was one of Zhejiang province's successful models for schistosomiasis control. In 1951, responding to the Ministry of Health's schistosomiasis control directive, as well as the policy of putting prevention first, the Zhejiang provincial authority chose Sanhuanfan as its first schistosomiasis prevention pilot district. Personnel, along with technical and financial resources, were poured in. To guarantee a successful result, grassroots cadres and activists – from the village party secretary to the heads of local mass organizations such as the peasant association and the women's association – filled positions on the Sanhuanfan Schistosomasis Prevention Committee. They took charge of the mass mobilization work to free up those experts sent by the provincial authority so that the latter could focus on the mass therapy and the more technical aspects of preventive work. These grassroots committee members set an example by handing over their own families' night-soil and went around to the villagers' homes to persuade them to hand theirs over. They did not give lectures. Instead, they helped villagers to wash vegetables, to sew shoes, or to harvest grain. They also came up with the innovation of redistributing the collective night-soil to each family according to its size. Attracted by the economic benefit, villagers began to hand over their night-soil. Villager Jiang Huanfa had been re-infected with schistosomiasis three times and had lost faith in the efficacy of any therapy. From the day that he was admitted for further treatment, he had been planning to escape, but having sensed his reluctance to undergo schistosomiasis therapy, cadres sent activists from the local women's association to influence his mother. After repeated visits and conversations about how treatment plus prevention would bring her son back to health, Jiang's mother was won over. Persuaded by his mother, Jiang stayed in the treatment centre and successfully completed his treatment. After his health had been restored, he was invited to share his experience at a public meeting. Jiang became the living testimony for the virtue of the state-run schistosomiasis control.[51] There were many other such public meetings where villagers learned about the horrific economic cost of the disease. They were told that schistosomiasis *and* the exploitative local landlords had driven them to poverty. Thus, in order to achieve economic betterment they had to fight the disease *as well as* the landlords. Such meetings often ended with party activists shouting slogans such as 'To fight against schistosomiasis was to fight against the enemy' and 'Just as we need every villager to fight against the landlords, we also need every villager to fight against schistosomiasis.' Enthusiasm soared, and with this repeated propaganda effort, as an archival report elucidates, the local schistosomiasis prevention work could be carried out effortlessly.[52]

Why did this area produce success where others failed? In addition to successful grassroots mobilization work, the same report also indicates that ensuring the 100 per cent success rate demanded that no infected villager from outside the area be allowed to receive schistosomiasis therapy at Sanhuanfan pilot district.[53] By strictly limiting the patient population to the available resources, success could indeed be achieved. But such an approach only worked in the most tightly controlled and limited context and could not be ramped up for the broader population.

Buyung Township in Jiaxing County was Zhejiang province's other model of success. Here, the mass mobilization did not start well. Overburdened by different rural campaigns introduced by the CCP, local cadres had to make choices and weigh returns against risks. Some put all the township's resources on the CCP's core rural policy of agricultural collectivization and production. For them, schistosomiasis prevention was simply a waste of time. Faced with their initial failure to gain support from grassroots cadres and to engage the locals, the West Zhejiang Schistosomiasis Control Centre felt something had to change. Since they could not mobilize the masses, they decided to target only a small number of villages. Number Four village was chosen because the village cadre was supportive. It began with a snail-catching competition in which village cadres and activists took the lead. They were followed by children from the village school as well as elderly villagers who had lighter farming duties. The competition lasted a month, and nearly thirty kilograms of snails were caught. Winners were honoured as model workers and were rewarded with material goods according to the number of snails they caught and their practical needs. Some were given hoes, others axes and straw hats; children were rewarded with school bags, textbooks, and writing materials. Rewards were given at a public meeting to celebrate the village's achievement and to encourage other villages to follow their example. Sixty-year-old Chen Chuda was the champion snail-catcher, having caught 135 grams of snails, and was given first-class honours. He was invited to give a speech at the meeting: 'During the Nationalist era, I did not know anything about snails. After the [Communist] Liberation I began to see snails everywhere. Thank the Communist Party for leading us to catch snails.' Chen's speech was simple but sincere. Representatives of other villages were obliged to take up the vow: 'We had been too negligent. We must learn from Number Four Village and to carry out our [schistosomiasis control] work properly and well.' But the provincial health authority was not overly enthusiastic about either

Buyun Township's purported success or their method of snail eradication. In their reply to the West Zhejiang Schistosomiasis Control
Centre's report on success, they warned: 'A snail-catching exercise
is dangerous if those involved don't wear protection.' Despite the
warning from their superiors, the West Zhejiang Schistosomiasis
Control Centre took the decision that the local control program was
to centre on the snail-catching competition, even though they were
fully aware of the danger of infection as well as the improbability of
the total elimination of snails. For them, snail-catching was the only
mobilization work they had managed with some success so far, and
it cost the local authority little money. Since there was no funding for
implementing sanitation work such as building new wells or latrines,
catching snails made better sense economically and was therefore
more likely to gain support from grassroots cadres and villagers.
Based on their experience in Number Four village, they calculated
that on average one villager could catch fifteen kilograms of snails
within three hours. Men had to work in the fields to meet the state
quota for grain production, but women and children had little to
do; they rather enjoyed the fun of catching snails. Local mass organizations such as the Women's Association, the Communist Youth
League, and the Peasant Association had built up considerable experience during earlier mass campaigns, such as for the elimination of
illiteracy as well as Land Reform. Subsequently, they played a key
role in organizing snail eradication teams of women and children. In
the first half of 1953, it was reported that 138,000 snails had been
caught and killed in west Zhejiang.[54] Yet the ever-expanding number
of snails killed seemed to have little or no effect on the actual spread
of the illness, given that the true focus was the expansion of agricultural collectivization and the increase of yield. Increased agricultural
activities also increased the chances of infection. In Jiaxing region,
for instance, 24,166 people tested positive. In 1953, the number of
people testing positive grew to 30,030. The rate of infection was
23.38 per cent – 0.10 per cent higher than the previous year.[55]

CONSOLIDATING

The goal of controlling the disease was nowhere near accomplished.
In the drive to meet the quantitative target that prioritized therapeutic
intervention, prevention was largely neglected. Treatment also failed
to deliver satisfactory results. In parts of Zhejiang province, although

the local authorities offered free treatment for those classified as poor peasants, many patients withdrew from their treatment halfway through the course because they could not afford to pay for the meals at the treatment centres. Even amongst those who completed their treatment, the rate of re-infection was high. Take Jiaxing, for example, Zhejiang's flagship region for schistosomiasis control. Here, the rate of re-infection was as high as 42 per cent.[56] Villager Dong Liyin was one of those who were re-infected: 'The treatment was useless. One month after receiving the treatment, I became re-infected, even though I followed the prevention advice by keeping away from waterways or paddy fields,' he complained, with a hint of a whine in his voice. Faced with such failures and to ensure a consistent rate of success, some local authorities gave the order to treat only those in the early stage of disease who had less severe symptoms.[57] When sick villagers confronted the authorities for breaching the stated policy for access to treatment, in the context of the New 'Three Anti'-Campaign to struggle against growing 'bureaucratism, commandism, and violations of law and discipline' at the grassroots level, the Zhejiang provincial Party Committee charged grassroots schistosomiasis control organizations with growing too fast and getting too large. Their growing bureaucratic structure was said to have contributed to 'commandism', a result of 'going over the head' of local organizations to achieve their political objective. In turn, 'commandism' had resulted in the low quality of local control work, with a poor outcome as well as excess waste – at least according to the local officials who clearly understood how they could retain their power over those now wresting it away from them in the struggle for control of the public's health. 'Counter-revolutionaries', right or left opportunists, were also 'unmasked' for being the underlying cause of corruption. They were accused of violating the party's decrees and thus contributing to the overall failure of local schistosomiasis control work. As such, ninety-nine schistosomiasis control cadres in Qu County were found guilty of different political crimes. Yet it is often not clear why and how they acquired those labels. For instance, amongst the 117 'unmasked' as Nationalist spies, their 'criminal' activities did not involve spying but the fact that they were 'narcissistic'.[58] In addition, just as there were 'models of success', there were also 'models of failure'. The latter were named and shamed.

More severely, the Zhejiang Provincial Party Committee accused the grassroots schistosomiasis control work of jeopardizing agricultural production, thus undermining the CCP's core rural policy. As

their 'rescue' plan to remedy past failures, the Zhejiang Provincial
Party Committee closed many local schistosomiasis control centres
and drastically cut back on the number of grassroots schistosomiasis cadres. According to the provincial deputy party secretary He
Shilian, this was to 'clean up' the grassroots organizations and to
avoid making errors of 'left deviationism' as well as 'right deviationism'.[59] As the leading province in schistosomiasis control work,
Zhejiang boasted of having better resources, since it inherited many
of the health and disease control institutions as well as experts and
trained personnel from the former Nationalist government. During
1951–52, it had made impressive progress in building up a grassroots
schistosomiasis control workforce. By 1953, Zhejiang's flagship
schistosomiasis control region, Jiaxing, had successfully recruited
and trained 763 full-time schistosomiasis control cadres. Many
more were mobilized to take part in what they saw as a historical
mission. In November 1953, all grassroots schistosomiasis control
cadres in Zhejiang province were summoned to the beautiful provincial capital of Hangzhou for a 'rectification meeting'. Zhang Ziwei
was the party representative initially assigned to the takeover of the
former Nationalist health institutions in the areas around Jiaxing.
He also took charge of building up the region's schistosomiasis control workforce. Many years later, in his memoir written in the early
1990s, he could still recall how his team were filled with great excitement and enthusiasm when they first arrived at Hangzhou.[60] They
learned quickly, however, that their hard work over the past three
years was condemned for undermining the party's core rural policy
and for jeopardizing agricultural production. They were criticized
for using styles of 'bureaucratism' and 'commandism' in schistosomiasis control work as well as for building too many wells, latrines,
and septic tanks that led to enormous financial waste. Elsewhere, in
Jiaxing region, 489 schistosomiasis control cadres, 64 per cent of
the total number, were dismissed from duty. Some were presented
with the option of pursuing further training in leading grassroots
political work, others were 'mobilized' to go and work for the local
railway and mail services, and a small number returned home to
look for other livelihoods. Disheartened, they grumbled: 'We had
been mobilized to take part in schistosomiasis control work, now
we are mobilized to leave. What's the point?'[61] In the meantime, the
province's mass therapy program was dismantled. The number of
people who could receive treatment was reduced from 50,000 to

15,000. As the CCP's priority changed, it took the entire country into the phase of 'political consolidation'. In its struggle against 'bureaucratism', 'commandism', and violations of law and discipline, schistosomiasis control as well other aspects of public health were also to be 'consolidated' and compromised. People's health was at stake. In Zhejiang province alone, an official report showed that some 35,000 villagers suffering from the disease were deprived of treatment and care as a greater number of schistosomiasis control organizations were consolidated.[62]

From then on, grassroots schistosomiasis control work in Zhejiang province, as well as in other parts of the country, was compromised to a large extent. It was primarily made subordinate to agricultural production and the concomitant development of agricultural co-operatives. As the remaining schistosomiasis control cadres helped villagers to fight drought, plant rice, control pests, and harvest crops, they served as 'the thread that tied the people to the party' and thus played a key role on the ground in assisting the party to consolidate its rule in the endemic regions. In the meantime, managing night-soil and water became central to fostering agricultural collectivization. Snail elimination, too, became integral to land reclamation as well as water conservation – both were essential for China's agricultural development, as will be discussed in chapter 3. The PRC's schistosomiasis control entered the phase of 'two managing and one eradicating' (两管一灭), and more basic scientific research would be conducted to provide scientific backup for the program. In practice, integrated management meant an abandonment of local mass efforts and the amelioration of the anti-commandism campaign as it became evident that centralizing management structures always risked the charge of greater commandism.

Eliminating snails by engineering modifications to agricultural irrigation canals, such as clearing vegetation and cementing, was first developed in Japan. Construction of cement ditches was incorporated into the 1950 amendment to the National Parasite Prevention Act in Japan. A couple of years later, in China, Chinese researcher Wang Peixin began to pilot the use of cement-lined ditches in some endemic regions of Zhejiang province.[63] Back in 1947, as part of his master's degree study, Wang had spent a few months researching schistosomiasis control in mainland Japan and Taiwan. After returning to China in 1948, Wang joined the Nationalist Jiangsu Medical University and spent much of his time observing the movement of snails in the marshland along the Yangtze delta. After his institute was taken over by the Communist authority, Wang was transferred to the nearby Zhejiang province to lead schistosomiasis' control research in west Zhejiang. The new co-operative agricultural system that began to emerge after 1952 made it easier to organize schistosomiasis control by burying the old snail-infested canals. Initially, a number of local authorities welcomed such undertakings because it allowed them to kill two birds with one stone: water conservation as well as schistosomiasis control, through mass participation. But at this early stage, the quality of such work was very poor. Villagers often complained that after the burial work, the surface of the earth became uneven and made walking between the ditches hazardous.[64]

Around the same time, a team of researchers from Hunan in central China came up with another idea of eliminating snails through land reclamation. Hunan province, bordering the Yangtze, is famous for hot chilies and fiery food and for having produced many revolutionary leaders of modern China. It also has the longest recorded history of being a schistosomiasis endemic region. Archaeological evidence of *Schistosoma* eggs from an unearthed female corpse excavated in the Mawangdui Han burial site dates the disease back more than 2,000 years. Indeed, as mentioned in chapter 1, it was by the shore of Dongting Lake that Cao Cao's army suffered a massive defeat after succumbing to a strange disease. Scholars in China identified the disease as schistosomiasis. It was also in Hunan, in 1905, that the American missionary doctor O.T. Logan reported the first clinical case of schistosoma japonicum in China.[65]

In June 1950, Chen Huxin, another graduate of Hunan-Yale College and a believer in saving his troubled motherland through the benefits of bio-medicine, was assigned the task of leading schistosomiasis control work in the Dongting Lake region. During their field research, Chen and his team came up with the hypothesis that land reclamation could help to eliminate snails by destroying their habitat. Their study was published in 1952, a few months before a catastrophic storm hit the southern regions around Dongting Lake. The storm flooded nearly 30,000 acres of farmland and claimed more than 2,000 lives. Around 90,000 people living along the lake were affected. That year's harvest was dealt a fatal hit, and agricultural development in the region suffered a heavy blow. There was therefore an urgent need to open up more land for cultivation.[66] The south Dongting Lake reconstruction project began in December

1952. The committee in charge of the project decided to put Chen's hypothesis of eliminating snails by reclaiming the marshes to the test. The marshland of Xiangyin County, infested with snails, was targeted for agricultural cultivation, and Chen and his team were invited to monitor snail numbers in the reclaimed land. Their survey data over the next two years showed a considerable reduction in the snail population. The reclamation project, however, involved more than 120,000 construction workers toiling in the snail-infested marshland and contaminated water, and as a result many (including those from non-endemic regions) were found to have contracted schistosomiasis.[67] Although Chen Huxin was concerned about this, what mattered more for the authority, however, was that the number of snails decreased significantly. The positive outcome of eliminating snails by land reclamation in Xiangyin County was timely and so was the experiment of linking water conservation with snail elimination in west Zhejiang. Such comprehensive approaches would grow ever more important and were adopted into the national program in the following decade as the CCP Central Committee marched the country into full-scale agricultural collectivization, matched by an even greater scale of the expanding nationwide schistosomiasis control program, as will be discussed in chapter 3.

In 1953, the First Five-Year Plan was put into effect and ran until 1957. Its goal was to rapidly industrialize China and transform the country into a modern industrial power, following the model of the five-year plans in the USSR. Because the largest amount of state investment would go to heavy industry and a much smaller amount would be made available for agricultural development, there was an urgent need to speed up the process of agricultural collectivization. Hence, to bring a full socialist transformation to the Chinese countryside would entail a radical restructuring of the national schistosomiasis control program and thus an improvement in the people's health.

3

Eradicating Schistosomiasis as a Political Undertaking

THE STORM OF SOCIALISM

In the Chinese Agrarian Calendar, 1955 was the 'Year of the Wooden Goat', signifying productiveness and success. In the history of the People's Republic of China (PRC), 1955 was a year of great significance: it marked the end of a period of makeshift years to a year of economic planning and the final adoption of the First Five-Year Plan. Although the First Five-Year Plan was actually inaugurated in 1953, work on the draft plan was only completed in February 1955 and was approved by the First National People's Congress in July 1955. It was followed by corresponding plans at the provincial level. 'We have won a new China, we must redouble our efforts in economic construction to protect and consolidate this new China. This construction is, in the main, a task of socialist industrialization,' as Li Fuchun, the vice premier of the State Council of China and chairman of the State Planning Commission, announced with a level of optimism when delivering the lengthy *Report on the First Five-Year Plan for the Development of the National Economy of the People's Republic of China in 1953–1957.*[1] At the same time, Li and his colleagues at the State Council and the State Planning Commission were aware that the new China they had won was faced with the problem of decreased agricultural production due to poor harvests in the previous two years as well as persistent grassroots resistance to agricultural co-operativization (合作化).* With

---

* Before 1958, collectivization of agricultural production took place in the form of co-operatives. The official term for this stage of collectivization was 'co-operativization'. In 1958, agricultural co-operatives were merged into people's communes.

less food to export, there was not so much equipment to be imported from the USSR and other European countries for 'socialist industrialization'. China had to rely on its own resources for the implementation of the First Five-Year Plan, and austerity was to continue. Since the state had invested huge amounts in heavy industry, there was little cash to invest in agricultural development. Thus, in addition to more efficient and rational management, there was an ever-greater need for agricultural co-operativization as well as for increased enthusiasm in encouraging production. 'Under the present conditions, the agricultural producers' co-operative is a means of increasing agricultural output that involves small investment and speedily yields good results. It is also a necessary step leading the peasants to socialism ... The enthusiasm which individual peasant households show for increasing production must be taken into consideration, and vigorous assistance and leadership should be given to them to develop all their resources to the full and raise per unit area yields,' Li Fuchun's report reasoned.[2] Yet on the ground, 'vigorous assistance and leadership' would pan out quite differently from what Li and the Chinese Communist Party (CCP) leadership envisaged.

Among the measures laid out in the draft Five-Year Plan to increase agricultural output, Li's report prioritized land reclamation, water conservation, and intensive farming methods: 'Since our population is large while the area under cultivation is still limited, we must take energetic measures to open up arable land in a planned way so that we can finally solve the problem of shortages in agricultural produce ... Water conservancy work can extend the irrigated area to increase agricultural output as well as preserve crops from the ravages of flood or drought. The increased agricultural output and other benefits brought about by the elimination or reduction of natural calamities through water conservancy works in many cases to pay back within a few years the funds invested ... Peasants should be encouraged to cultivate their land still more intensively, to put in more fertilizer and step by step adopt more advanced farming techniques ... The use of improved animal-drawn ploughs ... vigorous efforts to store and prepare manure ... are effective ways of raising farm output.'[3] However, all of this was easier to propose than to actually realize.

The minimal target for the expansion of cultivated area as laid out in the First Five-Year Plan was 38,680,000 *mu* (ca. 6,372,024 acres): 'Every effort must be made and means used to surpass it. One method is for state farms to reclaim land. Where local conditions permit, all state farms should expand their cultivated area by a reasonable amount. At the same time, wherever there are large tracts of reclaimable wasteland, efforts should be made to reclaim them and systematically build up new state farms. Another method is to use machines and other means to reclaim wasteland and to organize cultivation by pioneer emigrants,' Li announced in his broad Hunan accent. A man with big eyes and bushy eyebrows, Li had skilfully handled the supply lines for the Communist Red Army during the Long March in the 1930s. He was known as a competent manager but a cautious planner. Having envisaged even larger-scale, nationwide land reclamation for the Second Five-Year Plan, he also anticipated the complexity and difficulties of such a grand undertaking. A gradual approach to agricultural development ('in a planned way', in his own words) was central to his report. While urging the state to work closely with local authorities to draw up a good overall plan, he also encouraged them to undertake smaller-scale reclamation projects in this interim period.[4]

On 31 July 1955, twenty-five days after Li Fuchun delivered his report, Chairman Mao Zedong of the CCP delivered a speech titled 'The Question of Agricultural Cooperation' at a meeting attended by provincial-level party secretaries. The chairman's speech scaled up several targets that had been set out in Li Fuchun's report. Mao, eight years senior to Li, had been friends with him since they were middle school students in their native province of Hunan. Later, they had both joined the CCP and journeyed together on the Long March. While Li skilfully managed the supply lines for the Red Army, Mao had led and won many difficult battles. In 1935, on the Long March, Mao rose to become the supreme leader of the CCP. As the leader of the new China, which he had fought for and won, Mao had little interest in the detailed planning and the day-to-day management of the country; it was too tedious for him. Aspiring to the 'great historical experience in building socialism', as modelled by the Soviet Union, for Mao building socialism was a way to continue the revolution. Having led his forces to win many battles, he was ambitious to win this one too. 'Fight no battle that is not well prepared, no battle whose outcome is uncertain,' he urged provincial leaders. Building gigantic industrialized state farms, such as those in the USSR, across the Chinese countryside in the next twelve years (toward the end of the Third Five-Year Plan) with 500 million *mu* of cultivated land (ten times the figure laid down in the First Five-Year Plan), as well as speeding up agricultural co-operativization, was for him a critical step toward the successful outcome of socialist construction.[5]

Mao was also aware that his speech went against the tide. The situation on the ground had been rather ominous. Following the 'little upsurge' of agricultural collectivization in the last quarter of 1954 during which more than 600,000 co-operatives were organized, the movement suffered serious setbacks. By the first quarter of 1955, it had reached a crisis point. A few months prior to Mao's 31 July speech, the failure to organize agricultural co-operatives in Zhejiang province had raised serious alarm at the Central Committee's Rural Work Department. Reports by government work teams had shown that many middle peasants in Zhejiang province had ganged up and left the co-operatives.[6] Some killed their livestock to protest co-operativization, and many more retained their night-soil for private use. This action in particular had a serious impact on local schistosomiasis control. In the meantime, a poor harvest as well as the increased amount of grain being appropriated by the state left millions of poor peasants without food. A great number of them turned to local authorities to beg for aid. Responding to the emergency, the policy of 'drastic compression' was introduced by the Zhejiang provincial authorities. As a result, 15,000 agricultural co-operatives out of 53,000 were dissolved. In Jiaxing region, where schistosomiasis was endemic, the dissolution rates reached a high of 40 per cent.[7] Amid such confusion, some villages and counties simply reverted to private ownership. As villagers abandoned co-operatives, a good number of villages were left uninhabited. Rumours began to spread, and those peasants who had supported the co-operativization felt betrayed: 'Chairman Mao no longer wants us to organize co-operatives,' they cried.[8]

Some top leaders used the situation in Zhejiang as a warning about the speed of agricultural collectivization. Yet Mao was not someone who was easily cowed. He had acquired the habit of conducting investigations on local conditions back in the 1930s while he was a young CCP leader struggling to build up grassroots support. Once again, he took a trip south to study the local situation himself. More important, he wanted to take control of the chaos of 'mass dissolution' and put a stop to 'rightist mistakes'. During Mao's stay in Shanghai, Ke Qingshi, the first secretary of the Central Party Committee's Eastern China Bureau, gave him unwelcome news. Because of the fierce opposition of peasants seeking to be 'free', up to 30 per cent of grassroots cadres in eastern China no longer wanted to practise socialism in the countryside.[9] Ke's words set Mao on fire: the chairman was ready to strike and turn the tide around. A month later, in June, despite his busy schedule as the paramount leader of a colossal country, Mao returned to eastern China. While in Zhejiang, Mao learned from his bodyguards that schistosomiasis had damaged the health of many working-age male peasants in the region and prevented them from doing agricultural work. One desperately ill patient told Mao's bodyguards: 'If Chairman Mao could find a way to cure us from this deadly disease, he would be a living Buddha, our saviour.'[10]

The words 'living Buddha' and 'saviour' of the people went straight to Mao's heart. He already had some awareness of the damage inflicted by schistosomiasis in rural Zhejiang. Some fifteen months previously, Shen Junru, one of modern China's most respected political figures, who was the first president of the Supreme People's Court of the PRC, wrote a letter to Mao detailing the damage caused by a schistosomiasis outbreak he had witnessed during his trip to sweep his ancestral tomb in his native Zhejiang province's Jiaxing County.* In the same letter, Shen pleaded with Chairman Mao and the people's government to introduce strict measures to control the disease. Mao passed the letter to Xi Zhongxun (the father of Xi Jinping, the future president of the PRC). Xi was then the minister of propaganda, in charge of cultural and public health work.[11] Fifteen months later, however, in the midst of fighting for socialism, Mao envisaged that the battle for the health of ten million Chinese peasants who had been injured by schistosomiasis – the disease was also said to be endangering 1 billion more people living in the countryside – was not merely a matter of political propaganda, it should be on the revolutionary agenda. According to Lenin, 'the fight for socialism is at the same time the fight for health.'[12] In China in 1955, as Mao was to bring forth a socialist storm (in an edited version, this become 'an upsurge in socialist transformation') to sweep across the entire Chinese countryside, he was determined to fight the war against schistosomiasis, whatever the price. For him, ridding the people of this disease that plagued rural China was a necessary step in bringing socialism to the countryside, and his crusade against the disease would be a revolutionary experience that would involve the masses.

---

* Shen also served as the vice chairman of the Chinese People's Consultative Conference as well as the chairman of the Standing Committee of the People's Congress.

In 1933, the year when his mass military warfare tactics came under heavy criticism from the CCP leadership, Mao, a relatively young local branch Communist leader, was removed from the Communist Party Central Committee's Revolutionary Military Council. Faced with this setback, Mao went to Jiangxi province's Changgang Township, the model township of the Central Soviet Area, for an investigation of local conditions. His detailed investigation showed that in one after another mass campaign, from agricultural production to eradication of illiteracy, army recruitment, and public health work, every villager in Changgang Township was, to one extent or another, involved in revolutionary activities. Mao concluded that Changgang's revolutionary success rested on their programs that represented the interests of the people as well as the leadership methods that involved as many people as possible in the implementation of those programs. 'The revolutionary war is a war of the masses; it can be waged only by mobilizing the masses and relying on them,' Mao declared in summarizing his position. To win the support of the masses, Mao reminded the CCP, cadres must attend to the everyday needs of the people. One such need was health: 'Many people suffer from boils and other ailments. What are we going to do about it? All such problems concerning the well-being of the masses should be placed on our agenda ... We should convince the masses that we represent their interests, that our lives are intimately bound up with theirs. We should help them to proceed from these things to an understanding of the higher tasks which we have put forward, the tasks of the revolutionary war, so that they will support the revolution and spread it throughout the country, respond to our political appeals and fight to the end for victory in the revolution.'[13]

In Zhejiang province in 1955, as Mao gathered information on the severity of schistosomiasis in the countryside, he ordered officials at the Ministry of Health to come to the south to discuss eradicating the disease once and for all. He also gave orders that those who were affected were to be given free treatment. Confident that he had turned the tide, Mao left Hangzhou and went to Changsha in his native province of Hunan. There, disregarding all warnings, he symbolically swam across the River Xiang against the current. While still a young student, Mao had loved the thrill of venturing into the middle of the River Xiang to strike against the rapids. In 1925, pondering the future of the Chinese revolution, he had written 'Remember still / *How* venturing midstream, we struck the waters /

And waves stayed the speeding boats.' On 31 July 1955, after having furiously criticized colleagues who cautioned him to slow down the speed of agricultural collectivization, Mao delivered his speech on the 'Question of Agricultural Cooperation'. In addition to scaling up the targets set by the State Planning Commission in the First Five-Year Plan, Mao ended by announcing 'an upsurge in socialist transformation will soon come about all over the Chinese countryside.' He was prepared for an aggressive assault, and no one and nothing would stop him. Straight after the speech, he again went swimming at the Beidaihe summer resort, about 300 kilometres to the east of Beijing. Plunging in as a storm was arriving, Mao exclaimed, 'the storm of socialist transformation will soon come about all over China, we must go deep into the current!'[14] When the Leader swims against the stream, the stream changes direction. On 11 October, the Central Committee of the CCP adopted a decision calling for the completion of elementary co-operatives by the spring of 1958.

ERADICATING SCHISTOSOMIASIS WITHIN SEVEN YEARS'

In the next few months, 'the storm of socialist transformation' in the shape of agricultural collectivization swept across the entire countryside. In November, Mao was back in his favourite city, Hangzhou, to meet with provincial leaders from southern China and reveal his draft Articles on Agricultural Work. This time, he put schistosomiasis control on the agenda for discussion and invited the deputy minister of health, Xu Yunbai, to join the discussion. In Hangzhou, Mao preached that the primary aspect of socialist transformation was to improve economic well-being: the living conditions as well as the physical and cultural health of the rural population. Because there had been a rapid advance in developing agricultural co-operatives, the eradication of diseases such as schistosomiasis that were harming the health of rural peasants needed to catch up with the speed of socialist transformation. He commanded that eradicating schistosomiasis would become a political undertaking to which every local party organization was to give 'all-round' leadership. Of equal importance, he told them that this would be a mass campaign that was to involve as many people as possible.[15] Although not everyone at the meeting shared Mao's utopian vision, having lived under the constant strain of 'watching out for the wolf in front and the tiger behind' during the New 'Three Anti'-Campaign for the past two years, some had hoped that a 'storm of socialist transformation' would allow them to release all the nervous tension that had built up. Another focused campaign would also mean a chance for upward mobility if they managed to win the 'lottery' of meeting the eradication target. The decision was reached that schistosomiasis control, as well as the control of other 'local diseases' harmful to rural villagers and livestock – such as filariasis, bubonic plague, encephalitis, cattle plague, and hog cholera – would be included in the Seventeen Articles of Agricultural Work. This would be implemented across the entire country.[16] As soon as Mao obtained the 'full commitment' from regional leaders, he wasted no time in sending Xu Yunbai to Shanghai that same evening to prepare for the first national meeting on schistosomiasis eradication.

Ke Qingshi, the party secretary of the CCP Central Committee Eastern China Bureau, the man who had sided with Mao a few months earlier to put a stop to the 'right conservatism' in the party, was appointed the party boss of the CCP Central Committee's Nine-Man Subcommittee on Schistosomiasis Control, even though he had no experience in medical or health work or in leading them. Bo Yibo,[*] then China's minister of finance and the chairman of the State Planning Commission, remarked that Ke Qingshi was someone who always knew the right thing to say to Chairman Mao. It could be said that in the storm of socialist transformation that swept across the Chinese countryside in the second half of 1955, there was no one Mao trusted more than Ke to push forward a nationwide mass crusade against schistosomiasis, that 'enemy of socialism' from the natural world.[17] In Mao's heart, Ke was the person who could stand up to bureaucratism and answer only to the chairman himself. Suddenly, what had been a problem of public health to be combatted by trained experts in the field came to be seen as a clearly political undertaking: the people's health was and would be a focus for the utopian promises that were inherent in the new state's political ideology. A healthy people defined the perfect state. The Nine-Man Subcommittee was to take over the Ministry of Health's power over schistosomiasis control, since Mao had intended the eradication of schistosomiasis as a political undertaking to be led by party authorities, not technocrats. In this way, the Anti-Schistosomiasis Campaign

---

[*] The father of the disgraced politician Bo Xilai.

would not to be hindered by ministerial bureaucracy; the expert had been demoted to a subordinate role in this political attempt to improve the people's health.

On 22 November 1955, although the chairman was not present at the first national meeting to kick-start the nationwide Anti-Schistosomiasis Campaign, Ke Qingshi spoke to the ninety delegates from all the affected regions of southern China and made sure that 'Chairman Mao' and 'the Party' were constantly invoked. 'We must eradicate the disease within seven years (at the completion of the Second Five-Year Plan). This is the task entrusted to us by Chairman Mao and the Party,' Ke proclaimed. To win his points, Ke relied on political rhetoric, not expertise. According to him, the Anti-Schistosomiasis Campaign was an integral part of the chairman's and the CCP's plan to realize a specific socialist way of life in the Chinese countryside by transforming rural villages into a disease-free 'socialist garden' overflowing with 'socialist culture'. Hence, 'in the seven years, in addition to eradicating diseases, we would eradicate illiteracy too. Each villager would learn to read 1,500–2,000 words,' he announced.[18]

For the first time, the term 'eradicating' replaced 'control'. Yet Ke, as well as the Nine-Man Subcommittee, were either unaware of or overlooked the magnitude of the challenge. Among the data from the thirteen provinces where the disease was endemic, they learned that there were 224 endemic counties and that around 10 million people were infected. The same data also suggested that the severity of the disease in eighty-four of these counties was questionable. More worrying, no data was collected from Shanghai County, one of the worst affected regions. Furthermore, local reports from different parts of the country showed that the majority of those testing positive showed few or no symptoms. Those affected did not see the point of treatment, never mind eradicating the disease. Even the incomplete data that was available to them did not seem to deter Ke. Because the chairman had depicted public health as an integral part of the revolutionary war of the masses, it could only be won by involving the masses. To win over the masses would involve propaganda: 'I used to hear people talking about big bellies, but I never saw one. When I saw photographs of villagers with big bellies, I got frightened. Let's make films about the harm of schistosomiasis to wake people up and to warn them that the enemy is very canny ... To eradicate the disease, we must involve the masses as well as science. We must combine mass mobilization with mass science ... By next year, 80 per cent of peasants would join agricultural cooperatives. That would make it easier for us to mobilize the masses to join the battle [against schistosomiasis] ... Science is not to involve a few scientists. Science is to involve people to come up with innovations.' But how? And in what form? Ke Qingshi had envisioned the eradication of schistosomiasis as a propaganda war that could be won through exhortation. He gave provincial leaders three goals for its implementation: be optimistic; identify successful models; and make local plans. Following his boss, Wei Wenbo, the deputy party head of Shanghai municipal as well as of the Anti-Schistosomiasis Campaign, drew up an eradicating timetable of 'Two years of preparation; Four years of fighting; Two years of cleaning up'. In addition, the Nine-Man Subcommittee sent delegates away with a regular schedule of meetings (one each month at the county level and one every four months at the provincial and national levels) to discuss, review, and report on the progress of the campaign. To help the provincial authorities reach the goal of eradication, Wei Wenbo also urged them to utilize folk medical practices, or Traditional Chinese Medicine (TCM) as such practices had now become known.[19] This was the first time the incorporation of TCM had been emphasized at a high level. The abandonment of the 'expert society' simultaneously meant an abandonment of allopathic medicine as the sole model for the diagnosis and treatment of illness.

TRADITIONAL CHINESE MEDICINE (TCM) AS A REMEDY BUT NOT A CURE

In reality, the practice of combatting schistosomiasis with folk remedies had already begun. Two years previously, in the context of the New 'Three Anti'-Campaign (as discussed in the previous chapter), the heightened risk of accidental death as well as the need to reduce costs had led the Changshan health centre in Zhejiang province to abandon treating patients with sodium antimony tartrate. Instead, they involved some local physicians who treated severely ill villagers with a folk remedy made of the herb *veronicastrum axillare*, which grows abundantly in southern China. This had fewer negative side effects than sodium antimony tartrate, and it did relieve symptoms in those severely ill of oedema, but it could not cure the disease.[20] Experts trained in allopathic medicine, such as Su Delong, did raise the shortcomings, as did healers who used herbal medicine. One traditional practitioner in the Shanghai region, for instance, cautioned that 'herbal remedies are only useful to give a temporary break'.[21] More problematic was that some remedies also contained highly toxic herbal plants – such as the rhizomes of *Veratrum nigrum*, traditionally used to kill parasites. When widely promoted without careful monitoring of administration and dosage, herbal remedies, purportedly 'safe', could sometimes lead to fatalities. In the case of *Veratrum nigrum* roots, it could also cause permanent damage to the central nervous system.[22]

Yet the concerns of the experts, as well as the possible health risks, were ignored in the increasing politicizing of the campaign. Prior to 1956, the Ministry of Health, the seat of the public health experts, had been in charge of controlling schistosomiasis. After 1956, the power was handed over to the purely political Nine-Man Subcommittee.[23] As a response to this politicization, the Ministry of Health encouraged the development or rediscovery of folk herbal remedies to combat schistosomiasis – as in Changshan: 'Changshan's innovation was of political importance,' it was argued.[24] Abandoning its earlier attitude that labelled traditional healing practices as backward practices of the feudal past, herbal remedies and acupuncture were now advocated as a cultural heritage of the Chinese people. The process had begun a couple of years earlier. In 1954, the Military Commission's Ministry of Health, the military rival of the Ministry of Health, launched critical attacks on the Ministry of Health for being overly ambitious, lacking leadership and clear goals, and for allowing too much waste, as well as for an overwhelming number of accidents. The Political Affairs Council's Commission on Cultural and Education was assigned the task of 'helping' the Ministry of Health to re-evaluate its work. This allowed some eminent figures from the community of traditional healers, as well as those advocating a new medicine that was distinctively Chinese, to attack the Ministry of Health's earlier policy to modernize Chinese medicine by synthesizing pluralistic traditional medical practices with bio-medicine (the slogan was to 'westernize or scientize Chinese medicine and to make Western medicine Chinese'). They criticized such policies as having marginalized traditional medical practices – the national cultural heritage of the Chinese people.[25] The event coincided with an outbreak of Japanese encephalitis in the summer of 1954 in Shijiazhuang, 263 kilometres south of Beijing. After failed attempts to control the outbreak using penicillin, a local herbal doctor suggested using White Tiger soup, a decoction made of gypsum *Fibrosum*, *Rhizoma anemarrhenae*, Radix Glycyrrhizae Preparata, and non-glutinous rice that had been used in China for more than 2,000 years to treat the early stage of acute infection with systemic inflammation. The decoction did help to reduce the number of casualties.[26] In response to both events and under the instruction of the Commission on Cultural and Education, the Ministry of Health was obliged to revise its earlier policy. Out of this debate arose a state-defined and certified program of systemized 'folk medicine' that was now under the label 'Traditional Chinese Medicine' (TCM).[27] In 1956, the Ministry of Health sent a team of experts from its new Research Academy of Traditional Chinese Medicine in Beijing, the first state-funded institution for TCM research, to Zhejiang province's Jiaxing County to experiment with using acupuncture and herbal remedies to treat schistosomiasis. Although these experts had never encountered a single schistosomiasis case before, the experiment did bear some fruit, and it helped to popularize the use of acupuncture to cut down the adverse effect of sodium antimony tartrate.

The local authorities in Jiaxing welcomed the call to engage traditional practices in schistosomiasis control for practical reasons, as did the authorities in some other regions, such as the provinces of Jiangsu and Anhui. In this new and more radical phase of schistosomiasis control, developing or rediscovering existing local practices would help to reduce costs and win the support of traditional healers, especially since the State Council and the State Planning Commission made it clear that austerity was to continue. In Zhejiang province, for instance, after the number of schistosomiasis control cadres had been reduced in the New 'Three Anti'-Campaign two years previously, there was a severe shortage of personnel to lead the mass campaign on the ground. This shortage was further exacerbated by the simultaneous launching of other public health campaigns, such as killing the 'four pests' (除四害) in 1958.[*] In December 1955, a few days

---

[*] The campaign aimed at removing disease vectors such as rats, flies, mosquitos, and sparrows, but it had devastating, unintended consequences because it upset the natural ecological balance. After sparrows were slaughtered, for example, locusts drove in and devoured the fields of grain, paving the way for the famine that claimed tens of millions of lives. For further readings, see Rebecca Kreston, 'Paved with Good Intentions: Mao Tse-Tung's "Four Pests" Disaster', *Discover* Magazine Blogs, http://blogs.discovermagazine.com/bodyhorrors/2014/02/26/mao-four-pests-china-disease/#.XKWxSKR7kaE; Frank

after the campaign to eradicate schistosomiasis began, the Ningpo regional health authority in Zhejiang province was bombarded by requests from counties and towns for more personnel: 'We need more schistosomiasis cadres.' Yet the local personnel department had no budget to increase the staff quota, and they had little alternative but to turn to traditional practitioners for help.[28] Herbal therapies did not require patients to take time off from working in the fields; thus, cadres in the agricultural co-operatives, as well as sick villagers, preferred them to hospital or clinic-based treatment. In regions where villagers had little contact with or no access to allopathic medicine, they were more willing to be treated by local healers, since they trusted them. As a result, and somehow unintended, traditional practices flourished, as did grassroots health workers. Although it quickly became clear that herbal remedies would do little to help achieve the goal of eradicating schistosomiasis, these health auxiliaries, some of whom were herbal medicine healers or who practised traditional techniques such as acupuncture, became indispensable in carrying out the campaign as well as further public health work on the ground.[29] They not only relieved local cadres of the burden of time-consuming public health work, but, more important, they were essential in delivering health care to the villagers, thus reducing the health care costs of the co-operatives, since the health workers were either paid directly or were reimbursed with work points. These grassroots health auxiliaries would eventually serve as the model for the 'Barefoot Doctor' program in the 1960s and 1970s.

The initial euphoria over folk remedies and acupuncture, however, quickly exhausted itself because they not only failed to deliver a cure but had almost zero impact on reaching the goal of eradication. In Zhejiang province, in the heavily infected villages of the coast, there remained some residual resistance to TCM among villagers who had gradually built up a belief in the power of allopathic medicine that was due, in part, to the efforts of the Western medical missionaries prior to Communist rule but also to the persistent public health propaganda in the PRC before 1954 that prejudiced traditional practices as 'feudal' or 'superstitious' practices of the past. With their ears full of testimony such as: 'In the old China we had no money to treat disease, so we prayed to Buddha and drank folk remedies. Now

Dikötter, *Mao's Great Famine: The History of China's Most Devastating Catastrophe*, 1958–62 (London: Bloomsbury 2010), 187–6.

the party has sent doctors to cure us', these villagers, too, wanted the 'miraculous' cure of the magic allopathic bullet. Some of them refused folk remedies, seeing them as less effective.[30]

SETBACKS

Further up the ladder, the authorities soon realized that herbal therapies and acupuncture would not help them in meeting their seven-year eradication target. In the meantime, the plan to educate the public on schistosomiasis prevention through the new medium of film was underway. Upon receiving the edict requesting their participation in the Anti-Schistosomiasis Campaign, the Shanghai Film Studio responded quickly. By January 1956, two short educational films on schistosomiasis prevention were produced and made ready for public viewing. Yet at the grassroots level, very few cadres were willing to organize any viewings, since most of them were pressed for time to lead agricultural production as well the task of reorganizing the newly merged, larger co-operatives. Some cadres sent a note to say they would be away, and others said they had too much work to do. A few used the cold weather and cloudless sky as excuses. Those cadres managing the mobile communities living on rivers and canals around Shanghai complained that the minimal fee of five *fen* (less than one penny) charged for the viewing was too expensive given the poverty of the boat people.[31] Thus, the films were never shown to their intended audiences.

Although the implementation of mass sanitation work seemed to be made easier with the instituting of agricultural co-operatives, as Ke Qingshi had anticipated, and produced more immediate results, such results were often short-lived. In addition, under severe pressure to involve as many people as possible and get the job done quickly, there was neither the means nor the time to check on the quality of the work. In Zhejiang province's Jiaxing and Shaoxing counties, regions that had piloted the technically sound method of controlling the disease by reducing snail numbers with earth burial – a measure thought to have been carried out in Japan with some success – officials sent to evaluate the alleged success were horrified to find that the majority of the snails survived after these mass burial campaigns. It turned out that the snails were not buried deep enough, nor was the work carried out with the frequency it needed to be to be successful. In some villages, after the snail-infested mud was cleaned out from old ditches, villagers mobilized to carry out the task were not given any instructions as to what to do with the mud. They dumped the mud randomly in fields as fertilizer or piled it up all over the ground, thus allowing the snails to simply migrate over even greater areas. Similarly, the collecting of night-soil seemed to hit the target, but it could not be used as fertilizer during the busy planting season because it had not been treated to destroy the schistosoma eggs. When used as fertilizer, it simply increased the risk of infection, causing wider outbreaks, but without this fertilizer the farming co-operatives concerned would face the penalty of not meeting the government's production quota – an even greater political risk for the grassroots cadres. In desperation, they purchased fertilizer from elsewhere, including other affected regions. They quickly learned that even this fertilizer was contaminated, but by then it was too late to prevent massive, acute outbreaks.[32]

FURTHER COMPLICATIONS

The situation was looking more desperate farther inland in China's southwest, with more and more counties being added to the endemic list. One such county was Xichang and its surrounding villages. A fertile valley situated on the edge of the Himalayas, Xichang, as part of the former Xikang province, had been ruled by the Chinese warlord Liu Kang prior to the Communist Liberation in 1950. The surrounding hill villages were occupied by different Lolo tribes. Growing illegal opium crops for the black market had been the main source of revenue for the local Han Chinese, who had migrated there as early as the eighteenth century with the Manchu military expansion into this region. These Han Chinese rented land from the nomadic Lolos and introduced agriculture to the region. After opium was banned in China, its price shot up, and it became ever more profitable to grow and trade in opium. In the late 1940s, just before the Communist army conquered the region, one kilo of opium could be exchanged for thirty kilos of rice. Therefore, local villagers had little or no incentive to grow rice or to engage in other agriculture activities.[33] After the Communists took over the region, tackling the region's opium problems was the one of the first measures the authorities introduced to consolidate the CCP's power – that and ridding the area of bandits, many of whom were opium lords or traffickers. By the end of 1952, the region was declared opium-free.[34]

However, the price for being opium-free was a devastating famine. Having had their opium confiscated, the opium fields wiped out, and the market closed or pushed underground, local villagers were deprived of their livelihood. With no opium to exchange for food, they resorted to eating grass and earth to fill their empty stomachs.[35] The authorities seized the opportunity to launch Land Reform in the region, although this had already been completed in other parts of the country. As part of the government's famine relief, starving local villagers, most of whom were Han Chinese opium farmers who had previously rented plots of land in the hills, were given small loans and seed for growing rice so that they could move down to the valleys around Xichang to begin rice cultivation. In addition, the local authorities helped them to build small irrigation networks and convert the fertile valley into terraced rice paddies. By 1952, the cultivable land in the region had increased by 30 per cent,[36] but coupled with this agricultural expansion was the concomitant spread of schistosomiasis. An official epidemiological survey conducted in 1952 found not a single schistosomiasis patient. By 1955, however, Xichang was declared an endemic region, with more than 500 cases of acute infection reported by the local hospital that year.[37]

On the other side of the hills, in Yunnan province's Dali and Lijiang prefectures, which were inhabited by different ethnic groups, hundreds of cases of *Schistosomiasis japonica* were also reported. Prior to that, there had been warnings about the dangers of the disease. In 1939, a series of malaria epidemics, aggravated by the construction of the Yunnan-Burma Highway, wiped out entire towns in Yunnan province in China's southwest.[38] Robert Cecil Robertson, professor of pathology at the University of Hong Kong as well as commissioner for the League of Nations Epidemic Unit operating in central China, was transferred to the region to oversee the matter. While surveying the situation of malaria in Xiaguan city on the highway, Robertson encountered some schistosomiasis patients from villages in the plain along the shore of Dali's Lake Erhai, where the altitude is about 6,900 feet above sea level. This alerted Robertson, since Xiaguan was the most important city for trade on the highway as well the rice basket of the region. Equally important was that the British were planning to open several transport depots there, so he decided to investigate the matter further. Assisted by a Chinese technician from the South-Western Hospital in Xiaguan, they managed to collect hundreds of molluscs, similar to those found in Fuzhou in southern China, on 'sloping banks of the irrigation ditches which led to the rice paddies'. Although the data he obtained on the prevalence of schistosomiasis in the region was 'very meagre', some of the Chinese doctors working in the region told him that the disease, often mistaken for malaria, was very common in the villages along Lake Erhai. Although Robertson and his Chinese assistant were unable to visit these villages, they found traces of schistosomiasis as far afield as the foothills, about twenty kilometres to the east of Xiaguan. As a public health commissioner, he was keen that 'the public should be warned about this matter and the employees of the transport companies who use ponds along the highway in this vicinity for washing, domestic purposes or cleaning down cars should realize that the waters of these ponds may be highly infected at certain seasons of the year.'[39] Perhaps Robertson's discovery was too much of a puzzle, or perhaps war interrupted his work, but there was no further study of schistosomiasis in the Dali region until 1952 when 246 cases were reported by the Dali People's Hospital, the former Gospel Hospital of the China Inland Mission. The majority of those infected were young people and children who had contracted schistosomiasis while swimming in the lake. After the incident, the local health department in Dali pleaded with the Yunan provincial health authority for resources to investigate the matter further. A year later, in 1953, the CCP Central Committee South-Western Bureau's Epidemic Prevention Department sent a team to Dali to open the Yunnan Provincial Schistosomiasis Prevention Centre.[40] They simultaneously opened a Pandora's box, however.

Yunnan province, situated at the border of the Chinese empire, was also a public health periphery. This changed briefly during World War II when Yunnan temporarily became an important global centre for malaria research and control, partly because major medical institutions from the coastal regions of China retreated to the southwest to escape the Japanese and partly because of the efforts of some international health organizations in the wake of the building of the Yunnan-Burma Highway. But with the end of the war in the Pacific and the advent of the Communist takeover of the region, malaria control work in Yunnan ceased. Prior to Communist rule, Yunnan was also a centre for Christian missionary activities, since many of the ethnic groups marginalized by the dominant Chinese culture were more amenable and easier targets for conversion. Western medical missionaries were the main force, competing with

Buddhist institutions and indigenous shamanic healers, in delivering health care to the local population. As the Communists moved to take final control of the area, Buddhist institutions were shut down, and shamanic healers were suppressed. Foreign missionaries as well as lay medical personnel were forced out. Missionary organizations stopped sending money to their mission hospitals, so without funding and personnel, these abandoned hospitals turned into a living hell. Many patients died of hunger, while those who were still alive cried out for succour. Officials sent by the new People's Government for the southwest region were so horrified by what they saw that they 'could not bear the sight' and wept in despair.[41]

For the provincial and local health authorities in Yunnan as well as in nearby Xichang, schistosomiasis was one more nightmare that was added to their public health quandary. In addition to the severe shortage of funding and personnel, they had no idea how to control schistosomiasis, a disease that had long been mistaken by the locals for malaria. The majority of cadres employed by the new Schistosomiasis Prevention Centre had only primary school education and did not even know how to fill in a form properly. With no clear instruction on how to collect epidemiological data, they simply made guesses as they went along. Some thought 'the more the better', so they made up the number of infected villagers as well as snail numbers, whereas others did not think it was necessary to examine all the villagers.[42] Furthermore, the local terrain in both Dali and Xichang was mountainous; this made snail surveys challenging, since snails tended to congregate in small groups concealed in grass or under stones and big trees. Nor were the reservoir hosts for the disease limited to humans. In the mountainous regions of southwestern China, cattle, goats, dogs, and even voles were more important than humans in the spread of schistosomiasis. This meant that the methods used in the lower reaches of the Yangtze and the lake regions along the Yangtze to control the spread of the disease were largely irrelevant or ineffective here. The nomadic population's cultural preference for defecating and urinating in the wild, as well as the overwhelming poverty of the more settled communities, also made sanitation campaigns an impossible task. For instance, after villagers were banned from using fresh night-soil in rice paddies, they stored it in open spaces or in animal barns, since they had no money to buy storage pots or to build latrines. When it rained, the night-soil flooded all over the place, causing an even greater public health menace.[43] In Xikang, to save money on the pesticide '666', as well as having no trained personnel to carry out the spraying, villagers were mobilized to go into the rice paddies to catch snails using their bare hands. Without any protection, many were infected with schistosomiasis.[44]

KILLING SNAILS

April 1956 was the time for the Nine-Man Subcommittee to hold its second national meeting to review the progress of the Anti-Schistosomiasis Campaign. Contrary to the optimistic image painted in the state media, reports put together by the provincial authorities showed a rather bleak picture on the ground. It became clear that relying purely on political will plus the party leadership and mass participation was no guarantee that the snails, the 'enemy of the natural world', would be eliminated. As with any public health program, to successfully control schistosomiasis would require an achievable goal with realistic targets, proper planning, coordination of relevant departments – from water conservation to agricultural and public health – and the financial commitment of the state, as well as the appropriate cultural and economic conditions on the ground. All these were missing, however, from the design of the Maoist schistosomiasis eradication campaign.

From the outset of the campaign in 1956, a number of experts questioned the feasibility of eradicating the disease in seven years. Drawing on the Japanese experience, Huang Mingxin, the vice chair of the Ministry of Health's new Experts Advisory Committee for schistosomiasis control, cast serious doubt on the goal of eradicating the disease: 'Japan's medical science is far more advanced. The affected region there is much smaller, and fewer people are impacted. Japanese scientists have been working on controlling the disease for more than fifty years. Still they have not managed to eradicate it ... Isn't the goal of eradication in seven to twelve years a bit too high for us?' 'How is it possible?' he asked.[45] Following his reading of the official statement concerning the eradication plan, Su Delong pencilled two words: 'wild boasting'.[46] He even confronted Chairman Mao on this. Eager to win the 'golden' prize of eradication, however, the Zhejiang Provincial Party Committee paid no attention to the experts' warning. Instead, it shortened the goal of eradication by two years. In other words, Zhejiang would take the lead in eradicating schistosomiasis by 1960. Reporting on this, a party-inspired editorial in the *Zhejiang Daily News* attacked the experts' questioning as a 'bureaucratic attitude'.[47] Later, in 1958 during the Great Leap Forward, Su Delong would once again be heavily criticized for questioning the seven-year eradication goal and doubting the effectiveness of TCM remedies. In the PRC, when politics confronted scientific expertise, politics always won.

Yet parasites are apolitical. They defied the politics and thrived. By this time, because of a lack of personnel as well as hospital beds, local sanitation work, and mass therapy in the control model region, Jiaxing was in total disarray. The local department of disease prevention protested that they would never be able to meet the eradication goal.[48] In the meantime, Madame Li Dequan, on behalf of the Ministry of Health, which had lost the authority over schistosomiasis control work to the Nine-Man Subcommittee, waged a powerful attack on the Anti-Schistosomiasis Campaign for its design flaws. Speaking at the Chinese People's Political Consultative Conference, she stated that 'there have also been many defects in this work. In some areas, there was a lack of understanding of the stupendous and complicated nature of the task, and this gave rise to a feeling of hastiness and of an inclination to belittle the enemy.'[49]

Watching the goal of eradication slipping away, yet holding no winning card against the unseen disease, the Nine-Man Subcommittee had little choice but to come up with proper plans. This time they turned to the experts for help. It was agreed that science had no national boundaries. 'We must take science seriously, be it the scientific achievement of the Soviet or the West ... Science is universal and impartial,' proclaimed Ke Qingshi on behalf of the Nine-Man Subcommittee.[50] Since the Soviets claimed little knowledge of schistosomiasis control, Soviet scientists could offer no help except for a few visits as a symbolic gesture. The best they could do was to encourage their Chinese colleagues to put more effort into utilizing TCM. In the end, help came from Japan, the only country in the world that had had some success in controlling the disease. Yet, as John Farley points out, Japan's ability to mitigate rather than eliminate the disease had little to do with elaborate control schemes; rather, it was a decrease in agricultural activities as well as improved standards of living and hygiene that had brought it about.[51] In addition, Japanese epidemiological studies showed that natural environmental change also 'resulted in the annihilation of snails' in a number of regions in Japan.[52] So only mitigation, not eradication, took place even under the best of circumstances.

It was Premier Zhou Enlai, the chief administrator of the PRC and the architect of the country's earlier foreign policy, who first approached the Japanese for help. It has been argued that Zhou Enlai was the 'midwife' responsible for turning Chairman Mao's radical visions (the Great Leap Forward, for instance) into concrete policies and delivering on them.[53] Zhou was anxious about the disease spreading northward and causing greater menace in further water conservation projects, as well as bearing in mind the agricultural expansion that aimed to increase agriculture output. On 7 October 1955, just over a month before Chairman Mao decreed the eradication of schistosomiasis, Zhou confided to Amrit Kaur, independent India's first minister of health, that schistosomiasis control would be a major public health undertaking in the PRC: 'Schistosomiasis is the most harmful disease in China. It's widespread along the Yangtze River. We are planning to open up more paddy fields in the north [in the Second Five-Year Plan period]. It is possible snails would migrate northwards to harm the population in the north. This is a serious matter. [Eradicating schistosomiasis] must be a major public health undertaking for the Ministry of Health,' he told Kaur.[54] Zhou Enlai already knew several things: that agricultural work had to be expanded (even though it is not clear that he even believed this) and that it involved risks to the people's health. But he also understood that the government must be seen to be avoiding these risks by every possible means. For Zhou, as for the State Council that he represented, the eradication of schistosomiasis as a major public health undertaking was integral to China's agricultural development, even though he also understood that the latter meant the people's health was at risk. Despite some experts' warning that under the economic and social conditions at the time, the eradication of the snail host was impossible and was even fraught with danger, a few weeks after his meeting with the Indians, at an official meeting to welcome the Japanese medical delegation, Zhou, with the false expectation of eradicating the disease, asked Japanese medical experts to help China eliminate the snails.[55]

On 16 September 1956, at the Eighth Party Congress, Zhou Enlai, in the Report on the Proposal for the Second Five-Year Plan for Developing of the National Economy, announced a planned further increase of agricultural output by 35 per cent in the period between

1958 and 1962. This would entail increasing the extent of water conservation work and land reclamation. In the same report, he also urged authorities to 'actively popularize our experience in combating schistosomiasis, and eliminate, by periods, by districts, and in a planned way, the most harmful local diseases'.[56] A few days after the meeting, the Japanese Delegation for the Prevention and Eradication of Schistosoma Japonicum, led by Komiya Yoshitaka, the head of the Department of Parasitology at the National Institute of Preventive Hygiene in Japan and an advocate of social medicine (and also a member of the Japanese Communist Party), arrived in the PRC. After spending nearly three months surveying in Jiangsu province in the east and Sichuan province in the southwest, the Japanese experts warned their Chinese hosts about the challenge of controlling the disease in China, let alone eradicating it. The differences between the two countries were massive. In Japan, the principal habitat of vector snails was limited to only five districts with a population of 400,000, whereas in China the endemic *foci* were distributed over twelve provinces with a population of 100 million. In addition to China being vast, the habitat of vector snails in the country was also rich in variety. This meant that the method of controlling vector snails in Japan, where the snails were only found on the margins of small irrigation ditches (except in the marshy areas along rivers) might not be applicable to many parts of China, where snails were also found on the leaves and stems of reeds or on the margins of small streams between mountains. Furthermore, the Japanese observed, the method of night-soil control, only partly successful in Japan, was much more difficult and complicated in China where control was closely related to protection of the water supply sources. In Japan, night-soil control only involved killing parasitic ova or preventing contact with snails, whereas in China, almost all the inhabitants in the endemic regions washed their night-soil containers, provided by local authorities, in the same water that was used for drinking as well as agriculture. Thus, the Japanese concluded, the long-term policy for schistosomiasis control in China should give priority to environmental intervention over physico-chemical methods to control the *oncomelania* snails. Environmental interventions suggested by the Japanese consisted of burying snails in soil, blocking the water margin of creeks with stone, cementing irrigation ditches, and reclaiming and developing marshland. Warning the Chinese that such work would entail serious financial commitments from the state, Komiya concluded that in the long run it would 'pay off when the control work is combined with agriculture, irrigation, and fishery development'.[57]

By claiming that environmental control of schistosomiasis was integral to agricultural development and water conservancy, the timing of this Japanese recommendation was almost perfect. The year 1957 began with the PRC getting ready to launch the Second Five-Year Plan. If China could succeed in combining the elimination of *oncomelania* snails with the development of agriculture, irrigation, and fishery production, as put forward by the Japanese experts, it would mean more land for agricultural cultivation, better irrigation systems, and increased fishery production, thus reaching the goals set in the Second Five-Year Plan. It would be seen to achieve multiple goals with limited resources. In April, on behalf of the State Council, Zhou Enlai decreed that all local authorities in the endemic regions had to include schistosomiasis control in their yearly plan for agricultural and water conservation for 1957. In addition, they should work at promoting research on environmental control of snails, pesticides, and the examination of treatments that included Western medicine as well as TCM remedies. Yet there was no mention of state funding to help local authorities to achieve these goals.[58] Furthermore, as 1957 moved on, it became clear that there would be no Second Five-Year Plan. Mao Zedong was to march his country into a disastrous Great Leap Forward.

In the Chinese calendar, 1957 was the Year of the Fire Rooster, the year of big tasks and great ambition as well as a year of disturbances. The year began with the Hundred Flower Campaign, which encouraged intellectuals to participate in policy-making. Mao's words 'Letting a hundred flowers bloom' in the arts and 'Hundred schools of thoughts contend' in science brought millions of people out onto the streets. Like fire roosters, they spoke out. They ferociously debated party policies and China's future. But as with the human body (according to ancient Chinese medical theory), excessive fire (heat) causes inflammation that results in pain. The optimism of liberalization was quickly crushed. With the arrival of the blazing summer, the CCP launched the Anti-Rightist Campaign to attack those who spoke out during the Hundred Flower Campaign. Like viruses, it was said, they had crept into the party and multiplied. To defend itself, the CCP used the Anti-Rightist Campaign to 'boot out' those purported 'viruses' that were thought to be threatening the party's existence. The country was turned upside down, with millions ending up in labour camps. The year ended with Chairman Mao Zedong executing the Great Leap Forward, marching his country into catastrophe.*

THE GREAT LEAP INTO SCHISTOSOMIASIS ERADICATION

At the end of 1957, in a drive to transform China into an industrial power, Mao launched the Great Leap Forward. A year earlier, in 1956, severe flooding, typhoons, and then an intense drought had already damaged agricultural output. The Great Leap Forward began with a massive drive to divert the water from the south to irrigate the arid yellow earth in the north as well as to control floods in the south. The colossal Great Leap water conservation project also aimed to power China's rapid industrialization. By January 1958, the official estimate was that more than 100 million people in China had been mobilized to take part in the Great Leap water conservation campaign. Not only were the masses the only tangible resource the party could call on, equally important for the CCP was the promise that to transform the countryside into the socialist garden was a political project that had to involve the entire population. The Great Leap Forward in agriculture would entail a great leap of schistosomiasis control. As a political undertaking, the Anti-Schistosomiasis Campaign would require the collective strength of the masses of peasants. Mass mobilization of the undereducated peasant population, however, required skilled grassroots leadership. Experts and doctors from major medical institutions were dispatched to different parts of the country to carry out snail surveys, treatment work, and the grassroots training of health personnel for the mass campaign. With great haste, 1,400 hospitals and research institutes, as well as control stations, were opened throughout the country, with more than 13,000 schistosomiasis control cadres. In the meantime, 84,000 grassroots health workers and 25,000 local cadres were recruited to lead the campaign on the ground.[59]

More did not mean better, however. It entailed cumbersome administrative structures that often hampered the actual control

---

* Mao was born in December 1893, the Year of the Snake. According to the Chinese Zodiac, he was a black water snake, which becomes dangerous when disturbed by fire.

work. For instance, by failing to understand that schistosomiasis was a seasonal disease, as treatment should also be, the newly opened schistosomiasis control hospital in Jiaxing overestimated the number of staff and beds needed. Since hardly any patients turned up in the winter, the more than 1,000 hospital staff members had little to do. Slacking became commonplace. The hospital administration reacted by reducing the number of staff and beds. In the meantime, the Great Leap Forward in agriculture led to increased agricultural activities, which, in turn, dramatically increased the prevalence and morbidity of schistosomiasis. When the spring arrived, the season of outbreaks, the number of villagers infected by the disease grew precipitously, and suddenly the number of patients far exceeded hospital capacity. As a result, all useable rooms in the villages, including villagers' homes, were used as temporary treatment spaces. Without beds, patients were asked to bring their own quilts and to lie on the grass. The remaining medical staff often worked more than ten hours a day kneeling on the ground to provide treatment to sick villagers. Short of medical equipment, they often had to come up with rudimentary alternatives and cut corners by compromising treatment or simply sending patients away.[60]

The pressure from above to hurry the Great Leap in eradicating the disease was felt throughout the country. In Yunnan province's Dali and Fengyi region and in Sichuan province's Xichang, for example, the newly opened schistosomiasis control stations quickly filled their vacancies with enthusiastic local youngsters who had just completed primary or middle school education and with women, who had fewer farming duties. While they were useful, often talented, and played a key role in mobilizing the masses for the snail elimination work, they lacked the necessary technical skills. Most of them took only a week-long schistosomiasis control crash course. Despite their commitment (they often worked long shifts and skipped meals), the quality of the work was generally poor. In Dali and Fengyi, for instance, after announcing that they had practically eradicated schistosomiasis with repeated 'assaults' on snails, teams of experts who went to inspect their 'success' reported that an equal number of snails remained alive as had been killed.[61]

The Great Leap marching forward at an ever-accelerating speed put even greater strain on skilled personnel. Nationwide construction projects (e.g., transport and telecommunication), water conservancies, iron and steel works, and agricultural production constantly competed for trained personnel to lead their efforts and to manage the masses. All state organs, public institutions, and agricultural co-operatives were advised to practise strict economy to make full use of manpower, materials, and money. Local authorities had to curtail unnecessary expenditures and personnel. They constantly weighed their immediate interests against the long-term interests of the collectives. 'Questions of Improving the Health of People' was one of the last items on the State Council's agenda. Thus, on-the-ground health work was seen as the least important of their multitude of tasks.[62] Health care delivery was debated at the very moment when large numbers of grassroots public health personnel were being transferred to support the other 'more important' projects intended to transform the country into an industrial powerhouse. In Sichuan province's Meishan County, one of the worst endemic regions in the southwest, for instance, after the nationwide steel and iron production campaign began in September 1958, many local schistosomiasis control cadres were transferred to support the expanding steel and iron production. In the meantime, pandemics such as measles, whooping cough, diphtheria, and other infectious diseases became rampant at irrigation construction sites, steel and iron production camps, and the people's communes (collective farms). As a result, the public health priorities turned to fighting these epidemics and their prevention. There were no spare personnel to lead the mass campaign against schistosomiasis. Schistosomiasis control work became next year's task or was simply removed from the list of local public health work completely.[63] In Hunan province's endemic Yueyang region, ten schistosomiasis control cadres were transferred to other departments. The director of the local hospital multitasked in order to lead the local eradication campaign, but overburdened with too much work, he was unable to focus. The absent leadership resulted in diminished activities in the local schistosomiasis control.[64]

On the ground, grassroots cadres not only were burdened by multiple tasks, they also had unobtainable goals. As result, choices constantly had to be made regarding what to do first, depending on what the priorities were at any given moment. Since public health work such as killing snails or treating sick villagers required much time and effort, local cadres often saw them as a bother or hindrance to their winning medals in the race for the Great Leap Forward. In Jiaxing, for instance, Zhejiang province's schistosomiasis control flagship county, at a meeting to pledge mass effort to eradicate the disease, a grassroots party secretary stated: 'Eliminating snails is a waste of money and manpower. It decreases productivity. I strongly oppose it,' he shouted loudly.[65] In Guangdong province's Qujiang County, due to the enormous pressure to collect fertilizer to increase the agricultural yields, the plan to eliminate snails was simply withdrawn. Instead of incorporating snail elimination into local irrigation projects, as advised by the government policy, the two campaigns constantly competed for local resources. Fighting for labour became the most common scenario throughout the country. In Guangdong province's Hua County, all labourers were engaged in irrigation construction or steel and iron work, leaving the schistosomiasis control cadres alone to eliminate snails. Unable to meet their projected target, they abandoned the work altogether. As soon as the people retreated, however, the snails returned. Similar situations were also reported in Jiangsu and Zhejiang provinces.[66]

SCHISTOSOMIASIS: THE NEW PLAGUE OF THE GREAT LEAP IN AGRICULTURE

In the lake regions along the Yangtze River, propaganda images of bumper harvests and healthy, happy-looking workers gathering crops were replaced by the reality of acute infection. The environmental control method by land reclamation and water conservancy work exposed hundreds, indeed thousands, of healthy labourers to the disease when such projects were carried out with little or no protection for those who participated in them. This was the case during the PRC's great rush to Leap Forward. Earlier experts had already warned about the potential health risks. Chen Huxin, the expert who had led the pilot study of controlling schistosomiasis by reclaiming the marshes for agricultural cultivation during the South Dongting Lake Reconstruction project of 1953–56 (as discussed in chapter 2), testified that among the 250,000 labourers who had participated in that reconstruction project, more than half toiled in the contaminated water. Many previously fit and healthy labourers, imported from non-endemic regions, became infected with schistosomiasis as a result. Against such massive risk, Chen warned that it was necessary to wait until all the snails had been destroyed before the reclaimed land could be cultivated. He also urged all local authorities to regard the protection of labourers against infection as imperative when planning for land reclamation and water conservation projects as well as for agricultural work.[67]

But the Great Leap Forward would wait for no one and nothing. On 15 November 1958, addressing a question asked by a Polish delegation visiting the PRC regarding the huge number of industrial accidents, Marshall Chen Yi, the vice premier and foreign minister of China at the time, put it crudely: 'these accidents will not prevent us advancing forward. Such is the price worth paying. No need to get hysterical over this. So many lives were lost during the war. A few accidents and sickness are nothing.'[68] The masses may have been the CCP's most tangible resource, but human life was also cheap in the PRC. For local authorities with their eyes fixed on winning the prize, making sure labourers and farmers were thoroughly protected against infection was the last thing on their mind. Furthermore, because of the severe shortage of cotton (all cotton produced was procured by the state, mainly for export), local authorities could not supply enough of the fabric needed to make protective socks and leg wrappings for all the workers labouring in the contaminated water or paddy fields.[69] The worst season was from March to August. This was also the busiest farming season, and the increased agricultural activity multiplied the chances of infection. In the meantime, the warmer and humid climate allowed the parasite to breed more quickly. The warmer and humid weather also added further difficulties to treatment work: 'The more we treat people, the higher the morbidity,' a health official from Hunan lamented at the fourth national schistosomiasis control conference.[70]

An increasing number of people were infected as more land was reclaimed and more irrigation canals constructed. Between 1958 and 1962, along Hunan province's Dongting Lake and Jiangxi province's Poyang Lake, two of the worst endemic regions along the Yangtze, more than 18,121 acres (110,000 *mu*) of marshland were reclaimed. Thirty-three state farms were built on this reclaimed land, and more than 30,000 workers, many of them from non-endemic regions, were drafted to work on these new, makeshift farms. Schistosomiasis was the new plague for these farm employees and their families. Official statistics show that from 1960 to 1961, more than 4,000 workers from twenty different state farms suffered acute infection in that year alone. Among them were more than 170 workers from state farms in Hunan who died of schistosomiasis.[71]

Yueyang Prison was one of the first prison labour camps in the PRC. Euphemistically called the 'Jianxin (Constructing New) National Farm', it was on the shore of Dongting Lake and was jointly run by the Hunan Provincial Bureau of Public Security and the Yueyang County authority. It was the 'home' of the PRC's major political prisoners, including a huge number of Rightists. When Liu Fengxiang, the former editor-in-chief of the *Hunan Daily* and a prominent Rightist, first arrived at the farm, he told his fellow prisoner Yang Xiaokai (Yang was twice nominated for the Nobel Prize in Economics): 'Mao Zedong has sent us here to die.'[72] This so-called farm was built on a reclaimed marsh surrounded by water. Prisoners lived in shoddy pop-up tents built out of reeds, which were also an ideal habitat for snails. During spring and summer, large parts of the farm were flooded. Prisoners had to endure living and working in the contaminated water unprotected during the day, wearing their torn clothes. At night they shared their primitive living spaces with infected snails. It is not surprising that many became ill with schistosomiasis, and indeed many died as a result. According to an official estimate, during the busiest planting season in 1958, 613 prisoners suffered acute infections within a few days, increasing the infection rates from 23.7 per cent in the previous year to 27.3 per cent. The situation worsened as the speed of the Great Leap accelerated. Between 1960 and 1963, more than 9,400 prisoners suffered acute infections, and the disease claimed eighty-five lives. Although unintended, schistosomiasis had indeed become a means of getting rid of political dissidents.[73] If human life was cheap in the PRC, political prisoners such as Rightists were treated as the scum of earth and died as a result.

Along the east bank of Dongting Lake is the Miluo River, a minor tributary to the Yangtze.* In October 1958, under the Great Leap

---

* During the war against the Japanese, the Miluo was highlighted by the patriotic historian Wen Yiduo, who tied the river to the legend of Qu Yuan as well as to the Dragon Boat festival. Qu Yuan (340–278 BCE) was a court official and poet of the Chu state (nowadays Hunan province) who lived in the Warring State period. He committed suicide by drowning himself in the Miluo after being driven in disgrace from office. Throughout history, the suicide of Qu Yuan has represented many things to different people at different times. During the Sino-Japanese War, Qu Yuan was turned into a patriotic martyr. At the same time, the Dragon Boat festival, a lunar festival celebrated by communities living on the water in southern China long before the time of Qu Yuan, became a commemoration of Qu Yuan's death. The Miluo River was turned into the birthplace of the festival.

banner of 'Going all out, aiming high, and achieving more and faster economic results', Hunan province's Xiangyin County authority embarked on the Miluo River Water Conservation and Reclamation project. This was one of the many ambitious projects of the Great Leap Forward aimed at reclaiming the marsh for agricultural cultivation and diverting the water from the Milou into Dongting Lake for flood control. More than 14,000 labourers were thrown into the project to excavate canals and fill the marshes. They toiled around the clock with no sleep and little to eat so that they could complete the project before the arrival of the monsoon season. But the monsoon arrived a few days earlier than forecast. On 4 June, the river's water level rose so high that the dyke was about to burst. The newly reclaimed land, which had already been planted with crops, as well as the half-built irrigation canals, were in danger. In an attempt to prevent the dyke from bursting, the authority sent 550 labourers, including 470 political prisoners (most of them Rightists) down to the flooded river carrying twenty logs. Despite their herculean efforts, the dyke burst in the end, and the deluge washed over 1,977 acres (12,000 *mu*) of newly reclaimed and cultivated land. Half-grown crops as well as more than 200 dead bodies of workers floated away with the floods. One survivor named himself 'Iron Torrent' to commemorate the incident. At the age of eighty-one, he could still recall the horror of one fellow worker's body being swallowed up by a giant fish.* As soon as the water receded, snails returned, carrying schistosoma eggs. The prisoners and peasant workers who survived the flood were ordered to return to the construction site. Without any protection, many became infected with the disease.[74]

None of this mattered, however. The news of the total 'eradication' of schistosomiasis resounding from Yujiang, a small and unremarkable county along the Yangtze in central China, was to save the failing campaign, as well as inspiring Chairman Mao Zedong to write his often-cited poem 'Sending off the Plague God' that would immortalize the campaign. Both the claim and the poem were the fictions needed at the time to confront the brutal realities of the disease and its impact on the people's health. In Mao's China, the exigencies of national politics often trumped the provision of the public's health.

---

* This man was recently arrested by public security and imprisoned in southwestern China for speaking out about this tragic event that took place nearly sixty years ago.

4

The Propaganda War

YUJIANG MAKES THE NEWS

Situated in eastern Jiangxi province, just south of the Yangtze River, Yujiang County is a hilly area. The River Xin links it to Poyang Lake, the largest freshwater lake in China, which is also one of the worst endemic schistosomiasis regions along the Yangtze. In the 1800s, as part of the Qing imperial government's ambitious water conservancy initiative to develop agriculture – to end the chronic problem of famine in the region – a network of ditches was built to irrigate the surrounding countryside with water from the lake as well as the river.[1] These irrigation schemes, alongside increased agricultural activities, brought prosperity to Yujiang and the surrounding regions. At the same time, they increased the prevalence and morbidity of schistosomiasis, since irrigated farmland is the ideal environment for snails. The spread of schistosomiasis meant that the region's prosperity was short-lived. It weakened the manpower economy and eventually destroyed the once thriving agriculture. A local record suggests that between 1919 and 1949, schistosomiasis claimed more than 29,000 lives here. Hardly anyone was left to plant and tend crops, and more than 20,000 *mu* of fertile farm fields were soon abandoned and covered in weeds; in the meantime, snails multiplied in them. Villagers remembered that it was impossible to avoid stepping on snails in these fields. Calling them 'killing fields', those who were lucky enough not to be infected by the disease ran away from the area as if running from the plague. As a result, more than forty-two villages were abandoned.[2]

In 1951, Yujiang was declared a schistosomiasis endemic county. The highest number of casualties was reported at the construction site of the White Tower irrigation project in Dengjiapu, the new Communist authority's scheme to revitalize local agriculture. In 1946, as part of the post-war reconstruction, the Nationalist government had opened an experimental farm there. This new farm, a modernist development project, pioneered the use of machinery to replace traditional farming methods in order to increase agricultural yields. In November 1949, the newly established Jiangxi provincial Chinese Communist Party (CCP) authority sent army representatives to take over the farm and turn it into a model farm for teaching modern farming methods. Soon after, the White Tower irrigation project began. The White Tower project set out to build a major irrigation canal to bring water from the River Xin to the farm and to the surrounding agricultural fields. But the shock of a schistosomiasis outbreak meant the project had to be suspended.[3] In the mid-1950s, however, the draft of the First Five-Year Plan demanded that all state farms expand their cultivable areas. This was followed by the CCP Central Committee's proposal to raise the grain output for the Second Five-Plan Year period to a total of about 2,200,000 million catties and the cotton output to a total of about 210 million catties.[4] The farm in Dengjiapu was converted to a national experimental centre for breeding improved varieties of rice and other agricultural crops. In the meantime, another state farm named Genxin (which literally translates as 'Improved' or 'Renewal') was opened next to it. The provincial water conservancy bureau was pressured to resume the suspended White Tower irrigation project to bring about the projected high yield, despite the danger of creating further outbreaks of schistosomiasis.

In 1955, Fang Zhichun, the former People's Liberation Army (PLA) commissioner who oversaw the takeover of Dengjiapu state farm and the deputy party secretary of Jiangxi province, was named the head of the Jiangxi Provincial Five-Man Anti-Schistosomiasis Subcommittee, the parallel provincial organization to the CCP Central Committee's Nine-Man Subcommittee. In other words, Fang was the party boss appointed to lead the eradication campaign in Jiangxi province. Fang was also a distant cousin of the former CCP military leader and revolutionary martyr Fang Zhimin, who was a native of Jiangxi province as well as a veteran revolutionary experienced in party political and propaganda work. 'A new office applies strict measures, and a newly appointed official works hard to show his efficiency' is an old Chinese saying. As soon as Fang Zhichun received the mandate from the First National Schistosomiasis Eradication Conference, while still at Shanghai he consulted experts on how to effectively eliminate snails and thus control the disease. He was told to use sodium pentachlorophenate (NaPCP), the molluscicide widely recommended by international experts in favour of the chemical control approach. In China, the 'old folk' in Jiangxi are famed for being shrewd and calculating. As one of them, Fang did not simply follow the experts' recommendation; he did a quick calculation and decided that molluscicides were not affordable. At the time, China had not developed the technology to manufacture NaPCP; it would have to be imported and would cost around 500 *yuan* (ca US$90) per 0.165 acre of land. In total, there were 494,211 acres of farming land in Jiangxi – which would mean a cost of 2.5 billion *yuan*. Fang could not get his head around such an enormous figure. Subsequently, the provincial authority did not budget for molluscicides at all. Instead, they opted for buying umbrellas and shoes for local schistosomiasis cadres whom they sent to the countryside to study local conditions so that they could come up with cost-effective innovations. However, nothing came about, despite the umbrellas and shoes. Less costly methods such as using toxic herbs to poison snails or burning down the reeds with gas fires produced temporary but not lasting results. The method of converting paddy fields into dry fields reduced the number of snails, but it also killed the crops. As a result, agricultural productivity plummeted, exacerbating the food shortage that had already been underway.[5]

In neighbouring Anhui province, the local authority had promoted the method of draining the paddy fields, but acres and acres of rice crops had withered after the paddy fields were drained.[6] Anhui experienced much worse food shortages than Jiangxi, and the famine there killed more villagers than schistosomiasis. The villagers in Jiangxi were luckier in comparison. After a short period of eliminating snails by draining the paddy fields, the local authority quickly abandoned the method as they realized that it was hampering local grain production.[7] For the same reason, the method was also rejected by authorities in the rice-growing provinces in the southwest. In the mountainous regions of Sichuan and Yunnan, for instance, the increased amount of terraced fields in previous years had boosted rice production significantly. At the same time, however, the moist environment created the ideal habitat for *oncomelania* snails, thus helping to spread the disease. Weighing up schistosomiasis control against agricultural productivity, the local authorities in those areas rejected the drainage method from the outset.[8] In addition, epidemiological studies conducted after the drainage program took place showed that morbidity had increased in both Gaoan County in Jiangxi province and in parts of Anhui province, despite the decrease in the number of snails. It turned out that to carry out the drainage project, villagers and labourers had to work in the contaminated water for an extended period, and furthermore the increased number of local water conservancy projects had also increased the chance of infection. As a result, local data gathered in March 1957 showed that the number of people infected had doubled compared to the previous year.[9]

Faced with these shortcomings, Fang spotted an opportunity. Part of the White Tower irrigation scheme was to build networks of new ditches and reservoirs while blocking off the old, decaying ditches and muddy ponds that had been built in imperial times. During the 1955 annual snail survey, which took place in the winter, the team carrying it out reported that the number of snails had decreased significantly in places where old ditches were blocked off, whereas no snails were found in the newly built ditches. This was not really news, however. As epidemiological studies of the landscape had shown, although there had been some success in reducing snail numbers by the earth burial method in regions on the plain dotted with waterway networks, as in parts of Jiangsu and Zhejiang provinces, the method was not applicable to those endemic regions in the lake basins along the Yangtze River. In this low-lying, wet, and waterlogged land, characterized by the local popular saying 'Land in winter, water in summer', the low temperature in the colder and dryer winter months caused the snails to become dormant. The dry and cold weather is suitable for snails to lay their eggs and for hatching, but during the warmer, wet months the land becomes submerged under water. This wet and warmer weather is ideal for the growth of young snails; thus, the water quickly becomes contaminated with schistosomiasis.[10] Even in Jiangsu and Zhejiang provinces, work reports in the 1950s had shown that, despite some local success, in general the quality of snail burial work was not satisfactory.[11] But Fang Zhichun had neither the time nor the patience for probabilities or uncertainties in science. He had his eyes fixed on the decreasing number of snails. He had been given the task of leading the provincial eradication campaign in addition to a target of producing high-yield crops. Yujiang was going to be his model of success, and he was determined to make it happen.

In December 1955, a snail burial 'shock work' was carried out in Yujiang County's Magang Township. The quality of the work was so poor at first that it failed to meet the projected target. Yet this initial failure did not discourage Fang Zhichun. With a long career in party propaganda work, he knew how to mobilize the masses. In January, he gave orders to repeat the 'shock work'. Four thousand snail burial 'stormtroopers' camped onsite. They worked against bitterly cold wind and snow and often skipped meals and sleep. To safeguard their morale, women and children were also mobilized to bring hot tea to their hard-working husbands and fathers. After a three-day stormy 'shock work', two days ahead of schedule, Magang Township authority announced that their 'stormtroopers' had heroically completed the task. The shells of the dead snails were presented as evidence of this first victory. Smiling at the white shells, Fang wrote a jingle titled 'Song of Eradicating Snails'. With years of experience in party propaganda work, Fang was a firm believer in winning the masses through propaganda: he had the jingle published in the provincial daily newspaper.[12] According to Deng Tuo, the first editor-in-chief of the central party newspaper, *People's Daily*, news media such as newspapers were the party's most potent weapon 'to educate, and to lead the broad masses of people in the revolutionary struggle and the construction of the new life'.[13]

Picturing Magang as the 'blossoming flower' of the local eradication campaign, Fang Zhichun envisioned turning Yujiang into a 'blooming' county. He instructed every township in the county to send a team to Magang to be inspired by its 'successful' revolutionary experience. Fang also urged Yujiang's schistosomiasis control cadres to prepare for even bigger battles. 'He followed the snail burial campaign very closely, gave us full support if we encountered any obstacles. Whenever the campaign suffered setbacks, he called or wrote to Yujiang county authority immediately. Sometimes he even went to the campaign site personally to supervise the campaign, thus to hasten the success,' recalled a local cadre who was involved in the campaign.[14] With Fang pushing at his back, Li Junjiu, Yujiang County's party secretary and the executive manager of the Yujiang eradication campaign, camped at Magang Township to prevent the 'blossoming flower' from withering. Li, a former railway worker from Manchuria who joined the PLA during the Chinese civil war, was often seen taking part in the snail burial work, holding a shovel in his hands.[15]

In the meantime, Fang invited experts from Shanghai to put a stamp on Magang Township's purported 'success'. Su Delong, Wu Guang, and Huang Minxin, three of the People's Republic of China's (PRC) most revered experts in schistosomiasis control, laboriously arrived at Magang by taking a small boat and then walking halfway across the river. After being taken to see how snail burial was done in some villages, Su turned around and asked the following questions: 'How many ditches have been filled? How many cubic metres of earth have been dug up? How many acres of farm land have been increased? Has the agricultural yield increased, and how much per acre? How many labourers have you involved in the work? What is their cost? How many of them are volunteers?' The cadres in charge of the snail elimination work mumbled in response, unable to come up with any precise answers. Staring at their puzzled and embarrassed faces, Su sighed: 'Maybe you could try killing snails in this muddy pond with molluscicides. If it doesn't kill all the snails the first time, try spraying more the second time, and see what happens? I think this method is more cost effective than engaging so many labourers in burying snails.' Considering the fact that the environmental control measure was simply too costly given China's economic conditions, Su was in favour of using molluscicides to kill snails to control the disease. Yet, as mentioned above, according to their calculations, Fang Zhichun and the Jiangxi provincial authority had concluded that using molluscicides to kill the snails was simply not affordable considering the local circumstances in Jiangxi province. They had opted for the earth burial method because they counted on their ability to organize the local masses of cheap labour in order to get the work done. Yet the technical disagreement between the local authority in Jiangxi and the experts from Shanghai on the precise method to use to control the disease was immediately politicized, given that the control of schistosomiasis was an important political undertaking. Some months later, during the Great Leap Forward's political campaign of *'Pull down the White Flag'*, Su was criticized for 'blowing the cold wind' by undermining the power of the masses in eradicating the disease. Wu and Huang managed to escape being purged by making public statements acknowledging Yujiang's success in destroying snails through earth burial.[16] In recent years, there have also been attempts to reinterpret Su Delong's words to resurrect the 'successful story' of Yujiang's eradication and hence the triumph of the PRC's Anti-Schistosomiasis Campaign.[17]

With the 'white flag' pulled down, the 'red flag' was hoisted. To raise the 'red flag' in Jiangxi was a symbolic ritual. Jiangxi is often called the cradle of the new China. In the 1920s, it was in Jiangxi that the then-young CCP leader Mao Zedong and his close ally Zhu De, the military strategist, built up their Soviet base among the peasants and waged guerrilla warfare against the Nationalist army and the local powerholders. It was during his time in Jiangxi, as discussed earlier, that Mao came to understand that public health work was an integral part of the revolutionary war of the masses. According to Bing Xin, one of modern China's most celebrated female writers, the earth of Jiangxi was tinted red. To keep up with Jiangxi's revolutionary tradition, Yujiang was to raise the first 'red flag' in the PRC's Anti-Schistosomiasis Campaign. To win the battle was to involve the masses. In order to call up the masses, a red poster was put up outside the Yujiang County authority office. Li Junjiu, the man assigned to lead the battle, remembered that he could not sleep for many nights. 'When I put up the poster, I had tears in my eyes. After the Land Reform, the campaign to eradicate schistosomiasis was to bring villagers the second LIBERATION.' Su Xiangmao, the head of Magang Township, also recalled that 'The campaign was carried out with the great power of a thunderbolt and the speed of lightening. Within four days, we had completed the planning, and kick started the campaign.' Between 1956 and 1957, more than 20,000 labourers were involved in the Yujiang campaign to eliminate snails. Villagers shouted slogans such as 'If we don't destroy snails, we will never close our eyes and will never rest in peace.'[18] Each township organized its own 'stormtroops' for snail elimination. Altogether, there were fifteen teams, each carrying their own red banners. The competition was fierce. The slogans included 'We are not men if we don't eliminate snails.' Each team had their own work song to synchronize their physical movements, and one person led the singing. Some villagers who participated in the campaign remembered that during one 'shock work' session, which lasted three days and nights, the earth in Yujiang was shaken by their loud singing and shouting.[19] Those who were not engaged in the 'shock work', such as the elderly and women and children, were also out on the streets, picking up snails with pairs of chopsticks. Inspired by Fang's jingle, schoolchildren made up their own snail eliminating song: 'I am the Little

Guards of the Anti-Schistosomiasis Crusade'.[20] Within a matter of days, eliminating snails became the most important political event in Yujiang.*

After failing to impress the experts such as Su Delong, Fang approached Zheng Gang, the deputy head of the Office of the Nine-Man Subcommittee responsible for running the Anti-Schistosomiasis Campaign. The Office of the Nine-Man Subcommittee, situated in Shanghai, was the administrative agency set up by the CCP Central Committee's Nine-Man Subcommittee in January 1956 to jointly manage the campaign affairs with the Schistosomiasis Prevention Bureau, a subsidiary of the Ministry of Health. A younger revolutionary than Fang, Zheng Gang had joined the New Fourth Army in 1938 after China entered into war with Japan. In military ranking, he was Fang's junior; he addressed Fang as 'Commissioner Fang' and was respectful of everything Fang had to say. After having toured Magang Township's snail burial sites with Fang, Zheng and his delegation – which consisted mainly of bureaucrats administering the national eradication campaign from their office in Shanghai – were impressed by what they saw. They turned to Li Junjiu and local schistosomiasis cadres and urged them to carry on with their 'good work'. Both Zheng and Fang also gave speeches at a public meeting to inspire villagers to continue fighting the battle against the snails.[21] Yujiang was established as a national model for potential public health success in the PRC. The politics of eradication came to be coterminous with a range of claims about the efficacy of the new system. The underlying claim was that the health officials and experts at the centre, whether in the Central Committee or in the health establishment, knew what was inherently best for the people. Thus, the claims about the people's health and its improvement were an index of the success of the centralized planned economy.[22]

In the winter of 1957–58, when more than 100 million people across China were reported to have been mobilized to take part in the Great Leap Forward's water conservation projects, thousands of villagers in Yujiang were filling up old muddy ditches and ponds. By January 1958, the last few old ditches and ponds had been filled up. In the meantime, snail numbers had decreased substantially. Again, the snail survey was carried out during the winter months

---

* Today, local school children even play a snail elimination computer game to commemorate the Yujiang campaign.

when the low temperatures slowed down the snails' development. The news of the retreating snails excited Fang Zhichun in Jiangxi as well as Zheng Gang in Shanghai. Zheng immediately sent a team to report on Yujiang's 'success'. Together with local schistosomiasis control cadres, they drafted the 'Investigative Report on Yujiang's Near Eradication of Schistosomiasis'. For the draft to be finalized, however, and for Yujiang to become the Anti-Schistosomiasis Campaign's national model, it needed the official stamp of approval. To make sure that Yujiang passed the final test, Fang instigated an even more ferocious battle against snails. This time another 7,000 villagers were called up for duty, and snail elimination 'shock work' lasted for nearly three months. Every village wrote their pledges and posted their challenge letter to the contest, as well as their responses to the challenge. It was only during this final phase that the mass treatment work was carried out in Yujiang. A makeshift treatment centre was set up in the former Daoist temple, although it was too small because there were so many patients. In the end, villagers were moved out of their homes to make space for the treatment work. In May 1958, the team sent by Fang Zhichun to carry out the final check reported that only forty-three live snails were found. The same report also showed that amongst the 159 victims who received treatment, 95.6 per cent had been cured.[23]

Concurrently, however, the bi-weekly work reports published by the Nine-Man Subcommittee – which were based on the investigations of government work teams that regularly went around the countryside to survey the local work – painted a rather gloomy picture of the Anti-Schistosomiasis Campaign throughout Jiangxi province. The 1958 January report had shown that overall, the Jiangxi province's schistosomiasis control work was shoddily planned and haphazardly carried out. Many local cadres resisted the Anti-Schistosomiasis Campaign by complaining that 'there are too many snails to kill' and 'the disease is so widespread that it's impossible to control it. It would take forever.' The February report stated that the situation was worsening: 'Jiangxi province's schistosomiasis control work has stagnated. Local authorities there claim the pressure of water conservancy and agriculture work is too great. Villagers want to earn more work points, so they often resist joining snail burial work or receiving treatment. On the other hand, local cadres did not want to bear the blame of jeopardizing agricultural productivity and water conservancy. They dragged sick villagers out of treatment centres and hospitals and forced them to work in the paddy fields or to dig canals.' By 17 April, the work report from Jiangxi province was equally disappointing: 'A number of regions in Jiangxi province produced only slogans but no actions. The thunder is very loud there but we see no rain. A few counties and municipalities haven't produced any plans for schistosomiasis control. They kept on postponing control work from one month to another, and from this year to the next. We have not seen any progress being made at all.'[24] Yet all of this was quickly erased and forgotten as soon as Yujiang County in Jiangxi province raised the first 'red flag' of the PRC's Anti-Schistosomiasis Campaign.

THE PROPAGANDA OF HEALTH IMPROVEMENT

On 10 May 1958, an article entitled 'How Did We Eradicate Schistosomiasis' appeared in the *Jiangxi Daily News*. Thirty-three years later in 1991, the author of the article, Li Junjiu, the former Yujiang County's party boss who led the Yujiang's eradication campaign in 1958, conveyed to Zou Yihua (a native of Yujiang who had a distinguished career in local media and journalism) that Fang Zhichun had cowed him into writing the article: 'Yujiang was the model set up by Commissioner Fang. He constantly reminded me that good leadership is knowing how to evaluate the success. He impelled me not to fight a battle behind the closed door but to write articles to evaluate its success and to publicize it to inspire others.'[25] For Fang Zhichun, the man experienced in party propaganda work, the Yujiang campaign was propaganda from the outset. In the following months and years, the propaganda was to be presented as news and broadcast across China and globally.

In 1955, at a party politburo meeting, Chairman Mao Zedong of the CCP proposed that the Xinhua News Agency, the mouthpiece of the CCP and the new China, expand its activities around the globe: 'To let the world hear our voice,' Mao proclaimed.[26] Three years later, in the midst of the Great Leap Forward, the world was to hear the exciting news of how the new China, under the leadership of the CCP, had successfully eradicated schistosomiasis – acknowledged by the 1949 Second World Health Assembly and the international experts as the most widespread debilitating disease, after malaria, in many parts of the world, as well as a global social, economic, and health problem.

The spring of 1958 was unusually busy for the Chinese villagers and their cadres. In April, as soon as the Soviet Union launched Sputnik II into orbit, Chayashan on the north China plain – the reputed cradle of Chinese civilization – gave birth to the PRC's first People's Commune and launched the first agricultural 'sputnik' of the Great Leap Forward. Provincial party leaders throughout the country were challenged by Chairman Mao to join in a race to launch their own 'sputnik fields'.*27 Being a 'metal snake' himself, Fang Zhichun was in no hurry to join the 'dog race', however.† In his mind, Yujiang had won a smashing 'victory' by hoisting the first red flag of the Anti-Schistosomiasis Campaign. Their 'sputnik' had been launched already, and it was time for jubilation and publicity. Fang planned a three-day celebration and called Xinhua News Agency's Jiangxi branch to cover the event. A young and eager Liu Guanghui was given the assignment. New to journalism and to Jiangxi, Liu was a native of Hunan province; he had been one of the talented high school graduates recruited in 1956 by the ever-expanding Xinhua News Agency. After a short induction, he was dispatched to work at the Xinhua's Jiangxi branch. As the cradle of new China, Jiangxi province was also the birthplace of the Xinhua News Agency itself. The Yujiang celebration was Liu's first major assignment, and he was to travel there with Commissioner Fang, Jiangxi province's party boss and the chief engineer of the Yujiang 'victory'. 'Little Liu', as he was called by everyone then, was excited and proud to have been chosen. On the way, he learned from Fang how Yujiang, the land once rampaged by schistosomiasis, had eradicated the disease after three years' hard battle under the party leadership. A quick learner and a rising star at Xinhua's Jiangxi branch, Liu understood that Yujiang's story of fighting disease was a story of fighting for socialism. This battle against the threats of the natural world was also a heroic struggle of the Chinese peasantry, under the leadership of the CCP, against the old 'feudal' system, the Nationalist past with its corruption, and imperialist/capitalist medicine that relied on experts and denied the masses access and participation. In the context of the Great Leap Forward, Liu's responsibility as a news reporter for

---

* Inflated high-yield experimental farming fields.
† According the Chinese zodiac, 'metal snakes' are confident, quick at spotting opportunities, and always determined to accomplish their goals; 1958 was the Year of the Earth Dog in the Chinese calendar.

the state news agency, the mouthpiece for the party, was to report praiseworthy examples of implementing party policies as well as individual models who would inspire his readers regarding socialist reconstruction. For him, Yujiang's 'heroic battle' against schistosomiasis would make a perfect example. This was the victory narrative of the eradication in Yujiang that would appear in the *People's Daily* on 30 June 1958, and it was to become the epitome of the ever-victorious Anti-Schistosomiasis Campaign in the PRC as well as the model for the victory of the socialist road to public health.[28]

At first glance, this more than 5,000-word special report, entitled 'The First Red Flag: Jiangxi Province's Yujiang County's Experience in Eradicating Schistosomiasis', co-authored by Liu Guanghui with Chen Bingyan, a local journalist from the *Jiangxi Daily News*, was written as a typical, formulaic editorial of its time, which, according to Deng Tuo, the editor-in-chief of the *People's Daily*, always began 'with a discourse on current conditions, followed by a presentation of good examples and a criticism of a few bad examples. And then, the subjective causes of each. Toss in a few lessons from experience, and repeat a few generalities on advancing our work, which everyone already knows anyway. Finish up with a few sentences on how under the leadership of the Party this task will be completely achieved.' In 1955, lecturing editors and journalists working for the *People's Daily*, Deng Tuo had remarked that such a formulaic editorial was so dull that it made people want to vomit.[29] But in 1958, Deng was being pushed out of the role, even though he publicly praised and supported the Great Leap Forward. One of his faults was that he had opposed the Hundred Flowers Campaign in 1957. As the editor-in-chief, he had deterred many employees at the *People's Daily* from publicly speaking out, although perhaps more important was that he had sided with technocrats in the party, casting doubt on Mao's effort to speed up socialist transformation in the Chinese countryside.

Liu and Chen's special report, 'The First Red Flag', began with a sentence stating that the red flag of Yujiang was a new chapter and historic victory for the PRC's achievements in science. The report ended with a paragraph highlighting that it was the CCP's General Line for socialist construction that had led to the great victories in cultural and health work, and thus the eradication of schistosomiasis was an integral part of the Great Leap Forward. The positive message was also told through the mouths of a wide range of

individuals. They included Chen Chongyi, a Jiangxi province schistosomiasis control committee member as well as the director of
Jiangxi Medical College, who stated: 'For sixteen years I worked
for the medical establishment in Old China. I had not heard or seen
anywhere about schistosomiasis being eradicated. I have not seen
any papers from the capitalist countries saying it's possible to eradicate schistosomiasis. But today, I have not only heard it's possible,
I have seen it with my own eyes.' (Chen was a renowned medical
educator who advocated saving China through modern medicine
and education, and Jiangxi Medical College was one of the most
prestigious state medical colleges during the Nationalist period.) The
article also quoted nameless villagers from Yujiang county rejoicing
that 'The Party and Chairman Mao saved our lives ... In the future, if
Chairman Mao and the Party give us any more directives, as long as
our cadres build the ladders, we are willing to climb up to the sky.'[30]

Yet the report on Yujiang was far from a dull formulaic editorial.
It had a narrative that was told in a typical Great Leap Forward literary style that combined 'revolutionary realism' and 'revolutionary
romanticism'. In the spring of 1958, at the CCP Central Committee's
Chengdu conference, which lasted three weeks and was attended by
leaders of different CCP Central Committee departments as well as
eighteen provincial party bosses, Mao succeeded in further energiz-
ing the Great Leap Forward. In addition to the plan for greater speed
in economic construction, he also pushed through agendas launching technological and cultural revolutions, continuing criticism of
right revisionism, and 'smashing the blind faith in experts' (profes-
sors and bourgeois intellectuals) and Soviet practices. According to
Mao, Soviet-style literary social realism did not reflect the reality in
China. It was therefore inadequate for portraying the Great Leap
Forward and the new China's progress toward a glorious communist future. He proposed a new Chinese formulation that combined
revolutionary realism and romanticism.[31] For the next months or
years, the PRC's leading cultural theorists and literary figures, such
as Zhou Yang and Guo Morou, debated over and expounded on
the fundamental meaning of combining realism and romanticism.
This entailed arts and literature putting an emphasis on the 'romantic' projection of ideals in ordinary life, or, as Zhou Yang put it,
to 'describe the wide world of the people, depict the great struggles of the labouring masses, reflect the rise and prosperity of the
new socialist world, the birth and development of the new men and

women of communism'.[32] The life story of Deng Rumei, the heroine of Yujian's eradication narrative, as featured in Liu Guanghui and Chen Bingyan's special report, turned out to be a textbook example of this interpretation of the romantic projection of ideals in ordinary life. Deng's real name was not Rumei, however. While researching for this book, I learned that the error in her name was the result of a missing Chinese character on the authors' typewriter. This did not matter to the authors, however, since she was to represent the collective rather than any real individual.

The story of Deng was supposed to permit the reader a close-up view of an 'individual's experience of the disease that was said to have resulted from China's feudal past as well as Nationalist corruption'. As a woman, Deng had twice been a 'victim' of the old China. After marrying a man in her village, she became infected with schistosomiasis: 'She lost her spirit as well as so much weight, and her skin turned sallow. The disease left her with a distended abdomen, and for some years she was unable to conceive,' the authors informed the reader. As result of her infertility, Deng's marriage fell apart, and even her own mother turned against her. But the reader quickly learned that in 1956 the socialist upsurge in the Chinese countryside led by Chairman Mao Zedong brought profound transformation to the life of Deng as well as to her family. She was cured of the disease and returned to health. She even got her husband back, and a year later became pregnant and gave birth to a baby. 'This thirty-year-old woman has a naturally tanned face with a shade of red colour. The first glance tells us that she was healthy and strong. She was holding a baby in her arms when being interviewed … With the arrival of the baby, their family life has turned ever more happy and harmonious.' And 'now the whole family work hard in the field,' the authors exclaimed. The story of Deng's pregnancy was not a mere detail; it was important to the PRC's claim to the singular triumph of its socialist road to improve the people's health. In the post-war world, one reason that schistosomiasis rose to become a major public health concern was that it caused infertility and dwarfism – both seen to be detrimental to the manpower economy of many newly decolonized countries in the developing world, from Egypt to countries in Southeast Asia and Latin America. The story ended with Deng telling the authors: 'The party and the Chairman are our saviour.' By linking social progress to individual benefit, and more specifically linking personal health with economic and social justice, the authors brought out one key political message of the Great Leap Forward: 'This transformative experience of the Deng family is an epitome of the transformation experienced by hundreds and thousands of families in the endemic Yujiang County.' To make the narrative newsworthy, this individual life story was paired with 'sputnik' statistics: after more than 4,000 victims were cured of the disease, more than 247 acres of improved agricultural land were reclaimed, and after eradicating schistosomiasis, Magang Township, which in previous years had relied on government subsidy, handed over an extra 15,000 kilograms of rice to the government, while the annual income of individual villagers had nearly doubled from 38 RMB per year in 1953 to 74 RMB (in previous years, 40 per cent of local villagers lived on government loans).[33]

THE CHAIRMAN WRITES A POEM

The newspaper report on the success of the eradication campaign caught the eye of Chairman Mao Zedong. Jiangxi had occupied a special place in his heart. Nearly thirty years earlier, it was in Jiangxi that Mao, a young Communist leader, had succeeded in commanding a revolutionary war of the masses that would lead to the creation of the new China. The seed of revolutionary spirit that he had planted then seemed to have borne fruit again in the Great Leap Forward. Mao called the victory narrative of Yujiang's eradication of schistosomiasis the 'heroic display' of the Chinese people's revolutionary struggle in bringing about the Great Leap Forward, and he wanted this to be the narrative for the whole of China. Not long before – after reading the report from Henan province's Fengqiu County in north China boasting about how under the agricultural co-operative system local villagers in the Yingqu co-operative had eradicated poverty, freeing themselves of annual floods by building extensive water conservancy networks with their bare hands and thus bringing dry land under irrigation and converting alkaline land into paddy fields – Mao had written an essay in praise of agricultural collectivization. The essay was published together with the report from Fengqiu County in the inaugural edition of the *Red Flag* magazine, a theoretical journal of the CCP. Having just succeeded in driving the Great Leap further forward, in his essay the high-spirited Mao trumpeted that more and more Chinese people had joined his socialist revolution in transforming their 'poor and blank land' into a pest-free 'communist paradise': 'Never before I have seen so many people so high in spirit, so strong in morale and so firm in determination,' he exclaimed.[34] To him, it was with the same high spirit, strong morale, and firm determination that the people of Yujiang had 'broken down superstition, and let [their] initiative and creativity explode'. They had not only achieved the impossible by '[making] the high mountain bow its head and the river yield the way', they had also eradicated the disease where the imperialist West had failed.[35] For Mao, Yujiang's claim to success was his answer to those who doubted his Great Leap Forward policy, including the technocrats in the party who criticized the 'rushed advance' as well as medical experts such as Su Delong who doubted the feasibility of eradication: 'Until now our modern Hua Tuos [doctors and experts] had been rather reluctant. They lacked faith. Under the good party leadership, the situation is slowly improving. The masses have been mobilized to fight this battle. Now we need to get the scientists to join the battle too. By working together, they can send the Plague God back to heaven,' Mao proclaimed.[36] A month earlier, in a Politburo meeting, he had also said that 'it won't take us long to catch up with the United States and Great Britain.'[37] As his thoughts drifted back and forth, Mao could not sleep. On the spur of the moment, he grabbed a pen and jotted down a few verses in his favourite classic, eight-syllable quatrain style and with romantic passion. These verses would become his placard to 'propagate Yujiang's success, and to give [the Anti-Schistosomiasis Campaign as well as the Great Leap Forward] a push'.[38]

The poem mirrored one of the most influential late Qing reformist thinkers Gong Zizhen's cycle poem about the role of human agency in bringing cosmic change. On the eve of the First Anglo-Chinese War – commonly known as the First Opium War – Gong quit his office for good. On his way home to Hangzhou, he stepped into a temple. Watching worshippers bowing to different gods, Gong felt alone. In anguish and wrath, he burst out, envisaging the cosmos being brought to a standstill, followed by the power of human agency in bringing about radical changes: 'From Gale and Thunder comes the Chinese Nation's Vital Force; How pitiful then, that thousands of horses all struck dumb; I urge [you], the Lord of Heaven, to shake us up again, and grant us human talents not bound to a single kind.'[39] In 1958, set to promote radical collectivization or the People's Commune against all opposition, Mao cited these words of Gong's several times to invoke human agency's role in undertaking radical change. In his poem to propagate Yujiang's 'success' to eradicate schistosomiasis, Mao began by picturing the 'diseased' China as a land of desolation where all vegetation withered and life perished: 'Green Mountains and Emerald Streams, so vast and to what avail? Hua Tuo ["doctors" and "medical experts"] were made powerless by a mere microbe. Thousands of villages became overgrown with brambles while men wasted away. So silent and desolate, only the ghost was left to mourn for the dead.'[40] If, in the nineteenth century, the 'beastly opium' that had caused men in office to 'sleep through spring never waking in the Cold Food Festival' and turned China into a wasteland evoked Gong Zizhen's pathos – which was widely shared by many late Qing reformist literati and inspired them to a romantic passion for nation-building – for Mao, schistosomiasis, 'the mere microbe', was the 'living beast' endangering the new China that he had fought for and achieved. 'This disease is causing more damage than the imperialists. It has killed more people in our country than the Eight-Nation Alliance military collation and the Japanese Army. It's endangering our one hundred million people,' he declared.[41] Charged with the same chivalrous spirit that Gong Zizhen had, Mao went on: '[I] sit on the earth motionless, but I have been travelling [eight] thousand kilometres each day, patrolling the sky. As I see into eternity, time flies back thousands of years. Back then, the Celestial Herd Boy had cared for his people. Still, the same suffering went on year after year.' As did Gong Zizhen, Mao envisaged human agency (the means to a superhuman breakthrough) as producing change: 'The spring wind blows amid ten thousand willow branches, six hundred million Chinese people have turned into heroes like Yao and the Great Yu [the mythical founders of China. The latter is claimed to have built the Chinese civilization by controlling floods]. By the [utopian] will and their wisdom [they have transformed the nature and created an ecological condition to allow for the rejuvenation of the Chinese nation]: crimson rain has turned into fertile billows, and green mountains have turned into bridges. They dug into high mountains, and moved the earth and rivers with their mighty arms.' Having envisioned China, the 'bleak and poor' blank canvas, being painted over and turned into a beautiful landscape of 'communist paradise', Mao, staring into the future, went on to evoke the scene after expelling the schistosomiasis that plagued his country, when people rejoiced and sent the Plague God back into heaven: 'Try ask where the Plague God has gone? It has been sent off in a smoke with a burned paper boat.'[42] Here, Mao was recalling how, since the seventeenth century, communities in southern China had celebrated the Plague God Festival every spring, the peak season for the outbreak of diseases. The festival was a prophylactic measure against epidemics. It always ended with a large, collective procession to expel all remaining plague demons and send the Plague God back to heaven. This was done by placing the Plague God on a massive boat made of paper that was then burned or floated away on the waters.[43]

Despite his revolutionary romanticism, Mao was aware that the 'demon' schistosomiasis was not so easily evicted. To mobilize the masses and to have them committed to the eradication campaign, hard-core propaganda was needed in place of the traditional exorcist offering rites. On 1 July 1958, in a note to his secretary Hu Qiaomu, who was also the director of the Press Administration as well as the deputy minister of propaganda, Mao admitted that 'eradicating schistosomiasis is going to be a hard battle'. He urged Hu to polish up what he had written and to have it published in the *People's Daily* in a day or two so as 'not to let people's high spirit run cold'.[44] Hu, however, waited for another three months until the right moment to let Mao's poem appear in print and aptly titled it 'Send off the Plague God'. In the meantime, on 29 August, the CCP Central Committee had passed the resolution approving the People's Commune as the new and only form of organization for rural China. The resolution claimed that this would 'accelerate the speed of socialist construction ... thus prepare actively for the transition to communism. It seems that the attainment of communism in China is no longer a remote future event.' The transition to communism would, however, involve 'raising the entire people's communist consciousness and morality to a higher degree' and destroying those 'legacies of the old society ... and remnants of bourgeois inequality'.[45] 'Send off the Plague God' hence became a perfect metaphor for a new China and its people, prepared to move toward the future utopian communist society.

'SPRING COMES TO A WITHERED TREE'

With the publication of Mao's 'Send off the Plague God' poem, those in charge of the implementation were compelled to revamp the rather troublesome Anti-Schistosomiasis Campaign. There was a far more enthusiastic atmosphere in 1958 than in 1955 when the campaign had first been inaugurated. At the height of the Great Leap, with Chairman Mao marching the people of China toward his vision of a future communist society, the Nine-Man Subcommittee took on the challenge of eradicating not just schistosomiasis but also malaria, filariasis, ancylostomiasis, and kala azar. All were viewed as diseases of rural poverty. In November 1958, a month after the publication of the chairman's poem, the All China Conference on Parasitic Disease, under the direction of Wei Wenbo, resolved that China would achieve the basic eradication of all five parasitic diseases within one year, in time for the tenth anniversary of the founding of the PRC, their socialist Motherland. To reach this goal would entail a superhuman breakthrough in disease control. This meant 'doing away with the mysterious notions about science' and 'combining scientific research with technological revolution and the mass campaign'. In the meantime, experts such as Su Delong were publicly denounced for 'right conservatism' and being restrained by 'bourgeois conventions'. Medical and Health Technological Revolution conferences and exhibitions were held in major Chinese cities. In the autumn of 1958, the first National Health Technological Revolution Exhibition in Beijing showcased the PRC's Anti-Schistosomiasis Campaign and Yujiang County's putative victory in eradicating the disease, as well as local medical and health innovations from all over the country. As with agricultural 'sputnik fields', provinces competed to win the trophy in medical and health innovations bringing about disease eradication. Having done away with right conservatism, the masses were invited to participate in this technological revolution.[46] A campaign to collect folk remedies spread across the country. Many previously abandoned and excluded traditional practices, as well as long-lost home remedies, were rediscovered as innovations or national treasures and given the 'Traditional Chinese Medicine' (TCM) label. Within a few months, Sichuan province alone had collected and published 666,000 folk remedies, including a herbal mixture that contained Ahizoma Atractylodis, Angelica Dahurica, Szechwan Lovage Rhizome, and Cassia Twig, traditionally used to treat headache and chills. A local practitioner had been using it since the 1930s to relieve malaria symptoms with some success. The local health authority, eager to add their mark to the Great Leap in disease eradication, publicized it as a malaria cure, and it was soon promoted in the rest of the country.[47] Yet not all the herbs were widely available, and there were no spare workers to collect them; efficacy also varied from province to province because of the lack of quality control. In 1959, based on their laboratory studies, researchers at the Chinese Academy of Medical Science's Parasitic Institute announced that this malaria cure had no effect in treating malaria. To achieve the Great Leap in eradicating malaria, hospitals and parasitic disease treatment centres relied on Cycloguanil – the most widely used anti-malaria drug before China obtained the technology to domestically produce choloroquine, primaquine, and primethamine in the 1960s.[48] Similarly, to reach the target of eradicating schistosomiasis, many local health authorities also opted for using NaPCP to kill snails, even though it was more expensive and harmful than plant-based TCM pesticides made of *Camellia oleosa* or *Croton tiglium* (this will be discussed further in the next chapter).

Promoting technological revolution and mobilizing the broad masses would involve further propaganda. In an article titled 'The Labouring Mass Should Become the Master of Culture', published in the inaugural edition of the *Red Flag* magazine, Ke Qingshi, the party boss in charge of the Anti-Schistosomiasis Campaign once again stressed that public health work was an integral part of the cultural revolution to transform the dirty, backward, and diseased Chinese countryside into pest-free socialist towns and cities with 'new style housing filled with sunshine and fresh clean air, boulevards and sports facilities'. 'There will be willow branches dangling outside each home like curtains as well as running water in front of every house,' Ke proclaimed. According to him, villagers would learn socialist and communist ideologies as well as how to live a healthy, clean, and cultured socialist way of life. For Ke, this would entail rural communities (which by then had been transformed into production brigades) forming their own drama groups and watching revolutionary-themed movies. At the same time, villagers would adopt the habits of hygiene as everyday norms, from regularly washing their hands with soap to bathing each day.[49] To deliver this cultural revolution would require involving the masses, with the masses, of course, functioning under the direction of the centralized state authority.

Wei Wenbo, by then actively running the campaign, was experienced in party propaganda work amongst the rural masses. A keen calligrapher and poet himself, he adapted Mao's romantic poem into a popular jingle so that the undereducated villagers would learn to recite it in their literacy class. This paid off, and 'Send off the Plague

God' soon became an everyday buzz-phrase in many endemic regions as the Anti-Schistosomiasis Campaign became the new Plague God Festival. Ironically, in recent years the exorcist rites of 'Send off the Plague God' are back in fashion in some parts of rural China, although this has little to do with the resurgence of schistosomiasis – villagers now regularly hold 'Send off the Plague God' processions to protest the wide-scale corruption that plagues China.

In her study on 'Emotion Work in the Chinese Revolution', Elizabeth Perry argues that, for the CCP, theatre was 'a critical means of eliciting an emotional reaction that was used intentionally to solidify popular commitment'.[50] With his long experience in party propaganda work, Wei Wenbo understood how to harness emotional excitement to further the revolutionary cause. Prior to turning 'Send of the Plague God' into a popular jingle, he gave instructions to adapt Mao's romantic poem and Yujiang's victory narrative into a popular spoken drama so that the masses would be moved to throw themselves with renewed vigour into the chairman-led Anti-Schistosomiasis Campaign. The reason Wei utilized spoken drama to move the villagers to act was that traditionally in rural China, public theatre and spectacle had played a central role in promoting social cohesion. Wei named the play *Spring Comes to the Withered Tree*, partly in the hope that it would help to revive the dying campaign, and scheduled it to be performed before a mass audience during the PRC's tenth anniversary celebration. Wang Lian was the young playwright chosen for the task, and for several years Wang was assigned to the PLA art troupe with the task of supporting the Land Reform and the Communist takeover of the Lower Yangtze regions by producing and directing revolutionary dramas as well as rice-planting dance musicals (*Yangge*). The latter was a popular performance form with its roots in rural northwest China. It was first adopted by the CCP in Yan'an in the 1940s to disseminate the message of revolution and socialist transformation. After the Communist Liberation in 1949, *Yangge*, as well as revolutionary spoken drama, was introduced to southern China by the new Communist authority as a vehicle for propaganda.[51] They did, however, encounter competition from local operas. Prior to the Communist takeover, a vibrant operatic theatre culture had existed in southern China, with each region having its own local operatic traditions. Since most of them had told local narratives that conflicted with the CCP's narrative of revolution and the new Communist nationhood, they had had to undergo reform or reconfiguration.[52] Wang Lian and his colleagues in the art troupe participated in this process.

In addition to his duty to mobilize the masses through theatre work, Wang Lian could draw on his own personal experience, since he himself had been infected by schistosomiasis and subsequently recovered from it. The experience gave him the motivation to tell the party narrative as a human drama experienced by individuals and families. A native of Shandong province near the Korean peninsula, Wang was one of the thousands of southbound cadres who crossed the Yangtze to bring the revolution to the south. Upon arriving at the ancient canal town Suzhou, Wang Lian was diagnosed with schistosomiasis. While recovering in hospital, Wang had befriended another sick soldier. Too ill to write, this soldier had asked Wang to draft a love letter on his behalf to his wife back home in northern China, telling her how much he missed her but that for the greater cause of bringing the revolution to southern China, he had to stay away from her and the family until the work was done. After surviving the disease, for years Wang could not get the sick soldier and his wife out of his mind. He imagined his play, about how the new China had achieved the Great Leap in eradicating schistosomiasis under CCP leadership, as a family drama of separation and love but with a happy ending. Furthermore, the love story was a genre familiar to the mass audience in the Lower Yangtze region, since it had been an enduringly popular genre for local operas in all the endemic regions. It would therefore make the play appealing to them.[53]

Five years prior to Wang taking on the task of writing the play, the Shanghai Film Studio had turned a famous local *Yue* opera (which originated from regions around Zhejiang and Shanghai), *The Butterfly Lovers*, into a technicolour movie. It was the first colour feature ever made in the PRC. Subsequently, on an official visit to Geneva, China's premier Zhou Enlai entertained his Western guests, including the British prime minister Sir Anthony Eden, by showing them the film. Zhou gave the film its English name: *The Chinese Romeo and Juliet*. The Western guests were said to have been deeply moved by its tragic love story as well as mesmerized by the outlandish performance and exotic scenery. The movie was subsequently shown in French cinemas with great success. We are told that George Sadoul was moved by the long line waiting outside a Paris theatre and that even Charlie Chaplin praised the film as extraordinary. It also won awards in international film festivals and was a box office hit in Hong Kong.[54] After this international success, *Yue* opera became even more popular throughout China. For culture cadres or playwrights like Wang Lian, there was an ever-greater desire to produce artwork that was revolutionary but distinctively Chinese,[*] while at the same time appealing to both international and Chinese mass audiences. On the one hand, the success of *The Chinese Romeo and Juliet* had shown that romantic love was a genre that cut across cultures and politics; on the other, by giving human tragic love a happy ending, it also became the story of revolution and thus of the new China. Indeed, for intellectuals and culture cadres like Wang Lian, the Chinese revolution itself was a love story about themselves and their troubled Motherland.

After its successful première in Shanghai, *Spring Comes to a Withered Tree*, Wang Lian's play about the successful eradication of schistosomiasis that he framed as a love story, was chosen to go on a national tour. In March 1960, when it was staged at the Capital Theatre by the Beijing People's Theatre, it caught the eye of Premier Zhou Enlai. He proposed to turn the play into a film. As he relished the international success of *The Chinese Romeo and Juliet*, Zhou was keen for film to be utilized as a propaganda medium to mobilize the masses as well as to promote the image of China to a world audience, winning over sympathisers who might not have subscribed to the revolutionary cause of the PRC – in this instance, the Great Leap Forward. With the Sino-Soviet split following Stalin's death and subsequent de-Stalinization of the USSR and with Sino-Western relationships in serious disarray, Zhou and Lu Dingyi, the PRC's minister of propaganda at the time, encouraged Chinese playwrights and filmmakers to create plays and films that bore no resemblance to 'Khrushchev's revisionist' as well as imperialist films and plays. In a later address to the Ninth National Conference on Schistosomiasis Control (1963), Lu stated unequivocally that the film of *Spring Comes to a Withered Tree* was a piece of political propaganda for the international and the domestic audience:

---

* Since the early twentieth century, it has been an enduring theme for Chinese artists and writers to create an art and literature that was modern or revolutionary as well as Chinese. In the PRC, this became a state-sponsored enterprise, since the arts and literature are an important propaganda tool. During and after the Great Leap Forward, there has also been a great push to produce 'folk' and 'Chinese' arts and literature that was of and for the masses.

We are the world leader in schistosomiasis control ... We have produced a film and a play about [the Anti-Schistosomiasis Campaign]. Recently, some Japanese experts marvelled over our success: 'You have achieved much more [in schistosomiasis control] than we could in Japan. This is because China is a socialist country,' they praised. We wanted the imperialists and revisionists to know that we are more successful in public health work than them ... Some people have failed to understand that the arts are powerful tools in building socialism. They debated for many years over the role of the arts, and ended up with revisionists like Tito and Khrushchev ... Under Khrushchev, the Soviet Union has produced many films, plays, and literature that are anti-revolution, anti–revolutionary war, and anti-Stalin ... We need to be prepared, and to fight against imperialist and revisionist arts.* To do so, we need to produce revolutionary plays and films that reflect the spirit of our time, and at the same time are anti-feudal, anti-imperialist, and anti-revisionist. This is an integral part of our cultural revolution.[55]

As an integral part of the cultural revolution, Lu urged that arts such as the cinema and drama must use their power to mobilize the masses at home.

There was an important political reason for this outburst of propagandistic exuberance. It is worth noting that by 1960, famine had spread across the entire country and had already led to the death of millions in the countryside. With Great Leap euphoria withering, the Anti-Schistosomiasis Campaign had literally ground to a halt. Struggling to fulfil the government's grain procurement target, as well as cope with the escalating public health emergency caused by mass malnutrition, local cadres and health officials openly refused to implement the campaign: 'Our task now is to provide food and clothing for villagers, schistosomiasis control has to wait for a couple of years.' 'Eradicating schistosomiasis is like trying to reach the stars in the sky, we will never be able achieve it ... Our hair will turn white, and our teeth will fall out, but we will never get rid

---

* Strictly speaking, in 1963 there was no revisionist art in the Soviet Union and eastern Europe. Revisionism was first crystallized in literature only in 1967. But for the Chinese, 'apparatchik' here refers to films that depart from the hard Stalinist line as well as the Socialist Realist mold. Even more important, Lu Dingyi was less interested in Socialist Realism. He was asserting the Chinese determination to carve its own path to socialism, independent of other existing experiences.

of schistosomiasis,' they lamented.[56] On the other hand, following Yujiang's 'successful' model in declaring eradication, a huge number of counties made a political gesture in carrying out 'shock work' eliminating snails and providing mass treatment for the disease. Having gone through the motion a couple of times, they, too, declared near-eradication and buried the campaign together with the snails. With villagers and their cadres losing the 'high spirit' for the Anti-Schistosomiasis Campaign – or more generally, for the Great Leap Forward – there was an urgent need to use a mass medium such as film to win back the masses. Echoing Ke Qingshi's earlier speech, Lu Dingyi once again stressed that arts and health workers should work hand-in-hand to bring about a cultural revolution aimed at changing prevailing social customs. According to him, while public health work would enable the masses to transform their everyday life and live in a socialist way, cinema and drama, as well as other forms of visual arts, were powerful tools for not only spreading the message of health and hygiene but also for changing the way people thought: 'that's not the same as injecting medicine into their body.' And 'we need to teach our five hundred million peasants new socialist morals and ideologies, and transform them into builders for communism, in particular our youth who had never seen a landlord or an imperialist.'[57]

Although the policy of austerity was to continue, with millions starving to death in the countryside (it was rumoured that Chairman Mao Zedong had even given up eating his favourite fatty pork, while Premier Zhou Enlai had switched from drinking tea to plain boiled water), the leadership at the Shanghai Film Studio backed the *Spring Comes to a Withered Tree* film with full financial support as well as manpower. They understood it was to be an important piece of political propaganda. Zheng Junli, modern China's most celebrated film director, was named director. Xu Sangchu, the PRC's top film cadre and producer, who was the producer for this film, had hoped it would become another classic, on a par with Zheng Junli's immensely popular wartime epic *A Spring River Flows East* (1947). Initially, Zheng hesitated to take on the film project because he had been criticized for glorifying bourgeois urban intellectuals and misrepresenting the masses in his earlier film *Husband and Wife* (1951) and was cautious about taking on another film project about the masses. In addition, he had just finished making *Lin Zexu* – an epic film about the First Opium War

– that was chosen as the visual centrepiece of the tenth anniversary celebration of the PRC. Zheng was at the high point of his career and had his heart set on making a landmark film about modern China's cultural icon, Lu Xun, because the eightieth anniversary of Lu Xun's birth was coming up.[58] But Zheng could not refuse to take on the film project *Spring Comes to a Withered Tree* for several reasons. He was told that the film was Premier Zhou's idea; he also learned from Xu Sangchu, who was a native of Zhejiang province, that Xu's father as well as the children of two of Xu's relatives had died of schistosomiasis. Perhaps equally important, Zheng was energized by the Great Leap claim that his Motherland would soon surpass the imperialists in the West in all fields, from public health to the arts.

To prepare for the film, Zheng retreated to the countryside to be 'closer' to the masses, hoping to avoid being accused again of being 'detached from the masses'. The rural environment, as well as the euphoria over breaking down bourgeois conventions, encouraged him to experiment with a relatively new cinematic style that employed folk arts (thought to be spontaneously 'mass culture') as well as an ink and wash technique evocative of Chinese landscape painting. This allowed him to justify that the film was *about* the masses and yet also *of* the masses while at the same time being distinctively Chinese. To capitalize on the success of *The Chinese Romeo and Juliet*, Zheng invited one of the immensely popular local opera singers, Yu Hongxian, to sing Mao's poem 'Send off the Plague God' to an enchanting *Pingtan* melody.* Zheng also gave priority to the love story of Bitter Sister and Winter Brother, the heroine and hero of the film (modelled on the story of Deng Rumei in Yujiang, as had first appeared in the *People's Daily* special report). It is also worth mentioning that both Zheng Junli and his crew became bored with shooting scenes of village cadres and health professionals arguing about the relative importance of agricultural productivity and schistosomiasis control. They found such debates tedious to film. So they spent more and more time building up a melodramatic plot between Bitter Sister and Winter Brother and the latter's mother (played by one of modern China's most popular actors, Shangguan Yunzhu).[59] The crew also shot a great deal of Orientalist background 'wallpaper' scenes

---

* *Pingtan* is a popular local storytelling opera from Jiangsu and Zhejiang provinces.

of beautiful canal towns, stone bridges, traditional Jianglan style courtyards, flowing rivers and mountains, and dangling branches of willow trees. Fully aware that this film was a piece of political propaganda, the crew filmed many scenes of bumper harvests and the masses happily working in the fields or digging canals. Despite Zheng's ambiguity, *Spring Comes to a Withered Tree* managed to use the cinema to reinforce the narrative of Yujiang's heroic battle against schistosomiasis that was first reported in the *People's Daily* in 1958. In the context of the increasingly severe famine, plus the Sino-Soviet split, the authorities were scrambling around for resources. Since eradication was nowhere in sight, there was an ever greater push for a technological revolution. To this, the film added the theme of Bitter Sister being cured by the TCM doctors after the Western bourgeois doctor denied her treatment. This was a theme beloved by authors and artists in the Soviet Union, since medicine and health care were tangible programs that made socialism, either Stalinist or Maoist, appealing locally as well as abroad. Furthermore, the tension between medicine for the masses and Western bourgeois medicine would become an important feature of public health in the PRC and abroad in the following decade. This was exemplified by the decentralization of health care delivery in the PRC, later marked by the Barefoot Doctor Campaign, another public health centrepiece in the PRC, which still lay some years ahead.

In the meantime, with the goal of eradication slipping further away and the failure to deliver the promised health and well-being, the film *Spring Comes to a Withered Tree*, together with cheap public health posters, were used by authorities to bridge the gap between the increasingly harsh daily reality and the Maoist utopian future as well as to inspire villagers to participate in the official Anti-Schistosomiasis Campaign.

Screenings were organized for villagers in the endemic regions to watch the film in the open air. In 1964, an official estimate showed that the film had been screened more than 1,100 times in schistosomiasis endemic regions, with 440,000 viewers.[60] In rural Jiangsu province, mobile projection teams screened the film 57 times, with a reported more than 58,000 viewers.[61] According to Guan Wenwei, Jiangsu province's deputy head at the time who was also a PLA

Figure 4.1 'Involve the Masses. Adopt Integrated Approach. Constantly Fight [the Disease]. To Eradicating Schistosomiasis Is to Greet the New High Tide of Agricultural Production'. (Poster produced by Zhejiang Province Disease Prevention Centre, 1964.)

Figure 4.2 'Earth Burial Is an Excellent Way to Eliminate Snails'.
(Poster produced by Zhejiang Province Disease Prevention Centre, 1964.)

Figure 4.3 'It Is Also Necessary to Apply Chemical Control to Eliminate Snails'. (Poster produced by Zhejiang Province Disease Prevention Centre, 1964.)

general who had led the revolution in Jiangsu province,* the film inspired many villagers to participate in the local control work.[62] In urban Shanghai, however, when the film was first released in the spring of 1964, cinemas across the city reported having real difficulty selling tickets because urban residents did not want to watch another propaganda film about rural China. To attract an audience, urban dwellers were handed free cinema tickets, and government work units made it compulsory for employees to watch the film. After watching the film, the audience response suggested

* Guan was a native of Jiangsu province and had extensive experience in peasant-mobilizing work in different parts of Jiangsu. After the PLA liberated Jiangsu, as the new Communist authority's party representative who led the rural work, for some years Guan oversaw the local schistosomiasis control. As of the late 1980s, his daughter Guan Xiaohong was an academic researcher who participated in the Anti-Schistosomiasis Campaign. I interviewed her informally some years ago. Some of the research questions for this book have grown out of that interview.

Figure 4.4 Poster for film *Spring Comes to the Withered Tree* (1961).

that they were deeply moved by the love story as well as impressed by the beautiful scenery and the *Pingtan* melody but much less so by the official victory narrative of the Anti-Schistosomiasis Campaign.[63] During the Great Proletarian Revolution, the film was temporarily banned after Wei Wenbo was officially condemned as a 'counter-revolutionary' in 1967 and subsequently 'disappeared'. (Later, it turned out that he was incarcerated in a political prison.) Zheng Junli, too, was put under house arrest and died.

After the death of Mao, Wei Wenbo was rehabilitated, as was the film. It again played to mass audiences in the endemic regions to 'educate and promote awareness about schistosomiasis'. Without adequate data, it is difficult to assess the film's impact on the PRC's Anti-Schistosomiasis Campaign. There is little doubt, however, that it inspired some individuals to identify with the heroine and the hero of the film. Recently, while visiting local museums dedicated to the Anti-Schistosomiasis Campaign in Jiangsu province's Qingpu County, Zhejiang province's Jiaxing County, and Jiangxi province's Yujiang County, I came across similar texts in each museum claiming that the film was based on their own 'heroic' experience of 'Sending off the Plague God' and that Bitter Sister or Winter Brother had been 'real' villagers from their counties. After speaking to some participants in the campaign, it dawned on me that for villagers who had endured extremely cold weather burying snails with half-empty stomachs, it was important that they remember the time as worth celebrating rather than as time wasted. The film *Spring Comes to a Withered Tree* allowed them to see themselves as 'heroes' who had taken part in a 'heroic battle' against a disease that had claimed the lives of many of the people they knew: in the lower reaches of the Yangtze River, almost every family had some connection to the disease. The film thus gave them a sense of self-worth. By sharing the happiness of Bitter Sister and Winter Brother, they could, at least for a moment, forget the darker side of the campaign, despite the bitter experience of the famine and the resulting fear of an uncertain future. As Gerard Lemos's illuminating study, *The End of the Chinese Dream: Why Chinese People Fear the Future*, shows, the majority of people in China remain worried about health problems.[64] Their anxieties over poor health are exacerbated because of the deficiencies in the Chinese health care system. This anxiety has its roots, to no little extent, in the memories of the famine and the mass death and illnesses that resulted.

For the post-Mao PRC government, *Spring Comes to a Withered Tree* continued to serve as China's 'cultural ambassador' and was screened to audiences in some African and Latin American countries as well as in Japan. The Anti-Schistosomiasis Campaign had become an ever more important piece of cultural propaganda for the PRC in winning over fellow travellers in Latin America, Africa, and Southeast Asia. Not lived experience but the propagandistic representation of the successes of the PRC in improving people's health, made accessible to all in the form of narratives and films, shaped not only the internal debates about health care but also their international resonance. The reality at the time was, however, radically different from such propagandistic representation. As the next chapter shows, the Maoist utopian project of transforming the Chinese countryside into a disease-free 'communist paradise' turned out to be a total disaster. While millions died of starvation, schistosomiasis morbidity was also on the rise.

5

The Great Leap Backward

THE WAR ON NATURE: BATTLING SNAILS

Nineteen-fifty-nine was the Year of the Pig in the Chinese calendar. For China's agricultural communities, the pig is associated with fertility and virility, but 1959 turned out to be a harsh and barren year. The Great Leap Forward demanded constant increases in production from the peasants. The State Council increased the target for agricultural output to 40 per cent higher than the previous year.[1] It compelled many local authorities, from provincial to county, commune and production brigade, to inflate their yield by tens and even hundreds of times the actual output. This came to be known as the 'Wind of Exaggeration'. As this 'Wind of Exaggeration' swept across the Chinese countryside, the famine that had already haunted parts of the country worsened and quickly spread. Oedema caused by malnutrition became the new plague, claiming more and more lives. Death and ill health put further stress on the ongoing labour shortage caused by the expanding demands for workers for the Great Leap Forward's industrial construction and water conservation initiatives. With less and less labour available for agricultural work, many half-cultivated agricultural fields – some of which were newly reclaimed fields – turned into wasteland overgrown with weeds. As human activity receded, the unheroic yet resilient snails, which had previously gone into hiding, slowly crawled out, and to borrow the words of the Nobel Prize–winning novelist Günter Grass: 'it seldom wins and then by the skin of its teeth. It crawls, it goes into hiding but keeps on, putting down its quickly drying track on the historical landscape.'[2]

The situation worsened as the warmer spring weather brought the first monsoons. In the lake regions along the Yangtze River, water quickly submerged the land, making snail burial work impossible. As a result, in the regions surrounding Poyang Lake, literally next to the 'victorious' Yujiang County, many local authorities abandoned the practice of schistosomiasis control by burying snails. There, schistosomiasis control work retreated to treatment only, conflicting with the government policy that had previously put prevention first.[3] Elsewhere, heavy rains also prevented the land reclamation needed to control the vector snail. In Guangdong province's Dawang state farm, for instance, 20,000 labourers were brought in to reclaim the snail-infested marshes and turn them into agricultural land. Heavy rain, however, halted the work, and as a result these workers had nothing to do except play cards in their makeshift tents. In some regions, such as Yunnan province's Tunxi County in the southwest, local authorities assumed that the snails would automatically vanish after new irrigation canals and ditches were built, so they did not even bother to plan for snail control. During the annual snail survey, 'routs' of young snails were found crawling cheerfully in the newly built irrigation ditches. Even in the eastern provinces of Zhejiang, Jiangsu, and Shanghai, where they had boasted for years of their experience in snail control work and where they enjoyed more resources and technical support, it was reported that buckets of snails were being harvested in many counties just a few months after their near-elimination had been declared. In the suburbs of Shanghai in Jinshan and Nanhui counties, it was reported that merely 30 per cent of snails were being killed as result of local snail burial work – nowhere near the projected target of elimination.[4]

Later, in 1961, in Shanghai's Songjiang County, the head of one commune health centre admitted: 'we declared near elimination twice in the previous two years [1959 and 1960], but this year we not only found a few snails, we actually found *lots* of snails.' His excuse for the failure to reduce snail numbers was the poor quality of the snail control work on the ground. According to him, this was partly exacerbated by the labour shortfall, but his colleague in Shanghai County's epidemic prevention centre disagreed. This colleague argued that 'the problem is not due to the poor quality of the work. I led the snail control work myself, and two or three of my colleagues went along to supervise the work and verify the result. We made sure there were no snails left before calling off the work.

But a few months later, snails repopulated those scoured canals and ditches. How do you explain that? My head aches whenever I think about snails. Some younger colleagues who recently joined the control work grumbled: "I fear snail control work more than I fear death."' He concluded that to eliminate snails was simply not feasible: 'No one has any idea when and how we can eliminate snails.' Drawing on years of experience, one schistosomiasis control cadre from Zhejiang province's Jiading County supported this view: 'Snails are difficult to spot because they are very small, and there are too many of them. Not only that, they can survive in both water and on land. Even if we don't see them today, they will pop out tomorrow. After more than six years of effort to eliminate the snail, none of us think it is possible to get rid of them completely.'[5]

Some experts, such as Su Delong, acknowledged that there were far too many challenges in controlling the snail vector by the environmental method. He saw that China's economic condition at the time meant that the environmental control measures such as cementing ditches, which had been applied in small areas of Japan with some success in mitigating schistosomiasis, was not feasible in China where the endemic area was so vast and the terrain and the soil composition so complex. They therefore sought to control the snail vector with chemical control measures, despite the Japanese recommendation in 1957 that had warned against it because of the toxicity to other species. In the long run, molluscicides such as sodium pentachlorophenate (NaPCP) 'may increase the resistance of vector snails,' noted the Japanese experts. The drug is also soluble in water; the creeks of the Yangtze delta region could be easily contaminated by it. 'In those areas the inhabitants often culture fish in creeks and sodium pentachlorphenate was proved to be poisonous for fish in a concentration of one ppm [1 ppm = 1 mg per litre]. There exists the danger against human beings because the inhabitants in these areas usually drink creek water.'[6] Chemical control measures were also rejected by the local authority in Jiangxi province for economic rather than health reasons.

Knowing the danger of pollution did not preclude the use of this easier method because immediate successes were vital for the political status of the leadership of the People's Republic of China (PRC). The late 1950s were also the moment when public health authorities around the world came increasingly to favour chemical control, seeing it as offering a rapid means of bringing the disease under control.[7] Eyeing the crown of being the first in the world to eradicate schistosomiasis, it was no wonder that many Chinese experts sought out molluscicides as the 'magic bullet' for getting the job done. Since copper sulphate was too expensive for China at the time, the molluscicides that were widely used were calcium arsenate and the synthetic sodium pentachlorophenate. Although spraying molluscicides could effectively kill the intermediate snail host, experts both inside and outside China were also aware that these chemicals were highly toxic to fish, crops, and humans, as well as damaging to the entire ecology. Furthermore, molluscicides such as calcium arsenate are highly soluble in water. The toxicity remains for many months and is extremely harmful to humans and animals well after the initial application.[8] On many occasions, Su Delong stressed the importance of training villagers to take special precautions when spraying.[*] Aware that synthetics became ineffective in cold weather, Su and other experts recommended carrying out the spraying in spring or summer for effective control of the snails because in warmer weather the toxicity of the chemical was enhanced in warm water and the snail was hungry after its dormant period over the cold weather. Equally important, they emphasized that the spraying should be repeated at least once a month.[9]

Against their advice, however, in many affected regions the chemical control work was carried out in winter when there was little agricultural work and excess labour could be used for this purpose. Generally, the severe labour shortage caused by the interminable Great Leap Forward construction work and the ongoing campaign to increase agricultural yields, as well as the subsequent famine, meant that the spraying was often carried out in an intense burst of activity, in a similar way to the snail burial 'shock attacks' in Yujiang County (as described in chapter 4). It is not surprising, therefore, that the result was disappointing. Reports from western Sichuan showed that in many locations where there was a high density of snails, spraying NaPCP only managed to kill a mere 3.9 per cent of the snails. While spraying calcium arsenate was reported to have a higher success rate of killing 25 per cent of the snails, it was,

---

[*] For instance, after spraying villagers should avoid using the water from the nearby creek or river for at least three days, as well as stopping animals from drinking water from ponds or any other still-water source for as long as two to three months. Also, they had to avoid spraying on grasses, or, if they did, the contaminated grass was to be removed completely, since animals might die of the poison from grazing.

however, ineffective in killing their eggs. In addition, because of a shortfall in trained personnel, the spraying was often carried out in a haphazard fashion without any proper planning. This reduced the limited efficacy of molluscicides and led to enormous waste. Since there was little time and labour for the spraying, some grass-roots cadres deliberately avoided taking a snail survey prior to the application of the chemicals. In these communes, they only sprayed major ditches and neglected smaller ones, assuming 'the bigger the ditch, the more snails'. When public health officials came to verify the result, they were stunned to learn that snail density there was as high as one per every five square metres.[10]

In the desperate rush to reach the goal of eliminating snails, the very real concerns over human and animal health were regularly compromised because of the severe shortage of trained personnel to carry out or supervise the spraying. In the suburbs of Shanghai, the local authority of the schistosomiases control model county Qingpu, for instance, gave an order to spray everywhere, irrespective of the warning to avoid spraying near residential areas and animal barns.[11] A similar 'spray everywhere' program was carried out in nearby Jiangsu province, where sixteen schistosomiasis control cadres were reported to have suffered severe toxic poisoning after continuously handling NaPCP for several days without any protective measures. Ingesting fish poisoned by the chemical made their condition even worse, and one person subsequently died. Eating poisoned fish was also widespread among villagers due to the increasing starvation caused by the famine. In Zhejiang province's model county of schistosomiasis control, Jiaxing, some communes planned to solve the labour shortage problem by carrying out spraying during the rainy season when farming work would be suspended. Because of the rise in water level, however, snails crawled out from the canals where NaPCP had been applied. At the same time, floods transported dissolved chemicals downstream into sections of the river used for breeding fish, and a huge number of fish were poisoned as a result.[12] Further inland, in Sichuan province's Mianyang County in the southwest, many female sprayers were asked to carry out spraying barefoot in the paddy fields over an extended period. Some subsequently vomited repeatedly, while others fainted after inhaling too much of the toxin.[13] Despite frequent reports of NaPCP poisoning, its application continued into the 1980s. As late as 1985, cases of death by NaPCP poison relating to the local schistosomiasis control work were reported in Yunnan Province's Dali region.[14] Dermabrasion was also a common ailment among the sprayers. In Mianyang County's Mawei Commune, seeing their skin peeling off, the villagers were extremely frightened. In shock, they began to scream and threw away the spraying guns as they ran out of the village and paddy fields. Here, the villagers complained that molluscicides killed more crops and grass than snails. Without any grass to eat, the cows and pigs also died of starvation. The locals began to view snail control work as directly contributing to the local famine, and they called the schistosomiasis cadres 'life snatchers'.[15]

In addition to the danger of molluscicides getting into the food chain and harming human and animal health, there were also concerns that the unrestricted use of chemicals over a long period of time would damage the quality of the soil. Studies show that copper salts and other molluscicides that kill snails and fish also destroy nitrogen-fixing algae (BGA). The latter is recognized as one of the bio-fertilizers necessary to keep the rice paddies fertile. After the application of copper salts and other molluscicides repeatedly over time, the BGA was destroyed, and thus the quality of the soil of the rice paddies deteriorated.[16] In light of the ongoing famine as well as a severe labour shortage, an increasing number of local authorities began to resist the method of controlling snails with molluscicides. Some rejected it outright on the grounds that it would damage the quality of the soil and thus decrease the agricultural yield. In Fengxian County on the south side of Shanghai, for instance, local authorities gave the order not to carry out any spraying in or near the rice paddies. It also forbade any spraying near the village for fear that insecticides would harm livestock and fisheries as well as the inhabitants.[17] This drove the snails to migrate to the untreated (unsprayed) areas to hibernate or lay their eggs, but after the spraying stopped and as spring approached, the snails would quickly repopulate the previously treated area. Here, control through molluscicides was not only ineffective but also wasteful of already scarce local resources. In addition, with little or no food to eat, those with the task of spraying complained about the lack of adequate diet that left them with insufficient energy to do the job effectively. Some made a calculation that to apply a whole bucket of liquid chemical mixture would involve 700 spraying movements. In the summer, when the daylight was long, their workload would increase. 'To carry out the spraying, we need sufficient calories. With the ration of 400g rice per day, where can we get the energy to do it?' they groaned. Some even composed a mocking bit of doggerel: 'We get up every morning to try to eliminate snails. All day long we only get some spoonful of gruel to eat and two bowls of salty water to drink. When is this going to end?'[18]

The work of controlling snails with molluscicides was further hampered by the supply shortage that was a result of the collapse of the overall nationwide distribution system during the famine, as well as poor management at the local level.[19] Goods perished or were degraded at transport depots because there were not enough trains, trucks, boats, or workers to move them. An increasing number of train robberies, triggered by the famine crisis, also prevented molluscicides from being delivered to their designated places in time for the control work.[20] The other national problem was simply the lack of available containers to store and transport the chemicals. For instance, the Nanjing pharmaceutical factory complained that they were seriously short of cylinders and acid-resistant tubs. Similar problems were also reported elsewhere. As a result, the demand for molluscicides far exceeded the supply.[21]

With molluscicides in short supply, local authorities were encouraged to practise 'self-reliance'. This meant coming up with local solutions to eliminate snails that required either no or little financial input from the state. From its conception, the PRC's Anti-Schistosomiasis Campaign was a crusade that would involve the masses. In the context of the Great Leap Forward, communities, including grassroots schistosomiasis institutions in affected regions, were further encouraged to come up with technical solutions or local innovations to eliminate snails. Bio-pesticides were widely promoted, such as an oil emulsion extracted from croton seeds and a paste made of *Camellia oleosa* because they were claimed to have produced some success in reducing snail populations. To further the dissemination of such methods, experts from research institutions were involved in testing their efficacy. *Camellia oleosa* is a plant found throughout southern China. Traditionally, fishermen and villagers in parts of China used it as a poison bait to stun fish and shellfish. Prior to the introduction of commercial soap, rural villagers also used it as a sanitizer to wash their hands and hair. In 1956, at the start of the Anti-Schistosomiasis Campaign, researchers, with the help of grassroots health auxiliaries in Zhejiang province, experimented with using it to kill snails. The initial experiment conducted in Jiangshan County showed that the efficacy of *camellia oleosa* in reducing snails was uneven: at a warm temperature (+32°C), the snail reduction rate could reach as high as 97.7 per cent, but as the temperature dropped, its efficacy also diminished. Furthermore, its impact dissipated quickly. A longer-lasting result would involve constantly applying it to affected paddies and ditches, which was impossible to undertake. Given the impact of other interventions on human health, Su Delong and his team of researchers at Shanghai Medical University (today's Fudan University Medical College) developed prevention techniques to protect villagers from infection. This required applying 30 grams of dust of freshly collected *Camellia oleosa* to a cloth and then using the cloth to wrap around villagers' legs prior to them stepping into contaminated water or muddy fields. The field study in Qingpu County, outside of Shanghai, showed that this method could be effective for up to eight hours. In light of an ongoing famine, however, using *Camellia oleosa* to reduce the snail population or protect villagers from infection proved impractical for a number of reasons: first of all, both methods were time-consuming and labour-intensive; second, no cotton cloth or any other fabric was available;[22]* and third, the overuse of *Camellia oleosa* paste (to kill snails rather than using it as a poison bait at lower doses) caused a huge quantity of fish, shellfish, and water plants to die. Since many villagers relied on fish and shellfish for food and water plants were an important source of fertilizer, it is understandable that the method was unpopular. In laboratory tests, the oil emulsion of croton (at 4–8 g/m^2) achieved a similar success in killing snails as NaPCP ($1 \ g/m^2$). In the field, however, its efficacy was much less. It was also even more harmful to human and animal health than *camellia oleosa* paste. A few grams of it could cause severe diarrhoea and even fatalities. Traditionally, it was an abortifacient, well known for causing miscarriage. At the time of an escalating famine crisis, with malnutrition and infertility being two of the most widespread health risks, many rumours arose that croton oil was a cause of the problem. There were also reports of villagers suffering from skin ailments after handling it. Thus, instead of viewing it as a beneficial intervention, villagers regarded it as just one more health risk. Furthermore, it too was constantly in short supply, since it was expensive and labour-intensive to produce by hand.[23]

---

* To make up the ever-increasing cotton procumbent target set by the government, villagers were forced to hand over their cloths and quilts.

Still, the goal of eradication could not be questioned. In the meantime, local authorities, with the help of experts, were compelled to come up with new cost-effective innovations. They used toxic industrial chemical waste – such as a residual of calcium carbamide and a sodium salt of coal tar acid and phenol – as a means of getting rid of snails by poisoning the habitat. In addition to reducing snail populations, the method helped to recycle industrial waste as well as saving local authorities the cost of purchasing molluscicides. Transforming industrial waste into a 'useful treasure' was part of a nationwide drive to mitigate the ever-increasing problem of industrial waste and pollution as China embarked on industrialization at an unprecedented speed. From the outset of the Great Leap Forward in the late 1950s until the 1970s, there had been frequent complaints of factories dumping large quantities of coal tar residue and other toxic waste into the rivers, poisoning fisheries, damaging human health, and killing crops. The situation was at its worst in the industrial zones of the northeast and the northwest of China. According to an official government report, in the first half of 1959 nearly 13,000 tons of toxic industrial waste was dumped into the upper stretches of the Yellow River along the banks of Gansu province's capital city Langzhou. In China's northeast, the centre of heavy industry, another government report in 1960 showed that the phenol level in these rivers had reached between 2 and 24 milligrams per litre as a result of the huge quantities of industrial waste dumped into local rivers. In the Nonni River (also known as Non lua), local fishermen trawled more than 600,000 kilograms of dead or half-dead fish. Further south in Liaoning province's Hun River, locally referred to as the 'Mother River' of the Manchu rulers' former spiritual home Mukden, because of the large quantity of toxic industrial waste in the water, fish (including sturgeon) had become extinct.[24] It was also reported that more than 10,000 *mu* (ca 16,473.7 acres) of rice crops in Liaoning were killed by toxins in the waste water discharged from local factories. Because of the water shortages in large parts of China, during the Great Leap Forward many local authorities diverted waste water from factories to irrigate agricultural fields. From the late 1950s to the 1960s, food poisoning resulting from ingesting fish poisoned by toxic industrial waste was commonplace along the Yangtze. An official estimate in 1963 indicated that more than 10,000 tons of industrial waste was dumped upstream each day into the Yangtze. As a result, there was a sharp rise in gastritis among the population who lived by the river.[25] Yet the practice of using waste water from factories to irrigate agricultural fields continued well into the 1970s.

Despite claims that people's health and well-being were integral parts of socialist social welfare, as promised by the Communist state, the state also saw that the rapid industrialization of China was ever more necessary in order to achieve the 'higher' goal of quickly attaining the communist utopia. Weighing the future against the present, and caught between development and backwardness, the public good and individual lives, Zhou Enlai, the premier and manager of the PRC representing the State Council, boldly announced that China would achieve the impossible: 'transform the waste into treasure that would bring benefit to the greater good of the people'. In 1959, while visiting a coke plant 270 kilometres south of the PRC's capital city Beijing, he pointed to the thick black smoke: 'This smoke is a real treasure, we must recycle it. This way we can also reduce pollution,' he stated in a voice that was simultaneously firm and determined.[26] Responding to the challenge set by the premier, the State Scientific and Technological Commission, the Ministry of Health, and the Ministry of Agriculture jointly held a national conference to address the matter. At the conference, it was agreed that to recycle toxic industrial waste for the good of the country and the people would be a political undertaking just as vital as the eradication of schistosomiasis. It was regarded as 'science with a higher purpose'. To achieve such a scientific breakthrough – another great leap – all provincial party authorities were to make the recycling of industrial waste a priority. On 19 March 1960, amidst an ongoing famine, the Chinese Communist Party (CCP) Central Committee handed down a directive requesting all provincial-level authorities to urgently propose solutions to deal with the problem of toxic industrial waste.[27] Because of the severe labour shortage, however, reality soon showed that the campaign to transform industrial waste into 'treasure' meant going through the motions with no proper planning. In the case of schistosomiasis control, since the goal was to eliminate snails with industrial waste, such as the residual products of calcium carbamide or the sodium salts resulting from coal tar acid, little attention was paid to what quantity would be safe for the purpose or even how they should be applied. As a result, the actual amount used, and the application procedure, varied from location to location. In general, to eliminate snails required at least one kilogram of such a chemical mix for every square metre area. But in many affected regions, in the haste to eliminate snails, the actual amount used far exceeded what was recommended. Writing in the 1980s, Mao Shoubai, the PRC's foremost authority on schistosomiasis control, discouraged such measures because 'they harm human and animal health, damage the quality of soil, and pollute water. There are more drawbacks than benefits. Such measures cannot be recommended.'[28]

Because such undertakings were always focused on short-term gains, either because of political pressure from above or because of the resultant social and economic gains among those undertaking the eradication, little or no attention was given to the longer-term consequences. Not only did the chemical control method cause harm to the environment as well as to human and animal health, but the two widely applied environmental control measures employed by the Chinese in the late 1950s and 1960s – burning grass to roast the snails and destroy their habitat as well as draining swamps and marshes to reclaim low and flooded land – also had long-term consequences on the environment. Burning the grass that grew on the banks of small creeks and ditches, as well as decimating the reeds in the lake regions, was initially promoted by experts and the relevant political authorities as a simple and cost-effective way of reducing the snail population. While the method was reported to have achieved some success, it turned out to be more time-consuming and labour-intensive than killing snails with bio-pesticides made from plants. More important, its efficacy was unreliable because it depended on the season and topography. Furthermore, it destroyed reeds, bushes, grass, and other vegetation, all of which were necessary to a healthy lake ecosystem. Reeds were also a source of vital economic revenue for villagers living in the lake regions. Traditionally, reeds were used as building materials and as the raw materials to make weapons, tools, and musical instruments, as well as fashioned into paper. During the Great Leap Forward and the subsequent famine, trees, bushes, and grass were also in high demand because they were essential to keeping starving animals alive, as fuel for local iron and steel production, and in everyday use as fertilizer. One interviewee remembered that in 1958, after a campaign to kill snails by burning grass, the two brigades involved lost 44,000 kilograms of grass fuel as result. It is not surprising, therefore, that many villagers in these regions resisted applying such methods.[29] While I was researching for this book, I was often told by former schistosomiasis control cadres that this method of burning grass and reeds was less harmful to people and the environment than the chemical control method. A 2016 study by a team of researchers from the PRC and Australia, however, argued the opposite. According to this study, continuous open-field biomass burning, sometimes over several days – as was done to reduce the snail population – caused severe air pollution with the attendant risks to public health and a potentially adverse impact on the climate.[30]

As was discussed in chapter 3, the environmental intervention to control schistosomiasis by reclaiming and developing marshland was highly recommended by the team of Japanese experts at the end of their 1956 mission to the PRC. Subsequently, between 1957 and 1962, with the CCP frog-marching China and its people into the Great Leap Forward, more than 18,121 acres of marshes along Dongting Lake in Hunan province and Poyang Lake in Jiangxi province were reclaimed. As a result, the cultivable land in these regions doubled, a boon, it would seem, both in the struggle against the disease vector snails and in the expansion of agricultural acres and the concomitant food production.[31] Yet the continuous large-scale land reclamation initiatives, which first began in the 1950s, were thought to be a contributing factor to the worst flood of the twentieth century on the Yangtze that devastated the regions along Poyang Lake and Dongting Lake in the summer of 1999.[32] Large-scale land reclamation not only proved extremely costly and wasteful, it also ran into conflict with the systems for water conservation and as a result contributed to severe flooding. Research showed that land reclamation caused siltation and reduced the size of the lakes, which in turn decreased the lakes' flood storage capacity. Land reclamation and siltation, as well as the construction of levees, also restricted flood discharge capacity, causing flood levels to rise even higher[33] – a truly vicious circle. Furthermore, unplanned, excessive reclamation as was undertaken during the Great Leap Forward and during the Anti-Schistosomiasis Campaign also had a serious impact on the lakes' ecosystem. While it reduced the number of snails, it also reduced the number of other aquatic species living in these lakes. As a case study in 1993 by local researchers Li Jingbo and Deng Luojin shows, land reclamation activities on Dongting Lake after the 1950s, carried out partly as a measure to control schistosomiasis, seriously damaged the lake's eco-environment. As a result, the number of fish (and therefore food stocks) decreased by more than half in less than thirty years. In addition, the expansion of agricultural activities led to an increase in water pollution through the use of fertilizer and other forms of polluting run-off.[34] By the early 1970s, due to strong opposition from water conservancy and agriculture departments, such methods of controlling snails by land reclamation were gradually abandoned.[35]

INCREASED AGRICULTURAL ACTIVITIES
AND RISING MORBIDITY

Land reclamation may have reduced the snail numbers, but it failed to mitigate morbidity. With the increased cultivable land, agricultural activity as well as livestock populations also increased. Accompanied by the expansion of human settlement, such shifts provided new hosts for the schistosome and its parasites, increasing the risk of disease transmission. Between 1957 and 1961, at the height of the Great Leap Forward, thirty-three state-owned collective farms were built on the reclaimed land along the shores of the Dongting and Poyang lakes. More than 30,000 people, along with livestock from different parts of the country, were forcibly relocated there to work on these farms. Since most of them had no resistance to schistosomiasis, they quickly became infected. Between 1958 and 1962, seasonal outbreaks were reported annually on these state-owned farms, causing many casualties. In 1960, at the height of the famine, some 1,300 cases of acute infection were reported on twelve farms. The number doubled in the following two years. Simultaneously, large numbers of livestock were also infected.[36]

At the same time, the push to increase agricultural yields in order to meet the authorities' ever-increasing procumbent quota demanded that these farms use additional fertilizer. Traditionally, local villagers used grasses, tree branches, and water plants to make compost, but as a preventive measure the public health authorities in the impacted regions had banned state-farm workers and villagers from harvesting the floating water plants that grew on the lake. As a result, sod houses were pulled down, and their rammed-earth walls were soaked in ponds to make compost. The snails quickly migrated to these ponds. Because the local villagers, as well as the employees of the state-owned farms, relied on the water from the ponds for drinking and daily activities, all were infected with schistosomiasis. Failing to meet their fertilizer quota, many farm workers and villagers ventured farther afield to areas of the lake that had not been reclaimed or sprayed with molluscicides so that they could harvest the floating plants to make compost. Most of them suffered acute infection. Their boats carrying the water plants also brought the snails back to their communities.[37] Intense farming activities, including spending long periods of time working collectively in water during the harvest and planting seasons, further increased the chances of an outbreak.[38]

Contrary to the claim of the CCP leadership, having more land for agricultural production did not bring economic betterment for the rural villagers. The campaign in Mao's China, directed at reclaiming pestilential lands for production through improved housing and farming practices (technically called *integral bonification*),* proved disastrous. The planned economy, large farming collectives, and the state grain procurement policy denied individual farmers the ability to make profits from market participation. This meant that a great majority of villagers continued to live in destitution. Agricultural intensification, when coupled with land overuse (i.e., deforestation, land reclamation, and overgrazing), damaged soil quality by causing alkalization and increased drought as well as waterlogging and flooding, which in turn damaged agricultural productivity. The attempt at a quick leap into the communist utopia – a superior form of modernity – resulted in the worst famine in human history, a famine that lasted four years between 1958 and 1962 and claimed an estimated forty-five million lives in the Chinese countryside. Its adverse effects on the environment can still be seen today.[39] The effort expended by the rural population to simply survive, as well as to recover from the famine, further increased the risk of disease transmission. In the schistosomiasis endemic regions along Dongting Lake and Poyang Lake, some of the worst regions hit by the famine, in order to secure food a huge number of farm workers and villagers waded into the lakes to pull up lotus roots and fished in the same water for basic sustenance. Many were infected with schistosomiasis. While researching for this book, I met several famine survivors who had been infected

---

* The term *bonification* was first used during the malaria campaign in Fascist Italy under Mussolini. In the late 1920s, the integral *bonification* was recommended by the League of Nations' Health Organization (LNHO)'s Malaria Commission as a radical measure for its global malaria control program. See 'Conclusions of the Malaria Commission, Health Section, League of Nations, at the Conference in Geneva, June 25–29, 1928', in *Public Health Reports* (1896–1970), vol. 43, no. 45 (9 Nov. 1928): 2957–61.

with schistosomiasis in this way. For the next fifty years, they continued to live with the disease because the state-sponsored therapeutic interventions remained largely ineffective or inadequate.[40]

The official estimate in 1962 showed that the schistosomiasis morbidity in that year was approximately 8,000–9,000 cases in the regions along Dongting Lake and approximately 6,000–7,000 along Poyang Lake.[41] The latter included the PRC's eradication model county, Yujiang. A year later, at the Ninth National Conference on Schistosomiasis Control, when presented with the high morbidity rate and the increase in the snail-populated areas, Su Yongjiu, Yujiang County's new party boss, regretted that impetuousness and inaccuracy had been two major problems in the local schistosomiasis control work. To calm his nerves while attributing this catastrophe to himself, the skinny, thirty-something-year-old former PLA soldier lit a cigarette and inhaled deeply while stating that 'cadres on the ground misunderstood, believing that the disease could be controlled with one big shock attack. After Yujiang declared eradication in 1958, they stopped the control effort completely. No wonder we continue to find patients every year, even patients in the advanced stage of the disease. In 1961, the snail-populated area was as high as 2,198 square metres. Inaccuracy was a common problem in the local schistosomiasis work.'[42] It was not merely inaccurate reporting but conscious, repeated falsification that caused these ever-greater numbers of infections through the sense that the mission had been accomplished as promised.

Reports from other endemic regions also showed the increasing numbers of areas now infested by snails. In Sichuan province's Qionglai County, for example, in 1957 the snail-infested area was 20,500 square metres. Leaping into eradication, as inspired by Yujiang's 'triumph' in destroying the snails, many communes here declared the near-elimination of the snails. Yet the snail survey in June 1961 showed that the snail-infested area had actually increased to 320,000 square metres.[43] In parts of Jiangsu province in eastern China, too, the snail-infested areas were reported to have increased by more than fourteen times in the three years following 1960.[44] Clearly, trying to control the vector, by means of either environmental or chemical control, was not helping the PRC to reach its eradication goal, and the seven-year time frame set by the chairman was running out fast. It seemed that the PRC's Anti-Schistosomiasis Campaign was quickly turning from initially being a win/win situation into a lose/lose disaster. The political claim that had fuelled the demand for the eradication of the vector and the interventions into the newly expanded agricultural land led to long-term disasters that swiftly followed the short-term claims of success. Given the context of this undertaking, the abandonment of expert advice and the coupling of the public health goals with the political ideology of the Great Leap Forward meant that the only claims that could be made were for the purposes of propaganda. Such claims were evidently seen as false, even corrupt, by those on the ground whose lives and livelihoods were impacted by the attempts at eradication, and this dissatisfaction soon became apparent at the very pinnacle of leadership.

ADDRESSING THE FAILURE

In 1962, the CCP leadership, led by the president of the PRC, Liu Shaoqi, acknowledged that the famine was a man-made disaster, and the Great Leap Forward policy was subsequently withdrawn. A few months afterwards, the Nine-man Subcommittee on Schistosomiasis Control, with its vice chair Wei Wenbo, reporting at a national schistosomiasis control conference, collectively acknowledged that the earlier goal of eradicating the disease within seven years was unrealistic. They also admitted that many of the widely publicized claims of eradication were simply false: 'Some places immediately claimed they had eradicated the disease after a few days of shock work, whereas those responsible for verifying the result were too sloppy. As such the estimates were often too high. Under pressure, 167 counties and municipalities hurried to declare near-eradication. In many places, the grassroots schistosomiasis control work has run into a vicious circle.' Careful not to discredit the Chairman Mao–led Anti-Schistosomiasis Campaign or to criticize the model function played by Yujiang County (the PRC's first 'red flag' for this campaign), the report laid the responsibility for the campaign's overall failure to the 'error of misjudgement' at the level of the Nine-man Subcommittee and on poor leadership on the ground.[45] This was in line with the approach that the CCP leadership and its subsidiary departments took in addressing the Great Leap debacle. Toward the latter period of the famine, faced with millions of people dying of starvation and widespread violence on the ground, the CCP leadership could no longer deny that this was a man-made disaster. It was impelled to come up with an explanation for such a major catastrophe. Instead of questioning the overall utopian goal of making a perfect communist society, however, they attributed the failure of the Great Leap Forward to simple 'errors of judgement'. To avoid being held accountable, which would have threatened the party's power, they turned against the grassroots leadership and waged yet another campaign, this time attacking the 'Five Winds': exaggeration, communism/egalitarian, blind directive/leadership, commandism, and bureaucratism.* In other words, it was not the directives from above but the ideological subversion from below that was the cause of this man-made disaster: it was the 'corrupt' cadres on the ground who were at fault because of their intentional incompetence, not the leadership and its goals.

In the historiography of the Great Leap Forward, the 'Five Winds' explanation is regularly used by scholars both within and outside China to account for what happened. Yet, in his recent reflection on the campaign attacking the 'Five Winds', Zhang Guangyou, the former editor-in-chief of the CCP-owned newspaper, the *Peasants' Daily* as well as an eyewitness of the campaign, was more thoughtful about the actual experience of those grassroots cadres and their practice on the ground: 'Those cadres with the task of implementing [party policies] carried heavy burdens on their shoulders. It's like being in a big play, they each had a part to play ... they had to deal with countless problems and variables on the ground. That's very different from writing a news report. No journalists would be held accountable for what happened on the ground, but the cadres were.'[46] By shifting the burden from the decision-makers to those required to carry out their policies, the leadership looked for and found the perfect scapegoat, the purposeful incompetence of those underlings whose goal was to undermine the striving for the perfect, utopian society.

Having come up with their explanation for the past failures, the Nine-Man Subcommittee needed to introduce interventions to rectify the damage caused by the false claims and authoritarian methods on the ground as well as to deal with the urgency of ever-increasing morbidity. The vector control had not only failed to achieve its earlier goal of eradication, but it was also too costly for a country struggling to survive a horrendous famine. There were simply no

---

* With Mao's permission, the campaign attacking the Five Winds began in the winter of 1960, more than a year before Liu Shaoqi officially announced that the famine was a man-made disaster in January 1962 at the enlarged party cadres conference, commonly known as the Seven Thousand Cadres Conference.

resources to carry it out, let alone for it to succeed. In a time of national emergency, therapeutic interventions regained prominence. This was further catalyzed by the excitement generated when, in 1961, China successfully synthesized the non-antimonial antibacterial drug furapromidum and other nitrofuran derivatives. Initial experiments in using them to treat schistosomiasis were successful, but the early enthusiasm was short-lived. Experts quickly agreed that these drugs were less efficacious and also toxic, and as a result they were withdrawn from clinical use and mass production.[47]

CONTROLLING SCHISTOSOMIASIS BY MASS THERAPY

As with any disease, an accurate diagnosis is of the utmost importance in determining the cause of any patient's symptoms. Yet this remained a major problem with schistosomiasis. In addition to the Kato-Katz smear, the hatching test was another common diagnosis test for schistosomiasis used in the PRC. This test determined whether the person was infected or not based on the observation of miracidias, the second stage of development of the parasitic eggs that were hatched from the patient's faeces. The test involves diluting faeces in water and allowing it to sediment. To achieve the highest possible accuracy, it also requires repeating the observation of any emergence of miracidias every three or four hours – in other words, several times a day. Like the smear test, the hatching test is normally inexpensive and requires minimal technical training. To perform the test, however, requires a certain length of time. Also, the sensitivity of both tests decreases with decreasing schistosome intensity. In the early 1960s, during the post-famine mass therapy work in the PRC, the sheer number of patients, combined with the severe shortage of both trained and untrained personnel and of equipment, put further stress on both forms of testing and thus undermined their accuracy. To meet the quantitative target often meant compromising or neglecting quality. Thus, the test procedure was frequently performed incorrectly. For instance, returning from their field inspection, experts from Sichuan Medical University and the provincial schistosomiasis control office were both appalled by how haphazardly the grassroots diagnostic work was being carried out.* They noted that there was no standard of diagnostic work across different rural counties. Some coun-

---

* Sichuan Medical University was formerly the Medical and Dental Faculty of the West China Union University, a joint venture of some Canadian missionary groups. It is now the Sichuan University Medical School.

ties only performed the hatching test, others only the smear test. This meant that it was impossible to do a comparative study of the results. Because of their lack of experience in detecting parasite eggs presented in faeces, grassroots health workers regularly confused the rather non-descript, round shape of the eggs with air bubbles or hookworm eggs, etc. In addition, many failed to understand that fluctuating temperatures would affect the speed of hatching, so they sometimes wrongly evaluated unhatched stool samples as negative and disposed of them without disinfecting. These false negative findings caused the disease to spread widely. Equally important, carrying out the Kato-Katz smear test requires the bulk storage of specimens as well as freezing facilities and transportation, but this was simply impossible due to the lack of resources and equipment and the general collapse of the transportation network. Because of the shortfall in equipment, grassroots health workers were encouraged to practise 'self-reliance'. They often had to make do by using unsterilized and not always leak-proof earthen bowls and tubs as stool containers. As result, the overall diagnosis results were unreliable; hence the poor treatment outcomes.[48] Similar problems were reported in other affected regions, including some schistosomiasis control 'model counties' such as Songjiang and Qingpu in the suburbs of Shanghai. There, when the actual treatment outcome failed to meet the estimated target, grassroots health workers would simply fabricate the figures. The cadres managing such work cared only that the assigned job was being done, and therefore they did not bother to verify the figures.[49]

On the ground, eradicating or even controlling the disease by mass therapy was easier said than done, nor was it any less costly. From the outset, the PRC's health blueprint that put prevention first was sought partly as a cost-effective solution to address the existing health crisis and also to meet the financial shortfall. But the state was simply unable to deliver the promised free health and medical care. The advent of the People's Commune in 1958 was a hoped-for solution, and communes became the newest and highest form of administrative, economic, and political organization in rural China.* Each commune was divided into large brigades (most of which contained several small villages), and each large brigade was in turn divided into smaller production brigades. Households were organized into production brigades. On the ground, production brigades

---

* These People's Communes were gigantic farming collectives; some were as big as a township.

were the units of accounting and farming production within the large farming collectives. This meant that the production brigade was responsible for financing health and medical care, although overall it was the commune that managed health care delivery and disease prevention. Mao envisioned that with the People's Commune, there would be a surplus of grain and an abundance of other commodities. This way, the production brigade would generate enough income to defray villagers' care and medical costs. However, the amount of funds available varied from brigade to brigade, depending on their productivity. Brigades with greater numbers of children, the sick, and the elderly had poor productivity and thus were unable to generate enough income to pay for their greater need for medical care. In the early days of the People's Commune, some wealthier communes subsidized poorer brigades or directly defrayed the villagers' medical and health care costs from the commune's centralized fund. This sometimes led to cadres, as well as villagers who had a good relationship with the cadres, abusing and overusing the 'free' care.[50] Toward the last months of 1960, in the campaign attacking the 'Five Winds', this practice came under fire as 'egalitarian' (一平二调) and was subsequently stopped and replaced by a collective medical system.[*] This collective medical system required villagers to contribute a small amount to a collective welfare fund and also to pay a registration fee if hospital treatment was needed. In return, these villagers would benefit from 'free' medical and health care. Although the concept looked rational and workable, in practice, as soon as it encountered the realities on the ground, it proved to have some important flaws. First, the cost of care was never free. A standard seven-day treatment would require the schistosomiasis patient to stay in the hospital/clinic/treatment centre for the entire period. This meant that he would lose seven days' worth of work points – a large chunk of income for the family, especially if the patient was the primary breadwinner. Under the commune distribution system,

---

[*] Some researchers, including Fang Xiaoping, confused the collective medical system with the earlier co-operative medical system. While the collective medical system under the People's Commune shared some features with the co-operative medical system that began in the early 1950s and was reintroduced after 1965, there were fundamental differences between the two systems. The co-operative system was financed by voluntary contributions, whereas the collective system was financed by the collective welfare fund, which was not voluntary. To build up the collective welfare fund, the commune or the large production brigade automatically deducted villagers' work points without their consent.

since the amount of food each family would receive depended on the amount of work points earned, the fewer the work points, the less food there would be. Even though there was some greater access to health care, its real costs, even under this system, resulted in many villagers who were carrying the disease refusing to seek treatment. For the severely ill and for the elderly as well as children, the collective medical system made them worse off. Since they were unable to work, or worked less, they earned fewer or even zero work points. To participate in the collective medical system in order to receive the needed medical treatment, they thus ended up in perpetual debt. In Hunan province's Yueyang region, the family of schistosomiasis patient Xie, from Binghu Commune, did not earn enough work points to exchange for sufficient food to feed all of the family's six members. They therefore had no extra work points to put into the collective medical pot. Xie was thus denied the much-needed treatment for his schistosomiasis.[51] Further north in Sichuan province's Langzhou County, the Feng family, who lived in a poor mountainous village, had five children and a sick mother as well as two elderly members who were in poor health. Since only one family member could work to earn work points, the family did not generate enough work points to contribute to the collective fund. So that the sick mother could receive the medical treatment she needed, the family ended up in debt. With insufficient work points to repay the debts, the family had to endure living in squalid conditions, with neither adequate food to eat nor clean clothes to wear. In 1960, because of the mother's ill health and the lack of food, the family watched their newborn baby die of malnutrition. Their poverty was only ameliorated after one of the children joined the army and was able to send money back home to pay for his mother's medical expenses. In 2006, when I interviewed Mr Feng, he told me the family was still paying back the debt they owed to the commune, even though the commune system had been abolished in 1983.[52] The Xie and Feng families' experiences were by no means unique. While researching for this book, as well as for my social history of the Great Famine, several villagers I interviewed told similar stories.[53]

Second, a further complication was that with the advent of the People's Commune, commune clinics (the larger ones were called hospitals) took on the overall responsibility of delivering the mass treatment that was previously carried out by specialized hospitals or schistosomiasis control centres/stations. Many commune clinics were staffed by traditional healers who had come from diverse medical traditions. Most of them were unfamiliar with or had doubts about bio-medical interventions such as treating infected patients with sodium antimony tartrate. Understandably, some were simply reluctant to administer it. A few even contested how schistosomiasis and malaria were transmitted, given their understanding of patterns of illness as explained by different medical systems. Some viewed these diseases as caused by *qi* deficiency, and they doubted the efficacy of sodium antimony tartrate (for schistosomiasis) or cycloguanil (for malaria) as therapeutic drugs. In addition, because of the enormous size of some communes, commune hospital/clinics often had to involve younger villagers in the delivery of this mass therapy.* Most of these younger people had some education, and indeed some were even enthusiastic about relieving sick villagers of their suffering, but they lacked the necessary training, knowledge, and experience to carry out the sort of mass treatment required, which was always demanded in a great hurry. For instance, in eastern Sichuan's Wan County, when some villagers challenged grassroots health workers about the efficacy of the drug, the health workers could not come up with an adequate answer except for saying: 'I have no idea whether they will cure your problem. The authority from higher-ups told us to use it. That's all I know.'54

Local authorities were confronted with the ongoing problem of labour shortages as a result of the Great Leap drive for more construction projects as well as the increased demands for higher agricultural yields. Therefore, they were constantly weighing the value of medical, political, and social risks and considering what work would bring them the maximum gain as individuals – for instance, their advancement in the party. Labour would be allocated according to such calculations. In Hunan province's Yiyang County, the local authority estimated that a male patient receiving a standard seven-day treatment would cost each production brigade the equivalent of moving five less cubic metres of earth.† With so many villagers in Yiyang in need of treatment, this would mean that they would fail the water conservancy target as set by the provincial authority. In addition to serious financial loss, it would also amount to a greater

---

* On average, each commune consisted of 5,000 households.
† Yiyang County in Hunan province was, and still is, one of the worst endemic counties along the Yangtze River.

political risk for them. Thus, the Yiyang County authority took the drastic decision not to treat any male patients at all. To make up for the treatment target handed down from the higher authority for the Anti-Schistosomiasis Campaign, they sent only women and children for the mass treatment. Since the untreated male patients continued to work on crowded construction sites that often involved standing in water or mud for a long period of time, the disease spread quickly. So it is no wonder that the morbidity rate continued to increase in spite of the claims made on paper for the large number of people treated. Similar situations were also reported in Zhejiang, Jiangsu, and Fujian provinces.[55]

At the height of the famine, faced with the sharply rising numbers of schistosomiasis morbidity as well as decreased financial resources and manpower, the production brigade (responsible for financing the mass treatment), as well as the commune (responsible for organizing and delivering the treatment), came up with ever-more erratic solutions. The quality of treatment, and patient safety, were regularly compromised in desperate attempts to meet treatment targets at great speed. Despite the caution from experts and health authorities to put patient safety first after earlier incidents of patients dying of overdoses of the drug sodium antimony tartrate, speeding up treatment by increasing the drug dosage and shortening the length of treatment was a common problem.[56] The situation worsened as the famine took hold. To meet the even greater labour shortfall (due to the mass deaths and widespread illness resulting from famine), many grassroots authorities gave orders to further increase the drug dosage and reduce the length of the course of treatment. Although experts advising the local mass therapy, such as Dr Zhou Xuezhang in Jiaxing, a renowned expert in mass therapy, were concerned about the potential risk, in the end they bowed to political pressure.[57] Over and over again, in the struggle between politics and science in the PRC, it was politics that always took precedence.

According to official data obtained by the American Schistosomiasis Delegation to the PRC, between 1958 and 1962 a record of five million patients throughout the country received the three-day intensive treatment.[58] Because of the high dosage of sodium antimony tartrate involved, sometimes administered by inexperienced grassroots health auxiliaries or local doctors who had little or no understanding of standard procedure in such bio-medical intervention, the treatment that aimed to cure often turned into a serious risk. In severe cases, it sent patients to the grave even more quickly. One commune hospital in Hunan province's Lilin County, for instance, treated nine patients with the dosage meant for twenty-six people. It was no wonder, therefore, that the outcome was 'seriously severe'.[59] In Zhejiang province's Jiaxing region, approximately 80,000 patients were treated within one month. Many were given two days of intensive treatment. Because of the high dosage of drug applied, eighty patients died during treatment. One victim's family, whose relative died after the two-day treatment, appealed to the local authority. Instead of reviewing the underlying problem and stopping the intensive treatment, the authorities simply arrested the doctor who had overseen the treatment, Dr Xu. Xu was a much-loved local doctor of Chinese medicine and one of the many local doctors co-opted by the authority to support the mass therapy work because of the shortfall of trained personnel. The authorities gave him a three-year prison sentence for causing a death for which he was not responsible. Deeply distressed by the event, Dr Xu died not long after he was released from prison.[60]

As a consequence of the famine, an increasing number of communes had to cut back on their salaried staff, including doctors and other health personnel. With fewer or no doctors, commune hospitals/clinics were dissolved, and the mass treatment work was handed over to the semi–state-owned united clinics.* The united clinics had been introduced in the early 1950s to co-opt private practitioners into the state system as well as to reduce the state expenditure on medical and health care for rural villagers, who accounted then for 80 per cent of the population. Until the introduction of the People's Commune in 1958, united clinics were the main source of medical and health care for rural villagers. Although these united clinics were part of the state medical system, they were, at least in theory, voluntary and run by a collective of practitioners. To partly finance themselves, they charged the patients fees. These clinics were also financed by the co-operative medical fund, which was based on voluntary donations. Each practitioner and member of staff received a salary according to their contribution. To be sustainable, these clinics needed to show positive outcomes. Since many of them were quite small (some consisted of only one or two doctors) and lacked preparation for and experience in mass therapy work, they opted

---

* 'United clinics' is also translated as 'union clinics'.

to treat only patients with minor symptoms. Inevitably, this meant that severely ill patients desperately in need of treatment were often deprived of medical care.[61]

EVER-RISING MORBIDITY IN THE AFTERMATH OF THE FAMINE

In the aftermath of the famine, the morbidity of schistosomiasis had shifted from mainly rural inhabitants to an increasing number of urban casualties. The flight of rural populations to urban centres for employment and food meant that the disease migrated with the population. In addition, the morbidity continued to rise at an alarming rate across all affected regions – partly because of the worsening of the famine as it spread to towns and cities. For instance, in metropolitan areas such as Shanghai and Hangzhou, the desperately hungry urban residents regularly stepped into nearby rivers to fish for food, and as a result many suffered acute infection.[62] Their severe malnutrition also made them more susceptible to the disease. More important, as during the Great Leap Forward period, the increase in morbidity was linked to the expanded agricultural activities and to the growing number of people now participating in such activities. As part of the state relief effort, the authorities often exerted overt pressure on many government employees, factory workers, and PLA soldiers, as well as university and high school students, to go to the countryside to support agricultural work. With zero resistance to schistosomiasis and no protection from exposure to the vector, many quickly became infected. A 1962 telegram from the Nine-Man Sub-committee showed a huge number of acute infections reported in more than fifty counties in Anhui, Hubei, Jiangxi, Hunan, Jiangsu, and Shanghai. In Hubei province's Hanyang, Xinzhou, and Yangxin counties, the attempt to save rice crops from flooded paddies backfired, with more than 10,000 male villagers being infected with schistosomiasis. Among them were 300 cases of acute infection. The high morbidity left little or no labour to carry on the agriculture work. A few months later, in 1963, another emergency report from Jiangsu province stated that in the forty-two endemic counties, the morbidity rate had increased by more than 40 per cent compared to the previous year. Among the 6,031 cases of acute infection, most were group infections. In some cases, entire production brigades were infected at the same time. Since 80 per cent of victims were

prime labourers, no one remained to transport the harvested grain
and fight against drought. In Anhui province's Guichi County, too,
in an emergency attempt to save the grain from flooded paddies,
cadres and students from thirty-six government offices and schools
worked in the contaminated water with no protection whatsoever.
The effort resulted in 772 people suffering acute infection, twenty-three of whom subsequently died. Among those who died, one
production brigade lost more than half of its prime workers. In addition to the rise in human casualties, an increasing number of cattle
also died of infection. In Jiangxi province, all of the 135 cattle on one
state farm were infected with schistosomiasis; fifty-two of them died
of it.[63] Fearing becoming infected, more and more people refused to
work in the rice paddies. In 1963, a team of public security soldiers
were sent to guard the local agricultural work in Sichuan province's
Lushan County. Since their duty involved walking into rice paddies,
96 per cent became infected with schistosomiasis. After some soldiers died of the disease, the remaining soldiers refused to enter the
rice paddies again. 'The leadership from higher up only cares about
production, not human life,' they complained. Some even protested
that they would rather be shot than step back into rice paddies.[64]

RESISTANCE BY THE LOCAL CADRES

At the grassroots level, too, an increasing number of cadres contested the Anti-Schistosomiasis Campaign, seeing it as a financial
loss or even a direct cause of the famine. In Sichuan province's Mianzhu County, some commune cadres and villagers blamed the effort
to eradicate schistosomiasis as of 1956 for directly causing the famine: 'We had spent the past [six] years trying to eradicate schistosomiasis. We not only exhausted many labourers, we also wasted lots
of money. To eradicate schistosomiasis is such hard work, which
pays no dividend. Please spare us from it,' they pleaded. Some put
it more bluntly: 'If you want to eradicate schistosomiasis, you send
a team, but we will have nothing to do with it.' Cadres and public
health workers assigned to implement the control work compared
themselves to 'rats trapped in a barrel, being bullied from both ends':
'cadres don't support us, and villagers don't like us, how can we
carry out the work?' they grumbled.[65] Aside from contesting schistosomiasis control, grassroots cadres throughout the country, as they
weighed the urgent need to feed starving villagers and animals – and

fulfil the state's grain procumbent target at the same time – saw health work in general as a bother, and it was handed down to the women activists in the commune to undertake. Despite being portrayed as 'half of the sky' by the state media propaganda, on the ground women were counted as 'half labour' in the agricultural fields. In Hunan province's Henyang County, the party secretary at Chashi commune passed the responsibility for disease prevention and health delivery to the heads of the production brigades. As in a basketball match, one brigade head turned around and passed it to the section head of the local Women's Federation. But the ball quickly bounced back: 'Health work was a lose/lose last year, and there is no way I am going to take it on again,' the head of the Women's Federation contended. Little or no support from the local leadership left many grassroots health workers feeling stranded. Frustrated, they began to slack off.[66] This was a pattern that repeated itself constantly: rather than confronting even the local authorities, their key to survival was trying to pass accountability to other groups on the ground.

The lack of cooperation from the grassroots cadres also contributed to the unreliability of the statistics. Besides slacking, as mentioned earlier some grassroots health workers, along with schistosomiasis control cadres, would sometimes simply invent figures: 'For many years, we had no resources or incentive to implement the control work. All we did was fill in the forms and hand them back to the high-ups,' explained a retired schistosomiasis control cadre in Hubei province's Jingzhou region, still one of the worst endemic regions on the Yangtze River. In an interview with her in 2003, this retired cadre admitted: 'We simply made up the figures. Officials from higher-up knew it all along. To avoid getting into trouble or being sacked from office, they needed us to inflate or forge figures.' She then pointed out to me some old dusty papers covered with spider webs and said: 'It's an open secret.'[67] In another interview, Professor Yin, a retired expert from a state-owned schistosomiasis control research institute in a nearby province, agreed: 'Every year, we went the countryside to collect data. Where to start? We simply went to see the grassroots health worker [who later came to be called the "Barefoot Doctor"]. We would write down whatever she or he told us. We did not verify their figures. How could we? We did not even know how to get from one end of the village to the other. They were our best and only source. Besides, we did not want to stay long in the village. We just wanted to collect the data and leave. We did not question the data.'[68]

This is the key to unravelling the conundrum of the repeated propaganda claims about the successful eradication of schistosomiasis followed by the public lodging of blame against specific groups, or even individuals, for the re-emergence of the disease. In Jingzhou, as elsewhere in China, the 'schistosomiasis plague' did not 're-emerge' in recent years as we had been led to believe.[69] It had never been controlled, since many of the 'near-eradication' claims were invented in the first place or were radically overestimated, as was later publicly acknowledged. The ever-shifting politics of public health trumped the reality of poor or mismanaged health care delivery and eradication. Success had to be the goal because the state had placed the overall improvement of the people's health at the centre of its social compact. Engage the masses, and the people's health would improve – and improve it had to, whether supported by the experiences of the people or not.

6

The People's Health in Crisis

SCHISTOSOMIASIS AS YESTERDAY'S
PUBLIC HEALTH PROBLEM

The health consequences of the nationwide famine were horrific. As of 1961, famine-related oedema, gynaecological problems, and child malnutrition – referred to at the time as the 'Three Diseases' (三病) – ravaged the countryside as well as the cities. This meant that there were even fewer resources and less manpower for health authorities in affected regions to implement schistosomiasis control through mass therapy. In Hunan province's Xiangtan region, in 1962 more than 5 per cent of the local population suffered the 'Three Diseases', and the number was reported to be on the increase each month.[1] Similarly, in Sichuan province, one of the largest agricultural provinces badly hit by the famine, in the first half of 1962 a huge number of people died of oedema and other famine-related illnesses. Child malnutrition and rickets were also prevalent there. With 50 per cent of commune hospitals/clinics in Sichuan preoccupied with treating oedema, and with a decreased health budget, there was neither money nor personnel left to implement schistosomiasis control through mass therapy.[2]

In addition to the famine-related 'Three Diseases', in 1962 many provinces along or south of the Yangtze River also experienced some of the worst epidemics of malaria in recent history, as well as incidents of 'El Tor' (a particular strain of the bacterium *Vibrio cholerae*, also called paracholera and named after the site in Egypt where it was discovered in 1905 by Felix Gotschlich). The malaria outbreak was partly linked to the Great Leap drive to irrigate the ever-expanding agricultural land as well as power the rapid industrialization by building more dams. More agricultural land and more construction also entailed unrestricted deforestation. Intensive agricultural practice, irrigation, and dam-building, as well as deforestation, not only caused long-term damage to the environment through alkalinisation and waterlogging of the soil but also increased malaria transmission through the explosion in the numbers of mosquitos.[3] The official estimate of malaria morbidity in 1962 surpassed 10 million people, with the highest number of casualties in Jiangsu, Sichuan, and Zhejiang provinces. All three provinces were also the worst endemic schistosomiasis regions.

In the meantime, an El Tor pandemic had spread across large parts of Southeast Asia. As with the outbreaks of SARS in 2003 and avian influenza in 2013, Guangdong province in southern China was identified by the World Health Organization (WHO) as the location transmitting the disease to the nearby international port cities of Hong Kong and Macau. Worried that the disease would spread to the West, the WHO simply reclassified El Tor as cholera so that its member states could impose draconian quarantines and other control regulations. The official health propaganda and media reports in the People's Republic of China (PRC), however, suggested that the disease was brought into China from overseas, not dissimilar to the PRC's media coverage of the AIDS pandemic in the late 1980s. Suddenly, El Tor was of international and political importance to the PRC authorities. Regional health authorities in southern China were instructed to divert resources allocated for schistosomiasis control to El Tor research and control. For a while, schistosomiasis became yesterday's public health problem. Despite the official figure showing that more than 20,000 people suffered acute infection of schistosomiasis, the highest since 1957, and with more than 200 people dying as result, Su Delong and his team of researchers at Shanghai Medical School were asked to suspend their schistosomiasis work and to support El Tor control.* In Shanghai and the nearby regions, public health propaganda also prioritized El Tor prevention.[4] The PRC authorities were much more concerned with the international image of China as the source of a new global epidemic than with

---

* The El Tor incident almost led Su Delong into further political trouble, since his research showed that the El Tor outbreaks in southern China were not transmitted from abroad; they were related to the high level of sodium chloride in the ground water.

continuing, no matter how feebly, to try and deal with what had come to be seen as 'local' problems.

THE BREAKDOWN OF THE STATE HEALTH SYSTEM AND THE EMERGENCE OF A PRIVATE MEDICAL MARKET

At the same time, the lack of funding, as well as the severe food shortages spreading to cities and towns, led to a cutting back on even salaried government employees. As a result, a huge number of state-owned anti-schistosomiasis units were dissolved. According to an official estimate, schistosomiasis control work groups, often consisting of experts responsible for advising on technical aspects of control work in the fields as well as for quality control, had been reduced by half since 1957. In Sichuan province, one of the largest agricultural provinces ravaged by the famine and the resultant 'Three Diseases' as well as schistosomiases and malaria, the annual funding in 1962 for parasitic disease prevention and therapy was 500,000 *yuan* (ca US$100,000). The shortfall in funding led to cutting back on personnel and the acquisition of drugs, hence leading to a reduction in treatment. Because of the shortage of staff and drugs, many treatments already begun could not be completed. In addition to these staff and drug shortages, there was also an urgent lack of equipment. It was reported that 80 per cent of the necessary equipment, initially bought with the state's schistosomiasis control funding, had been damaged or destroyed because of lack of care. This added further burdens to the already stressed local health fund.[5]

Further down the ladder, as mentioned earlier, an increasing number of commune hospitals/clinics were shut down. In Hunan province's Henyang County, out of 660 commune hospitals/clinics, nearly half had neither money nor food to compensate their staff. With no food to feed their families, doctors and other health workers lost all interest in delivering any health care. The lack of shoes, umbrellas, and torches for grassroots health workers also prevented them from implementing local public heath work.[6] In some places, such as Yunnan province in the southwest, commune doctors were sent back to their original production brigades to work in the agricultural fields so that the commune did not have to feed them. Although in theory they could practise medicine in addition to doing agricultural work, in reality doing medical work would mean that they would lose work points and thus access to food. As result, a number of them gave up practising medicine, whether Western or herbal medicine.[7]

Not only was the commune health care system collapsing, a growing number of state-owned county or township hospitals, which were the next level up in the pyramid of the PRC's centralized health system, were also faced with serious financial difficulties. As of late 1960, with less food, the state reduced the amount of the food ration. It also introduced a policy to drastically cut back on the number of government employees, similar to the policy of consolidation in 1953 during the 'Three Anti'-Campaign. Health departments throughout the country were some of the worst-hit sectors, since health work was seen as costing more money than it generated. Many doctors and health personnel became unemployed. Those who had originally come from the countryside were forced to return to their former production brigades where they could at least feed themselves and their families by doing agricultural work.[8] Those with good skills and reputations, as well as social contacts or connections (*guanxi* 关系), managed to remain in towns and cities. They opened private practices where they charged high prices. A private medical market emerged to compete with the state-owned and the collective medical system. With fewer hospitals and more patients, access became a privilege, and those with power to grant such privileges, such as officials at state-owned hospitals, often abused their power. In addition to introducing fees for treatment like their private and semi-private competitors, many health officials as well as some high-ranking doctors used their position to extract more food or other goods that were in short supply. Some also bartered drugs and medical equipment for personal favours or money.[9] In Sichuan province, for example, several state-owned county and city hospitals turned into narcotic black markets where medical personnel regularly prescribed morphine and other opiates for each other. The drugs were subsequently sold at a high price to newly opened private practices or were used as bribes.[10] Dissatisfied with their work conditions and low pay and faced with uncertainty and increasing pressure, some of the health workers in government units gave up on the Chinese Communist Party's promise of the communist utopia and returned to older practices and their equally amorphous promises of divine help from the Buddha, spirits, or diviners.[11]

SEEKING HELP FROM SPIRITS

Not only did medical and health personnel lose their morale, but the lack and low standard of medical and health care throughout the countryside led many villagers to question the professional competence of health professionals, the reliability of the collective medical system, the state health care delivery, and the socialist welfare system in general. As this section shows, many so-called old 'feudal' and 'backward' practices that the Communist authorities and the modernizers (including many medical and health professionals) had worked hard to eliminate re-emerged and gained an ever-increasing number of adherents.

High up in the mountains and clinging to the bank of the Yangtze River, eastern Sichuan province's Wanxian region (nowadays Wanzhou in Chongqing municipality), for example, was one place where state welfare provisions, including health and medical care were (and still are) appallingly poor. Although on paper there existed a collective medical system with several commune clinics, the reality was that only one doctor of traditional medicine, assisted by his apprentice, attended the medical and health needs of villagers for this whole region consisting of several communes. Commune hospitals as well as disease prevention centres, which were few and far between, were all situated in townships. Since travel in and out of villages was a real hazard for most villagers, they had little or no access to hospital care. Likewise, health workers working at disease prevention centres rarely travelled to villages to implement the government's disease prevention programs.[12] During the Great Leap famine, nearly half of the local population died of starvation or of diseases resulting from food deprivation.* To survive, some villagers even ate the flesh of their dead children.[13] Villagers lost their trust in the socialist state's welfare system. During the malaria outbreak in the summer of 1962, local villagers refused to go to the town hospitals or to take the Western drugs distributed by the state. Instead, they turned to local healing deities and performed spirit-healing rituals. Those who were healthy enough simply ran away to avoid

---

* In times of scarcity, food was a more powerful weapon than torture. Food deprivation was a common method used by local cadres to force villagers to work harder or to produce more food. Cf. Zhou, Xun, 'Violence during the Great Leap Forward', in *Cambridge World History of Violence*, vol. 4 (forthcoming).

being infected, just as they would have done prior to the Communist Liberation.[14]

The situation was thought to be worse in regions where the population consisted of a mixture of social and ethnic groups, who were treated as subalterns or officially classified as 'minorities'. A report from the Sichuan Provincial Bureau of Health and Hygiene indicated that since free medical and health care had been withdrawn as of 1961, the implementation of medical and public health work among 'minority' groups in rural Sichuan became increasingly difficult. On the eve of the Communist Liberation in 1950, public health work and free medical care that centred on allopathic medicine had been a key strategy employed by the Chinese Communist Party (CCP) to gain support from the lower and middle strata of society in many of these so-called minority regions. State provision of free health and medical care had become a crucial thread that bound the local population to Mao and the CCP. For example, in Angla (nowadays in Qinghai province), after the CCP medical team cured her illness, a sixty-year-old woman was convinced that Chairman Mao was more powerful than the Sangji Lama. Another Tibetan woman recited sutras while holding Mao's portrait over her head after being cured by the People's Liberation Army (PLA) doctors.[15] For these villagers, Mao had come to represent a new power at the top of the religious hierarchy of their world. The initial success of dispensing free allopathic medicine to cure illness, as well as the repeated state public health campaigns to engage the local population, had built up an expectation among many villagers for adequate state health provisions. They began to rely on the state to protect them against illnesses as well as to provide medical care in the event of them falling sick or in the occurrence of a disease outbreak.

After 1961, however, because of the lack of financial resources, free medical care was replaced by a pay-for-treatment system. In this new system, the patient had to pay either the total costs or part of them. Because most of the people living in these regions were economically worse off than populations in the other parts of China, they simply could not afford to go to the hospital for check-ups or treatment. Poverty also hindered public health work in these regions because many villagers could not afford to buy soap to wash their 'dirty' hands or to feed themselves an 'adequate' and 'healthy' diet as they had been taught to do by the state public health campaign.[16] The withdrawal of the promised free care, the low standard of care available, plus the state public health campaigns' persistent obliviousness to the cultural/social sensitivities and to the economic condition of the local population were perceived by these villagers as a breach of their trust in the CCP as the new ruler. As a result, not only did the number of outpatients as well as inpatients in state-run hospitals begin to decrease, but many villagers refused to even be treated by the government mobile medical teams. In contrast, lamas and shamans in many temples, which had been replaced by the socialist health care system in delivering health after the Communist Liberation, were again in high demand.[17]

Reports from the Yunnan provincial authority also sounded the alarm as a vernacular collective culture, including everyday healing rituals, strove to compete with socialism. This collective culture proved more capable than the latter in facilitating a convergence of programs and visions in this time of crisis.[18] In the schistosomiasis endemic region of Chuxiong, collective rituals such as exorcism or sorcery involving entire villages became a regular feature of community life. Nestled among high mountains on all sides in the Yunnan-Guizhou high plateau on the edge of Himalayas, Chuxiong had always been considered a backwater of Chinese civilization with its mixed population and multiple cultural traditions. Different ethnic groups – some of them with their own subgroups – had their own popular gods and supernatural rituals. Being far away from the centre of the 'high' Chinese culture, it had always maintained a greater degree of cultural fluidity. In times of extreme calamity such as epidemics, existing cultural and religious boundaries would often collapse. Villagers from different cultural backgrounds who otherwise worshipped their own gods and goddesses would turn up at a public healing session. There they would bow to someone else's god or goddess, who, it was claimed, possessed healing power over a certain group of diseases, and perform a customary sacrificial ritual. They would also collectively recite an appropriate healing text. With the advent of the Communist Liberation in the 1950s, for a while, as Erik Mueggler's ethnographic study of one village in Chuxiong illustrates, the socialist state penetrated communities here by 'installing itself within, at the centre of production and social reproduction'. With the radical collectivization and the subsequent famine, however, this centre quickly turned hollow and literally collapsed. For these villagers, the Communist authority or socialist state had been transformed into an avaricious 'wild ghost' with an empty mouth who impotently demanded ever more obeisance and acknowledgement.[19] While some resisted this 'ghost' by raiding the commune granaries and farming fields, others cursed or physically attacked local cadres who were seem as the 'ghost's' officials. Like elsewhere in the country, slacking became a more common way of resisting the Maoist collectivization program.[20]

As the power of the CCP was displaced, there was a resurgence of traditional practices. Villagers interpreted the famine, as well as subsequent outbreaks of disease and their poor health in general, as the pain inflicted by the 'ghost' and the 'ghost's' officials. As Mueggler's study and a number of sources that have emerged from the party archives show, in the aftermath of the famine, ghost exorcism was revived as a popular practice. According to an official report, between 1961 and 1964 villagers from one commune in Chuxiong performed at least 227 exorcisms. This was coupled with a growing number of 'superstitious' practitioners. According to the official estimate, in 1964 there were at least 117 such practitioners across eight different communes who made a living by practising 'superstition'. Among them, many practised supernatural healings. Not only villagers turned to these supernatural healers for help; even cadres and party members became increasingly weary of the poor quality and inadequacy of the state system in addressing their health and medical needs, and they, too, sought the help of supernatural healers. After falling ill, the wife of a brigade cadre at Mahuangjing Commune, for example, refused to seek hospital treatment. Instead, she sent for a diviner to read her fortune. In Mahuangjing Commune, it was also reported that between 1961 and 1964 an entire village spent a total of 1,762 *yuan* on vernacular healing rituals. Even more alarming to the authorities was that these vernacular practices were attracting a growing number of disciples. These disciples had taken up apprenticeships in these traditional practices, and the majority of villagers took these 'superstitions' very seriously.[21]

Closer to the PRC's political and cultural centre in Beijing, an official report estimated that there were more than 50,000 practising wizards, witches, and fortune-tellers in Hebei province. In the aftermath of the famine and with the weakening of local party structures given the failures and famines, many party members and cadres here also took a lead in 'superstitious' activities.[22] The extraordinary burden on the centrally organized state structures, many of which were only superficially supported by the overall population, meant that

the repressed older social networks of belief, local in their manifestation and flexible in their appropriation of a wide range of response,
resurfaced. The local beliefs and structures trumped the centrally
planned economy because they maintained the trust of communities
who were never quite sure of the consistency and efficacy of centralized responses.

What troubled the CCP leadership even more was an increasing
number of sectarian insurgencies. Many of them had a strong apocalyptic streak: a major famine that was followed by outbreaks of
diseases, as well as abuses in hospitals, came to be heavenly signs
that foretold the world was coming to an end. In China's agricultural heartland, official estimates show that between 1961 and
1962 there were more than 8,000 incidents of sectarian activities
in Hebei province and the surrounding regions.[23] Farther away in
the mountainous southwest, in Guizhou province's Zunyi County,
more than 1,000 villagers were reported to have taken part in the
five-day Hungry Ghost Festival in the autumn of 1962. At the festival, villagers recounted the 'bitterness' they had suffered under the
Communist rule and chanted verses such as: 'Oh, the dead, what
a terrible life you suffered, and how miserable was your death. In
1959 there was no food, so you starved to death, just like that.'
After quoting the Buddhist teachings on suffering and salvation,
some declared that 'the real salvation is coming soon from heaven'
and 'Chairman Mao's regime will last only another two and a half
years.' This was deeply disturbing for the Communist Party Central
Committee because Zunyi was a key location in the official history of the CCP. In 1935, during the Communist Long March, it
was at the conference in Zunyi that Mao first rose to power and
where the CCP and its Red Army (the PLA) succeeded in building
its power structure. (Nowadays, Zunyi is a 'Red tourism' destina-
tion for visitors wishing to evoke the revolutionary past.) But with
more than 5,000 villagers dead of starvation and illness within a
single month in the winter of 1960–61 and with 50 per cent of the
local population suffering from diseases of malnutrition and the
absence of clean water, villagers in Zunyi began to challenge the
official memory of the Communist revolution and its promise of
Liberation. As the news of suffering in Zunyi spread, the Guanyin
Laomu Dao sect, which the CCP had tried hard to suppress since
the early 1950s, became active again in the nearby border regions
across Guizhou, Hunan, and Sichuan. Beginning in 1962, this sect

had successfully recruited more than 1,200 new followers and built
up their own power order by appointing their 'emperor' and 'mar-
shals'. They had also built their own 'Central Altar' for the worship
of Heaven and Earth to challenge the central power stemming from
Beijing. The 'Central Altar' was surrounded by seven 'Branch Altars'
for the worship of different gods, including the medicine god (药王).
In the meantime, villagers seized a huge number of cattle owned by
the People's Commune and killed them for food or as offerings to
Heaven. Several party activists and cadres who had violently abused
villagers for resisting their implementation of the Land Reform and
the Maoist collectivization were assaulted. Violence was first undertaken by those suffering extreme hardship and then furthered by
those enthused by apocalyptic visions that depicted a life and death
battle between the Communist cadres and the starving villagers: 'We
have inconceivable hatred towards the Communist Party'; 'To follow the words of Communist cadres is to die a hungry ghost. To live
in human dignity, we must seek help from spirits.' Villagers shouted
as the 'spirit' revealed to them: 'To live a good life is to work for
yourself.'[24] Neither collectivization nor the utopian goals of the CCP
mattered any more.

DECENTRALIZATION

In the meantime, in different parts of the countryside, more and
more grassroots cadres and villagers began to push for agricultural
de-collectivization.[25] In early 1961, for instance, at a Zunyi region
cadres' meeting, grassroots cadres from different counties appealed
to the regional authority to allow individual villagers to keep private plots and to grant the production brigade the power to manage
grain collection as well as its local distribution. Since the regional
authority was reluctant to reach any agreement on the matter, some
local cadres, supported by villagers, took the matter into their own
hands. In a number of communes, the collective canteens were dissolved. As brigade cadres went up the mountains to pick ferns for
private consumption or to sell in an informal local market, villagers
chopped down trees in the publicly owned forests and brought the
wood home for private use. Opium, the main source of local revenue
prior to the Communist Liberation in 1950, was 'openly' bartered
in the illicit local market. Dozens of dens that had been closed down
by the Communist authorities after the Liberation re-opened their

doors despite the official restrictions. As ever-greater numbers of villagers died of starvation and famine-related illnesses, the survivors sought help from opium-smoking. Even cadres visited opium dens as a means of releasing their stress.[26]

The situation in Zunyi was by no means an isolated case. From elsewhere in the countryside, top CCP leaders also learned that the peasants no longer trusted the party's policy or socialism in general. The widespread famine and the subsequent outbreaks of diseases had led many to question the party's political legitimacy. In Sichuan province's Hongya County, after the authorities suspended the promised state food subsidy for oedema patients, a female villager from Huaxi Commune was said to have been miraculously 'reincarnated' as the 'superior immortal'. She was accompanied by two other 'minor immortals'. All three had been classified as 'poor peasants' during the Land Reform, and they had initially been among the most loyal supporters of the Communist Party. But the famine propelled villagers such as these three individuals to turn away from the CCP and to take their survival into their own hands. They took the lead in spreading rumours such as 'the world is turning into a chaos; patients are dying in hospitals; taking medicine by injection or oral administration is killing people.' Under their influence, according to a commune hospital report, more and more sick villagers refused to seek medical treatment at the hospital. No longer trusting the socialist welfare system, they turned to these 'immortals' for guidance and help and began to collect donations to build a temple in their honour. With the temple becoming the centre of village life, villagers handed over any food they harvested to the temple, leaving nothing for the state granaries. And in turn, the temple redistributed the food to those in need.[27]

Around the same time that this was happening in Hongya, Mao's nephew Mao Huachu went back to their home village, Dong Guantang in Shaoshan County, central Hunan province, to investigate local conditions. There, an elderly villager confronted him: 'Does your uncle [Chairman Mao] have any idea what has been going on in the past two years? You must let him know the situation here.' Here, in Mao's home county, according to an official estimate obtained by Mao's secretary Hu Qiaomu, the three years of famine had claimed more than 30,000 lives. By the end of 1960, the mortality and morbidity rates had reached a high of 70,000, and the situation was worsening at the time of Mao Huachu's visit. During a consultation meeting with Mao Huachu, some villagers cried out: 'Collectivization will never work ... If this [the collectivization] is not stopped, the problem will become even worse.'[28]

'MAKE THEM TRUST US AGAIN'

Mao was well aware of the problem. By the winter of 1960–61, the famine crisis in the countryside had reached a tipping point. For the CCP to hold on to power, it was necessary to win back the support of the peasants, the bulwark of the CCP's power in the countryside. The CCP Central Committee began to introduce a gradual decentralization. In November 1960, to curb the damage caused by radical collectivization, the CCP Central Committee approved the 'Urgent Directives on Rural Work' (commonly known as the 'Twelve Articles'), drafted by Zhou Enlai. This directive officially removed the commune's power to make decisions. It also relieved it of the burden of managing the labour shortage. In the following months, unofficial practices converged with official policy to bring about change. Some production brigades took advantage of this directive and began to allow villagers to work for themselves and to sell their output or barter it for other goods in informal markets. Quickly, a shadow barter economy emerged in parallel to the socialist economic system. Hearing what happened on the ground, President Liu Shaoqi responded: 'To work for themselves is better than not to work at all.'[29] In a meeting with some provincial leaders from Zhejiang province in February 1961, Mao also agreed that it was necessary to make concession by allowing villagers to keep private plots: 'We have to let villagers keep their private plots ... To make them trust us again, we need to make this loud and clear to them.'[30] The meeting led to a draft version of the 'Work Regulations on Rural People's Commune' (commonly known as the 'Sixty Articles'), which formally granted the production brigade the autonomy to manage its own production and labour, while members of the production brigade were allowed to keep their own private plots. After several months of trial implementation as of the spring of 1961, a revised version of the 'Sixty Articles' was launched throughout China that autumn.

With the implementation of the 'Sixty Articles', the task of organizing snail elimination as part of schistosomiasis control was given to the production brigades. This had several advantages: 1. the production brigade could plan the snail control work in the less busy season when the workload was lighter; and 2. the snail control work was carried out on a much smaller scale and gradually, thus requiring less labour each time. More important, under the 'Sixty Articles', the production brigade, as well as individual households, could generate extra income through side-line productions (副业) such as furniture-making or growing medicinal herbs. With this extra income, the production brigade could afford the labour for small-scale snail control work and even award villagers work points for their time. In Chuansha County near Shanghai (the county would later become famous for its village health worker or 'Barefoot Doctor' scheme), most production brigades organized middle school graduates and other unemployed youth to do the snail control work. This way, not only did the production brigade not dissipate its agricultural workforce, it also provided a livelihood for these youngsters. By awarding their time with work points, it gave them incentives to carry out the snail control work to a reasonably high standard.[31] In Chuansha and in nearby counties, some brigades applied a similar principle to the sanitary control work as well as other public health activities as part of disease prevention. In addition to rewarding villagers for the time they spent on collecting animal and human night-soil for fertilizer, these brigades introduced a coupon system, which drew inspiration from an earlier schistosomiasis prevention experiment first begun in 1952 at Zhejiang province's schistosomiasis control model district at Sanhuanfan.[32] To overcome the problem of villagers hiding night-soil for their private plots, each household would receive fertilizer coupons based on the number of people in the household. With fertilizer coupons, each household could buy back sterilized fertilizer free of schistosomiasis infection from the brigade to use on their private plots. In addition to the fertilizer coupons, these brigades also awarded grain coupons to each household based on the weight and quality of the night-soil they handed over to the brigade. At the end of the year, the household would use these coupons to buy food from the brigade.[33]

Granting the brigade the autonomy to manage snail and sanitary control work meant that the outcome was often uneven, depending largely on local agency and resources. Dividing up management responsibility meant that it was never clear who would be responsible for the ditches between different production brigades. Also, there was no standard monetary value for the snail and sanitary work across the brigades. Some brigades paid more and some less. This caused resentment among those villagers who received fewer work points for the time they spent on schistosomiasis control or any other public health work; this would, in turn, impact the quality of such work. Partly to address these shortcomings, after consultation with impacted counties, in its draft five-year plan for schistosomiasis control, the Shanghai Region Disease Control Committee proposed that, according to local conditions, the production brigade should train one or two village health workers (auxiliaries) who, in addition to carrying out their normal agricultural work, would lead the local schistosomiasis control as well as other public health activities. The time they spent on such work would be counted as doing voluntary service, and they would be awarded work points accordingly.* Economically better-off brigades could also pay these health workers from the brigade welfare fund. The exact amount would be based on the villagers' evaluation of their work.[34]

Like the coupon system, such a proposal for training village health workers was not entirely new. It drew inspiration in part from some earlier village health auxiliary schemes in counties around Shanghai, as well as in the nearby Jiangsu and Zhejiang provinces, prior to the Communist Liberation. In parts of Zhejiang province, such a scheme had been introduced in 1952 in the effort to control schistosomiasis. This scheme had suffered setbacks, however, after the introduction of the work points distribution system as of 1955, and with the advent of the People's Commune following 1958, the scheme had been abandoned.[35] Many brigades now welcomed it, for they saw it as an efficient way of utilizing manpower resources. In the aftermath of the famine, many former government or commune employees had been forced to return to the brigades to work for food. Many of these returnees were doctors or commune public health workers who were less capable of doing agricultural work. Their leadership in schistosomiasis control work would free other quality labourers to do agricultural work, and this would also spare brigade cadres from the burden of managing public health tasks. At the same time, given the rising mortality and morbidity, the impacted brigades saw the long-term economic benefit of schistosomiasis control, since it

---

* In the agricultural collective, non-agricultural work was called 'voluntary service'. Villagers would still receive work points for doing such work but much less than for doing agricultural work. Since a shortfall of labour was a widespread problem in many communes or brigades, these voluntary services were assigned to 'class enemies' or villagers who were physically unfit for agricultural work.

would help to prevent a further drain on labour. More labour would mean higher productivity and thus better income for the brigade and for the villagers.

In the next couple of years, the number of village health auxiliaries grew steadily in the counties around Shanghai, Zhejiang, and Jiangsu province. Since they normally worked in the paddy fields barefoot like other villagers, local villagers nicknamed them 'Barefoot Doctors'. For instance, Zhejiang province's Jiaxing County trained 440 health auxiliaries to support local schistosomiasis control work.[36] The number was to explode over the next decade with the official nationwide launching of the 'Barefoot Doctor' program, as we will see in the next chapter. Yet the initial idea of 'Barefoot Doctors' did not begin as a policy from above; rather, it began as one of many local innovations in response to the collapse of the state-run rural health system. With the quiet acquiescence, if not active cooperation, of local cadres, these initially quiet health revolutions in villages accelerated the post-famine decentralization of rural health care delivery in the PRC.

The overall status of health care remained confused and conflicted after the peak of the famine. While sensible structures seemed to be emerging to support the work of disease control, they were often badly implemented or faced active resistance. Their success was never guaranteed. The successes were often due to local, small-scale implementation rather than to the mass efforts heralded in the state's propaganda. On the ground, it was individuals who made things work; if they saw some opening for local success, or if they decided they had had enough of state bungling and resisted, they guaranteed the failure of any enterprise.

7

The Health Worker as 'True Revolutionary'

In 1962, as agricultural production in parts of rural China began to recover, the rural produce market, largely illicit, was thriving. Chen Yun, the vice chair of the Chinese Communist Party (CCP) Central Committee overseeing famine recovery, encouraged the limited free market as a measure for economic recovery. A variety of goods, including many food items such as pork and vegetables, as well as medicinal herbs that had disappeared for quite some time, remerged for sale. Because of the collapse of the state health system in the rural countryside, herbal remedies were greatly in demand and were thus a valuable cash crop for villagers. In Zhejiang province's Haining Country, prior to the collectivization medicinal herbs had been a major source of income for villagers at the Zhoujia market district. In 1962, almost every household there switched from food crops back to growing medicinal herbs.[1] In comparison, rice and cotton crops, as well as tobacco and oil seed rape, became less attractive for villagers because they would only be procured by the state. In some places, villagers opted to grow sweet potatoes or corn, since the state would not acquire such produce. As such, the state continued to face difficulties in procuring the projected quota of agricultural products. This meant that China would have to import 4 million tons of rice in 1962 and possibly 1.5 million tons in 1963, as well as 10,000 tons of cotton. The 5.5 million tons of rice would cost the state US$400,000,000, and 10,000 tons of cotton would cost US$8,000,000. After that, the state would have little or no resources left to purchase raw materials and machines for industrial development or to import drugs and 'white goods' such as refrigerators and bicycles. To save the state 4 million 'lovely US dollars', Li Xiannian, the vice premier of the People's Republic (PRC) and also the minister of finance, handed out procurement quotas to provincial leaders.[2] Sichuan province, one of the largest agricultural provinces, again won the trophy for fulfilling the state quota. The cost for winning it was that the famine in Sichuan continued for another year into 1962, with oedema and other famine-related diseases claiming further casualties.[3]

In the meantime, a free labour market was also thriving. Many villagers (mostly the strong or skilled males) sold their labour to private bidders from across the country. They relied on a fragmented private medical market that had emerged after the collapse of the state system in the aftermath of the famine. Millions were on the move from one part of the country to the other for employment in a growing private sector: from farming to manufacturing, construction, handicrafts, and healing. Huge numbers of people were crossing the border to escape the famine but also socialism. In Yunnan province in the southwest, entire villages embarked on an exodus. Between April and May 1962, nearly 40,000 people, including many doctors, crossed the border into Hong Kong to seek a better life and freedom.[4] The flight of health care professionals further undermined any reliance on the state system that centred on medical expertise. The authorities were anxious, since population control (in all senses of the phrase) was not only integral to central planning, it was also seen as essential to national security and the stability of the country. In May, the news of another 60,000 villagers crossing the border at Yili, a Kazakh autonomous prefecture in northwest China, and fleeing into the adjacent Soviet republics alarmed Mao and the CCP Central Committee. Mao was convinced that this was a conspiracy by the Soviet 'Revisionists' to undermine the PRC.[5]

Mao also became increasingly concerned about the growing 'revisionism' inside China. One cause for his anxiety was the ever-growing number of household farming plots and villagers' evident enthusiasm for individual farming. In parts of central Hunan, close to Mao's native home, according to Marshal Peng Dehuai's field research in late 1961,[*] almost 80 per cent of the land was,

* Peng Deihuai was one of the leaders to criticize the Great Leap Forward policy at the Lushan Conference in August 1959. It led to Peng's downfall; he was disgraced as the leader of an 'anti-party clique'. In 1961, Peng was permitted to return to his home region in Hunan province to conduct a field investigation of the local conditions.

because of local cadres' resourcefulness and inventiveness, privatized.[6] In north Zhejiang too, by allowing individual households to plough around collective farming fields, more and larger household plots were developed. In some villages, the collective fields had virtually vanished. The popular term for this was 'dug into the collective ground' (挖边). It would later be reinterpreted as 'undermining socialism' (挖社会主义的墙脚) when the authorities tried to put a stop to the expansion of these household plots. Describing their plots as a 'golden rice bowl', 'treasure basket', or 'money trees', villagers would come up with tactics to circumvent or violate the official restrictions. Some entire villages were involved in the growth and production of medical herbals as a cash crop. In regions where local authorities took a more hard-line approach to stopping villagers taking part in such illicit activities, the actions of the authorities often led to violent clashes. With the increasing sectarian activities, there was an increased danger of these grassroots-level disputes escalating into a civil war between the state and the peasants.[7]

Although earlier on Mao had shown he was willing to make concessions by allowing peasants to keep some household plots, he saw it only as a short-term solution to what he considered a 'temporary' food crisis. 'The household plot (自留地) is a mere leftover of private ownership. It is not dangerous [to the socialist economical system].' He was full of confidence about their transitory nature.[8] Between the spring and early summer of 1962, while touring around the country, Mao became increasingly obsessed about the idea that 'revisionists' were seizing the countryside. He saw villagers' enthusiasm for private ownership and markets as evidence of 'revisionist restoration': 'The revisionists are turning five billion peasants into petit bourgeois. Giving authority to the petit bourgeois is to embrace petit bourgeois dictatorship. It has never happened in history.'[9] On 7 July, Mao warned against Chen Yun and Tian Jiaying, who were in favour of a 'household contract' system as a measure for famine recovery, arguing that such a system would destroy the rural collective economy and ruin the People's Commune system: 'It is Chinese-style revisionism.' And Mao was determined to fight revisionism; for him, to fight against revisionism was to safeguard the dictatorship of the proletariat and hence the world communist movement. At the Tenth Plenum of the Central Committee's Eight Party Conference in the autumn of 1962, he launched a fierce attack on those party leaders who sought to restore the Chinese economy by allowing privatization. According to him, to uphold the socialist collective economy and fight against capitalism was a matter of 'class struggle'. 'Never forget class struggle,' the chairman exclaimed.[10]

Mao had always believed that private farming practice, as well as the 'backwardness' of the Chinese peasantry, was a root cause of rural poverty. For him, to attain and consolidate socialism, these 'undereducated' and 'self-centred' individuals needed to be 'socialized' into collectives. This meant educating and persuading the Chinese peasantry to embrace agricultural collectivization.[11] It was with this belief, when responding to peasants' resistance to collectivization in 1957, that Mao had pushed for the CCP Central Committee to launch the 'Socialist Education Campaign' in the Chinese countryside.[12] Four years later, in 1961, with the Great Leap falling apart and peasants demanding privatization, he found Tan Zhenlin on his side. In November 1961, at the Central Committee Politburo meeting discussing the difficulty of procuring projected agricultural products, Tan argued against the idea of permitting the rural marketplace:

> It's not a matter of buying and selling goods. This is a political matter ... We need to introduce socialist education ... Our problem now is not about the one or two catties more cotton we would be able to procure. Our problem is we don't even know how much has been produced in the countryside ... We can't allow this. This is not socialist economy. This is not planned economy ... to procure grains, cottons, as well as agricultural products of commercial values such as oil, tobacco, and tea was to fight against revisionism and uphold Marxism ... We need to explain to peasants what socialism and socialist construction is. We need to help them to understand the relationship between the state, the collective, and the individual. We must remind them of our fine revolutionary tradition.[13]

Deng Xiaoping, the man who would march China to embrace neo-liberalism some thirty years later, also added his voice and insisted on the need to change peasants' 'state of mind' so that they would be persuaded to grow cotton: 'Our party must enforce that. This is an important matter.'[14]

Gradually, the recharged Socialist Education Campaign was dragged out in different parts of rural China. Officials as well as

other government employees were encouraged to go to the countryside to 'unite with the peasantry' so that together they would 'pull
out the roots of revisionism'. Despite the constant pressure from
their immediate party boss, Ke Qingshi, who was also in charge
of the official Anti-Schistosomiasis Campaign, provincial leaders in Jiangsu were reluctant to implement the Socialist Education
Campaign. They argued that there had been too many campaigns,
including those aimed at improving people's health: 'Grassroots
cadres have suffered enough stress. The productivity has only just
begun to recover. They simply have no strength to carry out another
campaign.'[15] In the meantime, the practice of sideline production,
with illicit markets and household plots, including the production
and sale of medicinal herbs, continued in Jiangsu. On the other
side of the country, the feedback from Hunan and Hebei province
was cheering to Mao. There, the Socialist Education Campaign had
indeed led to class struggle against 'counter-revolutionary substage',
local 'capitalists and feudal powerholders'.[16] Mao decided to disseminate their 'successful' experiences and to push forward the Socialist
Education Campaign throughout rural China. In May 1963, Mao
approved Song Renqong's proposal to raise ordinary people's socialist consciousness by engaging them in a revolutionary oral history
project. 'To educate ordinary people, in particular young people,
by talking to them about their village history, family history, community history and factory history' should, according to Mao, be
widely promoted.[17]

In the countryside, the revolutionary public/oral history campaign often turned into mass political meetings where tales of
illness and disease suffered in the 'old' China were contrasted to
the CCP's care for the people in the 'new' China. In the schistosomiasis endemic regions, the schistosomiasis control in 'new'
China was the topic that was most evoked. Speaking at the Ninth
National Conference on Schistosomiasis Control, Wei Wenbo and
Xu Yunbei (Xu was the deputy minister of health and had had a
long career in party propaganda work) put it explicitly that the
harmful impact of schistosomiasis and its control under the CCP
leadership would 'arouse people's affection for the party' and
raise their political consciousness, thus inspiring them to fight the
disease – 'the enemy of the natural world'.[18] In 1964, an official
estimate claimed that the film *Spring Comes to the Withered Tree*

(see chapter 4) had been screened more than 1,100 times in these regions, with 440,000 viewers. More than 180,000 posters of the popularized version of Mao's poem 'Send off the Plague God' were distributed to villagers' homes and schools.[19] Yu Xiang was at the time a grassroots schistosomiasis control cadre in a remote mountainous region in Sichuan province. In a 2014 interview, he recalled that, throughout the Long 1970s, political meetings where tales of how schistosomiasis had been controlled under CCP leadership became a core part of schistosomiasis control on the ground.[20] Public health education was simultaneously political propaganda, whether true or not.

Equally important, as Xu Yunbei proclaimed, 'fighting schistosomiasis is a class struggle'. 'In the endemic region, class enemies are particularly active. [Outbreaks of diseases] provide them with opportunities to spread feudal superstitious ideologies, and to attempt to restore old orders. To fight disease is thus to struggle against class enemies.' Because the PRC's Anti-Schistosomiasis Campaign was an integral part of the socialist economy, the management of human and animal night-soil (to be used as fertilizer) and water was intrinsic to the sustainability of a rural socialist collective economy. But with an increasing number of villagers fighting to keep their private plots, they also refused to hand over domestic night-soil to the farming collective so that they could keep it for their private use. The continued success of schistosomiasis control, according to Xu, was thus 'crucial to uphold the socialist collective economy and improve agricultural productivities'.[21]

While agreeing with his colleagues at the Ministry of Health, Liao Luyan, the minister for agriculture, also highlighted the challenge ahead: 'We cannot just give orders to 500 million peasants, it won't work. We must convince them.'[22] To convince 500 million peasants, according to Ke Qingshi, the party boss in charge of the campaign, was to 'straighten out their thinking' (思想通). This would be achieved by educating the peasants: 'If we don't educate [peasants], how can we practise socialism?' 'We won't succeed by relying on a few [scientists]. Scientists' task is research. That's a different matter ... We must rely on the masses. We need to straighten out their thinking ... So they would fight the disease themselves,' Ke reminded the delegates at the Ninth National Conference on Schistosomiasis Control.[23] Echoing Ke, Xu Yunbai went on to stress that public health work was to 'change prevailing social customs': a 'class struggle at a cultural front'. It could be won only by following the 'mass line':*

> From managing night-soil to eliminating snails, washing hands and receiving the right kind of therapy, these have to do with changing peasants' mentality and their unclean habits. It is a behaviour issue. Health work is to change prevailing social customs. It is cultural work. We can't just rely on government policy or the effort of a few health professionals. We must educate and mobilize the masses to fight unclean habits and diseases.[24]

The Nine-Man Subcommittee set up Sichuan province's Zundao Commune in Mianyang County as the model for others to follow. Accordingly, by upholding the collective economy, by struggling against 'privatization' and 'class enemies', as well as by contracting night-soil collection and snail elimination tasks to politically 'reliable' villagers, from village cadres to party members and model workers – and with the spirit of the Foolish Old Man who 'moved high mountains', as advocated by Chairman Mao (see the next chapter) – Zundao Commune boasted that it had moved the 'high mountain' and successfully managed night-soil collection and fulfilled their snail elimination target. Three weeks after the Ninth National Conference on Schistosomiasis Control, on 24 January 1964, the *People's Daily*'s editorial entitled 'Advance Further Following the Victory, and Fight the War to Eradicate Schistosomiasis' called for 'All to follow the example of Zundao to control schistosomiasis by following the mass line'. 'To improve productivity, to reinforce the socialist economy and strengthen the People's Commune, to speed up building the socialist new countryside, we must put schistosomiasis prevention and eradication high on our agenda.'[25] The Anti-Schistosomiasis Campaign was once more at the forefront of the PRC's public health work.

---

* The 'mass line' is a leadership and organizational method first developed by Mao during the Chinese civil war. According to Mao, all revolutionary war was a war of the masses, and it could only be won by mobilizing the masses. Since the communist praxis was to change their manner of living, moving toward the modernization of the collective, to reach such goals, including those of public health, would have to involve the whole population.

THE HEALTH WORKER AS MORAL CRUSADER:
FROM LEI FENG TO NORMAN BETHUNE

Up to this point, the Anti-Schistosomiasis Campaign as the centrepiece of the PRC's public health work had been a top-down campaign led by the party, delivered by experts as well as health cadres, and aimed at disease eradication. With the collapse of rural health care delivery in the aftermath of the famine, the orientation of health work shifted to prophylactic medicine and the provision of basic, if often poor-quality, care. The burden of health care delivery also shifted from experts and hospitals to individuals, in this case grassroots health auxiliaries. This shift from top-down to bottom-up in health care delivery also changed the goal from disease eradication to an emphasis on the political rhetoric of 'serving the people wholeheartedly'. As Xu Yunbai stated, in this renewed war against schistosomiasis it was the health worker who was the 'pioneer' and the 'true revolutionary'.[26] Being the 'true revolutionary' was to be 'selfless' like Lei Feng and Dr Normal Bethune,* who had devotedly and selflessly served the revolutionary cause, the party, and the people.

Today, people in China still debate whether Lei Feng ever really existed. Whether he was a real person or a political myth, what matters is that Lei Feng left behind nine volumes of his diary and reading notes as well as more than 300 photographs. Generations of Chinese youth have read his words, and many were moved by Lei Feng's 'selfless spirit'. Song Renqiong, the man who proposed using oral history to raise ordinary people's socialist consciousness, was also the architect behind the creation of this 'selfless' revolutionary hero. A native of Hunan province, Song was also a New Cultural youth who joined the Chinese Communist Party in the 1920s and had since devoted his life to the revolutionary cause of 'saving' China and transforming it into a 'new, independent, and prosperous' society. Experienced in party political work, Song was the People's Liberation Army (PLA) commissary who took charge of the CCP's political consolidation of Yunnan province in the early 1950s. Bordering Burma, Vietnam, and Laos, Yunnan was, and still is, one of the most ethnically diverse regions in China, where the Chinese population was

---

* Norman Bethune was the Canadian physician and a noted communist who served as a medical volunteer for the CCP's Eighth Route Army in the Shanxi-Hebei border region of China between 1937 and 1939 during the Sino-Japanese War.

only a small minority. To allow a relatively 'peaceful' takeover of the region, Song focused on cultural work, including introducing farming technologies as well as providing free medical care based on allopathic medicine. To make the local population feel part of the socialist 'motherland', Song also organized many mass meetings where the Communist soldiers and cadres made 'friends' with the locals by singing revolutionary songs and dancing together (instead of giving them interminable public lectures). By being 'friends' with the local people, the CCP cadres also taught villagers the 'clean' and 'socialist way of life' – from washing their hands with soap to emptying their bowels in the modern toilets built by the new Communist authorities. To bring the socialist cultural revolution to the local population, under Song's leadership the CCP authorities also commissioned linguistic experts to help in the creation of 'indigenous' written languages and systematized cultures for these people. By learning to read and write and by singing revolutionary songs that had their roots in the genre of village ballads, these villagers could thus participate in the 'new socialist-ethnic' culture.[27] Yet in 1955, Song Renqiong did not hesitate to hand down killing quotas when the local population resisted joining the agricultural collectives as well as the subsequent policy of handing over their harvested food to the state.[28]

Following his successful tenure in the consolidation of the southwest, Song went on to lead the upgrading of the PLA and to direct the political work in the PRC's emerging nuclear industry. In 1960, Song was appointed the party boss of the northeast region (formerly known as Manchuria), the PRC's heavy industry zone bordering the far eastern region of the Soviet Union. Song was also the commissary of the Shenyang Military Region for the PLA. It was during this period that Song popularized, or indeed created, Lei Feng and resurrected the 'fine revolutionary tradition of the Eighth Route Army', the latter including the 'spirit of Dr Norman Bethune'. Health policy, whether real or invented, remained a central part of the vocabulary of the new national identity across all reaches of the PRC.

In 1961, as the state granary stocks were running low, the food crisis began to hit the large cities such as Beijing and Shanghai as well as the industrial centres in the northeast. In the previous year, responding to Song's appeal for help, the State Council signed off on 1 billion kilograms of food aid to the northeast. But in December 1961, at the State Planning meeting, Premier Zhou Enlai made it clear that there would be no more food aid from the state. Each province and region had to fulfil their state grain and cotton procurement quotas: 'If any region failed to fulfil the procurement quota, the local authorities must take the full responsibility,' the premier said adamantly. When Yang Yichen, the director of finance and commerce of Helongjiang province (the food-growing region of the northeast), responded with 'Tough!' Zhou Enlai turned around and asked: 'What does that mean? "Tough"? Why can't you just answer "Yes" or "No"?' When Yang explained to the premier that Helongjiang province was unable to 'climb up the hill' (meaning to fulfil the state procurement quota), Zhou insisted: '[Helongjiang] has to climb up the hill.'[29] In addition to the difficulties being faced in procuring the projected amount of agricultural goods, in 1961 coal and steel production throughout China had plummeted. If China failed to produce the projected steel output target of 18.6 million tons in the following year, it was thought that the whole world would 'spit on China'. 'This was a political matter,' Song Renqiong reminisced.[30] Since the northeast was the backbone of the PRC's heavy industry, Song was charged with the daunting task of seeing that the region was producing enough coal to power the entire country's increased industrialization. With the USSR having withdrawn its aid, being 'self-reliant' and 'walking on two legs' were more than just ideological statements; they were also necessary. The desperate situation reminded Song of the time when he led the Communist army's famine relief work in southern Hebei province in 1943 during the Sino-Japanese war. By uniting and relying on the local people, the Communist army successfully completed the task of transporting 325 million kilograms of grain across the enemy line to the famine-stricken villages. 'We could only do it with the help of villagers ... From our past experiences, we learn that by uniting with the people, we could conquer any difficulties. We must continue with such fine revolutionary traditions.'[31] This may have been true in wartime with an external enemy, but the reality on the ground at this moment was very different.

In the early 1960s, however, with corruption running rampant in the countryside, very few villagers trusted their local cadres. To 'reunite the people to the party', Song understood that a propaganda campaign was needed to 'humanize' it in order to succeed. Thus, Lei Feng, the hero of the new China, was manufactured. Most important, Lei Feng did not represent top-down authority. The official version of his story tells us that he was an ordinary soldier, born into a poor peasant family in Hunan province. He was a fellow countryman of some of the top CCP leaders, including Chairman Mao, President Liu, and Commissary Song. Like them, he was of the people. More important, he was the 'successor of the revolution'. Being a new soldier and a new party member, he was said to have inherited the 'fine revolutionary traditions' of the CCP and its army, the PLA. He donated his savings to famine relief; he used his pocket money to buy a train ticket for a stranger who had lost hers; he helped an old lady crossing the road. Equally important, he was not an ordinary individual. When strangers he had helped asked for his name, he would always answer: 'I am a PLA soldier, and my home is China.' According to Song Renqiong, one of the people responsible for 'discovering' this hero, Lei Feng was the embodiment of new China: 'Lei Feng is the hero of our time ... he is the model of our time. He is the pride of new China'.[32]

This hero of new China died at a timely moment on 15 August 1962 at the very young age of twenty-two, and, of course, he died while on duty, which made him a martyr. Until then, very few people in China had ever heard of him, even though we are told that he had become a local hero in Shenyang and had received numerous honours from the PLA Shenyang Military Region for his good deeds. A month later, after Chairman Mao reminded the party and the people of China 'Never to forget class struggle', the story of Lei Feng began to spread from Shenyang to Beijing. On 5 March 1963, the *People's Daily* published Mao's motto 'Learn from Comrade Lei Feng!' which officially launched the nationwide 'Learning from Lei Feng' campaign. To learn from Lei Feng, every young person in China, including schoolchildren, read and recited *Lei Feng's Diaries*. The success of the Lei Fang campaign was that this exemplary worker replaced the state-directed admonitions to increase production. By personifying the utopian goal in and through this perfect citizen of the new state, the authorities encouraged the individual's involvement in the goals of the state rather than in any type of mass action.

A month prior to the *People's Daily*'s publication of Chairman Mao's 'Learn from Comrade Lei Feng', on 7 February 1963 the newspaper had published a co-authored feature article entitled 'Chairman Mao's Good Soldier Lei Feng', paired with an editorial 'A Great yet Ordinary Soldier'. The paper also ran an entire page of excerpts from Lei Feng's diaries as well as photographs of Lei Feng doing good deeds and reading Chairman Mao's works. Through both the editorial and the diary excerpts, the reader also encountered yet another revolutionary hero, 'Dr Bethune': 'The embodiment of true spirit of internationalism and communism'. The editorial in the *People's Daily* explained to the reader that it was through reading Chairman Mao's essay 'In Memory of Norman Bethune' (1939) and by learning to emulate 'Comrade Bethune' that Lei Feng had become 'a great revolutionary soldier'. In the words of Lei Feng, the reader was reminded that 'To live is to be like Comrade Bethune, who devoted all his energy and gave his life to the revolutionary cause and the cause of building communism.'[33]

As with Lei Feng, until then very few people in China had heard of Dr Norman Bethune. In November 1939, while serving as a medical volunteer with the CCP's Eighth Route Army, Norman Bethune had died of septicaemia after he accidentally lanced his finger while operating on a wounded solider.[34] In other words, he died on duty as a revolutionary martyr. Twenty-three years later, Lei Feng also died as a revolutionary martyr while on duty. In December 1939, a month after Bethune's death, Mao apotheosized the dead doctor. He wrote the essay 'In Memory of Norman Bethune' and transformed Bethune into a living revolutionary symbol. It was Chairman Mao's memorial to Bethune, we are told, that inspired Lei Feng to devote his life to the revolutionary cause and communism. In his memorial, Mao told his readers that although he did not know Bethune well in person because they had only met once, he wanted every Chinese communist to learn from the 'Spirit of Comrade Bethune' – namely, 'the true spirit of internationalism and Communism'.

Shaped after Sergey Nechayev's eponymous 'Revolutionary' – the 'doomed man'– Mao's Comrade Bethune had no personal interests but was wholly absorbed by a single focus, his passion for revolution; he had neither friendships nor attachments but was devoted solely to his comrades – the collective – who, like him, were dedicated to the revolution:* '[Bethune's] utter devotion to others without

---

* In 1930, Mao's young wife Yang Kaihui, who was a fellow revolutionary (a comrade) of Mao's, was imprisoned by the Nationalists and was subsequently executed. After Yang's death, their three sons were put into orphanages. They were found many years later and were reunited with their father. The oldest one, Anying, was killed in the Korean War in 1953. In 1957, in a poem, titled 'Butterfly Courting Flowers', in memory of Yang Kaihui and another revolutionary martyr, Liu Zhixu (Liu was their friend and comrade), Mao turned them both into the revolutionary symbol of 'righteous and loyal spirit' who had sacrificed their lives in the revolution.

any thought of self was shown in his great sense of responsibility in his work and his great warm-heartedness toward all comrades and the people.' Only with this spirit of absolute selflessness, proclaimed Mao, can a man be of value to the people. Mao's Dr Bethune thus stood as the antithesis of those false or faltering communists

> who are irresponsible in their work, preferring the light and shirking the heavy, passing the burdensome tasks on to others and choosing the easy ones for themselves. At every turn they think of themselves before others. When they make some small contribution, they swell with pride and brag about it for fear that others will not know. They feel no warmth toward comrades and the people but are cold, indifferent, and apathetic. In truth such people are not Communists, or at least cannot be counted as devoted Communists.

Toward the end of the memorial, Mao also wrote:

> Comrade Bethune was a doctor, the art of healing was his profession and he was constantly perfecting his skill, which stood very high in the Eighth Route Army's medical service. His example is an excellent lesson for those people who wish to change their work the moment they see something different and for those who despise technical work as of no consequence or as promising no future.[35]

In 1939, Mao was certainly not writing about how to be a good doctor or commenting on medical ethics. His argument was that only a 'true' 'revolutionary' and 'communist' like Bethune could attain the fine skills needed to excel in any profession. Equally important was that as a person Norman Bethune, in analogy to Jesus Christ, was a healer. But in death, his 'spirit of true communism and internationalism' was immortalized by Mao. For Mao, only communism, not Christianity or any other religion, could bring the ultimate healing to his country, 'the Sick Man of Asia', and through the 'spirit of internationalism', communist revolution would bring about the salvation of all of mankind.*

---

* Norman Bethune was born a Christian. In 1935 he travelled to the USSR where he became a convinced communist, and upon returning to Canada he joined the Canadian Communist Party. He was an advocate of socialized medicine.

Transformed into a revolutionary symbol, Norman Bethune would be evoked differently at different times by different people. Thirteen years after Mao wrote his memorial essay, at the anniversary commemoration of Bethune's death, Dr Nelson Fu (Fu Lianzhang in Chinese), the president of the Chinese Medical Association (CMA) as well as the deputy minister of health, delivered a lecture titled 'What We Should Learn from Dr Bethune's Revolutionary Humanitarianism' (1952). Like Bethune, Fu was born into a Christian family. After graduating from a missionary medical school, he worked as the doctor for a local branch of the Red Cross as well as the director of a local Christian Gospel hospital. Fu later joined the Communist revolution and was instrumental in building a military health system for the Communist army during the Sino-Japanese and the Chinese civil wars. Fu was not a revolutionary like Mao; he was a communist sympathizer and a humanitarian who participated in the revolution in order to save individual lives. Fu only became a party member in 1938. In that same year, he worked alongside another new convert to communism, none other than the Canadian physician Norman Bethune, a veteran of the International Brigade in Spain, at the Eighth Route Army hospital. In his 1952 lecture, Fu recalled how impressed he was by Bethune's devotion to medical work and his 'unravelling skill, boundless sympathy for his patients, sense of responsibility and zeal in teaching others'.[36] In 1952, as the frontrunner of the PRC's medical and public health work, Fu was trying to provide a meaning and purpose for medical and health work in the new China. Dr Bethune, the revolutionary symbol first evoked by Mao, became his 'sterling example'. With his background in Christian medical work, Fu focused his exegesis of Chairman Mao's memorial on the 'spirit of selflessness', one of the fundamentals of being a Christian according to Christ's 'Sermon on the Mount'. Having been baptized a second time as a communist, Fu rebranded this old Christian teaching as 'revolutionary humanitarianism'.[37] Fu's Dr Bethune was a humanitarian like himself who joined the revolution to save the lives of individuals. This was markedly different from Mao's Norman Bethune as the revolutionary and the collectivist anti-humanist.[*]

---

[*] Like many other supporters of the Communist revolution, Fu was purged during the Great Proletarian Cultural Revolution. As a humanist, he pleaded with Mao, asking Mao to save his life on the grounds that he had once saved Mao's life. But Mao did not intervene; Mao was a revolutionary who had denounced the 'I' for the 'we'.

'REVOLUTIONIZE' HOSPITAL SERVICES

Twenty-five years later, in the post-famine Socialist Education Campaign, humanitarian values, such as individuals volunteering to do medical and public health work, would nevertheless be utilized as a tool to reunite the party with the people. Aggravated by the famine crisis, the PRC's already flimsy health system had collapsed. Most people in the countryside had very little or no access to even the most basic health care, whilst in cities and factories the medical treatment provided by hospitals was a far cry from the goal propagated by the party. Poor-quality hospital care was one of the greatest popular complaints. In addition, corruption in hospitals and government health departments was rampant, creating a gulf between the haves and the have-nots and causing further public resentment. The Ministry of Health, held accountable for the low standards of care as well as the widespread corruption in medical and health care establishments, was obliged to respond and to introduce measures to combat corruption and improve services. Even in government departments, the emphasis of the campaign was on anti-corruption. At the national conference on hospital governance in January 1964, Qian Xinzhong, the deputy minister of health, urged the attendees to carry forward the 'spirit of revolutionary humanitarianism': '[during the war years] we won a lot of praise from the people … they used to call military medical workers "the Old Eighth Route" and our military hospital "the hospital that saves lives" … Today we need to forward our fine revolutionary traditions by promoting good governance and improve services as well as to train health cadres [who would be equipped for such a task].'[38] 'Revolutionary humanitarianism', inspired by Norman Bethune, became the new catchword for a focus on individual-based health reform as opposed to the state-focused institutions that were seen by the public as not only corrupt but also incompetent.

In the following months, to reform hospitals into 'truly socialist hospitals', armies of urban medical and health workers throughout the country were sent to the countryside to support the 'Three Revolutionary' campaigns – namely, 'Class Struggle', 'Struggle for Production', and 'Scientific Experiment' – as well as deliver medical care to peasants in the fields, workers in the mines, and the sick in their homes.[39] To ensure that they would 'rectify' their 'attitudes' toward services so that they would be able to solve the question of 'service for whom' and 'how to serve', medical and health professionals read Chairman Mao's works, including 'In Memory of Norman Bethune'. Many, we are told, were inspired by the 'spirit of revolutionary humanitarianism' and had become 'one with [the people] in thought and feeling' as well as 'remoulded their ideology'. In addition to 'tirelessly' delivering medical and health care to the workers and peasants, they also 'cooked food and boiled water for [the people]' as well as helping with agricultural work.[40]

A few outstanding examples were named and honoured as 'Five Good' health/medical workers so that others would emulate them. The story of a young surgeon, Li Gong from Gansu province, who used skin grafts from his own legs and thighs to treat the burns on a Tibetan villager's body and donated his blood to save the lives of ten Tibetan cholera patients, was adapted into a narrative poem and two operas with songs in the Tibetan genre. Tibetan villagers would remember him as the 'Red Doctor', the 'Manba (Tibetan Doctor) sent by Chairman Mao', while medical and health workers throughout China would aspire to become like the 'Red Doctor' sent by Chairman Mao and the party. Labelled as another martyr who died while on duty, Li Gong was the Ministry of Health's own Lei Feng and the new China's Dr Bethune. Interestingly, in 2011, to celebrate the sixtieth anniversary of the CCP's 'Liberation' of Tibet, Li Gong's story was re-invoked in a Peking opera titled *The Manba of Grassland* to demonstrate the 'deep affection' between the Communist Party and the Tibetan people. It also served as an exemplary instance of fine moral professional conduct for the new generation of medical and health professionals in China to imitate.[41]

In 1964, in order to build a truly socialist hospital and health service that would 'contribute to the country's socialist revolution and construction' by protecting the health of the 'broad masses of working people', 25,000 new medical graduates, according to the Ministry of Health's statistics, were 'channelled into county hospitals and mining enterprises'.[42] The so-called 'minority regions', including Tibet, were given priority, partly because medical humanitarian work had proved a successful strategy in winning the support of local populations in the early 1950s. By the end of 1964, according to official statistics, medical personnel in these regions had increased by 30 per cent, and hospital beds had increased by 20 per cent compared to 1949.[43] The shift from an expert-centred, top-down health care to a focus on health care disseminated across the widest reaches of the state through the activities of individuals had begun in earnest. Ironically, in northern Shaanxi, however, as a result of this intense campaign, it had helped to 'immortalize' the 'spirit of Norman Bethune' but in a very unintended manner. As Adam Chau learned from his local informants, in the mid-1960s villagers there turned Norman Bethune into a local deity or 'the god Bethune' who travelled around northern Shaanxi to cure people's illnesses. Since there was no temple or shrine dedicated to 'Dr Bethune', villagers uttered Bethune's name in prayer and lit what was thought to be Bethune's favourite cigarettes as incense to obtain his divine assistance.[44]

'THE THIRD FRONT': CHINA PREPARING FOR A WAR

In 1964, the CCP Central Committee decided to embark on the 'Third Front' construction project in order to build a comprehensive system of defence, industry, energy, and transportation in the mountainous regions of the southwest in preparation for the possibility of an American invasion in the wake of the Vietnam War as well as an attack from Moscow. It became imperative that there be a concomitant effort to construct an adequate health infrastructure in these remote regions.[*][45] With schistosomiasis identified as one of the major health risks for the military and civilian populations in wide swatches of the 'Third Front' area along the upper stretches of the Yangtze River administered by Sichuan and Yunnan provincial authorities, the Sichuan provincial health authority allocated 120,000 *yuan* to build a brand new schistosomiasis treatment hospital with fifty hospital beds in Xichang City.[†][46] This was a huge commitment, considering Sichuan province's health budget had been in deficit over the previous three years.[47]

On the south side of Xichang is Panzhihua, the ancient Cycas forest at the intersection of the Jinsha and Yalu rivers, once the home of giant pandas. It was chosen as the location for a gigantic steel and iron mill complex because it was rich in natural mineral resources, in particular iron ore. Panzhihua's drawback was that it was bleak and desolated. The existing inhabitants were said to be rather 'uncivilized', since most of them were illiterate. It was also

---

* The 'Third Front' area was centred in Sichuan province; it also stretched into parts of Yunnan, Guizhou, Hubei, and Shaanxi.

† Xichang was to become the PRC's satellite launching base.

a region of endemic leprosy. There were rumours that even hens and chicks became infected with the disease after encountering lepers and that the chickens then passed the disease to other humans through the food chain. To eliminate such fears, the Ministry of Health was impelled to issue a statement affirming that leprosy was under control in the PRC and that the future workforce would not be at risk from the disease.[48] In addition to schistosomiasis and leprosy, researchers also identified large sections of the subtropical 'Third Front' industrial development zone as the natural *foci* of a number of infectious diseases, including Japanese B encephalitis, leptospirosis, orientia tsutsugamushi (also known as scrub typhus), and plague – thus, a hostile environment for human habitation.[49]

Although no major outbreaks of these diseases were reported, official records showed that the risk of morbidity from meningitis, malaria, gastritis, and anthrax did increase dramatically. In 1965, the meningitis morbidity in the border regions between Sichuan, Yunnan, Guizhou, and Hubei rose nearly 30 per cent compared to the previous year. The main cause of such a sharp rise, as suggested by the official analysis, was simply that greater numbers of workers had been brought into these regions to work on this colossal national defence project.[50] The crowded and unsanitary living conditions turned the 'Third Front' industrial development zone (including road and railway construction sites, mines, factories, steel mills, and power plants) into a hothouse for the spread of a wide range of infectious diseases. Malaria, gastritis, and influenzas, in particular, plagued such places. In Sichuan province, the centre of the 'Third Front' project, government health reports consistently showed that many railway construction sites became covered with puddles of filthy water when it rained, while piles of rubbish were to be seen everywhere. Workers often had to share cups, wash bowls, and towels. There was no hot water for showers and limited amounts of clean and boiled water to drink. As a result, one tenth of the workforce fell ill across all factories and construction sites in the development zone. At some construction sites, the sickness rate was as high as one-third, and in addition, many workers were infested with fleas and lice.[51] At the Yingxiu hydraulic dam construction site in western Sichuan, bordering Tibet, there were only six toilets for 6,000 employees and workers.* With no space to store night-soil or any

* Yingxiu was the epicentre of the 2008 Sichuan earthquake.

transportation to remove it from the construction site, it was simply dumped into the Ming River, a major tributary of the Yangtze. In the meantime, swarms of flies invaded the factory and construction site canteens.[52] Mass political meetings in the countryside, as well as public entertainment for employees of the factories and mines, also helped to spread disease.[53]

Despite the state's claims that the health care provision in these 'backward' regions had improved dramatically since the Communist Liberation in the early 1950s, there were not nearly enough hospitals, let alone sufficient physicians. The problem was exacerbated by the Central Committee's directive to drastically cut back the number of state employees and to reduce food rations because of the severe food shortages in the aftermath of the famine. Because health was seen as a 'wasteful' rather than a 'productive' sector of the economy, a huge number of county- and commune-level hospitals throughout the country were closed down. In many remote hinterland regions, such as the southwest, with fewer resources and no proper roads, many smaller counties and towns as well as communes had no hospitals at all. In eastern Sichuan's Fengjie County, along the bank of the Yangtze next to what is today the Three Gorges Dam, there was only one medical worker per 2,000 people. Next to Fengjie County is Wushan County, where nearly two-thirds of the medical workers were dismissed. Although on paper there were fifty-six union clinics in Wushan County, in reality many of them had no medical staff.[54] For the whole of Sichuan province, official statistics showed there were on average only 6.1 hospital beds for every 10,000 people in 1964. This was more than one-third lower than the national average of ten beds per 10,000 people. The situation was even more desperate for rural Sichuan where there was an average of only 3.7 beds per 10,000 people – again, one-third lower than the national average of 5.2 beds per 10,000 rural residents. Although nearly all railway and road construction sites, power plants, factories, and mines were supplied with doctors and other health personnel – and arms factories, as well as steel mills, often came with attached hospitals – in every case, the demand far exceeded the number of doctors and beds. For the 'Third Front' industrial development zone, there were on average only 1.46 health workers (including doctors and nurses) for every 1,000 employees and their families.[55]

Wu Junmin, the novelist, was born in the 1960s when the 'Third Front' project first began. Both her parents were drafted to work on the project. She recalled that many factories had only one health clinic with limited amounts of drugs and very few doctors. If a person fell seriously ill, they had to be sent to the nearest provincial-level hospital, which was often a long way away.[56] Furthermore, because of the shortage of medical staff and hospital beds, workers who relocated or were recruited to work at the 'Third Front' industrial development zone consistently competed with the local population for what were already scarce local health resources. For example, in Dechang County (locally known as *dep cha xiep*), the ancient trading centre between Panzhihua and Xichang that linked the Himalayas with the Chinese empire, the county hospital had forty beds, sixty beds fewer than the actual demand; the average number of outpatients had been 100. With the 'Third Front' project, the number of outpatients tripled. Unable to cope with the huge increase, the hospital sent more serious cases – those who needed X-rays or specialized care, for instance – to the Xichang regional hospital. The Xichang regional hospital quickly ran out beds, drugs, and equipment, and as a result, more than 200 patients there were denied medical care in June 1964.[57] Health care, while remaining a staple of state propaganda showing the efficacy of the new state system, became ever less important on the ground during and in the aftermath of the famine. The gap between the lived experience of those needing health care, figures that mushroomed during and after the famine, and the claims of the state that it was providing health care became ever more evident.

The shortage of doctors, beds, drugs, and equipment meant that only cadres and engineers or their friends had access to them. Since many of the temporary construction workers were local villagers or from elsewhere in the country, as soon as they left construction work, often due to ill health or injury, they ended up with no access to any medical or health care. Still, they counted themselves lucky if they came out alive, since pneumoconiosis and industrial accidents, two major health risks during the Great Leap Forward period, were made worse with the 'Third Front' project and claimed tens of thousands of lives. In many arms and chemical factories, one accident would often kill hundreds of people. The high level of coal dust in the atmosphere meant that pneumoconiosis casualties were not limited to factory employees or mine workers. Inhabitants of the nearby villages, particularly schoolchildren, were also at risk from the disease.[58] One other major re-occurring public health menace to which all were exposed was the regular discharging of waste water by many of the factories into nearby rivers, releasing toxic gas into the environment that was harmful to the health of the local population as well as to food crops. Infectious diseases that first began at construction sites, mines, and in the new industrial towns and cities would often spread to nearby villages and towns through contaminated waterways or to the villages when the construction or mine workers returned home at the end of their jobs or during holidays (similar to the spread of the SARS epidemic in 2003). All of this added further stressors to the already inadequate health provision in the countryside.[59]

As poor health undermined productivity, and in a desperate attempt to battle the ever more evident public health emergencies, the relevant authorities were advised to organize mass clean-ups or other public health activities. In the Luzhou Gas Field in southeastern Sichuan, bordering Guizhou and Yunnan, employees and their families resisted such activities, seeing it as a waste of time and effort because employees' children regularly defecated on the newly cleaned ground. 'What is the point?' they complained. Others protested that their accommodation was overcrowded and poorly built (some lived in makeshift straw huts) and were thus impossible to keep clean. Instead of introducing measures to improve the quality of life, the authorities handed out brand new, coloured public health posters to 'brighten up' the workers' otherwise shabby accommodations. They also organized mass study meetings for workers and their families to read the diaries of Lei Feng and Chairman Mao's essay 'In Memory of Norman Bethune', replacing open-air cinema or opera – the most common forms of mass entertainment for factory workers. After these study sessions, workers and their families would clean up the communal kitchen as well as visit nearby villages to help villagers repair the pig barns. Anyone who showed any reluctance would run the risk of experiencing the 'class struggle' first-hand.[60]

In the context of the Socialist Education Campaign, public health activities that centred on prevention served the double function of attempting to mitigate health risks and mobilizing the masses in the struggle against the revisionists who doubted the efficacy of socialist health care. With prevention now re-elevated as the core strategy to protect people's health, as well as a political tool in the struggle against revisionism, preventive services expanded at a far greater pace than hospital services – in mining and industrial areas as well as in the countryside. Furthermore, as China prepared for war, mobile medical units, rather than big urban hospitals, were seen not only as cost-effective but also as strategically important. At the same time, the struggle against schistosomiasis continued to be seen as a factor in increasing military preparedness and efficacy and became one of the models for this more expansive model of health care.

Mao, who had had extensive experience in fighting guerrilla warfare during the revolution, often reminisced about the 'good old' military tradition of the revolutionary army engaging with the masses to fight disease as well as their enemies. In June 1964, in a conversation with a team of Vietnamese guerrilla fighters, styled as a true revolutionary leader as opposed to the Soviet revisionists, he remarked that health care in the PRC had been modelled after the Soviet system and had 'too many specialized doctors who can't treat a range of diseases. That's not good. It needs to change.'[61] When these words of Chairman Mao spread to the Ministry of Health, they triggered panic. There was awareness that centralized, expert care had already been undercut by the inefficient, unequal, and corrupt pattern of its availability across the nation. A month later, the ministry's Party Committee drafted a proposal to cut back on the health care services provided to high-ranking officials. The proposal began by apologizing that the health care system in the PRC had been oriented toward high-ranking officials and had failed to deliver services to the broad masses, thus encouraging selective privileges. But the proposal gave Mao one more excuse to pass the blame for the crisis in the countryside onto the 'privileged few' or 'revisionists': 'There are too many doctors in hospitals, they far outnumber patients. Our hospitals have become the hospital of old lords. It must open up.' For Mao, to 'open up' did not necessarily mean to provide more services for the greater population; rather, it suggested changing the doctor's 'false worldview'. 'The doctor views the world as a microorganism. That is a false worldview,' he had remarked earlier at the height of the Great Leap Forward. In his canvas of a perfect future world, there was little space for bourgeois doctors whose view of the world was different from that of the masses: 'There is no need for too many doctors. They should be sent to lead public health work such as killing flies and cleaning streets. We could keep a few top doctors, but they don't need to see too many patients. They could use their spare time to sing opera. Health workers should do health work. Spending all day with patients undermines their morale.'[62] Mao's irony was often misread as comments on practice rather than on the core nature of health care in the promised communist utopia.

The Ministry of Health neither closed down the Bureau of Health Care for Senior Officials nor moved toward closing the gap between urban and rural health care. But as of January 1965, an ever-greater number of hospital medical staff, as well medical students from universities and researchers from medical research institutes, were being regularly sent to the industrial and mining areas and into the countryside to 'revolutionize' hospital services by bringing bio-medical knowledge to remote corners of the country. In the spring of 1965, Huang Jiasi, the president of the Chinese Academy of Medical Science and one of the PRC's top surgeons, led a medical mission of top doctors from the Peking Union Medical College (PUMC) and the Chinese Academy of Medical Science to Xiangyin County in Hunan province. Reporting on the trip, Huang commented: 'the best way to convince the peasants of the significance of prevention was to do propaganda through treatment.'[63] The ambiguity of this statement underlines its inherent contradictions. It actually means the opposite of what was intended by 'putting prevention first' – a widely circulated slogan of the time. It was not prophylactic public health interventions with long-term effects but the immediate treatment of the existing ills of the population that provided the greatest propaganda benefit to the state.

On the ground, however, the effort to draw on urban resources to provide health care to the rural areas encountered many problems. One evident problem was the chronic shortage of urban medical personnel. In Sichuan province, the centre of the 'Third Front' project, where most new medical graduates had already been sent to support medical and health work in the newly built 'Third Front' factories, mines, and power plants, the provincial hospital authority resisted sending any more medical and health personnel to the countryside: 'How are we going to run hospitals if we send everyone away?' Existing personnel shortages were regularly used as an excuse for not carrying out preventive programs at all or to do them superficially and thus inadequately: 'Since we are short of personnel, we can only carry out the work poorly. If we have more staff, we will do it better.' Contrary to the official propaganda that many of the health care workers enthusiastically embraced the Ministry of Health's call, a great number of those who were drafted to serve the countryside and the remote 'Third Front' industrial development zone complained that such schemes split up families, damaged their health and well-being, and undermined their professional development. Many more worried about losing their existing benefits. One nurse in the Sichuan Traditional Medical Hospital openly announced: 'If I am called to go to the countryside, I will resign.'[64] For the villagers and their cadres in the countryside, doctors and health cadres from the cities often proved more of a burden than a help. In Sichuan province, nearly 1,500 schistosomiasis control cadres were sent to the countryside to support grassroots control work as well as the rural Socialist Education Campaign. They took with them the food rations they were assigned while living in the city, but the amount of food often turned out to be inadequate. To fill their stomachs, they would consume the villagers' food, placing an extra burden on the already impoverished rural peasants.[65]

Furthermore, as Chen Zhiqian (commonly known in the West as C.C. Chen), the doyen of public health in modern China, observed, the 'Mobile [health] units could go only where the roads took them, however, and so proved to be of limited use.' More important, they were 'stunned with the multitude of needs they encountered in rural market towns and villages, especially by the incidences of infectious diseases'.[66] For brigade cadres and communities on the ground, however, sending mobile medical units to do public health work conflicted with the ideal of inspiring community participation. It undermined local agency and autonomy and gave cadres the perfect excuse not to organize any public health activities for their brigades on the local level. Communities often left urban medical and health teams to carry out sanitation work or snail elimination on their own.[67]

Although authorities attempted to overcome such shortcomings by introducing measures of prevention, their ideas about prophylactic medicine were often, as Chen pointed out, vague.[68] To save state expenditure on public health and grassroots health personnel, the authorities in charge tended to put stress on the locals to practise self-reliance, but this did little to help in building a sustainable rural health system. In January 1964, at the Ninth National Conference on Schistosomiasis Control, Ke Qingshi, the party boss of the Anti-Schistosomiasis Campaign, urged all local authorities to follow the mass line and utilize local resources:

The state only has so much money. It's impossible to completely rely on the state. We won't be able to achieve our goal if we don't rely on the masses. We probably have the highest number of state employees in the world ... We can't just rely on these people to do the work. We need to rely on the masses ... We have not utilized our resources efficiently. For instance, in Shanghai, during the school holiday seasons, you see students all over the streets, playing with slingshots, gang fighting, climbing trees. Why can't we organize them to do some street cleaning or to kill flies? The same goes for children in the countryside. We could teach them how to prevent infection. We could ask them to dig ditches. Dig a little each day. This is something we can do. It's important that we rely on the masses.[69]

Echoing his boss, in 1965 Zheng Gang, on behalf of the Nine-Man Subcommittee, instructed Sichuan province's health authorities 'to uphold the spirit of self-reliance. To fight the battle to prevent the disease by relying on grassroots resources, from grassroots party leadership to cadres, villagers and health workers. To eradicate schistosomiasis with or without little financial and personnel aid from the state.'[70]

Such projects seemed to cause logistical nightmares and could only be answered by ignoring them and evoking the mantra of local self-reliance, a euphemism for the simple inability to appropriately distribute scarce recourses from the urban to the rural arena. Yet, as Chen Zhiqian rightly argued: 'intermittent visits by mobile health teams simply cannot do the job. Without systematic organization, the tendency is toward hit-or-miss measures of prevention.'[71] Before the preventive program could be carried out, a true rural health system had to evolve.

'MORE PART-TIME GRASSROOTS HEALTH WORKERS FOR THE COUNTRYSIDE': THE BEGINNING OF THE BAREFOOT DOCTORS

In Chen's native Sichuan province, because of a huge deficit in health and medical care as well as a shortage of resources and increased morbidity, the provincial health authority had proceeded to franchise health care delivery, partly by prompting the training of greater numbers of grassroots, part-time health workers (health auxiliaries) to use traditional therapeutic medicine and to undertake public health work. This was well before any policy change emanating from Beijing. In January 1965, at a meeting for regional health officials, the provincial leadership instructed local authorities to engage in training part-time health workers for the countryside and the mines. The training would focus on traditional medicine and would take place in the less busy agricultural seasons; those enrolled in the course would work in the fields or the mines for five months of the year while attending training during the other seven months. In the context of the Socialist Education Campaign, to deliver health was also to deliver class struggle. Thus, not surprisingly, the training curriculum also consisted of studying the works of Chairman Mao as well as politics. These auxiliaries were nominated by the communes and the brigades as well as the mines, with an emphasis placed on their political reliability. They were, for instance, from middle (class) or poor peasant families. Unemployed educated youth from the cities could also enrol in the training program, provided they were from the correct 'class' with the 'right consciousness'.[72]

In the countryside, a number of communes also opened after-hours health training courses for villagers. In January 1965, within a few months, some sixty villagers in Gaoliang commune in Neijiang County had attended the commune's part-time, health training school where they learned to carry out first aid and preventive medicine. The latter included recognizing most common parasites and diseases and giving vaccinations, as well as managing night-soil and water.[73] By the autumn of 1965, according to an official estimate, the number of grassroots, part-time health workers (including midwives) in rural Sichuan grew to 25,000. Because Sichuan was the centre of the 'Third Front' area, the majority of village-level part-time health workers also took part in militia training. This included military paramedics in preparation for the feared war. In addition to carrying out public health work like schistosomiasis control and administering vaccinations, many would also treat minor illnesses and deliver babies.

The shift to local urgent care lifted health burdens down the line. With the growing number of grassroots, part-time health workers in parts of rural Sichuan, as the data gathered by provincial health authority suggests, the demand for hospital services as well as the services of mobile medical teams decreased by almost half in 1965. In Mianyang County's Zundao Commune, after becoming the model for successfully controlling schistosomiasis by following the mass line, as mentioned above, the commune authority invested in training more than 100 village-level part-time workers in 1965. In the autumn of that year, these health auxiliaries carried out small-pox vaccination for the entire commune within fifteen days. In addition, they treated 6,700 villagers for minor illnesses and injuries and thus saved villagers more than 690 *yuan* in hospital registration fees. 'It's great to have health workers at our village. We don't need to go all the way to the town to find a doctor. They saved us the hassle as well as money. Great idea,' villagers noted.[74] In northern Sichuan's Langzhong County, an official investigative report dated 1965 showed that the plan to build more rural hospitals and united clinics was not economically viable, nor was it what the rural popu-lation desired: Villagers want what's cheap and what works ... They prefer herbal medicine and they always decide on which doctor to see.' As such, Baishan Commune joined with a united clinic run by local doctors to train sixty village-level part-time health workers, including eight midwives. As part of the training, experienced local traditional healers were invited to share the medical knowledge that had been handed down in their families. After a seven-day train-ing, these health auxiliaries returned to their villages. In addition to health work, they were also assigned the responsibility of engaging their communities to take part in public health activities as well as to care for themselves. Village festivals and market days turned into public health information events, and villagers were even invited to produce public health ballads in the form of the local opera.[75]

In addition to training rural, grassroots, part-time health work-ers and encouraging communities to become involved in health planning, the authorities in Sichuan province also introduced the policy of allowing all medical institutions, from hospital to clinic to pharmacy, to procure medicinal herbs directly from brigades or individual villagers. By cutting out the 'middle-man' (the state), this reduced the cost of herbal remedies, thus enabling each com-mune or town to become 'self-sufficient' with its own pharmacies. For most villagers, this meant that, once again, traditional herbal remedies became affordable and accessible.[76] It also meant, how-ever, that it was difficult for the state to monitor the quality and distribution of herbal medicine, paving the way for an illicit and often questionable medical market to emerge in the following years, as will be discussed in the next chapter. This contributed to the increasing stigma around herbal medicine as less efficacious, while simultaneously reinforcing the idea that some type of local control or production in the arena of health care was at least possible, if not completely desirable.

Elsewhere, as in rural Henan province, the number of grassroots, part-time health workers was also increasing at a steady pace. Like Sichuan, Henan, China's agricultural heartland, had been hit by radical collectivization and the resultant famine. In the aftermath of the famine, most commune hospitals and clinics had been closed down because of staff cuts. After the latter half of 1963, as agriculture began to recover in Henan, a growing number of communes began to offer training courses off-season to villagers on how to treat minor illnesses and provide elementary acupuncture and some knowledge of common diseases and their prevention. Each brigade would choose one villager to attend such a course. Upon completing the course, he or she would bear the responsibility of providing basic health care to the villagers; this included treating minor illnesses and injuries as well as organizing public health activities. By the end of 1964, according to official data, there were more than 300,000 such grassroots, part-time health workers in Henan province, some at the village level, some at the commune level.[77]

In the meantime, some of the technical officials within the Ministry of Health began to see training more grassroots, part-time health workers as a way forward toward solving the rural health crisis and building an affordable and more sustainable rural health system. Reporting on the PUMC and the Chinese Academy of Medical Science medical mission to rural Hunan, the president of the Chinese Academy of Medical Science, Huang Jiashi, affirmed that 'medical teams from the city cannot completely change the picture of rural health or thoroughly solve the problem of medical care in the countryside. It is necessary to train local personnel.'[78] Even the experts had begun to see the double value in the decentralization of health care as an answer to what had seemed intractable problems of supply and demand.

FRANCHISING RURAL HEALTH CARE DELIVERY

In April 1965, the Party Committee of the Ministry of Health sent a consultation plan to expand the rural, grassroots, part-time health worker and midwife training program to all provinces as well as medical colleges. It foresaw each village having at least one health worker as well as a midwife within the next three to five years.[79] To a degree, this consultation plan mirrored a number of rural, grass-roots, part-time health worker programs that had already been set in motion in Sichuan, Henan, and in Zhejiang and Shanghai, as discussed earlier. The process of franchising rural health delivery was further catalyzed by the escalating political tension between Mao and Liu Shaoqi that had begun in 1962, partly triggered by the debacle of the Great Leap Forward. Liu, by publicly acknowledging that the famine was man-made, had undermined Mao's leadership.[80]

On 26 June 1965, in a conversation with Mao, Dr Li Zhishui, Mao's personal physician, remarked that published medical textbooks intended for popular readership neglected the fact that the majority of the population in China lived in the countryside. The occasion allowed Mao to attack his political opponent Liu Shaoqi, making him 'the enemy of the people' responsible for the appalling reality of the countryside. The Ministry of Health served as a more than convenient scapegoat. According to Mao, it had come under the control of the technocrats and bureaucrats who followed Liu Shaoqi's revisionist line: '[The Ministry of Health] is providing health care to only 15 per cent of the people in this nation. Of these 15 per cent, it is those lords in the national and local governments who receive the best care ... but the vast percentage of people in the countryside have no health care at all ... The Ministry of Health is not serving the people. It is not the people's ministry.' Medical education oriented toward training students to provide a high-tech, urban-based medical service was another target for Mao's attack. Quoting Mencius that 'believing everything in books is worse than having no books at all,' he urged the Ministry of Health to reform medical education by shortening the length of training and to promote practice-based learning. 'Medical students don't need to read so many books ... Medical schools don't have to enrol high school graduates. A primary school certificate should be sufficient to begin studying medicine. Medical skill is learned through practice. The type of doctor we need in the villages does not have to be so talented; they would still be better than witch doctors. Besides, this is the only type of doctor the villages can afford.' Having created scapegoats in the 'scandalous' Ministry of Health and 'useless' medical education, Mao once more established himself as the 'saviour of the people', hence the sole authority about health (and everything else) in the socialist state. He concluded that 'we should devote a major portion of our resources to what the masses need most ... Our future medical profession should concentrate its future work in the villages.'[81] After this conversation, Dr Li drew up a memo and sent it to the Ministry of Health and Peng Zhen, the mayor of Beijing and also a member of the Politburo. According to the doctor, writing in his memoir, he had no idea that this memo would become the famous 'June 26 Directive', the basis for decentralizing aspects of health care, which led to the launching of the nationwide Barefoot Doctor campaign three years later at the height of the Great Proletarian Cultural Revolution.[82]

Although this conversation between Mao and his doctor was not made public at the time, it prompted the Ministry of Health to switch on a green light to allow the franchising of health care delivery, a process that had already begun in parts of rural China, from Zhejiang and Jiangsu as well as in the suburbs of Shanghai in the east, to Sichuan in the remote southwest, and to Henan in the heartland. In the next couple of months, Qian Xinzhong met with top CCP leaders, including Zhou Enlai and Liu Shaoqi as well as Mao on different occasions, to finalize the decentralization of health care delivery in the countryside. Qian was rather anxious because he had just been promoted to minster of health. More important, as we have seen, the process of decentralization on the ground had already begun without approval from the top, and it seemed imperative to earn the endorsement of top leaders before he, and the Ministry of Health, could be penalized for allowing such grassroots health care development to flourish without official authorization from the centre.

While Primer Zhou and President Liu endorsed a partially centralized structure that relied on regularly sending urban medical teams to the countryside as well as promoting preventive medicine, the chairman showed greater interest in training village-level part-time health workers. For many months, Mao had been hearing news of peasants in the countryside becoming weary of the Socialist Education Campaign. One complaint concerned the harsh methods of the work teams sent by the authorities to 'assist' the campaign in the countryside. Mao was not pleased and began to contemplate replacing the Socialist Education Campaign with a new program that would rally the masses around him to promote and protect socialism in the countryside. In May 1965, a month prior to his conversation with Dr Li, Mao, at the age of seventy-one, climbed the

Jinggang Mountain in Jiangxi province, where he had led the revolutionary war of the masses some thirty years before. The trip cheered him up. He was pleased to see that the 'seed of revolution' he had planted had borne fruit, and he was determined to guard the 'fruit of the revolution' by once more mobilizing the masses on his side. At a planning meeting for the Third Five-Year Plan two weeks later, he warned against fuelling industrialization by increasing the state procurement quota for agricultural products: 'If we procure too much, people will rebel ... we mustn't push them too hard. The masses are the most important to us. We mustn't lose the heart of the people ... We will lose our way if we alienate the masses,' he stressed.[83]

Yet how to win back the masses – here, the peasants – who were individuals with little or no political ideology but self-interest? Mao, well versed in Chinese history, understood the propaganda power of promises of healing and health. Since the Yellow Turban Rebellion in the late second century, epidemic, war, and natural disasters, including famine, had been seen as signs leading to the downfall of many dynasties. In the post-famine PRC, with war potentially looming in the background, the collapse of rural health care could be the final mishap that might undermine the revolutionary project and bring down the political power of the Communist Party. Yet Mao also knew well that the Chinese understood that disease and illness were part of the human condition that demanded amelioration.[84] Beginning with the Zhang brothers, the leaders of the Yellow Turban Rebellion, almost all major sectarian insurgencies in Chinese history had involved some form of faith-healing. According to the received view of Chinese history, in the late Han period (25–220 CE), as a result of epidemics and natural disasters, the demand for medical treatment grew. Many people had complained that the cost of medicine was too high, especially considering the economic damage caused by various natural disasters, and while looking for cheaper alternatives they found faith-healers such as Zhang Jue, Zhang Bao, and Zhang Liang, the leaders of the Yellow Turban Rebellion. Those who were cured became 'believers' and joined the rebellion in different parts of the country.[85]

In 1934, when Mao's revolutionary army was under siege by the Nationalist army, in order to win the support of the masses, he had urged his comrades to 'be concerned with the wellbeing of the masses'. In his concluding speech that year at the Second National Congress of Workers and Peasants, he famously proclaimed that by becoming the 'true organizer of their well-being', from food to shelter, clothing, sickness and health, and marriage, 'the masses would rally around us and give us their warm support.'[86] Some twenty years later, in 1955, to rally the masses around him to support his socialist revolution in the countryside, Mao had called for the eradication of schistosomiasis. In 1965, in the aftermath of the Great Leap famine, in order to prove the infallibility of his socialist revolution project, he would attempt once again turn the masses into 'believers' with the promise of health and healing. Much to the Ministry of Health's surprise, during one of his conversations with Qian Xinzhong, the minister of health, and Zhang Kai from the Ministry of Health's Party Committee, Mao used the political history of 'magic medicine' to illustrate his point of the centrality of health for the political project: 'Magic medicine [the Yellow Turban leader Zhang Jue's healing techniques included using charm water as well as other forms of magic] has three advantages: firstly, it's safe, they won't poison anyone; secondly, it's cheap, it only costs a few coppers; thirdly, it's comforting; it makes people feel better,' he reasoned.[87]

But who would be trusted to be the 'apostle' to deliver the 'gospel' of healing and health? Certainly not the 'corrupt' health cadres and the 'bourgeois' doctors, who, according to Mao, were responsible for the inequality as well as the misery of the masses. His answer was the training of village-level, part-time health workers; they would spring from the masses. Standing at the opposite pole from the 'bourgeois' and 'impractical', therefore 'useless', expert, as well as the 'revisionist' officials, these health workers would form a new class in the countryside as the 'successors of the revolution' who would carry the spirit of the revolution forward. Mao went on at great length to discuss the criteria for choosing grassroots health workers: 'Middle school graduates would do. The important thing is they must be politically reliable. This is very important,' he reminded the Ministry of Health. With the looming war as another major fear, Mao also stressed the need to promote primary care as opposed to specialized medicine as well as to build an adequate health network that would cover all remote corners of the country: 'if the war breaks out, it won't be possible to attend hospitals in Beijing. [Planning] health work should be preparing for war ... When the war breaks out, doctors should be able to treat all kinds of illnesses as well as nurse the wounded. Specialized medicine is not good [for such a purpose].'[88] The new health workers would thus help to solve a wide range of existing and potential difficulties in post-famine China.

In September 1965, the CCP Central Committee approved the decentralization of rural health care delivery, and the nationwide rural, grassroots, part-time health worker training program leapt into top gear.[89] On the ground, however, there was confusion. Ever since the Great Leap Forward, the development of grassroots health organizations below the county level had been organized from the bottom up, first by the commune and then by the brigade. The latter came about with the introduction of the Sixty Articles to give production brigades the autonomy to manage their own production and labour more efficiently. It allowed local authorities to develop a grassroots health organization tailored for local conditions, such as those in Sichuan and Henan, as discussed earlier in this chapter, as well as in the regions around Zhejiang and Shanghai (see the previous chapter). Transforming it into a national program administered from the top down impeded local autonomy, thus actually undermining the initiatives. Decentralization turned out to be a centralized system with the grassroots health workers at the bottom of the health care pyramid, supervised by district or town hospitals and health centres. The provincial health departments responsible for implementing the Ministry of Health's policy coordinated and planned the grassroots health work, from training health auxiliaries to preventive activities. This often caused struggles on the ground. For instance, in many parts of the country the training schedule was decided by provincial and regional health departments, not by the production brigades, so it did not always parallel the agricultural seasons. When the training took place during the planting or harvesting seasons, it cost the brigades precious labour time, and so those brigades that were affected refused to send health workers to attend. Given that the same problem had previously occurred in the attempts at schistosomiasis control and similar public health work, it seemed that the centralized health authorities could not even learn from their own prior mistakes.

Uneven, often poor-quality training was another major problem. In a great rush to cover the entire countryside with health auxiliaries, in 1965 the Ministry of Health set the goal that over the next five to ten years, each production brigade would have at least one health worker equipped to attend to villagers' minor illnesses and be able to administer elementary acupuncture. On the next level up, each large brigade would have at least one part-time doctor who would be responsible for treating and diagnosing common diseases as well as leading public health work. In addition, each large brigade would train one or two midwives, whereas each commune would also have four to five well-trained doctors. Paradoxically, as Chen Zhiqian, who played a noteworthy role in developing public health in modern China, remarked, there was no guideline for developing a carefully structured system that linked these grassroots health workers to 'a hierarchy of more fully trained medical personnel at higher rural levels or to advanced scientific personnel in the cities'.[90] In Chen's native Sichuan province, there were in total 544,669 production brigades and 71,122 large brigades. This meant that across the entire province, if the Ministry of Health's policy were to be carried out successfully, there would be at least 540,000 village-level health auxiliaries and 70,000 midwives as well as 71,000 part-time doctors. This was a giant leap up from the 25,000 grassroots, part-time health workers/midwives the local authorities had already trained. Meeting the Ministry of Health's target meant an explosion of crash training courses, with many of them overlapping each other. With an emphasis on quantity, most of these courses compromised quality. The same problems that had emerged with the political goal of 'eradicating schistosomiasis within seven years' reoccurred. The inadequate training affected the efficiency of these health workers, and even after their training many did not have the basic skills to even diagnose diseases or administer drugs.[91]

Aside from uneven, often poor-quality training and by putting an emphasis on quantity, the program was further hampered by the cultural sensibilities of local populations in different parts of the country. Further south in Yunnan province's Ruili County, across the border from Myanmar, Zhimai, a fifteen-year-old Jingpo girl from an ethnic group who lived in the hills between Myanmar and Yunnan, was sent by her brigade to attend the health auxiliary/midwife training course at a local health school. Because her father was a devoted Christian convert, Zhimai was the only girl in the village who had completed primary school education.* For this reason, she was chosen to be the brigade's part-time health worker and the new-style midwife so that the brigade could fulfil

* Christian missionaries working amongst subaltern groups such as the Jingpo promoted education for girls.

the national requirement of at least one brigade/one health worker plus one new-style midwife. But Zhimai did not want to become a health worker or midwife; she wanted to learn how to weave cloth, not how to give injections because she feared them. Furthermore, in her village there were special childbirth rituals, and many of the villagers considered the new-style medicalized childbirth promoted by the PRC's public health authorities as taboo. In the end, the brigade head bullied her into attending the course. During the training, she could not face examining the different parts of the vagina; she felt ashamed, and during her first practical training session she was so scared that her body could not stop shaking. She sweated so much that someone in her class had to help her by wiping her face. In addition, because too many people were enrolled in the training, there were barely any chances to practise what she had learned. Yet, after only two training sessions on delivering babies, she was sent back to her village to serve as the front-line health worker.[92]

Despite many initial drawbacks, with the advent of the Great Proletarian Cultural Revolution, which began in the summer of 1966, the political importance of the rural village health worker program grew exponentially. In 1974, Wang Guizhen would become the PRC's 'model Barefoot Doctor' representing her country and speaking to the Twenty-Seventh World Health Assembly on China's Barefoot Doctor program. She had been in her twenties when the 'Learn from Lei Feng' campaign first began in 1963. Inspired by this hero, as her hagiography relates, she aspired to 'serve the people'. She was awarded the accolade of model worker for being a 'reliable successor of the revolution' and for that reason was chosen to attend the part-time village health worker training. After four months of training, she returned to her village in Chuansha County, Jiangsu province. In addition to attending to the villagers' health needs and leading local public health work, Wang worked barefoot in the paddy field like other villagers. Villagers nicknamed her 'Barefoot Doctor'. In the beginning, the brigade cadre admonished the villagers: 'Guizhen is our Lei Feng style model worker. Don't nickname her Barefoot Doctor!' But he was wrong. Three years later, at the height of the Great Proletarian Cultural Revolution, Wang Guizhen would become a national hero just like Lei Feng, and Chairman Mao would turn the nickname 'Barefoot Doctor' into a revolutionary brand.

THE BAREFOOT DOCTOR AS A
'NEWLY EMERGED REVOLUTIONARY THING'

In the final months of 1964, approaching the end of the Year of Dragon – the Dragon being the Year of Upheaval in the Chinese calendar – Mao had become increasingly dissatisfied with the results of the Socialist Education Campaign. He had also become weary of how Liu Shaoqi was using the campaign to overshadow his leadership. In his last attempt to prove to the socialist world that he alone was at the vanguard of the proletarian revolution fighting revisionism, in the summer of 1966 the aged Mao went for another symbolic swim in the Yangtze River and then launched the Great Proletarian Revolution. He began by delegating the task of purging those he considered undesirable elements in the higher level of power to young radicals – namely, university and high and middle school students, who became known as the Red Guards. In the next months, unprecedented chaos erupted across the country. China was on the verge of a civil war.[93] In the summer of 1968, Mao lost his patience and blamed the Red Guards for personally letting him down by destroying his revolution.

The problem with the Red Guards, according to Mao, was that the schools and universities continued to be dominated by the 'bourgeois intellectuals'. To liquidate the intellectuals and end their domination at schools and colleges, he brought in workers with the support of the army. He mandated sole power to them to bring about an educational revolution and transform the intellectuals' world view. They would build an 'army of proletarian intellectuals'. He also urged schools and colleges to be filled with students 'selected from workers and peasants with practical experience. After their study at school for several years they should return to practical production.'[94] In the countryside, Mao delegated the task of carrying out his educational revolution to the poor and middle (class) peasants – 'the steadfast ally of the working class'. On the basis of two investigative reports from his chief polemicist Yao Wenyuan, one of which was about the Barefoot Doctors in Chuansha County's Jiangzhen Commune, just outside of Shanghai, he launched the 'education revolution' in the countryside: 'The majority of the students trained in the old schools and colleges can integrate themselves with workers, peasants, and soldiers, and some have made changes and innovations; they must, however, under the guidance of the correct line, be re-educated by workers, peasants, and soldiers and thoroughly change their old ideology. Such intellectuals will be welcomed by the workers, peasants, and soldiers. Is there anyone who doesn't believe me? Look at the case of the Barefoot Doctor at Chuansha County's Jiangzhen Commune,' Mao proclaimed. Despite the title of the report, 'The Orientation of the Revolution in Medical Education as Seen in the Growth of "Barefoot Doctors"', Mao made clear that the true goal was the revolutionary transformation of the entire education system. Following the chairman's instruction, Yao published the report, accompanied by the editorial 'On the Re-education of Intellectuals', in the 10 September (1968) edition of the Party's *Red Flag* magazine.[95]

When Yao Wenyuan brought the report about the Barefoot Doctors to the chairman, Yao was also seeking to eliminate Wei Wenbo's influences in the health departments in Shanghai and eastern China. Wei was one of the chief opponents of the Cultural Revolutionary Group in Shanghai. After Ke Qingshi died a premature death in 1965, Wei succeeded him as the party boss of the eastern China region with additional responsibility to oversee the region's public health work, including the Anti-Schistosomiasis Campaign. Wei had been Ke's deputy for the campaign. From the onset of the Great Proletarian Cultural Revolution, Wei had not seen eye-to-eye with Zhang Chunqiao, the former head of propaganda for eastern China, and Yao Wenyuan. Both Zhang and Yao would become powerful leading figures of the Cultural Revolution Group. In autumn 1966, Wei intervened to prevent the Red Guards from Beijing going to hospitals in Shanghai to cause chaos, but his efforts would eventually fail. By the end of 1966, with the support of Zhang Chunqiao and Yao Wenyuan, Shanghai's Cultural Revolution rebels, led by Wang Hongweng, who would also become a member of the Cultural Revolution Group, ransacked Shanghai and seized power. Wei Wenbo was removed from office and publicly denounced for being a 'traitor' and the 'agent of China's Khrushchev Liu Shaoqi'.* But the purge did not stop there. 'Wei is a traitor. The urgent task is to clean the ranks,' Zhang urged. For the next months and years, the ongoing campaign to expose Wei's crimes continued to allow the rooting out of the 'traitor's' influences, as well as those of 'secret

---

* In August 1966, Liu Shaoqi was denounced as the number one revisionist in the Communist Party. He was put under house arrest.

agents' in different government departments in Shanghai and eastern China – from art to education and health. By rooting out the revisionist influences and their agents in these government institutions, the Cultural Revolution Group would also fill them with 'fresh new blood'. The report about the Barefoot Doctors in Jiangzhen Commune thus opened by condemning the 'agent of China's Khrushchev in Shanghai's public health' who 'unscrupulously pushing a counter-revolutionary revisionist line in medical and public health work, made a malicious report viciously slandering the health workers in the production brigades and ordering them to drop their medical work. The new-type public health force created in the period of the Great Leap Forward in the rural areas was thus destroyed; the number of health workers, originally over 11,900, was slashed to just over 300.' On other occasions, Wei and Liu Shaoqi were both accused of pushing their revisionist line in health work, and it was claimed that their 'revisionist line' was responsible for the failure of the Anti-Schistosomiasis Campaign, even though Liu had had little direct involvement in the PRC's public health work. To fight against the 'revisionist line in medical and public health work', the report quoted revised excerpts from the memo of Mao's conversation with Dr Li Zhishui: 'On 26 June 1965, Chairman Mao issued his brilliant instruction: "In medical and health work, put the stress on the rural areas."'* Mao was credited with giving birth to the Barefoot Doctors. With the growing number of Barefoot Doctors, the report trumpeted that the 'health protection network was thus developed all around'. The report went further by proclaiming that 'with the Great Proletarian Cultural Revolution, many more Barefoot Doctors have emerged. Tempered in the storms of class struggle and the struggle between the two lines, this force has expanded and been consolidated and made much progress.'96 The Cultural Revolution subsumed the Barefoot Doctor program, but in the meantime, because a huge number of experts and public health officials had been purged following Wei Wenbo's downfall, there was no one to lead the schistosomiasis control work in eastern China. In Chuansha, the Barefoot Doctor model county, all grassroots schistosomiasis stations were closed.

* In the beginning of the Cultural Revolution, this memo was seized by the Revolutionary Committee for All Medical and Health Institutions in Beijing (北京医药卫生界大联合革命委员会). The committee subsequently published it in one of the Great Proletarian Cultural Revolution pamphlets, *Red Medical Battle Bulletin* (红医战报), in their attack on the Ministry of Health.

The Barefoot Doctors had replaced the bourgeois experts in delivering the people's health.[97]

Four days after its first appearance in the *Red Flag* magazine on 10 September 1968, the same report about the Barefoot Doctors of the Jiangzhen Commune appeared on the front page of the *People's Daily* and then a week later in the English-language magazine *Peking Review*, the PRC's official propaganda tool targeting the outside world.[98] In October, at the Eighth Central Committee's Twelfth Plenary Session, Liu Shaoqi was publicly condemned as a 'renegade, traitor, and scab' and expelled from the party. At the same meeting, it was also proposed that the middle-level 'revolutionary intellectuals' such as Barefoot Doctors and school teachers would be nominated to participate in the National People's Congress, replacing bourgeois intellectuals. Having been reconfigured as a 'newly emerged thing (新生事物) that grew out of class struggle' as well as the struggle between revolutionary and revisionist lines, the rural, grassroots, part-time health worker training program took on a new political life. From then on it became universally known as the 'Barefoot Doctor' program: Mao's 'revolutionary approach to health'.

Health care had been a political keystone in the rhetoric of the founding of the PRC. By the 1960s, the state had moved to a greater if somewhat uneven ability to achieve actual health improvements over the primarily propagandistic claims of previous periods. In spite of the collapse of the centralized health system as a result of the famine, the Great Proletarian Cultural Revolution meant that the CCP under Mao's leadership had a more secure position, and economic development was beginning to become more consistent. The absence of any political alternatives to the state, especially after the official break with the USSR after 1962, meant that conflicts and inconstancies were seen as problems to be resolved rather than calls for the alteration or abandonment of the Maoist utopian goals. Health care remained in all cases a central concern of individuals, party, and state.

8

Delivering Rural Health:
From the State to Communities

RE-COLLECTIVIZATION AND
THE CO-OPERATIVE MEDICAL SERVICE

Despite the disastrous result of the Great Leap Forward, Mao continued to hold on to the view that substituting labour for capital was the key to achieving rapid 'socialist transformation' in China.[1] In the aftermath of the famine resulting from the Great Leap and of the 'Big Brother' Soviet Union cancelling its aid and withdrawing from major development projects, Mao evoked the spirit of the 'Foolish Old Man Who Removed the [Taihang and Wangwu] Mountains' at the Dazhai Commune and enshrined the 'Spirit of Dazhai'. Located at the foothills of the Taihang Mountain in the impoverished corner of Shanxi province, villagers at the Dazhai People's Commune had supposedly transformed arid earth into fertile agricultural fields without any aid from the state. Setting Dazhai as a model, Mao once more called upon the people's power, according to him China's most valuable asset and the 'only motivating force in history'.* In December 1964, the entire

---

* 'The Foolish Old Man Who Removed the Mountains' was originally an ancient fable from the body of Daoist texts known as *Liezi*. Mao first evoked the 'Spirit of the Foolish Old Man Who Removed the Mountains' in 1945, during the Chinese Civil War, in his concluding speech at the Seventh National Congress of the Communist Party of China (CCP). For Mao and the CCP, 'imperialism' and 'feudalism' were the two major obstacles – the two mountains – they needed to remove in order to achieve their revolutionary goal. He urged the CCP to unite with the masses of the Chinese people – the 'God' in this case – to fight against imperialism and feudalism. In 1958, at height of the Great Leap Forward, he again advocated 'the high spirit, strong morale and firm determination' that, according to him, had made 'the high mountain bow its head and the river yield the way'.

population of the countryside was called to 'learn from Dazhai' by practising 'self-reliance' in order to transform their lives with their bare hands. This simultaneously led to a process of devolution in rural health care delivery as villagers across China were left to their own devices to come up with the means to pay for the state-guaranteed social welfare, from education to health care.

Partially catalyzed by the official 'To Learn from Dazhai' campaign, but, even more importantly, driven by villagers and many grassroots cadres' desire to improve daily life, across different parts of rural China – from Hubei province on the bank of Yangtze River, to Shanxi province in the arid north, Sichuan province in the mountainous southwest, and the suburbs of Beijing – communes and brigades came up with similar but not identical schemes to help finance the costs of villagers' medical and health care. In northern Sichuan's Langzhong County, for instance, after the collapse of the commune health system some doctors from the former Baishan commune hospital used the social capital of the community to service villagers. With money donated by villagers, they purchased basic drugs and rented a small room where they opened the Baishan United Clinic. Partly to reduce the cost of drugs but equally in order to comply with the villagers' preference for folk herbal remedies, these doctors also sought out traditional formulas. To utilize local resources as well as to engage the community, the doctors and the commune jointly ran training courses to empower individual villagers to become caregivers for their own village. Villagers welcomed this initiative: it saved them the hassle of having to travel to town hospitals or clinics as well as money on drugs. Equally important, if not more so, they were more comfortable with traditional remedies as well as caregivers in their own communities who were familiar to them and whom they trusted. Many villagers also volunteered in their spare time to help with the refurbishing of the clinic room as well as constructing beds and other furniture for the clinic.[2] Similarly, in Xier Hedao Commune in the suburb of Beijing and in Xingao Commune in Shanxi province's Dai County, doctors from commune clinics – calling on their own knowledge of folk medicine as well as their desire to reduce the cost of treatment – regularly went into the hills to collect locally grown medicinal herbs.[3] Yet it was the Leyuan (which literally translates as 'Happy Garden') Commune's Co-operative Medical service model that fit best with the overall 'revolutionary' agenda of the time, and it was this model that was subsequently rolled out as a national program.

Already, in October 1959 at the height of the Great Leap Forward, in a conversation with a Polish delegation, Mao boasted about the advantages of the collective economy, more specifically the People's Commune in the People's Republic of China (PRC): 'With the People's Commune, we have achieved things which were unattainable [under the private economy], from commune-run reservoirs to factories, schools, and nurseries.'⁴ As of the summer of 1968, in the midst of the Great Proletarian Cultural Revolution and assisted by revolutionary committees in the countryside, Mao waged a 'revolutionary' war to revert the rural economy back to collectivization. To re-collectivize the rural economy entailed abolishing private plots as well as removing from individual villages – the production brigade, in this case – the autonomy to manage their own production and labour. Accordingly, the aim was to foster villagers' collective spirit to 'gradually bring about a complete break with the old concept of private ownership', thus 'realizing the goal of communism'. This included building or reinstating the collective welfare system, from health to education.⁵ Under such conditions, during the last quarter of 1968 and the first quarter of 1969 Mao's chief polemicist Yao Wenyuan orchestrated the appearance in the *People's Daily* of a series of articles praising the collective economy. Among them was the report (published in the newspaper on 5 December 1968) about how the Leyuan Commune had achieved free health and medical care for all the villagers by organizing a Co-operative Medical service. According to the official version of the Leyuan story, in 1966, as part of the Great Proletarian Revolution fighting against the revisionist power over health and medicine, villagers at the Leyuan Commune in Hubei province's Changyang County organized a Co-operative Medical service to provide their own inexpensive and effective medical care. To join the service, each villager contributed one *yuan* (RMB) each year toward the collective medical fund. For each contributing villager, their production brigade also added 10 per cent toward the fund. By joining the Co-operative Medical service, villagers would enjoy free medical care, ranging from therapy to drugs. As with the village health worker scheme, this initially unique, grassroots innovation was reconfigured as another 'newly emerged thing' that the Great Proletarian Revolution brought to health work.⁶ In the next months, the Rural Co-operative Medical System (合作医疗 RCMS) was implemented throughout rural China. It became the only approved system for rural health care delivery between 1968 and 1983. Villagers in rural China, many living in extreme poverty, were forced to help finance the Co-operative Medical service as well as the official Barefoot Doctor program.[7] Anyone who resisted or doubted the efficacy of Co-operative Medicine and the Barefoot Doctors would be charged with the political offence of 'not following Chairman Mao's revolutionary line' or sabotage. And sabotage brought draconian punishment.

The official Co-operative Medical service and the Barefoot Doctor program, analogous to the Anti-Schistosomiasis Campaign, were enacted at the centre of political power. In the process of being implemented, they frequently evoked a variety of responses from below that were often at odds with one another, given the sheer size and vast diversity of the country. When these conflicts were significant enough, they could lead to the non-implementation or the complete alteration of the official program. Although official accounts depicted the Barefoot Doctors and Co-operative Medical service in a highly favourable light, I have uncovered evidence from previously unseen archival documents from nine different provinces, as well as through conducting oral interviews with former Barefoot Doctors, villagers, local cadres, and health officials and experts, that suggest that the reality on the ground was often radically different from the official account.[*] Indeed, any positive or negative outcome of the Co-operative Medical service, as well as the perseverance (or lack of it) of the Barefoot Doctors, had much more to do with multifaceted factors on the ground than on the government policy superimposed from above. Often, locally based health workers and their cadre, as well as the villagers, were unaffected by the revolutionary vision of Mao and the Communist Party. While many were quick at discerning the advantages or disadvantages of the newly introduced health services, they did so on their own terms. In the process of implementation, these local actors regularly circumvented the official program to accommodate for local conditions and their own needs or to fit official

---

* These interviews were conducted by myself and others at the Institute of Health at the Kunming Medical University and Yunnan Health and Development Research Association (YHDRA) between 2000 and 2016. The interviews conducted by the team at the YHDRA are available in Zhang Kaining, Wen Yiqun, and Liang Ping, eds, *From Barefoot Doctors to Village Doctors* (Kunming: Yunnan Renmin chubanshe 2002). The English translations are by me.

policy into existing local schemes. As one former Barefoot Doctor from Shanxi province stated: 'Indeed, there was official policy regarding the [Barefoot Doctors]. When being implemented, many aspects of the policy were ignored. What has been implemented on the ground resembled nothing of what is said in the official documents.'[8] Although many of the previously existing grassroots health programs were rebranded as the Barefoot Doctor program and were then financed by what became universally known as the Co-operative Medical service, they remained specific to their locality and were noticeably different from those in other parts of China. In addition, folk healers ranging from witch doctors to exorcists and other ritual healers (most of them operating on their own) coexisted alongside the Barefoot Doctors in supporting sick villagers and their families through prayer and exorcism as well as in community and domestic healing rituals.

Social scientists have examined in detail the strengths and weaknesses of the policy design of the Maoist official health care.[9] However, we know very little about how both the Co-operative Medical service and the Barefoot Doctor program were carried out in practice and how they were experienced on the ground. By shifting our focus from the policy at the top to the diverse aspects of support, accommodation, and resistance on the ground during the process of implementation, we can get much closer to the pulse of everyday life. In doing so, we can better understand complex and often strikingly dissimilar experiences of a whole range of individuals struggling to cope with illness and disease when the state system failed to deliver the promise of 'health care for all', since such a system – with state support in addition via the county hospital – was delivering on the promise, with the state as the enabler if not the source of finance. By exploring how state health ideologies were communicated, circumvented, or sometimes simply ignored on the ground, we can see how the world views of not only the villagers but also of those grassroots cadres in charge of policy implementation and the caregivers – the Barefoot Doctors in this case – who were officially responsible for health delivery affected the actual outcome of the health of individuals and communities. This grassroots data is essential, for it provides an insight much more effectively than repeating the claims formulated in the central health policy as promulgated by the state.

THE 'DAWDLING' CO-OPERATIVE MEDICAL SERVICE
AND INEQUALITIES IN THE PEOPLE'S COMMUNE

After agricultural collectivization was relaunched in the Chinese countryside in the late 1960s during the Great Proletarian Cultural Revolution, villagers once more lost their enthusiasm for agricultural work. 'Sweating in the private plots, while dawdling in the collective fields' was a popular saying in Shanxi province at the time. Here, in the arid land where the 'Spirit of Dazhai' was born, more villagers were seen spending their time idling when working in the collective fields.[10] In S's village at the foothills of the Great Wall, the widespread problem of slacking, taken together with the chronic drought, meant the village was too poor to generate sufficient income to finance the Co-operative Medical service. Nevertheless, the brigade authority was determined to transform itself into a Co-operative Medicine model: 'To turn our village into a model, the whole village were involved. The big brigade sent us lots of medical equipment to make it look good,' S recalled. This Co-operative Medicine 'model' turned out to be a 'Potemkin's village': for many years, the village health centre remained an empty, dark room with no drugs, staffed by S, the Barefoot Doctor who had no basic medical training. It was only after 1978, when villagers were given the sole responsibility for making a profit or loss, that they were able to generate sufficient income to finance the Co-operative Medical service. Only then was the village health centre able to stock up on drugs, and it was only then that S received his basic training in medicine and care. To earn a livelihood for himself so that he could continue caring for the villagers, S admitted he had to introduce various charges for drugs and services because otherwise 'Co-operative Medical service would never work'. He was not ambiguous about this at all.[11]

Further south in Shanxi province's agricultural heartland, the Co-operative Medical service at Qin County's Koutou village ended after only a single year. It was economically unviable, and the villagers did not want it. At the time, Koutou village had about 1,000 inhabitants. According to the policy, to join the service each villager would contribute one *yuan* per year. Together, the village Co-operative Medicine fund generated just over 2,000 *yuan* annually to cover the villagers' medical costs. But the village cadres and the village accountant worked out very quickly that the 2,000 *yuan* would not go very far if even one or two villagers needed hospital care. With no other funds, and being unwilling or unable to subsidize the Co-operative Medical service, they modified the government policy by slashing the amount of reimbursement for hospital care in half. This meant that seriously ill villagers were denied any necessary treatment, since they could not afford the other half of the hospital fee. Between 1969 and 1970, Koutou village's Co-operative Medical service only funded the cost of village Barefoot Doctors and some vaccinations. After one year, most of the villagers refused to enrol in the Co-operative Medical service, since they saw no personal benefit in doing so. More important, as in the case of both S's village and Koutou village, under the People's Commune system, because individual villagers were denied the opportunity to make a profit by participating in the marketplace, most of them were too poor to afford even the one *yuan* health care premium. 'When I was the village cadre [in the mid-1970s], most villagers were very poor. As such I was unable to collect any money for the Co-operative Medical Fund,' recalled L, the village's former Barefoot Doctor and cadre.[12] Clearly, it was not so much health disparity and the state's lack of resources but rather the collective economic system that disincentivized villagers to engage in the service. How can they be blamed for not looking after their well-being when they had no actual access to basic health and care?

Equally, the political and social hierarchy in the People's Commune gave the village cadre and the Barefoot Doctor enormous power to decide how the Co-operative Medical fund was spent, whether and how to absorb the cost when there were shortages in the fund, and how to determine who had access to the service. The overt abuse of power and misuse of the services were regular features that rendered the universally promised Co-operative Medical service an empty political declaration. In such cases, the health disparity reflected political and social inequality in the People's Commune. On the one hand, even the Rural Co-operative Medical System (the RCMS), as enforced by the welfare state, was unable to protect the most vulnerable villagers from the structural inequality because they lacked social capital, in this case a good relationship with cadres and Barefoot Doctors. On the other hand, the radical re-engineering of the rural health delivery system, even if it seemed a positive innovation at the time, often created social stress as the insecurity led to ever-increasing intolerance.* As a result, instead of sharing resources as the system was designed for them to do, villagers and cadres regularly, and often viciously, competed for resources. At the shore of the Korean peninsula in eastern China, in the Daotian big brigade in Shandong province's Shouguang County (nowadays Shouguang Municipal), a former local cadre recalled that under the RCMS, because the power of managing the Co-operative Medical fund was solely controlled by the cadres of the big brigade, only those who had a good relationship with brigade cadres or Barefoot Doctors had any access to the promised service. Although in theory the RCMS entitled all villagers to an equal amount of reimbursement if they needed hospital care, in practice the amount of reimbursement depended not on the actual cost of hospital care but on whether the villager had a good relationship with the brigade party secretary. Only those who had a rapport with the brigade party secretary could get him to sign the piece of paper that entitled them to claim the cost of their hospital care. 'Ordinary villagers who did not have a good relationship with the party secretary did not even bother to try making a claim. They knew it was a waste of their time. They had no chance of claiming back the medical cost,' this former village cadre explained. With limited amounts of drugs as well as funds, 'ordinary villagers could only get painkillers for free. If they wanted more expensive drugs such as antibiotics, they would have to pay for it out of their own pocket.'[13] On the other side of the Korean peninsula, in Laoshao County outside of Qingdao, one former village cadre there also admitted that unfairness and abuse of power was fairly common: 'There was a shortage of drugs. Only those who had face [a good relationship with the cadres] had access to good and expensive drugs ... Villagers regularly complained about having no access to medicine, particularly good medicine.' Here, as elsewhere in China, the Barefoot Doctors were nominated by the local cadres. In most cases, they were chosen to be the Barefoot Doctor because they had good relationships with the local cadres and were seen as politically reliable. This had an effect on their service; in most cases, they were

---

* For centuries, villagers in China had sought medical counsel and obtained medication from fellow villagers who had greater knowledge than they did – from family practitioners, scholars, Daoist or Buddhist priests, village witches, exorcists, and other ritual healers.

more eager to serve the local cadres who appointed them and less inclined to help ordinary villagers. 'At the time, villagers were at the mercy of the Barefoot Doctor. They could not simply request services from the Barefoot Doctors,' the same cadre reflected.[14]

Furthermore, the lack of experience and resources of the grassroots cadres, and the conflicting interests, often meant that village cadres were incompetent in managing the Co-operative Medical service and the Barefoot Doctors program. They were often focused only on immediate gain. In this way, they mirrored the shift in the schistosomiasis control programs from the long range of the prevention projects to the more immediate models of treatment. Their incompetence would increase health inequality, even if this was unintended. As one retired village cadre from Shanxi province's Shiling County, responsible for managing the village health work in the 1970s, reflected: 'Most of us village cadres had little education, and we had no experience in health work. We were simply fumbling in the dark. We had not anticipated there would be so many issues. We only tried to solve them when they caused real problems. Most of them were badly dealt with. There were a lot of problems regarding how to manage money, equipment, and drugs as well as the quality control of Barefoot Doctors. Maybe that's why the Co-operative Medical service collapsed.'[15]

In Henan Province's Qingyang County, a government investigative report in 1973 showed that many brigade cadres failed to see the advantage of the Co-operative Medical service. Their view was that 'The Co-operative Medical service would not make any difference. Those villagers who could afford medical costs don't need any help in the first place. For many poor villagers, the Co-operative Medical service would not be much help as it can't [generate enough money to] pay for their total medical cost. It would be better to leave villagers alone to pay for their own medical cost. If they could not afford it, they could then apply for help from the big brigade.'[16] Up until 1975, because of the cadres and the villagers' lack of interest as well as funds, about 20 per cent of village-run Co-operative Medical services in Qingyang County failed. Even among the other 80 per cent, there were many complaints that the Co-operative Medical service had disadvantaged those most in need of help. The problem was said to be so widespread throughout the entire province that in 1975 Henan provincial authority waged a campaign to rectify 'the false attitudes and bad management' on the ground.[17] Rectification, however, ended with blaming 'corrupt' cadres and Barefoot Doctors. It failed to address the actual obstacles that crippled the RCMS in the first place: instead of utilizing existing local medical resources and motivating communities, the RCMS depended heavily on specialized urban medical facilities such as hospitals, while Barefoot Doctors were supervised and supported by hospital doctors and academics from urban medical schools. In the case of Henan province, as elsewhere in China, the demand for hospital care often exceeded capacity. To extend their services to an increasing number of non-urban patients, many already crowded hospitals charged non-urban patients radically more than the urban patients. This made the RCMS impractical, unviable, and undesirable.[18]

Furthermore, grassroots cadres at the village level often prioritized improving agricultural productivity over health equality. When there was a shortage of resources, they would use the Co-operative Medical fund for other purposes, such as water conservation. In the case of one village in Shanxi province's Qin County, after the village cadres misspent the money collected for the Co-operative Medical fund on other purposes, the village could not afford to pay the Barefoot Doctor his work points (wage). In order to support his family, the Barefoot Doctor was forced to leave the village and seek his livelihood elsewhere, and the already crumbling village Co-operative Medical service fell apart completely.[19] The experience of villagers across rural China was so diverse and often so negative that the only force that saw an overall improvement in the health care was the central administration of the CCP, which made claims of continuously improving health care outcomes, outcomes that were based, however, on the manipulation of data rather than on the actual experience of the people. However, the reality seeped out, even into the official accounts, as the local experiences became ever less satisfactory.

'WHY SHOULD I BE PAID LESS?'

Across the entire countryside, according to the official data presented at the National Health Conference in 1973, by the end of 1971 about two-thirds of the Co-operative Medical service had failed to deliver what had been promised.[20] Low pay plus heavy workloads and long working hours, as well as poor career prospects and job satisfaction, were identified as some of the major factors contributing to low retention rates for the Barefoot Doctors, undermining the effectiveness of the Co-operative Medical service on the ground.[21] H was the Barefoot Doctor in a village not far from the Yunnan provincial capital, Kunming. In an interview in 2002, H recalled bitterly how she had always received less food compared to other villagers who did full-time agricultural work: 'For nine years when I was the Barefoot Doctor, I took care of villagers day and night ... in the end I could not earn enough food to feed my children.'[22] Even in Chuansha County, outside of Shanghai, the national model for the Barefoot Doctors program, various official investigations conducted in the 1970s consistently showed that poor pay and a heavy workload had resulted in a growing number of Barefoot Doctors abandoning their duties and seeking their livelihood elsewhere or engaging in other activities to supplement their income.[23] By 1979, the report produced by the Shanghai Municipal Health Bureau showed that there were only 218 Barefoot Doctors left in Chuansha County compared to 750 prior to 1968. In a huge number of brigades, there was no one on the ground to deliver health services, from prevention to care.[24] An earlier investigative report from 1973 by the Chuansha County authority stated that a number of Barefoot Doctors in Jiangzhen Commune, the Barefoot Doctors flagship commune, complained that being a Barefoot Doctor made them economically worse off. Some moaned: 'Why should I be paid less than professional doctors? I would get paid more by doing something else.'[25] To supplement his income, one Barefoot Doctor at the Xiaoyu brigade was often seen dropping his medical kit by the road to take up some work as a builder or to help other villagers fishing.[26] In a more recent interview, one former cadre from a village outside of Qingdao in Shandong province summoned it up in a nutshell: 'Because there was no incentive, the majority of Barefoot Doctors were not proactive, and they showed no interest in learning. For them it was like being a monk in the temple who would go on tolling the bell as long as he is a monk. The only time they would show some enthusiasm was in front of cadres.'[27]

The problem of poor pay was so severe that it prompted some Barefoot Doctors in Youai brigade in Jiangsu province to write a letter of complaint to the editor of the *People's Daily* (10 November 1972), petitioning the state to intervene by making sure the Barefoot Doctors were paid an amount of work points equal to that of other labourers. The letter revealed that despite their increased political status, Barefoot Doctors, as well as other rural health workers, suffered structural inequality as the result of the rural work point system that prioritized agricultural work over health work. In the original design, the idea was that Barefoot Doctors should spend about a third of their time working in the fields; it had not been envisaged as a full-time job. But in the process of implementation, with the increasing political importance of the program as well as to save expenditure on public health activities, in many places being a Barefoot Doctor became a full-time job but without full pay.

The official propaganda that extolled Barefoot Doctors as 'revolutionary', 'working class' health workers, as opposed to the bourgeois medical professionals, further exacerbated this problem. Slogans such as Barefoot Doctors 'wearing no shoes' and 'covering their hands with dirty earth' allowed many brigades to impose heavy labouring rotas that demanded the Barefoot Doctor work in the agricultural fields for a certain number of days each year. In 1971, in order to uphold its national model status, Jiangzhen Commune launched the 'to learn from Wang Guizhen' campaign to prevent Barefoot Doctors turning into bourgeois doctors by spending too much time sitting in the village health station: 'their hands had turned pale and soft, and there was less dirt on their bare feet.' This campaign brought about a rota system, which required all Barefoot Doctors to spend at least one-third of the year doing agricultural work, regardless of the size of the village and the load of their public health duties. This resulted in there often being insufficient time for the Barefoot Doctor to care for villagers or to complete the necessary public health tasks.[28] Throughout the country, from Shaanxi province's Bin County in the northwest to Youai brigade in Jiangsu province in the east, a number of Barefoot Doctors complained collectively that the heavy workload, with the farming responsibilities as well as managerial tasks, had prevented them from doing health work. In the case of some villages in Bin County, because Barefoot Doctors were often away attending meetings or working in agricultural fields, sick villagers had to travel to the county hospital or seek help elsewhere. This, in turn, undermined the local Co-operative Medical service.

In addition, many Barefoot Doctors complained that constantly undertaking diverse tasks gave them little or no job satisfaction.[29] In Henan province's Minquan County, partly because of the labour shortage problem, the local authority increased the Barefoot Doctor agricultural rota to 240 days a year. For this to work, different villagers would have to take turns being the Barefoot Doctor. This not only led to confusion and the neglect of their health duties, but it also prevented them from receiving any consistent health training or even completing the training, since their agricultural work rota often ran into conflict with the training schedule.[30] Being a Barefoot Doctor turned out not to be a fulfilling role in a commune that prioritized production, since agricultural production was demanded by the authorities over everything else.

GENDER INEQUALITY

Structural inequality also led to a pay gap between male and female Barefoot Doctors that hampered the enthusiasm of the women in particular in delivering health care. Recently, Fang Xiaoping claimed, based on a case study of a Zhejiang village, that the Barefoot Doctors program granted young women in the countryside equal rights to study medicine and to participate in the rural public health program.[31] Yet as early as 1973, an official report showed that among eight large brigades in Jiangzhen Commune – the national model for the Barefoot Doctors program – the total pay gap between male and female Barefoot Doctors amounted to more than 1,000 work points.[32] Such misalignment had less to do with any policy design at the top but, rather, reflected the deep-seated cultural bias as well as the default of the work points system, which undervalued female labour in general. As with the female mill workers in Great Britain during the Industrial Revolution who were paid less than the male workers, in the PRC during the People's Commune (1958–83) female farmers were paid less work points than the men.[33] This was despite the official propaganda that boasted that women in the PRC enjoyed the same status as men for holding up 'Half of the Sky'.

The pay gap was but one aspect of gender inequality. In the case of the Barefoot Doctors, the inequality was also reflected in the allocation of roles. Based on the social and cultural bias that viewed the midwife and the nurse as roles for women, reinforced by the official policy and discourse, the majority of female Barefoot Doctors were assigned to gendered work such as midwifery and nursing. Some were only given the limited, relevant training. Villagers often treated the female Barefoot Doctor who did midwifery and family planning work, as well as nursing, differently from the male Barefoot Doctor who supposedly practised 'medicine'. In a village outside of Datong city in Shanxi province, for instance, the village clinic was staffed with three female Barefoot Doctors and one male one. As the only male, villagers called him 'doctor', and he spent most of his time in the clinic doing 'medical' work. Being the 'doctor', he was also given lighter farming duty, although he received the most work points in comparison to the three female Barefoot Doctors. Of the three female Barefoot Doctors, one did nursing work, another did midwifery, and the third took care of sick children. All three women were given heavier loads of agricultural work for which they received fewer work points. Among the three, the one who did midwifery work received the least work points, for, traditionally, villagers did not regard delivering babies as real 'medical' work.[34] Because the system and the social and cultural norms discriminated against certain kinds of health work such as midwifery and nursing, classing them as less important, such work became, as a result, undesirable. Not surprisingly, a number of female Barefoot Doctors were less enthusiastic about undertaking health work, and the increasing number of female Barefoot Doctors quitting impacted on the caregiver/villager ratio and hence the quality of care.

FURTHER IMPEDIMENTS TO PROVIDING LOCAL SERVICES FOR THE COMMUNITY

The ongoing problem of retention of the Barefoot Doctors was also exacerbated by the government's compulsory 're-education' program, which began in 1969 and lasted for more than ten years. The program brought millions of young students (知识青年) from cities to the countryside to 'learn from the masses'. Ling, who nowadays lives and practises acupuncture in London, was one of many hundreds of young students from Beijing who were sent to a remote village in Inner Mongolia in 1969. She had learned some basic acupuncture before leaving Beijing, and upon her arrival in the village, Ling volunteered for the Barefoot Doctor role. With 80 per cent of villagers illiterate and with most having had no previous contact with either allopathic medicine or systemized TCM, her request to volunteer was quickly granted. This was quite common at the time; because of the labour shortage as well as the villagers' lack of interest and education, grassroots cadres would often circumvent the government policy that required the Barefoot Doctor to be from the same village by allocating the role to young students from the cities.

From the village cadres' point of view, this was an efficient way of utilizing human resources, since many of the young students from the cities were more trouble than help in the agricultural fields. For the students from the cities, being the Barefoot Doctor was often seen as a perk for doing less agricultural work. But Ling quickly learned that being a Barefoot Doctor was, in her words, 'very tough ... Villagers came to me for many things. They knocked on my doors day and night. Whenever they called on me, I had to go, even if it was at the other side of the village,' she recalled.[35] Although at the time that I interviewed Ling in her comfortable clinic in London she reminisced about her Barefoot Doctor experience in the 1970s as 'spiritually rich', she felt little nostalgia about the harsh life in Inner Mongolia. In 1977, after the universities and colleges resumed, she returned to Beijing to pursue further medical training. Despite her empathy for the poor villagers, the temptations of future career prospects as well as a more comfortable life in the big city was hard to resist.[36] Ling was by no means unique. Throughout the country, the red Barefoot Doctor certificate had indeed become the golden passport for many educated youths to return to the cities to undertake further education in medical colleges. Initially, a great number were sponsored by the villages in the false hope that these young students would return to continue to serve the villagers after graduating. Almost none of them did, however.

In today's China, readers were given the account of the exemplary Barefoot Doctor Sun Lize in a 2016 best-selling volume titled *Memories of a Barefoot Doctor*. Like Ling, in 1969 during the Great Proletarian Cultural Revolution, Sun was one of tens of thousands of students from Beijing sent to the countryside to be 'remoulded'. Sun ended up in a village in northern Shaanxi province's Yan'an prefecture, the wartime Red Capital of the CCP, situated at the Yellow Loess Plateau. Villagers there had little to no access to any form of medical or health care. Although there was the commune hospital, health workers rarely turned up at the village. According to one witness's account in the book, these villagers had lived 'under the spell of Yama (the king of hell)' prior to Sun's arrival. Sun arrived with a self-help medical manual and some antibiotics, and he became the village's Barefoot Doctor as soon as he unpacked his luggage. For five years between 1969 and 1975, we are told, Sun 'selflessly' served the villagers with his fine medical skills. Christened the living Norman Bethune, he became a national celebrity. In 1974, after

Mao personally knighted him as one of the five model students who had successfully 'remoulded' themselves by learning from the masses and who had 'settled' in the countryside, he was escorted by the local Cultural Revolutionary Committee to the Norman Bethune Memorial Hall in Yan'an to give a public lecture propagating the 'Spirit of Norman Bethune'. The next year, as the tale of a national hero, Sun's story was adapted into a graphic novel and a television documentary. He was also appointed a member of the PRC youth delegations visiting Europe and Africa. Yet from the witness accounts of some of his contemporaries, we also learn that Sun had never wanted to 'settle' in the countryside to 'selflessly' serve the poor villagers; he had wanted to return to the big city to pursue further studies in medical school. But as he had been made into a political symbol for upholding Chairman Mao's 'revolutionary approach to health', Sun was initially denied that opportunity. He had to wait until the late 1970s to fulfil his dream of becoming a professional doctor. Following the death of Mao, in 1980 the Barefoot Doctors program was officially condemned as 'the poison seed' that the Gang of Four had planted in health work. Later, Sun and his wife settled in the United States, where he embraced neoliberalism and became a multi-millionaire entrepreneur in the publishing business. Yet in recent years, the romance of the 'selfless' Barefoot Doctor Sun Lize was excavated by some of his contemporaries in order to give a nostalgic veneer to their 'lost youth'. Labelled by his contemporaries as a 'Super Human', the Barefoot Doctor Sun Lize had once again become a symbol, but of a different kind.[37]

THE BAREFOOT DOCTOR VS THE WITCH DOCTOR

Despite Sun Lize boasting about having saved villagers from 'the spell of Yama (the king of hell)' with the 'Super Human' allopathic medicine, villagers saw him as just another 'magic healer' or 'wizard'. In his detailed study of the Barefoot Doctors program in Zhejiang province's Fuyang County, Fang Xiaoping argued that with the advent of the Communist Liberation in the early 1950s, and with the Barefoot Doctors program in the late 1960s, allopathic medicine – promoted by the state medical system – had effectively replaced the previous multiple medical systems and 'prohibited healers in supernatural and religious sects, and eradicated their practices'.[38] Mr Xu, the former Barefoot Doctor in Fuyang County, contested these claims. In a 2015 interview, Xu told me that 'even after the implementation of the Barefoot Doctor program, many villagers here continued to seek help from the Bodhisattva. That's what they believed.'[39] Contrary to the conventionally held view that Chinese medicine was the 'traditional medicine' universally available across China, historically it was predominately only the social elites that had had access to this system. In Zhejiang province, for instance, phenomena such as therapeutic rituals at temples and shrines were a commonplace. Even under socialism, state-sanctioned medicine, in both its allopathic and Traditional Chinese Medicine versions, did not completely replace village rituals for ordinary villagers in Xu's village. Bowing to the Bodhisattva or lighting some incense helped to manage illnesses that were understood as either misfortune or divine retribution, thus providing a prognosis and a path toward their management.

Despite the official discourse that was highly prejudiced against witchcraft, magic, and other popular healing rituals, labelling them as 'feudal superstitions', such practices persisted under socialism in different parts of the Chinese countryside, even with the advent of the RCMS. In Qin County throughout the RCMS era, as I learned from a recent interview with the former Barefoot Doctor, many villagers continued to seek help from the village witch doctor.[40] Compared to the often erratic Co-operative Medical service, the witch doctor was not only affordable, but, more important, she was always available to help the villagers with their anxieties, losses, and helplessness when the welfare state consistently failed to deliver the promised health care and denied their well-being. As Mr Liu, the former Barefoot Doctor, stated, 'if the village held a meeting to announce government policy, very few villagers would turn up. If the witch doctor turned up, it would be a very different scene ... You would see villagers busy preparing, cooking, singing, and laughing. A real community fanfare.' He recalled that when he was the village Barefoot Doctor, he regularly bumped into the witch doctor at sick villagers' homes. Even though Liu dismissed the witch doctor as 'unscientific', most villagers did not privilege Liu, the Barefoot Doctor who claimed to practise 'scientific medicine', over the witch doctor. As Liu admitted in the interview, on many occasions he was competing with the witch doctor for the villagers' affection. 'I don't understand why they believe in such superstition,' he sighed. Many of these villagers did not associate 'medicine' with science; what mattered to them was convenience, affordability, and efficacy. Their understanding of efficacy and healing differed substantially from the bio-medical concept of 'curing'. While the latter focuses exclusively on eliminating a specific pathogen, for these villagers healing was a process aimed at addressing the social causes of affliction, hence alleviating their harm on the individual patient as well as their family or community by addressing such causes. This is why, when one sick villager was recovering after Liu had treated him with an intravenous injection, the family continued to call on 'the witch doctor to perform magic'.[41]

The matter was further complicated by the fact that the official press often did not make distinctions between local practitioners of folk medicine and ritual healers. Many private practitioners of herbal medicine and acupuncture who were not nominated to be the Barefoot Doctors and who practised outside of the Co-operative Medical service were sometimes condemned as 'witch doctors'.[42] Since many Barefoot Doctors also used similar 'folk' interventions, it is not surprising that many villagers were confused. As one villager from Shandong province put it: 'I don't understand what was different about the Barefoot Doctor. I only know they are from our village. It's convenient to have them.' Quite often, for extra insurance, villagers simultaneously sought help from the local witch doctor, the herbal doctor, and the Barefoot Doctor.

This was even more the case in multi-ethnic regions such as Yunnan province in the southwest. In Chuxiong, as one former Barefoot Doctor recalled, 'most villagers never stopped seeking divine help from witch doctor and sorceress. They believe in them.'[43] In Chuxiong, situated on the periphery of the Chinese empire until the CCP took over the region, most of the population had only intermittent contact with both the codified 'traditional medicine', as documented in Chinese medical texts, and modern allopathic medicine. Historically, in these regions sickness had its specific local meanings. As Frances Hsu's detailed ethnographical study of local responses to the 1942 cholera epidemic in western Yunnan documented, ordinary villagers believed that the epidemics were a divine punishment for misbehaviour.[44] This meant that local therapeutic interventions that were familiar to ordinary people involved locally meaningful ritual components, from correcting behaviours to asking forgiveness or aid from supernatural forces through prayer, magic, or possession. To ease the stress, they may also have sought help from acceptable medical interventions, ranging from herbal medicine to bio-medical interventions such as injections. For them, as Frances Hsu has pointed out, 'the injection and modern measures of medicine were merely more devices against the epidemic, but they were neither the only devices nor the most important ones.'[45]

Although the Barefoot Doctors interviewed were aware that they were different from the other healers and that they sometimes dismissed supernatural healers and other folk healers as practising 'superstitions' rather than 'science', since they were simply another villager, many of them did not see that it was necessary to 'eliminate' therapeutic ritual practices. Indeed, as Mr Liu, the former Barefoot Doctor in Shanxi province's Qin County, admitted, often 'the witch doctor did her stuff, and I did mine. We did not interfere with each other. At most, we might look askance at each other.' At times, when they saw it 'appropriate', some Barefoot Doctors even took part in the 'superstitious' rituals. As Liu recalled, on one occasion a fellow Barefoot Doctor called him to help with his sick uncle. When he arrived at the patient's home, he saw the other Barefoot Doctor burning incense, following the witch doctor's instruction.[46]

BAREFOOT DOCTORS AND BIRTH RITUALS

When it came to delivering babies, however, quite a few Barefoot Doctors, almost all of them female and trained to implement the 'new-style' medicalized childbirth as well as the family planning program, admitted that traditional birth rituals often presented serious challenges. Worldwide, medicalized childbirth has functioned as the public face of the success of allopathic medicine. By focusing solely on the questions of mother and infant mortality and morbidity, success was measured by the ultimate survival of the individual. In modern China, maternal and child health served as indexes to national reconstruction. The training of new-style midwives first began in the late 1920s under the Nationalist government.[47] After the Communist Liberation of China in 1949, child and maternal health was viewed as integral to the building of the future utopian state. The new Communist state included child and maternal health as one of the Sixty Articles of its provisional constitution, the Common Program of the Chinese People's Consultative Congress.[48]

Concurrently, maternal health became a worldwide priority for the World Health Organization (WHO). Beginning in the early 1950s and aimed at reducing maternal and infant mortality worldwide, the WHO engaged the United Nations International Children's Emergency Fund (UNICEF) to train Traditional Birth Attendants (TBAs). The TBA programs were launched in many newly decolonized Third World countries. In the meantime, in the newly founded PRC, the program for training 'new-style' midwives (the official term in China for midwives who practised medicalized childbirth) that had begun in the Nationalist era grew considerably, with an emphasis on the rural countryside. Overwhelmed by the competing demands made by the state, from agricultural development to disease eradication, such as the Anti-Schistosomiasis Campaign, the training of new-style midwives, as well as the implementation of the new-style medicalized childbirth program in the countryside, remained haphazard until the advent of the Barefoot Doctors program in the 1960s and 1970s. In 1964, Zhimai, against her own wishes, was nominated by the village cadre to undergo training to become a 'new-style' midwife. Her role as the 'new-style' midwife was to mitigate 'risks' by replacing the old-style 'dangerous' childbirth with the 'safe' medicalized child delivery method. After 1968, Zhimai was designated a Barefoot Doctor, although her role remained the same. She remembered that it was hard work persuading labouring women and their families to embrace the new method. Zhimai's village was situated on the Chinese-Burmese border, and the majority of the people in the village were Jinpo by ethnicity. In her village, the traditional belief was that birth and death were two of the core generative functions of human life. As such, the survival of the mother and infant was entwined with the moral fabric of community and family, reaching deep into the past and focusing on the future. Villagers viewed protracted or painful labour as caused by 'ghost affliction'. The ghost was said to be one's ancestor. When that happened, the whole family would make offerings, often in the form of food, such as chickens or eggs, to feed the ghost. On many occasions the expectant mothers refused Zhimai's help. To send her away, they told her: 'No pain yet. It's not happening. Why don't you go home to rest for a bit?' But as soon as she left, they gave birth. '*They did not trust me*,' she said, blaming herself. In her role as the new-style midwife, she was also responsible for the implementation of birth control, yet she recalled that it was an impossible task. Traditionally in her village, fertility was associated with prosperity. Women were often compared to a fruit tree that should bear as much fruit as possible or a hen that should produce as many eggs as possible, while infertility was regarded as a misfortune for the entire family. It was believed that infertility could be passed down from mothers to daughters. As such, villagers considered the use of contraception a total taboo.[49]

Further north of Zhimai's village, in Chuxiong region's Nanhua County, Lanfeng, the former midwifery Barefoot Doctor, recounted that she had infuriated many villagers by trying to implement birth control: 'No one turned up to receive contraception devices. I ended up going around houses to persuade them. They were so annoyed with me,' she recalled. Equally, Lanfeng found it a daunting task to ensure that women underwent 'safe' medicalized childbirth in the hospital instead of 'dangerous' home births. In her village, childbirth always took place at home in the presence of the family. On one occasion, a 38-year-old expectant mother was complaining about terrible pain before labour. For the mother's safety, Lanfeng wanted her to go to the hospital to give birth in a 'safe' environment and be assisted by health professionals. The woman refused because she was frightened by the prospect of giving birth outside of her home, and moreover she considered it shameful to give birth in front of strangers. 'How can a woman give birth in the hospital? Even if I were to die, I would stay home,' she told Lanfeng. As expected, there were complications during labour as the umbilical cord broke. 'I did not know what to do. I had never encountered the situation before. I wanted to call the hospital, but there was no telephone,' Lanfeng recalled. In the meantime, some female villagers turned up asking Lanfeng to massage the woman, but Lanfeng turned down their advice because it was the 'old' method and hence involved 'risk'. By ignoring the 'old' village tradition, Lanfeng caused chaos. The female villagers argued with her, and their argument became louder and louder, adding more strain to the already stressed woman and her family. In desperation, Lanfeng put on sterile gloves and gave the woman an injection to speed up the delivery, while the others watched in awe. For the rest of the week, Lanfeng took care of the woman to make sure there was no infection. The incident won her respect and trust in the village. As her reputation grew, more and more women asked her to help in delivering their babies, although most of them continued to refuse to go to the hospital to give birth, often ignoring her warnings of health risks.[50]

Elsewhere in China, as we learn from Gail Hershatter's study of women's memories of the Maoist revolution in rural Shaanxi, until the

1970s many women also preferred a homebirth, whether with or without the assistance of midwives. Infant deaths from umbilical tetanus remained common in this rural area well into the 1970s. Hershatter suggests that this had to do with the villagers' indifferent attitude toward antisepsis.[51] In *Purity and Danger* (1966), anthropologist Mary Douglas argued that 'dirt is simply matter out of place'.[52] What defines dirt is a question of perception; for many women and their families living in different parts of rural China, childbirth was 'dangerous' and 'dirty' because they considered the placental blood 'polluting'. It could cause contamination, harming the mother, the infant, and the family, even impacting on the greater community. In one interview, a woman from rural Sichuan told me that her own grandmother had refused to help cut her umbilical cord after she gave birth for fear of being contaminated by the 'dirty' blood.[53] Traditionally in China, to prevent contamination after giving birth, the mother would be confined at home for a whole month of convalescence. This was known as 'doing the month', and it is still practised by some. When she was 'doing the month', the new mother would also be prohibited from cleaning herself, or exposing herself to the wind, or coming into contact with water in order to avoid polluting the environment. In addition, she would follow a strict diet to counter the 'imbalance' induced by the very pregnancy that had made her vulnerable. In contrast, dirt in the natural environment was not associated with 'impurity', nor was it imagined that it had the power to 'pollute'; hence, it was not seen as necessary to wash hands or disinfect the scissors used to cut the umbilical cord. While many infants died of umbilical tetanus and women died of infection, many also survived through relying on local indigenous remedies and methods as well as the restorative postnatal ritual of 'doing the month'. The woman from rural Sichuan quoted above told me that after her grandmother refused to help, she grabbed the scissors and cut the umbilical cord herself, but she suffered an infection as a result. To treat the infection, following the advice given by a local doctor, she washed the wound with an infusion made of mugwort, dried pomelo skin, and Sichuan peppercorns. She recovered, and so did the infant. Subsequently, as this ninety-year-old who was now a grandmother herself proudly told me, she helped to cut the umbilical cords for other villagers: 'I often cut umbilical cords for others. I would cut a very short length to avoid causing too much pain for the mother. In fact, the right length is about this much, but I was afraid of causing the mother and the baby too much pain.'[54] In 1954, this woman migrated to the city where she gave birth to her fourth child at a state-run birth clinic. By this time, any newborn baby not delivered by medicalized birth procedure was denied any legal status. Four years later, in 1958, this woman gave birth to her fifth child at home because she so distrusted the clinic. She also plotted to give the newborn away to a neighbour so that the child could be legally registered through adoption. It was by circumventing state policy in such ways that unassisted home births continued. Many unlucky newborns died at birth; because these babies could not be legally registered, their deaths were never officially recorded. In the following four years, as a result of the famine, the birth rate dropped sharply, which also contributed to the decrease in the infant mortality rate.

By the 1970s, with the advent of the Barefoot Doctors when all villages in rural China were required to have at least one female Barefoot Doctor who performed midwifery duties, unassisted births remained a commonplace in rural China. Even in regions with better access to transport, such as Juntong County in Jiangsu province, official statistics show that neonatal and infant mortality persisted.[55] In remote mountainous regions such as Guizhou province's Tianzhu County, the situation was considerably worse. There, many villages did not have any Barefoot Doctors or a new-style midwife until as late as 1976. Tianzhu (which literally means 'Pillars Supporting the Heaven') is a multi-ethnic region in southeastern Guizhou bordering Hunan province. More than 98 per cent of the local population is Miao and Dong. Nestled in the high mountains, Yang village had no accessible road until quite recently. But during the heavy rainy season, which happens every summer, the road into the village became dangerous because of mudslides. I experienced this in 2015 when I was conducting field research in the village, and I had to wait for many days until the rain had ceased. But when a baby is due, he or she cannot wait for days for the rain to stop. Yang Mama, the former Barefoot Doctor, was the first new-style midwife in the village. She received her training in 1976 and returned to serve the village in 1977. But even then, some villagers continued to have unassisted homebirths because they could not afford the 1.5 *yuan* fee for a birth assisted by Yang Mama, who, as the village Barefoot Doctor, was supported by the Co-operative Medical service.[56]

By the time I was conducting the research for this book, almost all midwifery Barefoot Doctors I interviewed agreed with the official statistics claiming that the spread of the new-style medicalized childbirth has significantly reduced maternity and infant mortality in the countryside. Informants told me in their interviews how the Barefoot Doctor program was instrumental in winning over the women in their villages to embrace medicalized childbirth as the unquestionably 'safe' way of giving birth. As with other bio-medical interventions, medicalized childbirth has undoubtedly helped to save the lives of many mothers and infants. Yet from the accounts of women in different parts of rural China, we also learn that 'safety' is a social and cultural construct, dynamic and always changing. In the eyes of these rural women, anything new and unfamiliar was a 'threat' and thus 'dangerous'. For them, the new-style medicalized childbirth 'ritual' challenged their symbolic cultural values, disrupted their family and community dynamics, and was far from 'safe'. It was simply threatening.[57] Equally, for many, to give birth in the alienating environment of a hospital, without their family and in the presence of strangers whom they did not trust, was not 'safe' but 'shameful' and stressful.[58] This may account for why even today the practice of homebirths – most of which are now, however, assisted – remains commonplace in rural southwest China, even though the government has introduced stricter rules aimed at eliminating the purported health 'risks'. During my research for this book, I observed that in different corners of southwest China, there are still many families who are too poor to afford giving birth in hospitals. Aside from affordability, for those living in remote villages such as Danbo village in Barkam in the Himalayas and Yang village in Guizhou, the majority of villagers had no means of travelling to the hospital. For them, homebirth was not a matter of choice. It remained risky for the family and the village doctor (after the Barefoot Doctors program officially ended in the 1980s, many of the Barefoot Doctors were renamed 'village doctors' if they passed the national exam), but today it is a very different kind of risk. If they get caught, both the family and the village doctor would be penalized by the state.[59] However, many consider it a risk worth taking, since they rely on the individual village doctors more than they trust the state system that often disadvantages them; these village doctors are valued members of their community and highly skilled in delivering babies.

TRUST

For Chen Zhiqian, one of the most eminent figures in the development of public health programs from the Nationalist period through to the PRC, developing trust between patients and health care providers was key to the development of local allopathic medical programs. Without the villagers' trust in those assigned to their care, little would have changed, no matter what the *ukase* from above. In 1929, a rural health experiment by the Chinese National Association of the Mass Education Movement began in Ding County in northern China.[60] It aimed at educating illiterate villagers through public health education and by introducing them to allopathic medicine. According to Dr H.Y. Yao, who headed the public health department of the Mass Education Movement: 'most of these [villagers] are poor, ignorant and superstitious, living in mud huts, blackened by soot and smoke, swamped with flies, mosquitoes, bed bugs, fleas, and rats.'[61] In the late 1980s, reflecting back on his earlier experience in developing the Ding County rural health program, Chen Zhiqian reminded us that the 'Barefoot Doctor' phenomena was nothing new: 'Since time immemorial, Chinese villagers had been seeking medical counsel and obtaining their medication from other villagers whose knowledge of medicine was only slightly greater than their own.' For him, it was 'theoretically plausible to use villagers – who lacked advanced technical knowledge – as the primary health workers: they were already there, and they were apt remain there. Whereas an outsider accustomed to more amenities and less isolation might well be reluctant to suffer the hardship of village life for very long, the inhabitants were accustomed to the local conditions and were bound to their communities by kinship and other ties. Villagers who were trusted by their fellow villagers, moreover, would have an advantage over outsiders, who would have to spend precious time demonstrating their reliability.'[62]

Zelang Muchu was in her seventies when I interviewed her in 2016. Muchu was one of the very few village doctors struggling to continue providing basic health care to villagers in and near Danbo village in the Himalayas, many of whom have little or no access to, or simply do not trust, the state system and hospital care. In 1973, while still a young girl, Muchu was nominated by her village to be the Barefoot Doctor, and she subsequently received basic medical and midwifery training. Up until 2016, she told me, she had delivered more than seventy babies in her village as well as in surrounding villages:

I went to help villagers whenever and wherever, often without pay. [Under the work point system] I would lose work points if I was found helping women from another village with their delivery. So, I often took the risk to help them at night. I never refused anyone. They were our neighbours. They came for my help because they trusted me. I could not let them down ... This applied to all sick villagers too. They asked for my help because they trusted me. I could not betray their trust ... I was born and raised here. My family had lived here for a long time. Villagers knew me well. They chose me to be the [Barefoot Doctor] because they trusted me. Ever since I finished my Barefoot Doctor training I have been here and I am always around to help. For forty years, the only time I left the village was to buy drugs in Barkam. Villagers knew they would always find me whenever they needed my help ... When I turned sixty-five, I told villagers I would retire. They begged me to continue [being the village doctor]. They trust me and my skill more than they trust doctors and the hospital ... They knew I would never charge them high fees like in the hospital. Villagers from other villages also asked me to stay on.[63]

Trust remained the defining quality of her presence in the village.

Similarly, in northern China's Shanxi province, Wanping, the former Barefoot Doctor from Qin County who stayed on to become the village doctor despite the low pay, told the interviewer that money was much less important than winning the affection of the villagers:

Villagers liked me because I always tried my best to help them. I never cared to bargain for money. Everybody was poor, why should I bother about money? ... I treated those villagers who could afford it, and I treated those who could not ... On one occasion, I charged one old villager less. It made her very happy. After that, she often asked for my help. We were all poor at the time. I never wanted to charge villagers more money than they could afford ... I slept at the health station so I could be available when villagers needed me ... It wasn't hard work for me. I took on the job because villagers trusted me ... When I saw villagers cry, I became very anxious. I feel for these people. Their problem was mine too. I wanted them to trust me.[64]

The familiarity and comfort that is echoed as a positive feature of the local doctors and midwifes is certainly not limited to rural China. In the extensive work of medical sociologists on allopathic medical delivery, it can be seen that trust in the physician has a curative function in health care.[65] Trusting the physician, no matter what the therapeutic intervention, is at the core of effective health care, and this is just as true in rural settings in China as in a Western medical context.

As we learned from Muchu and Wanping, above, in small rural villages where virtually everyone was a friend, neighbour, or relative, winning the villagers' trust and respect was precious. Such moral bonds, either by kinship or social ties, increased the health workers' commitment and empathy. Alu, the former Barefoot Doctor from Yunnan's multi-ethnic Ninger County, is a Yi by ethnicity. Although he was illiterate, he was nominated by the villagers to be the Barefoot Doctor because he had some knowledge of herbal medicine. Villagers respected him, he recalled in a soft and slow voice, 'more than they did cadres from the big brigade ... Villagers always pretended they were poor and had no food when cadres from the big brigade turned up. But whenever I went to villagers' home, even if they had hardly anything to eat, they would use the food they saved for their children to feed me ... Some villagers also sent me chickens and eggs ... In our village, I did not earn work points [when I was the Barefoot Doctor]. Villagers donated their food and money to me ... The food I ate, and the money I earned came from villagers. It did not matter how late it was ... or how heavy the rain, I always went to visit villagers as soon as being called. I was always ready for their call.' The younger villagers called him 'Daddy' because he had helped to deliver them. Being respected by villagers made him proud: 'I was very proud when I was chosen to be the Barefoot Doctor ... So was my parent ... When I proposed to the girl I like ... she agreed to marry me. It's partly because I was the Barefoot Doctor. It gave me a face [status] in the community.'[66] As seen in this instance, trust in the practitioner results in the establishment of the social capital that defines status.

Being the Barefoot Doctor brought status. For He Yongjin, the village doctor in Yunnan province's Nanhua County, this was far more important than financial gain. Yongjin only took up the Barefoot Doctor's role in 1983 just as other Barefoot Doctors were abandoning their duty because of the low pay and the state's lack of interest in continuing the national program. Prior to being officially nominated as the Barefoot Doctor, Yongjin had been treating villagers privately with herbal remedies. He had learned herbal medicine from his grandfather, who was a folk herbalist. Although Yongjin would have made more money by continuing his private practice, he wanted to become a Barefoot Doctor to win the respect of villagers: 'In our village, the [village] doctor is the most respected person. Villagers respect [the village doctor] more than they respect the village cadres ... Whenever a villager slaughtered a pig, they would invite me for dinner ... When villagers have difficulties, they would always talk to the village doctor.' Respect is reciprocal. Because villagers respected and trusted him, Yongjin cared more for the villagers: 'When villagers have difficulties or if they are bothered about something, they always come to tell me ... I always listen to them and try to understand ... If I have prescribed medicine to sick villagers or treated them with acupuncture, I always follow up with them. Whenever I run into them, I always ask how they got on with the medicine or treatment, whether I could do more for them. Because I care for them, that's why they respect me.' Yongjin understood that giving care is more than just giving out pills. He was also empathetic and always willing to spend time with his patients and listen to their troubles. For more than thirty years, the village clinic has been the heart of the village and Yongjin the advocate for the community. He recalls:

> Once, two families got into a dispute over a small plot of land ... it escalated into a serious fight. One person was hurt and damaged the soft tissue around his waist. He came to me and told me he needed to go to hospital and he would file a lawsuit against the other family. I comforted him and explained that he did not need hospital treatment for soft tissue injury. I also had a long talk with him about taking a step back and try making peace with the other family. Gradually he began to see my point and retreated. The man from the other family got frightened. The fear of being asked to pay compensation troubled him all night so that he could not sleep. The next day he came to see me about his insomnia. After I gave him some medicine, I had a long talk with him trying to persuade him to make peace with the family. There are many incidents like that.[67]

Having status in the community made Yongjin more sensitive to individual villager's needs and thus a more effective healer. By being part of the community, Yongjin better understood the local worlds and the values embedded in them, which would have been alien to an outsider. Although Nanhua was designated by the Communist state as a

Yi ethnic region, in real terms it is a multi-ethnic society. Being a Bai himself, Yongjin is sensitive to the diverse needs of this multi-ethnic community. Although he was originally trained as a herbalist by his grandfather, being attuned to the villagers' different needs and economic capacities, he is always willing to be eclectic in his therapeutic interventions. When he saw that younger villagers were reluctant to take herbal medicine because they disliked the taste, he would prescribe Western drugs for them. For those villagers who could not afford the standard treatment, he would try his best to provide a combination of therapies to lower the costs. Whenever he prescribed a medicinal herb that grew locally, he would tell the villager where to harvest the herb so that they did not have to spend the money to buy it. 'I would make less money this way. But being a doctor, I want to be able to help villagers with their pains. I don't mind if it means less financial gains for myself ... On occasions when some villagers had no money to pay for their treatment or drug, I would write down what they owe in a book ... If they have chicken or eggs, I would pay them market price for the goods. With the money I paid them, they would pay off what they owed for the treatment ... I don't like the method, but there is no other means. Villagers don't have enough cash.'[68] The social capital acquired by the medical practitioner outweighed any diminishment of their financial status.

After 1983, with the marketization of health care delivery, there arose the perception of a widespread problem of overcharging by health care providers, from individual doctors to hospitals. As part of the community, very few Barefoot Doctors would dream of cheating or overcharging villagers. In such a close community setup, dishonesty was not socially acceptable. Like Yongjin, Shimeng was a former Barefoot Doctor, in his case from Daotian village in Shandong province in eastern China. He also learned herbal medicine from his grandfather. 'Today, there are so many medicines on offer. They [doctors at hospitals] just want to fool us in order to get our money. In the old days, when Shimeng was the Barefoot Doctor, he would give us some herbs, it was cheap, and it always worked,' one villager noted, speaking of him fondly.

For this villager, as for many others in different parts of rural China, the other thing that made them trust the Barefoot Doctor in their village more than they would the current state system with its focus on hospital care was that the Barefoot Doctors were always there when villagers needed them. He or she was also both pleasant and approachable: 'In those days, in addition to Shimeng, there was a lady Barefoot Doctor ... There were two of them in the village clinic. Whenever they were called, they always went to [the villager in need] as fast as they could. They were very approachable, and they had a good attitude. Nowadays, if we go to hospital, the doctors charge us a lot of money. In addition, the nurses always treat us badly,' one interviewee lamented.[69] Agreeing with him, in a village from the other side of Korean peninsula, outside of Qingdao, one inhabitant told the interviewer: 'Because the Barefoot Doctor was in the village, if I had a problem I'd go to see her. If she could sort out my problem, that's great. Since we had no money, and I had nowhere else to go, it's good to have her around. Day in or day out, we saw each other all the time. She was always approachable and pleasant, and she was honest if she could not solve my problem. After all it doesn't really matter if she could not solve my problem because she was helpful to me. I wish the doctor today would be as kind-hearted and less obsessed with making money.'[70] Trust, as becomes evident in such comments, is an inherent component in the efficacy of the practitioner.

Social contexts define medical practice. Trust in the local and the therapy tends to be more effective, even if it is simply because of a willingness to undertake it. Distrust, whether caused by distance or cost, leads inevitably to poorer health outcomes. Hence, the Barefoot Doctors (and subsequently village doctors) were often more efficacious because they slowly assumed the reliable and locally recognized roles of the priest, the witch doctor, and the herbalist. Indeed, by integrating various modalities of intervention beyond the state-sanctioned allopathic medicine or TCM into their practice, they heightened their trustworthiness. These patterns could not be, and were not, directed from above. Their wide variation from region to region, from village to village, from individual to individual meant that the very syntheses were local and personal. Yet trust is not a stable concept. In times of radical political and social change, such as collectivization under Mao and the post-Mao economic reform, traditional family life and community structure were eroded. The existing systems of trust were at risk. In times of extreme scarcity, as during the time of the Great Leap famine (1958–62), selfishness became a means of survival. Under such conditions, even members of the same family did not trust each other, while, on the other hand, when self-worth is measured only in monetary value, as with the marketization in post-Mao China, connectedness and trust give way to competition and distrust.

DELIVERING HEALTH WITH
'A BUNCH OF HERBS AND ONE ACUPUNCTURE
NEEDLE' AS WELL AS ANTIBIOTICS

In converting the Barefoot Doctor scheme into a national program, its designers neglected the local. As a result, instead of motivating the community to care for their environment or the health providers becoming advocates for the community, the Barefoot Doctors were forced to act on their own with minimal support from urban experts, while redistributing the scarce national resources in delivering the promised 'Health Care for All'. On the ground, 'Health Care for All' was often reduced to mean 'one cure for all'. Such a reduction not only undermined community responsibility but also weakened the notion that care was a person-to-person exchange. The hegemonic identity of the Barefoot Doctor as the non-professional health worker who was *of* as well as *for* the rural masses, encapsulated by the propaganda image of Barefoot Doctors delivering health care with 'a Bunch of Herbs and One Acupuncture Needle' that adorned village health centres, further hindered individual Barefoot Doctors' competence to deliver care that addressed villagers' actual health needs. In the case of Tonbai County in Henan province, we learn from an official source that the growing popularity of the 'herbal panacea' saved local Barefoot Doctors from 'wasting' time on one-to-one encounters with patients. Although the source praised this as a positive, 'time efficient' health strategy, it is hard to imagine how it would generate a better health outcome than if the Barefoot Doctors spent more time addressing the health needs of individual villagers. In reality, it often facilitated Barefoot Doctors slacking.[71] Many of them had only minimal or no knowledge of herbal medicine.[72] Unlike the herbal medicines prescribed by traditional healers, who had tested the herbs and had years of experience in administering them, the 'herbal brews' or 'honey pills' decocted by many Barefoot Doctors in mass batches to prevent seasonal flu and malaria or to combat tuberculosis outbreaks were often untested. Yet, as part of Co-operative Medicine, entire villages were obliged to consume them collectively, regardless of the known assumption that individuals responded to different medicinal herbs differently. As with the old Chinese saying that 'all medicine contains some poison', it was not surprising that such intervention measures sometimes caused more harm than the cure or prevention they were deemed to effect.

To an extent, this problem of a 'herbal panacea' was little different from the 'magic pill' [placebo] problem in allopathic medicine.

More worrying was that Barefoot Doctors were often expected to perform medical miracles using traditional interventions such as herbal medicine or acupuncture. While this worked for a few who had been experienced practitioners prior to being appointed as Barefoot Doctors, others ended up carrying out 'revolutionary' medical experiments that could be potentially risky. For instance, many Barefoot Doctors who had no previous experience or training in acupuncture experimented by sticking needles into their own body while holding an acupuncture manual in their hands. Others competed to test newly decocted herbal medicine on themselves, sometimes leading to injury. In some cases, Barefoot Doctors lacerated their own body in order to test whether a particular herb could be used to treat wounds.[73] To help Barefoot Doctors in developing new herbal medicine, it was reported that one army medical worker ingested a poisonous herb and that he cut open an artery in his own jaw to test whether a herb could stop external bleeding. Despite awareness of the potential risks, the official propaganda encouraged such 'revolutionary' experiments. In one case, when a team of army medical workers experimented with some herbs on themselves, it was reported that 'some made them dizzy, others made them vomit or caused diarrhoea, but nothing stopped them. Finally, they found an effective treatment.'[74] Self-experimentation is nothing new; there is a long history of it in allopathic medicine. But historians of medicine have focused more on those cases of self-experimentation that were successful.[75] These have tended to be based on 'good science', such as Max von Pettenkofer's 1894 ingestion of cholera bacteria or David Pritchard's self-experimentation in 2004 with hookworm and asthma, rather than those that stemmed from false or ineffective theories and resulted only in health catastrophes. The Chinese cases were as mixed as might be expected, given the politics of health care in the PRC.

Rather than promoting Chinese or traditional medicines, these 'revolutionary' medical experiments were often amalgamated under the official label of 'Traditional Chinese Medicine', and encouraging the Barefoot Doctor to deliver a 'cure', rather than having one-on-one encounters, also paved the way for the long-term problem of antibiotic over-prescribing (and eventual resistance) in rural primary care in China. Although the state encouraged Barefoot Doctors to integrate Western medicine with Chinese medicine, in reality many Barefoot Doctors preferred delivering allopathic medicine, often complying with the demand of the patient. As Fang Xiaoping's study demonstrates, in the 1970s an increasing number of rural villagers came to prefer allopathic medicine as being quicker in treating acute illnesses and hence more effective than herbal medicine.[76] In addition, for some Barefoot Doctors, allopathic as well as patent Chinese medicine was more convenient to obtain and use: 'Initially, we were trained to use a combination of Chinese medicine and Western medicine. When I was younger, I used Chinese medicine a lot. But as I am getting older, my foot began to give me a lot trouble. It's difficult for me to go up to the hills to pick herbs. Thus I only use Western and patent Chinese medicine now. Western medicine is very effective,' explained Muchu, who lives in a mountainous village in the Himalayas.[77] Both types of medication could be found in regional pharmacies, and while patent Western and Chinese medicines were clearly more expensive, they bore the imprimatur of 'scientific' (e.g., urban) medical practice. Such changing perceptions have evolved over the past forty years with the erosion of traditional and local methods and the increased prominence and knowledge of both allopathic medicine and systemized TCM.

The problem was not, however, the preference for allopathic medicine or Chinese medicine. As Chen Zhiqian rightly pointed out, the risk lay in the many Barefoot Doctors – who were only given practical training on how to carry out some basic medical procedures and provide immunizations – who were impelled to do clinical work, from diagnosis to treatment, at the same level as a well-trained physician. Chen's daughter Fujun recalled that 'he often talked about the fact that this could lead to serious risk.'[78] And there were indeed many accidents. In the case of one village in Ningxiang County, Hunan province, the village Barefoot Doctor was also the head of the village Women's Association. This woman had neither medical nor public health training and knew nothing about medicine. She was given the Barefoot Doctor role because she was a relative of the brigade party secretary. Soon after she took the role, accidents began to happen – for example, by mistaking arsenic for talcum powder, she accidentally caused nine deaths.[79] Fujun's own experience in rural Sichuan also confirmed her father's concern. For several years in the early 1970s, Fujun was sent to the Sichuan countryside to assist with rural health work. She recalled that many Barefoot Doctors treated patients with injections. One model Barefoot Doctor did not understand that hypodermic needles and syringes needed thorough sterilization after each use, and instead of delivering the promised cures, this Barefoot Doctor had helped the spread of Hepatitis A.[80] Such cases as this left the Barefoot Doctors with the reputation of being 'shoddy' doctors.[81]

Fujun was most troubled by the problem of unrestricted and unsupervised use of antibiotics amongst the Barefoot Doctors: 'I witnessed many Barefoot Doctors in rural Sichuan doing things they were not qualified to do. One thing I noticed was that they randomly gave out pills. They often randomly gave antibiotics to any villager who presented with a fever. This was because they did not know the cause [of the fever]. They were simply not trained to do diagnosis.'[82] The problem of the Barefoot Doctors, the rural primary caregiver, over-prescribing or misusing antibiotics was by no means limited to rural Sichuan. A 2012 joint study by researchers at Kunming Medical University and the Medical Faulty of Prince Songkla University showed that in many parts of rural Yunnan, the problem of over-prescribing antibiotics to paediatric patients was still widespread amongst rural primary caregivers, almost all of them former Barefoot Doctors. In addition, the research found that the level of supportive care was poor.[83] Undoubtedly, as Fujun pointed out, the Barefoot Doctors' inconsistent and inadequate training had contributed to their clinical incompetence and heightened patient risk, hence the problem of their overreliance on antibiotics as a cure-all. On the other hand, the official promise of 'Health Care for All' that came with the Co-operative Medical service, as advertised by slogans such as 'It's Free to See a Barefoot Doctor', created a demand for a therapeutic 'cure'. This was made worse by the propaganda that exaggerated the Barefoot Doctors' 'infallible abilities' in 'curing' many severe illnesses, including removing tumours. Burdened by the demand and the heightened expectations, and in addition to their clinical incompetence, many Barefoot Doctors, as well as other commune hospital doctors, resorted to antibiotics, the 'magic bullet' of their time. For instance, in Chonming Island, just outside of Shanghai, an official report in 1975 showed that primary care doctors at the Xinmin commune hospital prescribed antibiotics as an 'insurance policy' to every sick villager they saw.[84]

The Long 1970s were globally the 'Golden Era' of antibiotic innovation and broadening use. In the excitement surrounding their successes in treating a range of previously incurable diseases and serious infections, a broad range of antibiotics were made readily available to the general public, first in the West and then around the world. In China, the mass production of penicillin had begun in 1952 with the outbreak of the Korean War, and that created the initial demand. Until the early 1960s, however, domestic production remained low, and as a result the price was high. The prohibitively high cost meant that antibiotics were generally out of reach for ordinary people.[85] By the mid-1960s, China successfully obtained the technology and the licensing to produce semi-synthetic antibiotics. This resulted in a huge increase in quantity, driving down the price. By August 1969, the price of more than 1,230 kinds of patented medicines had been slashed significantly, including a whole range of domestically produced antibiotics. The price of domestically produced penicillin, for instance, was 90 per cent lower than in 1952 and 46 per cent lower than the month before! Sulphanilamide tablets, too, became 63 per cent cheaper than in 1952 and 13.3 per cent cheaper than the previous month. This radical reduction in the price of drugs, according to the *People's Daily*, had reduced the health care burden of the masses living in mountainous, rural, and ethnic regions: 'It helped to promote and consolidate the rural Co-operative Medical service and hence the development of rural health care.'[86] Following this banner article was a news report about Barefoot Doctors in rural Shanghai delivering 'revolutionary' health care to villagers. The increased presence of the Barefoot Doctors as well as the increased affordability of Western drugs – with antibiotics showing the most significant drop in price – were portrayed as the victories of Mao's revolutionary approach to health for the rural masses. The imperative became for the Barefoot Doctor to deliver antibiotics whatever the need or the diagnosis.

Unrestricted and unsupervised use of antibiotics by the Barefoot Doctors, endorsed by the experts in the hospitals and sanctioned by the state, helped to create a drug dependency in rural China. As Chen Zhiqian observed, the majority of villagers in the rural countryside 'depended [on the Barefoot Doctor as their primary caregiver] on health matters and respected their judgement'.[87] Yet prior to the RCMS, the majority of villagers in rural China had had minimal or no contact with most allopathic medicine. This was even more the case with antibiotics due to their prohibitively high price and limited availability. Even in the early years of the RCMS, antibiotics remained a 'luxury' reserved for cadres and those who had good relations with the cadres or the Barefoot Doctors. This made them more desirable when they became readily available, since they had the prestige of status associated with their use. The craving for antibiotics was made worse by the little or no access to hospital care as a result of distance, unavailability, or unaffordability. For many rural villagers, antibiotics were a more affordable and accessible alterative. For the majority of them, the practice of self-medication was nothing new. Until the late nineteenth century, the rural masses in China smoked opium to manage a whole range of illnesses, from severe diarrhoea to malaria, or as a prophylactic measure against diseases. However, after the more powerful opiate, morphine, was introduced to China by medical missionaries in the late nineteenth century to 'cure' the Chinese of their opium 'addiction', opium gradually lost its importance as medicine.[88] By the end of the 1970s, as Fang Xiaoping has shown, many of the younger generation preferred allopathic medicine or patent Chinese medicine over herbal medicine. Antibiotics dominated the consumption of allopathic medicine for their perceived effectiveness in treating many common diseases.[89] Like opium in the eighteenth and nineteenth centuries, antibiotics gradually became the panacea for the masses in China in the late twentieth century.

In the early 1970s, villagers in different parts of China, often supported by their cadres, opened illicit factories, established black markets, and rented out collective plots for private use. This was partly driven by the official campaign to 'Learn from Dazai' by practising 'self-reliance', but more importantly by the human instinct to 'save oneself' (自救) from danger, in this case the extreme poverty imposed upon them by collectivization. An increasing number of villagers roamed around the country illicitly trading anything they could get their hands on, or which they had produced themselves, often with forged documents. Some Barefoot Doctors abused their power during this furtive move to a quasi-market economy by charging villagers higher fees or peddling medicines on the black market to supplement their income. Many grassroots cadres simply turned a blind eye to such activities, since they also profited from it. In northern parts of rural Zhejiang, where about 18 per cent of the skilled labour had left to start businesses elsewhere, agricultural collectivization gradually collapsed in the late 1970s without any policy changes from above.[90] In the years immediately following Mao's death, more and more villagers in different parts of China joined forces to push open the door for economic reform. From Sichuan province's Guanghan County to Anhui province's Fengyang County, local authorities gradually abandoned the People's Communes, introduced their own local policies, and allowed household contracting. By 1981, as Chen Tingyuan, the party secretary at Fengyang County, admitted: 'Household contracting was like an irresistible wave, spontaneously topping the limits we had placed, and it could not be suppressed or turned around.'[91] Despite its initial reluctance, as Kate Xiao Zhou has argued, the CCP Central Committee gradually came to the understanding that it had little power to stop the widespread illegal transfer of land to households. In Anhui's Fengyang County, previously famous for its huge number of beggars, it was very evident that the household responsibility system had improved grain outputs and increased household income. Villages throughout the country demanded that the same system be applied to them. To retain its legitimacy to power, the CCP Central Committee had to give people what they wanted, and in 1983 it officially abandoned agricultural collectivization.[92] With the People's Communes dissolved, the RCMS officially came to an end. Health centres as well as commune clinics were closed down, and Barefoot Doctors lost their livelihood.[93] In order to make a living, those with good skills opened private practices and charged high prices. Many also joined the illicit drug trade.

The problem of antibiotics abuse escalated with the post-Mao decentralization and marketization of health care. As of the early 1980s, the number of private drug manufacturers – many of which were illicit – mushroomed, coupled to a new network of drug distribution in the countryside. In the coastal province of Fujian, for instance, using forged approval documents and more than 100,000 boxes of fake trademarks, fifty-eight fake drug factories were built between 1983 and 1985. More than 700 peddlers were employed to promote the sale of these illicit products to thousands of hospitals or other health delivery units in twenty-nine provinces and cities using unethical measures such as undercutting costs. The total sales value of the counterfeit drugs was more than 35 million *yuan*. In Jingjiang County's Hankou village alone, twenty-two fake drug factories were built, and 80 per cent of villagers were employed in the business of producing counterfeit drugs.[94] Partly for convenience, partly for more profit, because many unlicensed private producers offered cheaper prices than those for the drugs bought through official channels, as well as further incentives, many rural primary caregivers (many of whom were former Barefoot Doctors) began to purchase drugs directly from these private producers. This new network of production, distribution, and marketing 'had troublesome implications,' warned Chen Zhiqian, since they were difficult for the government to monitor, 'posing the danger that quality of the private[ly] produced pharmaceuticals fell significant[ly] below that of those produced by the government'.[95] Chen was right. Between 1980 and 1987, official drug quality test results had shown that about 22 per cent (the range was 6.7 per cent to 38.5 per cent) of drugs tested failed to meet the quality criteria.[96] In addition to the huge number of low-quality counterfeits that flooded the market, interviews conducted by researchers from the School of Public Health at Fudan University have suggested that primary health providers in rural China often 'prescribed more drugs than necessary because of marketing activities or patient demand'.[97] Increased purchasing power and the easier accessibility created by this new network of production, distribution, and marketing also contributed to the prevalence of antibiotic overuse. Until recently, anyone in China could walk into a local pharmacy and buy antibiotics over the counter without a prescription. Yet the government was slow in addressing the problem. It was only in 2012 that the government introduced a regulation to prohibit pharmacies from the unrestricted selling of antibiotics. In the countryside, where demand remains high, the problem has persisted, partly because there are unlimited supplies of relatively cheap, low-quality, or ineffectual counterfeits but equally because in some remote, impoverished regions, villagers continue to have limited or no access to hospital care. Self-medication now relies not on herbal medications, as was earlier the case, but on allopathic interventions such as antibiotics, which may well have greater efficacy but can also lead to long-term health problems on the widest possible scale.

Since adopting the neoliberal market economy, and with a large number of rural villagers migrating into coastal cities, the PRC government began to opt for a market model for financing health services. It moved away from the former model that provided inexpensive and basic health services to a selective primary health model with an emphasis on expertise defined as excellence, with specialized (tertiary) health care and a focus on short-term economic gain. Health care services were reduced or denied following claims that they could not be sustained or afforded. Millions were disadvantaged in the process.[98] The unprecedented scale of urbanization further exacerbated the problem. For those who could neither afford nor had access to hospital care, antibiotics were affordable and readily available. For millions of migrant workers living in squalid conditions, antibiotics have often proved lifesaving, while simultaneously creating the sort of drug resistance that haunts allopathic medicine in the West. At the same time, in those remote rural corners of the PRC where villagers continued to rely on primary health providers for their health care, given the pragmatics of distance as well as cultural reasons of trust, more and more providers left because the system did not incentivize them sufficiently to enable them to continue. As Muchu, the former Barefoot Doctor and currently the village doctor who struggles with how to deliver care and health to her local village, told me (with a big sigh):

Most younger generation village doctors don't want to stay in the village because of the poor subsidy from the state. The amount of money they earn as the village doctor is not enough to take care of their families as well as to pay for their children's education. Anyone with good skills would look for opportunities to be transferred to work in the regional hospital. Even those who did not seek their livelihood elsewhere spent much of their time up in the mountain digging cordyceps sinensis or other precious medicinal herbs to supplement their income. You rarely see them in their villages ... They often complain about the drawbacks of being a village doctor. I think this is a serious issue ... I have been a village doctor for nearly forty years. If I stop being a village doctor, I'd receive no pension. Not even a penny. At one time, the [government] mentioned about introducing an old age insurance system for people like me. But until now, this has not been realized. I am very worried about the future. At the moment, my health is good enough to allow me continuing working as a village doctor ... When I become too old or too sick to continue, I don't have any family to pay for my living expenses. I don't have a pension, what could I live on?[99]

One factor that played, and continues to play, a role in the failure of primary health care systems such as the Maoist Barefoot Doctor program is that they were conceived of initially as aimed at the underserved rural population. Yet it was the movement of rural populations into large urban areas, and the increased speed of this movement during this period, that also characterized what is now called the 'Fourth Phase' of public health. Such movements had been inherent to the rise of industrialization, as in Great Britain in the eighteenth century. With the gradual end of colonization and the rise of twentieth-century nationalism, the speed of such movements of populations into urban areas in India, Mexico, and southern Africa, as well as in the PRC, meant that there was a gradual reduction in the actual numbers of underserved people living in rural areas. The Barefoot Doctor scheme was never imagined as functioning in the new megapolis, and the simple expansion of urban health care to include this new population never occurred. The problem of the people's health quickly became one of urban access to health care, where decentralized systems were inappropriate and centralized systems expensive and hence unaffordable for the displaced rural population in the cities.

China in Global Health: From the 'Sick Man of Asia' to the 'Chinese Approach to Health'

THE SOCIALIST ROAD TO THE PEOPLE'S HEALTH?

In 1948, John Black Grant, an 'old China hand' and a self-styled 'Rockefeller Bolshevik', writing for the Rockefeller Foundation, argued forcefully that the discipline of medicine must extend 'beyond clinical diagnosis to social pathology and therapy, thereby making it the task of medicine to assure a mentally and physically healthful community'.[1] For him, the 'full development and maintenance of mental and physical capacity' depended 'not only on adequate medical services but also on minimum standards of nutrition, housing, recreation, education, and social security'. The provision of these 'necessary non-medical factors' could not be attained by individual effort but solely 'by community efforts and government aid'. Grant stressed that the state had a role to create those welfare policies and legislation, which would guarantee that health was a right to be enjoyed by its citizens. Enthused by the post-war 'revolutionary' developments of health care in countries he visited, in particularly in South Africa, Grant was full of optimism: 'The pump is primed ... The universal establishment of this pattern of health care as a "social science in the service of society" would usher in a new and momentous era in human welfare.'[2] Change was going to come, but through which model?

However, one year later, in April 1949, Grant lamented the fact that 'nowhere up to the present time, has the concept [of extending medical care into health care] been experimented with, much less demonstrated.' Although in post-war Britain, the National Health Act 1946 had come into effect in July 1948, bringing together a wide range of medical services under one organization and establishing

a comprehensive health service for England and Wales, Grant also
noted the continued instability of international health policy. He
pondered whether 'in the evolution of the welfare of communities,
are the democratic or the totalitarian countries going to be the first
to provide adequate health care?'[3] This was the dilemma of the post-
war world: divided into 'totalitarian' and 'democratic' camps, the
reality of the Cold War was that it was not clear which was the best
way to ensure the improvement of the people's health, at least as
seen from the perspective of internationalist NGOs.

At this precise moment, despite the complication of a schistosomiasis outbreak that affected thousands of Communist soldiers, the
Chinese Communist Party's People's Liberation Army succeeded in
crossing the Yangtze River. After ten years of civil war, peace if not
stability had finally been achieved. The newest communist state –
the People's Republic of China (the PRC) – was founded. China was
once more united, this time under the leadership of a strong and centralized Communist government. The new Communist authority of
China pledged to transform the 'Sick Man of Asia' into a prosperous
country, a healthy nation that would eventually be free of disease. To
reach this nation's 'common goal', it would expand public health and
medical work by involving the masses[4] (as was examined in detail in
chapters 1 and 2). It looked as if Grant's 'China project' would finally
be realized and the CCP would be the one to turn off the never-ceasing
cascade of disease and affliction that Grant and other advocates of
social medicine had earlier tried so hard to accomplish but failed.

John Black Grant was born in Ningbo, eastern China, to what
he called a 'sainted' Canadian Baptist medical missionary, James
Skiffington Grant. According to Grant senior, trying to use medicine
to save the suffering masses in a country like China was like 'trying
to mop the water off the overflowing sink while the tap is still on'.[5]
Yet despite, or perhaps because of, his father's warning, J.B. Grant
had spent nearly twenty-five years in China trying to turn off that
tap by rethinking how medicine should be organized and practised in
this vast and impoverished country with multitudes of health problems. Between 1920 and 1921, before returning to China to take
up a permanent post at the Peking Union Medical College (PUMC)
(the Rockefeller Foundation's 'Johns Hopkins for China'), Grant did
a master's degree in public health at the Johns Hopkins' School of
Hygiene and Public Health.[6] There he met and studied with Sir Arthur
Newsholme, a retired medical officer from England who believed that

it was primarily poverty that exacerbated the spread and intensity of disease and hence advocated improving health through improvements in living and working conditions as well as better nutrition.[7] A champion of an organized system of state medicine as an effective tool to prevent and curtail 'a large mass of illness', Newsholme would also become an admirer of the new centralized comprehensive health system that combined medicine and public health developed in the Soviet Union under Stalin. In their co-authored book *Red Medicine: Socialized Medicine in the Soviet Union* (1934), Newsholme and John Adams Kingsbury commended the Soviet system as the 'vast and fascinating experiment of socialized health ... that the rest of the world cannot afford to ignore'.[8] Kingsbury was the director of the Milbank Foundation, as well as a leader of social work in the United States, who advocated for improving the conditions of the poor.[9] In their preface to *Red Medicine*, the two authors began with the following passage: 'When a Russian becomes ill the Government does something about it. In fact, the Government has already done something about it, for Soviet Russia has decided that the health of the individual is the concern of society as a whole. Indeed, the Soviet Union is the one nation in the world which has undertaken to set up and operate a complete organization designed to provide preventive and curative medical care for every man, woman, and child within its borders.'[10]

The new USSR, seen through the idealistic model of state engagement promulgated in the West by John Reed immediately after the Bolshevik Revolution, was to be the model for improving people's health.

After completing his studies at Johns Hopkins, in 1921 J.B. Grant returned to China, seconded by the Rockefeller Foundation to build a brand new, modern public health program.[11] In addition to advocating the teaching of preventive medicine as a core of the medical curriculum, he designed the new public health program at the PUMC in such a way 'that the fundamental techniques in preventative medicine and public health in the community could be practiced and taught'.[12] He also collaborated with the Peking Municipal government to establish the first Public Health Experimental Station in China. A community-based public health experiment such as this was not only new for China; in the early 1920s, such community health undertakings were new and relatively rare throughout the world. Having concluded that 'the low economic standards with their resultant bad social conditions', including overcrowding and malnutrition, were 'important factors in the high incidence of [GI TB] and other diseases',[13] Grant as well as his Chinese collaborators – who included Robert Kho-Seng Lim (more widely known in the West as Bobby Lim), Lim Kho-Seng (an eminent physiologist and the first Chinese professor for the PUMC), and Chen Zhiqian – envisaged that the sole solution to the complex health needs of the Chinese was a system of state-supervised medicine. It would be similar to the Soviet system in that it would '[render] available for every member of the community, irrespective of any necessary relationship to the conditions of individual payment, of all the potentialities of preventative and curative medicine'.[14] Such a system would also encompass the development of a social machinery to ensure standards of living adequate for the maintenance of health.[15] In order for such a system to sustain itself, Grant believed it was also necessary to extensively involve members of local communities. To engage these communities entailed organizing special courses to train health delivery 'auxiliaries', including vaccinators, sanitary inspectors, and other semi-professional groups of health personnel.[16]

The American-trained public health expert Selskar Gunn, who had been the vice president of European operations for the Rockefeller Foundation and was an expert in infectious diseases, arrived in China in 1931. Grant and Gunn then worked together to develop a public health experiment in China for the foundation that would form a part of a larger plan of social reconstruction, with an emphasis on raising the economic and social level of the rural masses. They envisaged China becoming 'a vast laboratory in the social science, with implications that would be international in scope'.[17] Their pioneering social experiment in rural China did eventually fail, however. Many later scholars attributed this failure to the Japanese occupation of China after 1937, which had resulted in the termination of all of the social medicine experiments undertaken by the Rockefeller Foundation. However, on a close study of Chinese sources from this period, it could be argued that the failure of these social medicine experiments in China was largely due to Chiang Kai-shek's Nationalist government's increasing orientation toward a model of positive eugenics as the central vehicle for tackling the country's health problems. With the advent of the New Life Movement as of 1934, rather than addressing rural health needs, Chiang's Nationalist government advocated that the Chinese peasantry 'participate' in creating a new rural lifestyle, from eradicating their 'barbaric and superstitious' customs to changing their 'unclean' habits and practising 'superior birth' (优生 *yousheng*) or 'race reform'. It was believed that the latter would facilitate those 'retarded' peasants to 'breed out' their 'inferior' and 'unhealthy' genes.[18] Social medicine, as in Germany during National Socialism, gave way to positive and negative eugenic solutions to the people's health. Fascism was not the sole origin of ideas of eugenic improvement, however; in Germany such ideas had already been present in the 1890s, as they had been in Britain, and it became party policy in the late Weimar republic.

With the founding of the People's Republic of China (the PRC), the new Communist authority's commitment to improving the well-being of the common people, as well as its seeming willingness to work with non-communist political groups and individuals in a democratic united front to bring about socialist progress, including public health to China, won many supporters at home and abroad. As Chen Zhiqian, Grant's former Chinese collaborator, recalled: 'I looked forward to contribute to health improvement in the new socialist society.'[19] Among many others, Madame Li Dequan, who became the first minister of health of the new PRC, wholeheartedly supported the new Communist authority's pledge to transform the 'Sick Man of Asia' into a healthy and prosperous socialist country.

The founding of the PRC also came at the intersection of competing global models for the people's health. According to the United Nations Relief and Rehabilitation Administration (UNRRA) in 1948, China presented 'the greatest and most intractable public health problem of any nation in the world'.[20] At this exact moment, the UN's newly founded World Health Organization (WHO) rectified and enacted its constitution and gave expression to many of the ideas of social medicine that had been advocated by public health advocates of the left during the interwar period. After World War II, with a mounting problem of worldwide reconstruction and its attendant health crises, a number of these advocates pushed forward their earlier ideas through the new post-war international organizations such as UNRRA and the WHO. Dr Andrija Štampar, the Croatian health reformer and a crusader for agrarian reform who was also an 'old China hand', was elected chairman of the first World Health Assembly held in June–July 1948. Before conflict had broken out in Asia, Štampar had spent several years in China as the League of Nations Health Organization (LNHO)'s representative. While in China, he announced to his mentor Julius Tandler, the Viennese

Jewish physician and social reformer who was instrumental in creating a new welfare and health care system for Vienna in the 1920s and 1930s (and who was also simultaneously a eugenicist), that 'my sympathies lie in China, not with the rulers but with the oppressed.'* Štampar was convinced that in order to build a successful health system it was necessary to first remove 'social grievances, such as the sense of exploitation by the landlord'.[21] After China, Štampar also visited the Soviet Union. The trip was said to have imbued him with enthusiasm for communism. He envisaged that communism would bring about a state health system that would meet the agrarian needs in his native Yugoslavia as well as in China. To his great disappointment, however, the post-war USSR under Stalin had moved further toward a rapid industrialization and urbanization that was accompanied by a more centralized health system. In the meantime, Tito's new communist regime in Yugoslavia, while defying Soviet political hegemony in 1948, adopted a health strategy that was parallel to that of the Soviet Union but which failed to address the radical regional differences and complex agrarian needs of the multi-ethnic state.[22] At the same time, as Randall Packard has argued, the WHO's initial efforts to integrate disease control and broad development programs, including the UN's Food and Agricultural Organization's rural welfare program, fell victim to Cold War politics. The model of social medicine integrating rural health with agrarian reform advocated by Štampar and Ludwig Rajchman and their supporters at the 1937 LNHO's Conference on Rural Hygiene in Bandoeng in Dutch Indonesia (also known as the Bandoeng Conference) was pushed to the margins. Supporters of the vector control method that relied on new bio-medical technologies (for instance, the massive spraying of DDT for malaria control) dominated the field of public health.[23] While these advocates of vector control discounted the social and economic variables that shaped the local epidemiology of diseases such as malaria and schistosomiasis, they trumpeted Western bio-medical expertise and continued to deny local participation.[24] In contrast, the new Communist authority of China's agrarian reform policies, such as the Land Reform, the collectivization of agricultural

---

* After a lecturing trip to China in 1933–34, Tandler then immigrated to China in 1936 because the fascists came into power in Austria. While in China, he was invited by the Soviet government to help reorganize Moscow's sanitary system. He died within a few months of arriving in Moscow.

production, which aimed at the rapid modernization and social transformation of rural China, and the CCP's efforts to engage the masses in its socialist transformative project in which public health undertakings were a core part, stood out as a promising alternative model of a socialist road to public health.* Yet, as we have seen in earlier chapters, many of the CCP's methods to involve the masses were noticeably 'imperialistic' and coercive.

Among the PRC's purported achievements in public health, the nationwide campaign to eradicate schistosomiasis by involving the masses became the most celebrated showcase for the efficacy of the new Chinese approach to the people's health. As Wei Wenbo, the deputy party head in charge of this mass public health campaign proudly announced at the 1959 Nine-Man Subcommittee's Enlarged Meeting for all grassroots managers of the campaign held in antic-ipation of the tenth anniversary celebration of the founding of the PRC, 'visitors from capitalist Europe, who have nothing good to say about industrial construction in our country, are impressed by our Anti-Schistosomiasis Campaign.'[25] Such undertakings came to mark the unique successes claimed by the young state as well by as global public health authorities.

'POLITICAL COMMITMENT' AND 'COMMUNITY PARTICIPATION'

As of the second half of the 1950s, in many of the newly decolonized countries in Latin America and Africa and in countries of the indus-trialized West, a growing number of advocates of social medicine in the field of public health and medicine – most of them anti-capital-ist and anti-imperialist – became attracted by and willing to accept the PRC's claim to have transformed the 'Sick Man of Asia' into a healthy nation without any dependence on Western aid. The PRC was seen to have accomplished this through the political commit-ment of a strong and centralized socialist government and with the enthusiastic mass participation of local communities.

Among the first Western medical visitors to the PRC was a group of British physicians. In August 1957, a couple of months before Mao

---

* A growing number of studies in recent years have shown that both programs under-taken in the PRC under Mao were disastrous in terms of the loss of individual life and a true failure of agricultural expansion.

marched China into the disastrous Great Leap Forward and at the invitation of the Chinese Medical Association (CMA), nine prominent figures in the field of public health and medicine from Britain visited the PRC on a 'medical tour'. The delegation, led by Brian Gilmore Maegraith – the dean of the Liverpool School of Tropical Medicine (LSTM) and one of the most outspoken critics of the imperial model of tropical medicine in the post-war West – included Sir Theodore Fox (more widely known as T.F. Fox), the editor of *The Lancet* and a Quaker, as well as Sir Francis Avery Jones, the renowned gastro-enterologist who was also an ardent supporter of the new National Health Service (NHS) in Britain. During their three-and-a-half weeks of carefully choreographed stops in the PRC, restricted to larger cities and the more developed eastern rural regions, the British visitors conceded the innate superiority of the PRC's health system under the CCP's leadership: 'The standard of hygiene reached already is ... most impressive ... the successful control of flies, the litterless streets, and fanatic household cleanliness are having profound effect on the spread of gastro-intestinal infections, especially in children, in whom, we are told, bacillary dysentery is much less common than it was,' marvelled Maegraith and his fellow British travellers.[26] For them, it augured well for this strong, centralized government, as T.F. Fox put it explicitly in his lengthy report of their visit: 'This defeat of the flies, which astonishes every traveller in China, illustrates what can be done by a regime which can so easily enlist man, woman, and child against a common enemy.'[27]

Before World War II had broken out in Europe, T.F. Fox had visited the Soviet Union. He had been deeply impressed by how the Soviet experiment had reallocated medical services 'to the better advantage of the community as a whole' by 'abolishing the common idea that medical care was a commodity on sale for a fee'.[28] In post-war Britain, in his capacity as editor of *The Lancet*, T.F. Fox advocated for an organized state medical service for Britain that would free medicine from the marketplace. He was thus actively involved in the discussion about setting up the NHS. He was also an advocate of birth control and primary health care as well as its equitable delivery.[*] In October 1965, during the Harveian oration delivered before

---

[*] Theodore Fox's father was a Quaker doctor who served a rural community in the Scottish Highlands at the turn of the nineteenth and twentieth century. It was a regional community health innovation to serve the poor communities in the rural Scottish Highlands in the early twentieth century (it became known as the Highlands and Islands

the Royal College of Physicians, Fox famously proclaimed that medicine must serve a moral purpose. The primary role of doctors was to help people rather than to advance science, he proclaimed.[29] Three years prior to his China visit, Fox had revisited the USSR. This time he had found the more advanced Soviet health service less exciting, partly because his post-war Britain had achieved the provision of a free medical service to the entire British population. But like an increasing number of contemporary Western observers, he found the Soviet authoritarian system morally objectionable. Despite the fact that 'it is capable of promoting rapid progress up to a certain point', he asked 'whether medical practice and medical science can reach their full stature under an authoritarian regime'. Furthermore, Fox was disappointed to see that Western materialism had become 'part of a new gospel' in Stalin's USSR.[30] In contrast, Fox was enthused by the visit to the less developed and newly founded Communist China. This, according to him, was partly because he found the enthusiasm of his Chinese hosts for their new country 'infectious' and 'persuasive', but he was equally enthused by the Communist authority's ability to manage this vast nation and to 'motivate' the 600 million Chinese.[31] Contrary to the Victorian view of a diseased, filthy, poverty-stricken, and retrograde China, Fox's impression of the new China, which was echoed by a growing number of China observers in the post-war West, was noticeably more positive. While China was enchanting and timeless, as imagined by Westerners from Marco Polo to Fox's Quaker missionary father, it was substantially more than this. The new China was, according to Fox, a progressive and independent modern nation, which was undergoing 'rapid' and

Medical Services after 1913) that provided the basic structure of the NHS as adopted in 1948. At the time, Fox was known for his support of the NHS. He was also known for his part in the publication of the highly critical Collings Report (1950) of general practitioner (GP) practices in post-war Britain and the subsequent creation of the College of General Practitioners that aimed at improving the standard of general practice as well as generating a growing awareness of the importance of primary care. For a history of the Highlands and Islands Medical Services, see M. McCrae, *The National Health Service in Scotland: Origins and Ideals, 1900–1950* (Edinburgh: Tuckwell Press 2003); D. Hamilton, 'Highlands and Islands Medical Services', in Gordon McLachlan, ed., *Improving the Common Wealth, Aspects of Scottish Health Services 1900–1984* (Edinburgh: Edinburgh University Press for Nuffield Trust 1987): 481–90. For an evaluation of the Collings Report, see Roland Petchey, 'Collings Report on General Practice in England in 1950: Unrecognised, Pioneering Piece of British Social Research?' *British Medical Journal*, 311 6996, 1 July 1995): 40–2.

'astonishing' transformation by following the socialist path. While he was pleased to note that Western medical missionaries' efforts to 'save' China, as well as the Rockefeller Foundation's earlier initiative to modernize and improve medical education in the country, seemed to have had some lasting impact, in the post-war world such endeavours came increasingly under criticism as the 'white man's burden' in public health. In the search for a new and positive model to improve people's health, he was enthused by the Chinese Communist state's 'great effort to prevent diseases and improve medical services'. Equally, he was excited that the PRC had supposedly achieved this without the help of the West: 'the feet of these 600 million people have been set on the concrete path of hygiene and mechanization that is to give us all long and happy lives in a utopia of nuclear physics.'[32] Although he cautioned that the new Communist China was an authoritarian state like the Soviet Union and Nazi Germany, and indeed that in the latter medicine had been a tool in the genocide of the Jews, he was willing to accept the claim that the CCP was exercising its power for the good of the people: 'This power, which can be used for good as well as for ill, is the chief reason for its remarkable achievements, in medicine as in so much else.'[33] Sharing Fox's view, Avery Jones, too, was impressed by how the authoritarian system of the new China had enabled the Communist authority 'to bring its policies most effectively to the attention of each individual and enabled the anti-fly campaign, for example, to be so effective'.[34]

If both Avery Jones and T.F. Fox had some reservations about the PRC's authoritarian system, Brian Gilmore Maegraith applauded it. As one of the most prominent figures in the field of tropical medicine in the post-war West, Maegraith was a fervent opponent of the prevailing view that diseases can be eradicated by simply eliminating the parasites. During the war, Maegraith spent several years in Freetown, Sierra Leone, heading the Royal Army Medical Corps' mobile pathology laboratory.[35] This 'real experience' in the tropics, according to him, broadened his views of tropical medicine. It made him increasingly critical of the imperialistic approach that viewed the local population as inherently inferior (such views were held, for example, by many in the LSTM's rival institute, the London School of Hygiene and Tropical Medicine [LSHTM], such as Patrick Manson (whom we encountered in chapter 1), and therefore denied the locals any participation in the planning and implementation of medical aid. Calling the 'official attitude' in Britain that defined tropical medicine merely an 'ordinary medicine' as transplanted to the tropics a fallacy, which at its worst was truly 'dangerous', Maegraith argued that tropical diseases such as malaria and schistosomiasis were not merely caused by the specific parasites but were also the result of social and economic conditions in the tropics, in particular communal poverty, low standards of living, and a lack of health education. He also opposed the view 'cherished' by many economists in the post-war West, particularly in the United States, that socio-economic 'progress' would inevitably lead to better health. Maegraith warned that 'unless the health aspects have been included from the beginning, the socio-economic development may well become a menace to health not only in the building areas but in the contiguous population.' He argued that 'a healthy economy demands a healthy community' and that 'health aspects must be included at all stages of major socioeconomic developments as an integral part of the complex organization of the planning.'[36] 'Modern tropical medicine', as opposed to the established imperial tropical medicine in the United Kingdom, was for him 'above all, a multidisciplinary subject, taking into account social, economic, and environmental factors which influence the whole pattern of disease in the community, as well as in the individual'. Maegraith advocated for local involvement, from local governments and the impacted communities, in the planning and delivery of health care. Importantly, the latter included training medical auxiliaries.[37] According to him, local people, with their experience and knowledge, were the 'essential building blocks' in designing a sustainable and efficient health care system, and they could 'take the available medical care to the periphery where professionals [could] seldom operate'.[38] Driven by his motto, 'Our impact on the tropics must be in the tropics', Maegraith worked closely with his Thai colleague Chamlong Harinasuta to build the Faculty of Tropical Medicine at Mahidol University in Bangkok, a research and teaching institute to provide 'ordinary medical undergraduates training towards rural and urban community health and to provide trained scientists to work in the field problems'.[39] He had hoped that 'one day the Bangkok project would extend beyond the national boundaries into the [Southeast Asian] region' to 'countries bordering on the South China Sea that might be interested in collaborating in graduate medical training programs and in research into the local endemic diseases which were depressing living standards in the region'.[40] The seeds for local knowledge, if not local control, in providing care for the people's health were already sown.

Maegraith visited the PRC while he was working on this joint venture of 'new' medical education. On this visit, the British were shown 'the nation's all-out totalitarian attempt to "liquidate" the threat of schistosomiasis to the future of the new China'. They were also invited to join 'the hordes of village children picking up roasted snails'.[41] Persuaded by the official rhetoric, Maegraith felt the urge to broadcast revolutionary China's national Anti-Schistosomiasis Campaign to the Western medical and public health world: 'This monumental modern struggle against an ancient disease will interest and excite you as much as it did me.'[42] For him, the Anti-Schistosomiasis Campaign as well as the PRC government's public health efforts were perfect cases of how keeping the farming communities healthy would, in turn, improve agricultural productivity and hence people's well-being – at least in the rural areas.[43] According to Maegraith, not only had China achieved 'nutritional independence' in producing sufficient food to feed an 'astonishing number of 800 million souls' without any Western aid, by controlling diseases and keeping its population healthy, 'this happy state of affair is likely to continue for some time'.[44] Equally, for Maegraith, the PRC's Anti-Schistosomiasis Campaign was a perfect example of how 'the local community is acting for itself in its own interests and cooperating at the same time in the wider national scheme.'[45] Yet, as my earlier chapters have shown, while the PRC's Anti-Schistosomasis Campaign did involve the community, it was a centrally planned and expert-led campaign. It was also hastily implemented, often encountering local resistance. Far from a case of local communities acting in their own interests, to a great extent many of the methods used to involve the masses were noticeably 'imperialistic'. Furthermore, Maegraith also lauded the PRC government's intensive public health propaganda campaign as 'essential' to ensuring the cooperation of the communities: 'The Chinese Government quite rightly regards propaganda as an essential technique in the antischistosomal scheme and has organized public information services in the endemic areas on an impressive scale, with the twofold object of achieving control of the disease and of obtaining a more general improvement in social health and cleanliness, and, even more important, a genuine desire for an improving standard of living.'[46] It is ironic that Maegraith, the expert voice known for advocating that the locals were the 'essential building blocks' in designing a sustainable and efficient health care system, also endorsed the view, held by Chinese health officials and earlier medical missionaries such as Barlow, that local communities were 'ignorant' or 'under-educated' and that they needed to be 'enlightened' about important health concerns such as hygiene and disease control based on a Western bio-medical model. So, what was the local health experience and knowledge worth if he considered the locals inherently 'unenlightened'?

Maegraith was in favour of the equally, if not greater, top-down authoritarian model in the PRC, seeing it as providing an advantage in coordinating the public health authorities and other allied services, from agriculture to forestry and water conservancy as well as communities, in a what he called a 'cooperative effort' to control schistosomiasis: 'The remarkable degree of integrated cooperation already achieved, perhaps more easily in China than in nontotalitarian countries, augurs well for the future success of the whole scheme. The Chinese have set as their target the practical control of schistosomiasis within twelve years from now. Their cooperative enthusiasm, skill, and dedication to the task should enable them to achieve this objective.'[47] Yet, as we have seen throughout this book, this highly centralized top-down campaign was very far from a 'cooperative effort'. The local responses to it had proved fragmented and often contradictory; there was also a fair amount of resistance at different levels, from various state ministries to local authorities and in the impacted communities. Equally troubling was that Maegraith and his fellow travellers cheered as they watched local children take part in snail control activities without protective measures. As an expert on tropical medicine, he might have been expected to know that such activities carried a potential health risk because it would expose these children to the disease.

In the meantime, the British doctors' positive 'medical' impressions of the PRC were propagated to a much wider audience by pro-China journalists in the West, notably Felix Greene. With the exception of Edgar Snow, widely known as the main advocate for the CCP in the West, Greene was the most read journalist and broadcaster reporting on Mao's China during the Cold War. His book, *What's Really Happening in China?* published in 1959 by City Lights Books (the San Francisco publishers known for advocating radical left-wing politics and social justice), was one of the first volumes of eyewitness reports on the PRC published in the West. The book portrayed the CCP and its new China in a highly favourable light. With growing criticism of the USSR in the West following the gradual revelation of the horrors under Stalin's rule and the suppression of the Hungarian uprising by Soviet armies after Stalin's death, Greene was eager to assure his Western readers that Mao's new China was different from other totalitarian states, which for him included Hitler's Germany as well as the USSR. The new PRC, according to Greene, 'is being led by a group of historically conscious, strong, and enormously competent men who identified themselves with the people, who knew the changes the people wanted and sponsored those changes. They won their revolution because they voiced the demands of a people driven to extremities of suffering, who were determined to end the disease, hunger and corruption which had held them in subjection for centuries. If ever in history there was a people's revolution – this was it.' For Greene, the PRC's achievement in public health was a fruit of this 'people's revolution': 'the [Communist government of China] has succeeded, despite the violence of the civil war, in bringing unity, order, honesty, food, education, health, and above all hope, to the Chinese masses ... No one visiting China today fails to be impressed by the degree of cleanness and order which is found now throughout China.' To prove his claim, he turned to the accounts of Maegraith, Fox, and Avery Jones: 'top-flight British doctors who visited China in 1957 to see what had happened to medicine in China since the revolution'. [48]

Remember that Maegraith had argued that the 'disease situation in the community is further influenced by ... the background of malnutrition and overall shortage of protein, the agricultural and veterinary products available.'[49] In the four years following the British visit, the PRC's all-out totalitarian attempt to transform the countryside into a 'communist paradise' turned it, rather, into a living hell. Existing rural communities were destroyed; millions died of starvation in the worst famine in history that lasted four years between 1958 and 1962.[50] In the meantime, diseases such as schistosomiasis were to remain an intrinsic part of the daily experiences of millions of villagers living in the endemic regions.[51]

'THE SICK MAN OF ASIA HAS BECOME THE HEALTHIEST MAN IN THE WORLD'

In the early 1960s, while a number of editorials in the Western press, as well as documents from CIA files, suggest that the West was aware of the widespread outbreak of diseases associated with malnutrition (particularly oedema and hepatitis) and the resulting sharp increase in the mortality rate in China in 1960 and 1961, news of the Chinese famine and the high mortality rate was dismissed or ignored by many China sympathizers in the West as anti-communist propaganda.[52] Instead, they turned to Edgar Snow, who visited China at the height of the famine in 1960, and then to Dr Joshua Horn, an English surgeon who was living in China during that time, to argue in favour of the PRC's superior primary health care system under Maoist communism.*

Edgar Snow, an 'anti-colonial, anti-imperialist, pro-independence' radical leftist from Missouri and the author of the earlier global bestseller *Red Star over China* (1937), was one of the most widely read propagandists for the CCP in the West, as well as, according to John S. Service, the 'chief contact' between the United States and the PRC during the first two decades of the Cold War.[53] In his first-hand account of his 1960 visit to Maoist China, *The Other Side of the River*, Snow denied that there was a famine or any signs of mass starvation: 'Whatever he was eating, the "average Chinese" maintained himself in good health, as far as anyone could see.'[54] To further prove the 'average Chinese' was in good health, he cited the 'authoritative' voices of the British doctors who visited China in 1957 as well as the 'authentic' voice of his old friend Shafick George Hatem, the Lebanese-American physician who became the first foreigner to acquire Chinese nationality after the CCP came to power and was another 'brilliant apologist for the Chinese Communists' during the Cold War.[55] Originally from Buffalo, New York, Hatem went to Shanghai in 1933 during the Great Depression as a medical student looking for an 'Eastern adventure' as well as a livelihood. While in Shanghai, he came to know Madame Sun Yat-sen (Song Qingling), the widow of China's revolutionary leader and the most influential fellow traveller of the CCP after the Nationalist party broke their alliance with the Communists in 1927.†

---

* In the 1960s and 1970s, Chinese communism, often branded as 'Maoism' as opposed to 'bureaucratic' communism in the West and the Soviet Union, appealed to a huge number of radical young leftists (born in the interwar period) in the West as well as in Latin America and Africa.

† After the success of the Northern Expedition, in April 1927 Chiang Kai-shek, who secured his power in the Nationalist party during the Northern Expedition, broke the alliance with the Communist Party and executed a bloody purge of Communists and Communist supporters in Shanghai. Three months later, in July 1927, Wang Jingwei, the Nationalist party's leftist leader, who was seen by many as Sun Yat-sen's anointed heir, followed Chiang Kai-shek's lead by turning on the Communists in Wuhuan. Angered by the massacres of thousands of Communists in Shanghai and Wuhan, Song Qingling

In the 1935 'August First Declaration', the CCP strategically shifted from its former position in what had amounted to a Chinese civil war against the Nationalists to be willing to form a new United Front in the wake of the Japanese invasion. Madame Sun, who wholeheartedly supported this new United Front and the 'sacred' cause of resisting the Japanese and saving China, began to actively recruit sympathetic foreigners. This included finding medical personnel as well as raising funds for the International Peace Hospital at the CCP's revolutionary base at Yan'an in the northwest of China. Hatem became increasingly attracted to communism during this period. In 1936, partly in response to Madame Sun's appeal, Hatem decided to go to the Communist base at Yan'an to support their wartime medical work. Madame Sun, who organized the trip, introduced him to Edgar Snow, who was also on the way there. In Yan'an, Hatem subsequently joined the CCP and became involved in its health planning and after 1949 took an active role in the PRC's public health work, in particular the prevention and treatment of venereal diseases and leprosy.[56] During their reunion in 1960 in Hatem's beautiful but modest little courtyard house in the back of the former imperial palace, the two old 'China hands', Snow and Hatem, bemoaned American racism, McCarthyism, and the appalling state of public health in the United States, comparing the latter with the PRC's achievements in 'eradicating', or the 'near eradication', of a raft of diseases, from cholera and plague to typhus and smallpox, as well as 'controlling' venereal diseases and malaria.[57] Yet a year after Snow's visit, in 1962 many provinces along or south of the Yangtze experienced a serious pandemic of paracholera caused by a particular strain of the bacterium known as *vibrio cholerae*. At the same time, many of these provinces also experienced some of the worst malaria epidemics in recent memory.*

---

publicly withdrew from active political work in the Nationalist party. In the following years, she sided with the international leftists and actively supported the Communist underground movement in Shanghai as well as the Communist rural reform programs and its anti-Japanese cause.

* While there were no incidents of cholera and plague reported after 1951 until the time of Snow's visit, the actual vaccination program for both diseases had begun during the Nationalist period. Furthermore, as we know, diseases such as cholera and plague as well as malaria, while there might not be any pandemic for a number of years or in certain seasons in the case of malaria, hence zero or low morbidity, this might have more to do with the condition of the environment and the movement of people and animals than with the actual disease control program.

Echoing Hatem and Snow, Dr Joshua Horn, in his widely read biographical account of his time in China, *Away with All Pests* (1969), proudly presented to the world the story of 'how China, once the so-called "Sick Man of Asia", became the first country in the world to conquer syphilis' thanks to the political will of the CCP and the 'voluntary' effort of the Chinese people.[58] Joshua Samuel Horn was born in east London to Jewish parents during World War I. In the interwar years, while still a medical student at University College Hospital (UCH), he became actively involved in the struggles against fascism and unemployment, and he subsequently joined the Socialist Medical Association and the Communist Party of Britain. In 1936, he went to China as a ship's doctor. During his short stay in China, he was appalled by what he saw: 'China was truly the Sick Man of Asia, rampant with poverty, disease and corruption,' and he believed that this was caused by feudalism, imperialist oppression, and social evils such as concubinage. 'China needed a revolution' was the thought that occupied his mind at the time. In 1949, when the People's Republic of China was founded, Horn was among the British leftists to embrace its social claims. In 1954, Horn, by then an established surgeon in Britain, took the first opportunity to return to the new China of which he had dreamt. This time, he moved with his family, and they lived there for fifteen years. What he saw, or tended to see, this second time was markedly different. Horn's new China was an equal and 'democratic' communist society where 'doctors, nurses, orderlies, boiler-men, administrators, Party functionaries, maintenance workers and gardeners, nearly 900 of us all eat together in one huge dining room' and where 'rotten' diseases of the feudal past such as syphilis had been wiped out. According to Horn, by the same political will of the CCP and the 'voluntary' and 'cooperative' effort of the people, China was on its way to becoming the first country in the world to 'wipe out' schistosomiasis – 'one of the world's greatest scourges' and one of the 'most difficult diseases to eradicate'.[59] The 'Sick man of Asia' had been transformed into 'the most healthy man in the world', and politics was the driving force behind China's remarkable public health achievement, Horn argued forcefully in a public lecture he delivered in New York in 1971, which was subsequently broadcast in May 1972.[60] In another lecture at the University of Hong Kong a year earlier, Horn had marvelled at China's Barefoot Doctor program: 'There are more than one million health workers [in China], and most of them live in the countryside. This means one health worker for every six hundred Chinese. For the first time in the five thousand years of Chinese history, China has successfully achieved to deliver health services to its people no matter where they live. China is the first one in the world to achieve this. Yet in wealthy countries such as the United States millions of people have no access to health care.'[61] This last sentence was endorsed by many leftists in the United States who advocated for China as the bastion of a new health care model and who, like Snow and Hatem, were of the generation born and raised during the Great Depression. As Birn and Brown have argued, the impact of McCarthyism and racism in the United States and the Cold War had driven this generation of 'health-leftists' to channel 'much of their political energy beyond U.S. borders, subsumed under the promotion of other bold and worthy causes'. Thus, while Jack Geiger became attracted by the anti-racist, community-oriented primary health care experiments he encountered in South Africa, Victor and Ruth Sidel promoted the Barefoot Doctors they found in Maoist China.[62] From the Sidels' first visit to the PRC in the summer of 1971 to the WHO's Alma Ata Conference in September 1978, the global enthusiasm for the 'Chinese approach to health' increased exponentially. What represented the successes of this system and stood for China's 'supreme' health care system were the examples of the Barefoot Doctor program and the Anti-Schistosomiasis Campaign. However, the entire edifice was a Potemkin's village created to be attractive to visitors passing through the PRC, and the gold-star attractions came to be these two exemplary programs.

THE 'CHINESE APPROACH TO HEALTH'

Fourteen years after the British doctors' 'medical mission' and ten years after Snow's trip to the PRC, in the summer of 1971, in the midst of the Great Proletarian Cultural Revolution, a group of prominent physicians and leaders in the field of public health from the United States, again at the invitation of the CMA, visited the PRC. The visit had been initiated by none other than Edgar Snow, who by this point was in political exile from the United States and living in Switzerland – but for Chinese political leaders such as Premier Zhou Enlai, Snow remained a central conduit to the Americans. Between 1970 and 1971, after his second trip to the PRC at the invitation of the CCP Central Committee to observe and report on the Chinese Great Proletarian

Cultural Revolution, Snow published numerous articles about his trip and his interviews with Chinese leaders in *Life* magazine as well as in its popular Italian counterpart *Epoca*. In several articles for *Epoca*, he detailed the PRC's achievements in medicine and public health, in particular the birth control efforts and the Barefoot Doctor program.[63] While it stirred up a great deal of interest in the United States, his reporting also attracted criticism. A number of critics discredited Snow's account on the grounds that he had no professional training in medicine or public health. To defend himself, Snow arranged for his friend E. Grey Dimond, a respected cardiologist, medical educator, and innovator who had founded the University Missouri-Kansas City School of Medicine, to go to the PRC and make his own professional observations and report on them.[64]

This was the first time in twenty-four years that health professions from both countries had made 'official' contact. It has often been referred to as the 'historical visit'.[65] Dimond was accompanied by Paul Dudley White, the distinguished cardiologist and President Eisenhower's personal physician; Samuel Rosen, the internationally acclaimed ear surgeon; Victor Sidel, the chair of Social Medicine at Montefiore Medical Centre and the professor of Social Medicine at the Albert Einstein College of Medicine; and Ruth Sidel, a social worker at a primary care paediatric health centre at Einstein College who was also committed to the cause of women's and children's rights and well-being. During their twelve-day guided tour, the Americans were taken to see twelve model medical and health facilities and had thirty hours of scheduled discussions with officially chosen Chinese physicians. While none of the Americans had been to China before and while they spoke not a word of Chinese, according to Dimond the *lingua medica* such as stethoscope, ophthalmoscope, electrocardiogram, and laboratory data 'bridged whatever other language gap existed'. The trip impressed Dimond deeply: 'Eight hundred million people, one-fourth of the world's population, are hard at work, disciplined, honest, courteous, intelligent, healthy, and give every evidence of enthusiastically learning and practicing a Communistic way of life.' Writing about the trip for the *Saturday Review* – a widely circulated weekly magazine that promoted liberal causes such as nuclear disarmament and world peace – Dimond warned the American public not to be blinded by the 'Bamboo Curtain' that 'has only obscured our view, including that of medicine ... I think we Americans do ourselves harm, blind ourselves to facts, and perpetuate myths.' To support his argument, he compared the Chinese 'achievements' in public health and the PRC government's ability to provide ready, inexpensive, and convenient health care to its rural population of 700 million to the failure of the American government to provide adequate health care to the American people. 'China is more than Communism,' he concluded forcefully.[66]

Echoing Dimond, his fellow delegate Victor Sidel also felt strongly that China's 'revolutionary experience' in health and medicine could offer valuable lessons for public health and community health work in the United States as well as for the rest of the world. Also born during the Great Depression, Sidel's own commitment to community primary care grew as a reaction to McCarthyism and Cold War politics. Like many in the American left of their generation, Victor Sidel and his wife Ruth were strongly committed to causes for greater social and economic justice both at home and abroad. As a physician, Victor Sidel channelled much of his political energy into public health work, in particular community health undertakings, and he co-founded Physicians for Social Responsibility, the largest physician-led organization, aimed at 'creating a healthy, just and peaceful world'. In preparation for their first China visit, the Sidels read Edgar Snow and Joshua Horn, as well as William Hinton's *Fanshen*.[67] Their writings presented health care in the PRC in the most favourable light possible, and according to the Sidels, the 'detailing [of] the extraordinary changes in China during and after the revolution, were particularly useful'.[68] It was from these works that they developed their questions about health care delivery and community primary care in rural China. In another words, it was through these clearly propagandistic texts that China's public health achievement as a major medical and political success was to be approached and evaluated.

Their 'historical visit' to the PRC also antedated Nixon's visit and the diplomatic opening to China in 1972, both of which had been brokered, in an odd way, by Edgar Snow's 1970 discussions with Mao and Zhou Enlai, reported in *Time* magazine, where the idea of Nixon's trip was first broached. Suddenly, China became a 'hot topic'. Upon returning to the United States, the Sidels and Dimond, as well as Joshua Horn (who had by then left the PRC), spent much time lecturing and writing to promote the PRC's purported public health achievements. Their lectures and publications were enthusiastically received by a wider audience, from the FBI agents who shadowed them to the general public who were fascinated to hear that 'starving children in China' had turned into happy, healthy, and 'cooperative human beings'.[69]

Amongst the Sidels' 'new audience' were also critical voices of the 'medicationization of life' who were pushing for the 'deprofessionalization' of medicine. In the West, the scientific and technological revolution in medicine that had begun with the end of World War II had seemingly peaked by the late 1960s. Great changes in medical care and access were, however, slower in coming. There was a growing consensus that medicine in the Western world was in a state of crisis. Despite huge efforts and wealth being invested into health care and medicine, the reality was that the general health of the population was deteriorating. In his highly controversial but influential work, *Medical Nemesis* (1975), Ivan Illich, the Viennese-born radical thinker, famously argued that modern allopathic medicine and hospital-centred health care had become a major threat to health in the world: 'After a century of pursuit of medical Utopia, and contrary to current conventional wisdom, medical services have not been important in producing the changes in life expectancy that have occurred. A vast amount of contemporary clinical care is incidental to the curing of disease, but the damage done by medicine to the health of individuals and populations is very significant.'[70]

This was 'the closest I ever came to a religious experience,' said Richard Smith, who later became the editor of the *British Medical Journal* (BMJ) and 'a pillar of the British medical establishment', recalling the effect of Illich's words on him at the time: 'I dropped out of medical school that day [after hearing Illich]. Three days later I dropped back in again, unsure what else to do.'[71] Smith's anxiety was shared by a great number of people in medicine and public health in the West. There was a strong sense that 'new ideas are needed, new systems of health care have to be explored.'[72] Accounts by Joshua Horn and George Hatem, as well as other Western health observers of the PRC – particularly in the popular works by the Sidels and echoed in the 1972 documentary film *Barefoot Doctor of Rural China* produced by a group of scholars from Stanford University – claimed that the health care delivery system in the PRC that relied on non-professional health workers (the Barefoot Doctors) offered a radical new approach to the people's health. This 'Chinese approach', understood as a draconian government measure aimed at providing ready, convenient, and inexpensive health care to the 700 million people who lived in the rural countryside, became increasingly attractive to Western health professionals and policy-makers who were seeking a way out of the perceived Western health crisis. One needs to note here that the health care crises in the United States at the time were perceived as centred in the deteriorating urban landscapes. The fascination earlier in the century with rural poverty and health care, such as that represented by Joseph Goldberger's work on pellagra, had given way to the perception that greater urbanization had created even greater risks to the people's health.[73]

In the next decade, a growing number of American health professionals were offered opportunities to visit the PRC. Like Dimond and the Sidels, they were impressed by the PRC's purported achievements in public health, particularly how China had managed to resolve the problem of providing health care to its 700 million people living in the countryside, whereas the United States had failed to do anything like this. One such individual was Phillip Lee, professor of social medicine at the University of California's School of Medicine in San Francisco. In 1965, Lee had participated in the first White House Conference on Health when the Secretary of State, Dean Rusk, famously declared the export of American health capacity as one of the strongest aspects of US foreign policy.[74] For the next decade, in his capacity as a medical educator, Lee advocated for health professionals to work in concert with the United States government to meet the growing demands of a changing society and globally. In 1974, after spending several months in China as the guest of the CMA, Lee joined the Sidels and Dimond in promoting the PRC's health care delivery system back home:

It is clear that there has been a pronounced decline in the death rate, particularly infant mortality. Major epidemic diseases have been controlled, and in some cases apparently eradicated. Nutritional status has been improved. Massive campaigns of health education and environmental sanitation have been carried out. Large numbers of health workers have been trained, and a system has been developed that provides some health service for the great majority of the people ... How, in so short a time, did the Chinese manage to transform a country where the death rate was among the highest in the world, epidemic diseases were widespread, sanitation was primitive and modern medical care was essentially limited to the urban elite, into a country where the health status of the population now ranks well ahead of that of most developing nations, most of the people have an appreciation of sanitation and the great majority have access to health care? Is there anything Americans can learn from the Chinese experience in medicine and public health?[75]

To learn from the Chinese experience, Lee joined others in pushing the United States government to prioritize public health programs at home and globally, centred on community health programs. In the meantime, modelled on the Chinese Barefoot Doctor program as well as on parallel programs in Cuba and Chile, the Sidels helped to build a Community Health Participation Program in the Bronx, New York, that recruited, trained, and supervised neighbourhood health workers.[76] The Bronx, in the 1970s, was very poor and underserved but also very urban. The Sidels' focus had moved from rural China to urban America.

HEALTH DIPLOMACY

While medicine had been part of European 'soft power' in China before the CCP's seizure of power in 1949, as of the late 1950s the PRC government skilfully utilized Western fascination with its mass public health achievements, in particularly the Anti-Schistosomiasis Campaign, to win support internationally. By the second half of the 1960s, an increasing number of Western critics of existing health disparities in industrialized nations and advocates of social medicine came to view the PRC's Barefoot Doctor program, fashioned as Mao's 'revolutionary approach' to the people's health, as able to deliver ready, convenient, and inexpensive health care to the millions living in rural China as a true alternative model for primary care and health care delivery. This complemented increasingly positive images of the PRC and its totalitarian government purveyed by its cohort of Western sympathizers, who contrasted Communist China with the American aggression in Vietnam that was seen as aimed at suppressing a popular revolution. In developing countries and the United Nations, the rise of the 'Third Way', championed by Yugoslavia and India, offered China a global space to effect its political goals through exporting its model of health care.

In 1972, a year after their first visit, the Sidels were invited by the CMA to return to China and undertake more detailed and extensive observations about China's public health innovations. In the same year, Dimond brought the first PRC medical delegation to the United States. From then on, together with Joshua Horn, they became the PRC's most useful 'international friends' in the arena of international public health. While the Sidels acted as spokespeople for the PRC, Dimond took many groups, both medical and lay, to visit China to promote cultural exchanges between the West and the PRC. As a reward for his 'friendship', he was given honorary professorships at several medical schools in China as well as rare access to many key events in the PRC. The Chinese Minister of Foreign Affairs Huang Hua was among one of his 'close friends' in China.

At the same time, governments in postcolonial Africa, Southeast Asia, and Latin America, where healing and indigenous medicines played an integral part in the political struggle for a new postcolonial identity, had become impressed by China's reported ability to redress health care disparity. They were particularly interested in the way the Chinese had managed to reduce the health burden of the state by incorporating existing or traditional medical practices into its national health service.[77] In 1967, for example, a medical delegation from Tanzania visiting China was said to be 'impressed by the stage of development of health services, which have been revolutionized and transformed by the new China'.[78] The training of Barefoot Doctors, as well as the integration of indigenous methods and allopathic medicine – the latter was often branded 'modern' – were seen by these Tanzanian officials as a useful model by which to develop a new national health care delivery system that would cater to its rural populations.[79] Partly driven by their commitment to non-aligned socialism, a number of African countries, as well as socialist countries in Southeast Asia and Latin America, approached China for health collaboration that included training and health aid.

The PRC leadership quickly capitalized on this, viewing health cooperation with these Third World countries as 'inexpensive but profitable' undertakings that could help its effort to promote a new international order – a 'people's revolutionary movement in Asia, Africa and Latin America' against 'colonialism, imperialism and hegemonism'.[80] After learning from Luis Echeverría Álvarez – the president of Mexico who had just embarked on a populist political and economic reform that included massive state spending on improving the people's health – that he was planning to promote the PRC's Barefoot Doctor program in Mexico, Mao, for instance, advised Xiong Xianghui, the PRC's first ambassador to Mexico, to spend some time in the Chinese countryside to study the Barefoot Doctors.[81] A couple of years earlier, on 5 June 1971, in a conversation with the government delegation from Somalia, Zhou Enlai had carefully emphasized that health collaborations between the two countries were intended to serve the local interests and thus to promote friendship. Chinese medical teams had to avoid the 'superpower chauvinism' associated with the Americans.[82]

Beginning with sending a medical team to 'aid' newly independent Algeria in 1963, the PRC continuously dispatched medical teams to more than twenty-two countries in Africa over the next decades. Different provinces in China were twinned with African nations. For instance, Sichuan was responsible for developing malaria and schistosomiasis control projects in Mozambique, whereas teams of doctors of both allopathic medicine and traditional Chinese medicine (TCM) from Shandong went to Tanzania and other African countries.[83] In addition, China provided medical and health training to a large number of students from Africa, Southeast Asia, and Latin America, competing with the extensive parallel programs of training such physicians in the Soviet Union, such as that at the Lumumba Friendship University in Moscow. China also regularly sent 'friendship delegations' to these countries; the delegations always included at least one health worker as a model 'Barefoot Doctor'. With this expansion, China's influence on health care delivery in Asia, Latin America, and Africa grew exponentially. China's 'friendship', centred in health collaborations, also paved way for the re-emergence of traditional medical practice and a fast-growing herbal market in postcolonial settings such as Tanzania.[84] In Mozambique, on the other hand, acupuncture imported from the PRC as part of the newly created 'Traditional Chinese Medicine' became widely popular.*[85] At the same time, China's Barefoot Doctor program worked particularly well in the local rural conditions in many African countries.[86] In contrast, the centralized Soviet model was perceived as less effective.

Contemporary sources that have recently emerged from Chinese archives also show that politics was always an integral part of Chinese medical activities and its selling of Sino-African friendship. Chinese medical teams were fully aware that their mission was to spread

---

* In September 2017, the Ministry of Health in Mozambique announced the introduction of acupuncture into main provincial hospitals in parts of the country.

Figure 9.1 Africans revering a Mao portrait.

Figure 9.2 Chinese doctor performing acupuncture in Africa.

'The Thought of Mao Zedong' (毛泽东思想 or Maoism) in addition
to their medical work. For example, while researching the African
variety of schistosomiasis in Somalia, the Chinese medical team put
up an exhibition showing how under the leadership of Mao, China
had successfully eradicated this deadly disease. Those invited to the
exhibition included workers, rural residents, officials, middle school
students, and policemen. Not only was the medical and public health
propaganda rampant, the villagers even learnt to sing 'The East Is
Red'. This medical and cultural propaganda bore fruit. After seeing
the exhibition, one local official went to the Chinese team and said:
'Thank you. Compared to the American, the British, and the Italian
doctors, the Chinese are our most loyal friends.' Another government technician was convinced that the 'Thought of Mao Zedong'
was the only guarantee that could bring happiness to the people of
the world. During the Somalian New Year celebration in 1971, a
group of workers and rural villagers sang 'The East Is Red' while
holding Mao's portrait aloft. After singing and dancing, they also
shouted: 'We thank the Chinese doctors for helping us', 'The Chinese
bring us food and cure us from diseases', 'China brings us life. Don't
invade China'.[87] Whether the medical interventions were as successful
as the propaganda claimed is questionable, but the end effect was to
establish China as the model for improving the people's health.

At the UN, the PRC's increasing medical 'humanitarian' activities and the bonds of friendship created through such undertakings
helped the PRC win its battle against the Republic of China (Taiwan)
for the permanent 'Chinese' seat at the Security Council and mem-
bership in the General Assembly. At the 1971 UN General Assembly
meeting, twenty-six African nations voted in favour of legitimat-
ing the status of the People's Republic of China in the UN.[88] At the
same time, the PRC was seen as a crucial player in the so-called
'African issues': 'China could outdo the Soviet Union rhetorically
and also sponsor action that is too rich for Moscow's blood,' argued
American television correspondent Richard Hottelet, covering the
United Nations at the time.[89] In placing the PRC in the UN, the sense
was that it would prevent China from supplying military aid to the
various national liberation movements in Africa, given the Chinese
support for such activities in Southeast Asia. In comparison, Taiwan
was considered too marginal a player in this matter.[90]

With its entrance into the UN in 1973, the PRC was invited to
rejoin the World Health Assembly.[91] The PRC began to use the World

Health Assembly meetings as the diplomatic arena to promote its new Third World policy and to combat the First World 'superpowers', particularly the USSR. For instance, in May 1974, a few days after the PRC's vice prime minister Deng Xiaoping presented the Third World policy at the UN General Assembly, the model Barefoot Doctor, Wang Guizhen, was briefed by the new minister of health to use the Twenty-Seventh World Health Assembly meeting to defeat the PRC's enemies by propagating Mao's 'revolutionary' foreign policy, in addition to disseminating the 'revolutionary' approach to health preached by the PRC with the Barefoot Doctors and the integration of Chinese and Western medicines. On her return, Wang proudly reported that the meeting was a great triumph for the PRC and for Chairman Mao. According to her, many Third World countries, as well as the WHO officials, welcomed the PRC's new Third World policy and praised the PRC's cooperative health system and the Barefoot Doctor program for being truly grassroots, while criticizing Soviet medical training and its aid to the Third World as not applicable to these countries.[92]

FROM 'HEALTH FOR ALL' TO THE DECLARATION OF ALMA ATA

The post-war scientific and technological revolution, as well as the collapse of the remaining colonial empires of Great Britain, France, and the Netherlands, also brought about major changes in the world, presaging what is now called globalization. This led to greater awareness of growing global disparities, especially in health care and access. The emergence of decolonized nations and the spread of national and anti-imperialist socialist movements in the less developed Third World countries (nowadays labelled the 'Global South'), with more limited economic resources, also demanded a new health care delivery model. In the meantime, the International Health Division of the Rockefeller Foundation had more or less retired from the active global scene in direct health care interventions. The people's health had begun to enter a new post-imperial stage, now labelled as the 'Fourth Phase' of public health. China's rural health delivery system – the Barefoot Doctor program – which involved a massive training program and a major mobilization and organization of health services, linked with mass political campaigns, soon became a major inspiration for the burgeoning, worldwide Primary Health Care movement.

In 1967, John Bryant published *Health and the Developing World*, based on a collaborative project sponsored by the Rockefeller Foundation to assess health care delivery in developing countries. Bryant had been one of the foremost leaders of international public health over the previous three decades and a member of the Christian Medical Commission – a member of the World Council of Churches and the Lutheran World Federation, created in the late 1960s by medical missionaries, which advocated primary health care. While warning that 'large numbers of the world's people, perhaps more than half, have no access to health care at all', Bryant argued against transplanting hospital-based health care from the West to the developing countries: 'for many of the rest, the care they receive does not answer the problems they have ... the most serious health needs cannot be met by teams with spray guns and vaccinating syringes.'[93] Also around this time, medical missionaries working in developing countries, notably those of the Christian Medical Commission, were pushing for primary health care, with an emphasis on training grassroots health workers and adequate but inexpensive care.[94]

At the WHO headquarters in Geneva, the perceived failure of single-disease programs, also known as the vertical health approach, as promoted by the WHO and many US agencies in the 1950s and 1960s, provided a further context for moving away from hospital-centred health care and expert-based medicine toward primary health care and preventive medicine. In 1967, Kenneth W. Newell, an epidemiologist at Tulane University in New Orleans, was appointed by the WHO to lead the new Research in Epidemiology and Communications Science Division. Newell began his career as a medical officer at the Te Araroa Maori region in New Zealand where he had been actively involved in developing community health projects. The Ngati Porou tribe there sold their cattle to raise money to fund his further training in public health in the UK. For many years, Newell had been arguing for an integrated horizontal approach to control zoonotic diseases such as *salmonellae*.* He stressed that the control measures for the developing countries where 'there was lack of safe water supplies and methods of excreta disposal' had to be

---

* In recent years, such an approach has been rebranded and modified as the One Health approach and adopted by a number of global institutions such as the World Bank. See World Bank, *People, Pathogens and Our Planet, Volume 1: Towards a One Health Approach for Controlling Zoonotic Diseases* (Washington: World Bank 2010).

different from those used in the developed countries.[95] After joining the WHO, Newell began to advocate for wider attention to primary health care and became interested in China's Barefoot Doctor program and in comparable developments in Cuba and Tanzania, which in the latter had been carried out with Chinese help. Consequently, he invited the Sidels to the WHO headquarters in Geneva to consult on a WHO and UNICEF joint project entitled Alternative Approaches to Meeting Basic Health Needs in Developing Countries. They were to contribute a case study on the health system in the PRC. The project was both organizations' attempt to 'develop fresh policies and approaches' to assist developing countries in improving people's health by 'examining successful or promising systems of delivery of primary health care'.[96] The project also led to a landmark publication, *Health by the People*, edited by Newell, which included a chapter on the PRC's health care delivery system contributed by the Sidels.[97] Among the nine countries studied, two communist countries, the PRC and Cuba, stood out as the 'really successful' examples of achieving 'better health care coverage, and improve levels of health' with limited resources. Drawing on their 'positive' experiences, the project identified that the government's 'political commitment', 'the integrated approach to health and development', 'mass mobilization', and 'community participation' were keys to building a successful primary health care system that would meet the basic health needs in the developing world. The project report recommended that 'successful' programs such as those in the PRC and Cuba should be 'fostered, extended, adapted and used as examples for a large-scale global program'.[98]

To take the recommendation further, Halfdan Mahler, the director general of the WHO at the time and another driving force behind this joint project, proposed 'health for all citizens of the world'.[99] Before becoming assistant director general in the summer of 1970, Mahler had served as a WHO senior officer attached to the National Tuberculosis Program in India where he had been committed to causes for social justice. During his tenure as the assistant director general, Mahler worked closely with Newell to build the new Division of Strengthening of Health Services. 'Both men were visionaries who shared common values that included dedication to the pursuit of human development and justice,' recalled Socrates Litsios, the former senior scientist at the WHO's Division of the Control of Tropical Diseases.[100] Like Newell, Mahler responded enthusiastically to the widely cited example of the

PRC's successful experience in tackling health problems with limited financial, technological, and human resources and thought it should be promoted around the world. During his speech at the Twenty-Ninth World Health Assembly in May 1976, Mahler spoke of the need for radical change: 'Many social evolutions and revolutions have taken place because the social structures were crumbling. There are signs that the scientific and technical structures of public health are also crumbling ... we are on the threshold of a new era in community health ... it is our duty and our sacred privilege to shape this new era and to chart the ways that lead to it.'[101]

'Health for All' was formally adopted by the Twenty-Ninth World Health Assembly as its goal, to be achieved by the year 2000, and this became the rallying call for the worldwide Primary Health Care movement during the Long 1970s.

While major Western powers accepted the Mahlerian notion of Primary Health Care, the USSR, still very much in favour of centralized health care, opposed it, condemning it as a step backward from the advances in science and technology that had been made since the beginning of the Cold War. In addition, from their perspective, the notion of Primary Health Care was seen as a victory for the developing or 'Third World'. This would, in turn, undermine the USSR's claim to be the world leader in health care delivery and the people's health provider. This was impacted by, and became an intrinsic part of, the open and growing hostility between the PRC and the USSR since Khrushchev's denunciation of Stalin in 1956. Since the goal of 'Health for All' drew its inspiration heavily from the Chinese experience, particularly the Barefoot Doctor program, Moscow felt strongly that it could not 'permit Peking a victory within the Third World'.[102]

After the PRC delegation to the WHO first proposed the idea of an international conference on Primary Health Care, the Soviet Union began to lobby hard to host the conference.[103] In January 1976, the day before the WHO Executive Board meeting, the Soviet Minister of Health Dimitri Venediktov turned up at David A. Tejada de Rivero's home (the assistant director general of the WHO at the time) in Geneva and made an offer: 'I will give you US$2 million for an international conference on Primary Health Care.' Despite Tejada de Rivero's reluctance to accept the deal, at the Executive Board meeting Venediktov once again presented his proposal. It was only after Venediktov agreed that the conference would not be held in Moscow but instead in a developing country that the Executive Board accepted his offer and the conference was scheduled for 1978.[104]

The search for a suitable location in the 'Third World' was a difficult one. Since the USSR was sponsoring the conference, the PRC – the world's putative leader in and certainly a major inspiration for the Primary Health Care movement – had to be excluded. Other countries favoured by the WHO were Costa Rica, Egypt, and Iran, but none could successfully secure the additional US $1 million needed for the conference. After some extensive travel around the USSR, Venediktov and Tejada de Rivero agreed on Alma Ata (today's Almaty), the capital of the Kazakh Soviet Socialist Republic (today's Kazakhstan) as a suitable location for the conference. According to Tejada de Rivero, Alma Ata was chosen for two reasons: it had a very impressive conference hall and a very dynamic minister of health, Professor Turgeldy S. Sharmanov.[105] For the Soviets, however, Alma Ata was also significant because it was geographically proximate to China. Furthermore, it had become the USSR's showcase of socialist achievement in providing health care for the 'backward' Kazakhs through a centralized, state-run health delivery system and bringing modern bio-medicine to rural villagers.[106] (It should also be noted that it was the site of the politically inspired famine of 1932–33, known today as the Goloshchekin genocide, which caused the deaths of approximately two million people.[107] While the Chinese famine was a recent public health horror, the Soviet famine had become a distant memory, occluded by the new ideal of a Kazakh health program.)

Back at the WHO headquarters in Geneva, Kenneth Newell was put in charge of drawing up documents for the Alma Ata conference. There were extensive conflicts over the concept of 'Health for All' as well as the wording of the official text of the declaration. According to Tejada de Rivero, with 'Health for All' Mahler 'made it clear that he was referring to the need to provide a level of health that would enable all people without exception to live socially and economically productive lives ... It was a social and political goal, but above all a battle cry to incite people to action.'[108] Yet, as Mahler pointed out in a 2008 interview, 'Primary Health Care will not succeed unless we can generate participation from individuals, families and communities, but this community participation will not work unless there is support from the health system.'[109] Not only the USSR and many WHO member states supported a centralized health system approach, but a number of delegates also 'fought to include details that had more to do with medical specialties than with health'.[110] 'It wasn't easy,' as Mahler remembered it. 'There was a lot of fighting during the months of preparation and at the conference itself ... For example, to include "family planning" alongside "maternal and child health care" in the declaration virtually caused the whole thing to break down ... But the Secretariat was anxious about getting a consensus, which was vital. That did not mean trying to convince our adversaries they were wrong, but trying to unite ourselves with them at a higher level of insight. This was exactly what happened in Alma Ata. It was almost a spiritual atmosphere, not in the religious sense, but in the sense that people wanted to accomplish something great.'[111] The Chinese model came to be redefined by the debates but remained at their core.

Between 6 and 12 September 1978 at Alma Ata, 3,000 delegates from 134 member states, sixty-seven international organizations, and a dozen NGOs from around the world attended the world's first Primary Health Care conference. At the conference, the Final Declaration of Alma Ata was read aloud to all delegates. This declaration made it clear that health is 'a fundamental human right and that the attainment of the highest possible level of health is a most important worldwide social goal whose realization requires the action of many other social and economic sectors in addition to the health sector'.[112] 'Lots of people had tears in their eyes,' Mahler recalled fondly in an interview twenty years later. 'We never thought we would come that far. That was a sacred moment. The 1970s was a warm decade for social justice. That's why after Alma-Ata in 1978, everything seemed possible.'[113] Yet the reality of the next decades was to be quite different from the emotional sentimentality of the declaration. 'Health for All' remained a distant promise for most of the globe. The end result of the popular acceptance of this 'mirage of health', as labelled by Rene Dubois, based on the Chinese model, was not only its failure in those nations attending the conference but also in the one conspicuous nation missing at the conference: the People's Republic of China.

Medicine and health always have a political dimension, and it is no wonder that it came to have an explicit one during the Cold War, especially in regard to the PRC and its relationship to the First as well as the Third World. Standing in opposition to the perceived inadequacies of American health care and the Soviet centralized health care structure, the PRC held out the promise of a true alternative – one that proved as ephemeral as the success falsely attributed to the Barefoot Doctor program and the Anti-Schistosomiasis Campaign. The Long 1970s was the pivotal decade in which this model seemed at the verge of success, only to collapse into the morass of global neoliberal capitalism by the late twentieth century when health care became less and less an exportable model of cultural propaganda. The promise held out by the PRC health care model to deal with the people's health turned out to falter on a number of factors, primarily on the false perception of the coherence of the system itself and its radical focus on rural health in an age of increasing urbanization. Here, we can contrast these promises to the reality, no matter how partial and incomplete in the 1970s, of the access that improved the people's health through the National Health Service in Great Britain. Mortality and morbidity in Great Britain and the PRC radically decreased beginning in the 1950s.[114] Yet the overwhelming initial decreases in the PRC were certainly countered by the mass deaths during the famine years, even though they rebounded thereafter.[115]

Foreign advocates of public health innovations in the PRC were, in the end, much less interested in health care as an end in itself than as a means of achieving social and political reform. To them, success in one dimension – the people's health – demonstrated success in the other: the political realm. The reality was that in attempting to define the improvement of the people's health as an indicator of the utopian success of the political system that furthered it, for good or for ill, they accepted its putative success without question. In the details were, of course, the problems that caused the system to fail or the inability to implement it. Ideas may well have the power to transform. Karl Marx did not think so, however: Marx firmly believed that the material basis of society was the source of all ideology. Ideas and visions may well have an influence on the social beyond being a means of justifying a material structure. But ideas are plastic: they can be twisted and misused easily simply because they do not have a material presence. The health policy of the PRC and its reception is a classic case of this dilemma. The desire for 'Health for All' remained after the death of Mao, as well as the Alma Ata Conference, a goal unequally sought and rarely accomplished across the globe.

Afterword

The jubilation at Alma Ata that enthroned the People's Republic of China (PRC) as the model for improving the people's health most appropriate for the 'Third World' quickly dissipated. Despite the euphoria at the time, merely a year after the Declaration of Alma Ata, Kenneth Warren, who had been appointed director of health science at the Rockefeller Foundation in 1977, and his colleague Julia Wash proposed a radical alternative that vitiated the utopian promises made at Alma Ata. Their Selective Primary Health Care model introduced 'low-cost' but 'high-impact' targeted interventions as an 'interim' strategy for disease control in developing countries.[1] A number of UN agencies quickly adopted this selective approach, seeing it as less costly and simply more pragmatic than the more integrated approach advocated by Halfdan Mahler and Kenneth Newell. Even UNICEF moved away from its earlier commitment to the integrated and holistic model of Primary Health Care in favour of Warren's selective approach.

The background of this decision is important. Kenneth Warren was an expert in schistosomiasis research and grasped the complex reasons for the failure to curb the disease. According to him, it was an earlier 'transformative' experience of watching infants and children die by the roadside in Kenya that gave him the great impetus of using scientific mechanisms to alleviate the health problems in poor countries.[2] Sometimes described by those who knew him well as 'contemptuous' and 'dynamic', Warren was obsessed with health quality and information.*[3] Under his leadership and financially backed by the Rockefeller Foundation, the Great Neglected Disease of Mankind Programme (GND) was established with the intention to create 'a network of high-quality investigators who would constitute a critical mass in this field, attract brightest students, and conduct research of excellence'.[4] No longer was the panacea of universal health care seen as possible.

This unexpected shift was a great disappointment to Mahler and Newell and their supporters: 'That brought us right back to square one,' Mahler lamented in a 2008 interview. 'We had started with selective health-care programmes, single diseases such as malaria and tuberculosis in the 1950s and 1960s. Then we had this spiritual and intellectual awakening that came out of Alma-Ata, and suddenly some proponents of primary health care went back to the old selective approach again. Perhaps, paradoxically, Alma-Ata had in such instances the opposite effect to the one intended, as it made people think too much about selection, rather than following the Alma-Ata gospel of health for all.'[5] Reflecting on why their 'ambitious and worthy' dream of 'Health for All by 2000' failed to realize, David Tejada de Rivero's view was that the concept of 'Health for All' had often been misunderstood, confused with a simple concept of programming that is technical and bureaucratic rather than social and political, whereas 'the conceptualization of "primary health care" was based on erroneous and biased perceptions of the experiences of Third World countries in providing health care with limited resources. In particular, the Chinese experience with "barefoot doctors" was interpreted simplistically and superficially.'[6]

If the PRC had been excluded from the Alma Ata conference as the result of Cold War politics, it was, however, by choice that at virtually the same moment that Warren proposed the Selective Primary Health Care model, the post-Mao government began to gradually abandon the Barefoot Doctor program. The program was officially ended in 1983 as the post-Mao PRC government under Deng Xiaoping's leadership abandoned the Maoist collective economic system in favour of neoliberal market capitalism – labelled as 'socialism with a Chinese face'. As the PRC government opted for a

---

* Interestingly, 'information-sharing', as advocated by Warren, is also the core part of the One Health approach, currently advocated by the WHO.

Selective Primary Health Care model, it began to privatize providers. Barefoot Doctors were reconfigured as village doctors, and they opened private village clinics. To earn a living as well as to sustain their services, they charged the patients fees. Those who could not afford the fees were denied health care. Although the government tried to remedy this by introducing measures to regulate prices for services, drugs, and equipment, it resulted in many providers focusing their activities on high-margin services by investing in high-tech equipment and expensive drugs. This meant health care became even less affordable for many villagers as the providers moved their efforts away from low-margin activities such as day-to-day patient care. These villagers turned to relatively cheaper local indigenous remedies or to cheap antibiotics and other products with unknown side effects. In the 1990s, there were efforts by some local authorities to revive the Rural Co-operative Medical System (RCMS), but most were unsuccessful because the majority of villagers had lost their trust in the co-operative system. Some were simply too poor to make the RCMS economically feasible.[7] While researching for this book, I also learned that after the government had abandoned the program, in one village not far from Hangzhou in Zhejiang province, the local villagers opted to keep the RCMS. This village had a small but profitable hardware factory, and the villagers collectively decided to use the profit it generated to set up a village health fund to finance the health care costs of those villagers who would need it. 'This had nothing to do with the government policy. It's what villagers wanted,' one villager told me.[8] This case as well as the other examples I have given in this book suggest that, to a great extent, if the PRC's Rural Cooperative Health System was ever successful, it had more to do with local agency spurred on by the shared aspiration to improve the communities' health care that contributed to that success.

From the early 1990s, in a drive to modernize China once again, the PRC government embarked on an epic-scale urbanization project. Millions of Chinese farmers were uprooted and displaced into coastal cities where employment in the new quasi-capitalist industries provided better economic incentives than the rural communities could provide. However, the rigid, state Hukou system of household registration meant that they had little to no access to health care and other urban welfare provisions because a person's local identity

defined their access to the faltering state system of health care.* You
had to be treated where you were officially registered – a fact that
excluded millions.

The new Selective Primary Health Care model – but even more
importantly the large-scale urbanization – also impacted the control of schistosomiasis in the PRC. In 1981, two years after Warren
proposed Selective Primary Health Care as 'an interim strategy for
disease control in developing countries', he led an international team
to China to conduct a joint study on schistosomiasis mortality in rural
Anhui province, a marshy region along the Yangtze River. His resulting evaluation discredited the earlier Chinese strategy of eradication
as not only too costly and ineffective but also harmful to the people's health.[9] Although Su Delong, Warren's Chinese co-investigator,
argued that to effectively control the disease it was still necessary to
eliminate the snails, the Ministry of Health, which had had its power
reinstated to manage disease control in 1986, agreed with Warren's
evaluation that using newer single-dose, oral, nontoxic chemotherapeutic agents in treating the disease was more cost-effective than
trying to eliminate snails.[10] This also coincided with, in 1984, the
World Health Organization (WHO) expert consultation committee
changing its strategy and objective from controlling snails and the
environment to reducing morbidity and mortality by focusing on
chemotherapy and health education.[11] In subsequent years, the earlier integrated eradication strategy was abandoned in the PRC, and
the morbidity control strategy intended to reduce the prevalence and
intensities among local populations and livestock was implemented
in the lake regions along the Yangtze.[12]

Between 1992 and 2001, with a loan from the World Bank, the
chemotherapeutic intervention favoured by Warren was introduced
in the PRC as the key to reducing the rate of human infection and
the intensity of schistosomiasis. An official statistic suggests that as
a consequence of this, the number and morbidity of cases of the disease were reduced by half in endemic regions.[13] In the next decade,
the PRC government published the Schistosomiasis Prevention and

---

* Hukou is a comprehensive family registration system to control population mobility
first introduced in 1958. This system discourages migration by limiting individuals'
eligibility for regular urban welfare benefits or social services (e.g., urban pension plans,
public housing, and medical and health care) – a means of preventing the rural population from moving into cities.

Control Regulation, which resulted in the implementation of a more comprehensive strategy for disease control. Such controls ranged from the construction of lavatories with running water to the institution of drug treatment and health education.[14] The introduction of this new national schistosomiasis control program also coincided with the modernization of agriculture, with the reduction in the number of agricultural workers through mechanization and with the simultaneous urbanization and the moving of displaced rural workers into the ever-expanding industrial centres that has occurred since the end of the twentieth century. With the coterminous shift of agricultural land being contracted to individual households, a greater number of villagers also switched from growing labour- and water-intensive crops such as rice to cash crops like tea, medicinal herbs, fruits, or vegetables. While a combination of sanitary interventions and Praziquantel drug therapy have undoubtedly contributed to the decrease in the number of infected people in the endemic regions, the shifts in the means and modes of agricultural production had a much greater effect.[15] These shifts in agricultural practice radically decreased the proportion of people and farm animals engaged in agricultural activities as well as the acreage taken up by rice paddies. The farmers' working hours were also shortened, and the resulting overall improvements in the standard of living were at the core of the upgrading of the people's health.

The depopulation of rural regions and the mass abandonment of agriculture also radically reduced the incidence and prevalence of what were actually primarily rural diseases, such as schistosomiasis. By 2015, official published statistics showed that all endemic regions had achieved control of the infection, with the number of infected people falling by 91 per cent.[16] Just as malaria disappeared from the East Anglia Fens in England in the nineteenth century after the local population moved away, in many regions of China where schistosomiasis had been endemic the greatest challenge for those in charge of local treatment today is finding sufficient patients, since virtually all male labourers have migrated to the coastal cities for their livelihood.[17] The occasional acute outbreaks are mostly among rural children who become infected after playing in contaminated water.[18] However, many infected villagers from endemic regions of rural Anhui, Hunan, and Hubei moved to coastal cities seeking employment in factories or work on construction sites, and as a result there was an increased danger of acute outbreaks of the disease in these urbanized areas where the infection had previously disappeared precisely because of urbanization and the consequent draining of fields and swamps.[19] Many of these displaced rural workers lived in crowded accommodation with appalling sanitary conditions. If the water supply became contaminated, there was a real danger of schistosomiasis quickly becoming endemic again in these urbanized areas, especially as an increasing number of snails were now found in many of the reclaimed wetlands in the lower reaches of the Yangtze River near the coast because of the rise of water levels and the absence of a budget as well as cheap labour for snail control.[20] Adding to the existing complications has been the increased Sino-African cooperation in recent years. There have been reports of Chinese contract workers, as well as travellers, returning to the PRC from African countries carrying variant forms of schistosomiasis after becoming infected in their host countries.[21] At the same time, after the PRC adopted the Selective Primary Health Model and in the wake of the SARS pandemic in 2003, a number of local schistosomiasis control institutions were simply dissolved and restructured into local centres for disease control.[22] Just as antibiotic overuse has led to the reappearance of a wide range of infectious diseases long since considered under control, so, too, have patterns of diseases such as schistosomiasis continued to shift – from its spread by the movement of Communist troops immediately after World War II to the displacement of rural workers into the cities, as well as the PRC's economic and political expansion into Africa half a century later.

With radical system change and concomitant social upheaval, insecurity prevailed, and the basic trust necessary for health care was at risk. Local trust had vanished with increased urbanization and the dispersal of ever-greater numbers of people who were now crowded into what have become massive urban slums with increased rates of infectious disease and malnutrition. Such was the unintended consequence of urbanization as well as the utopian projects to modernize China. Urban health care, relying on centralized medical expertise, never earned the trust of the new migrant patients. Indeed, the urban system even lost whatever trust their original urban patients had had in it as it became overloaded, inefficient, expensive, and chaotic. Violence directed against doctors, euphemistically called 'medical disturbances' (医闹), has become a regular feature of urban health care.[23] Distrust of the state's primary care system has resulted in increasing rates of self-medication, which relies on cheap counterfeit drugs smuggled in from India or on out-of-date clandestine remedies.[24] In 2018, Wen Muye's film *Dying to Survive* was the top box office success in Chinese cinema that year. The film tells the true story of how the leukaemia patient Lu Yong became a folk hero when he imported unapproved anti-cancer drugs from India to supply fellow patients in China suffering from chronic myeloid leukaemia (CML) who could not afford the cost of the medication on the domestic market.[25] At the same time, allopathic medicine is undermined by corruption at all levels, from the pharmaceutical industry to the hospitals. Folk remedies have also been rendered unsafe because practitioners employ equally questionable remedies with little or no training in their application or are driven by the profit motive. Repeated unsafe vaccine scandals have further undermined people's trust of the state: 'If a government can't deliver safe vaccines for children, is it fit to rule?' one asks.[26] People's anger has prompted the government to again attempt to alter the health care system by tinkering at its edges. The sense on the ground is of chaos in the health care system; the public response is wide-scale distrust and anxiety.

The Mao era has long since passed. China is now the world's second largest economy. The previously dirty and diseased countryside, 'the Sick man of Asia', has given way to megapolises with hyper-modern facilities. Yet China is long way from being the disease-free 'socialist garden' imagined in Mao's utopian plans. The cities create continuously greater health risks; air pollution and flu pandemics have become the largest threats to people's health in urban areas. In the meantime, health disparity continues and expands across the board. Although the divide imagined by Mao in the 1960s between the urban and rural populations has vanished, health disparity is everywhere.

THE LEGACY OF THE
PEOPLE'S HEALTH IN THE PRC

By the end of the twentieth century, the trajectory of the wide range of undertakings to improve the people's health in the PRC had taken a markedly downward turn. What had begun after the successful seizure of power by the Communists in 1949 in linking health care to their revolutionary agenda ended precipitously after Mao's death in the late 1970s. As I have shown, social upheaval, political change, and health care were, and are, intimately linked in the PRC. Health care delivery, public health interventions, and the changes in medical practice occasioned by shifts in political needs at the centre and on the periphery have changed health care in the PRC, sometimes for the better but often, because of the unintended and secondary effects of other state policies, for the worse. The legacy of the 'Chinese approach' to improving people's health is thus as complex as all of the other tales of improving health care. While many of the indicators of the people's health, such as the gross statistics of morbidity and mortality, tended to improve over time, the way individuals experienced such changes was often radically different from the official claims. The experience of those engaged in these processes, both the experts from above and the grassroots cadres, the health workers and villagers from below, as presented in this book, points to the importance of undertaking careful examination of the many complexities involved in the implementation of large-scale public health initiatives. China serves as a good example of the complexity of creating a monolithic health system for a vast and varied country.

By moving away from a narrow focus on policy formulation and the published official accounts, and by examining the reality of health care and medicine at the local level, this book has provided a fuller and more nuanced account of how and whether the PRC's internationally acclaimed mass public health undertakings – the Anti-Schistosomiasis Campaigns and the Barefoot Doctor program – worked on the ground and the many difficulties and contradictions that emerged as they were implemented over time and in various geographic and cultural locations. By contrasting the views of those impacted, either as patients or as experts and health cadres, with the officially stated goals to improve the people's health, a better sense can be achieved of the accuracy of the claims of these programs, as well as the attitudes toward them, for the first time. By bringing those directly impacted by the campaign into my account of this complex history and seeing them as active participants in the state public health campaigns, it can be seen how great designs on paper often turned into makeshift solutions, with little resemblance to the original project, as soon as they encountered human reality.

What is vital in this account is that the progress of both campaigns varied from province to province, from location to location, and over time. They depended less on the political vision and the policy from above than on a whole range of local factors: from the precise nature of the relationship between agencies at various levels of local authority to the vagaries of the local economy, the range of resources, and the cultural sensibilities of both villagers and grassroots health workers, as well as other more 'practical' considerations. To overcome these obstacles, the frontline workers or the CCP cadres managing the campaigns on the ground understood the need to be persuasive rather than authoritarian in their approach. This was reflected in the efficacy of the public health propaganda as well as in local organizational work. It was not national norms but local conditions that defined success.

Of equal importance to the vagaries of local experience is the simple fact that health planners at the centre never understood how communities at the periphery perceived their health needs. The state's attempt to improve the people's heath with modern allopathic medicine and systemized Traditional Chinese Medicine (TCM), by stamping out existing popular healing practices as 'feudal practices', was regularly contested on the ground. A wide range of vernacular healing rituals, from witchcraft to exorcism as well as other forms of collective, everyday healing rituals and self-help strategies, continued unabated under socialism.

As the promise to improve the people's health had been, from the beginning of the new state, a central tool utilized by the CCP in establishing political legitimacy, the state's failure to deliver it nearly cost the CCP its legitimacy. When bureaucracy hindered Mao and the CCP from exercising power from the centre, slogans such as 'To Serve the People' and 'Revolutionary Humanitarianism' were evoked as a means of papering over the difficulties on the ground and of easing tensions between the people and the party. Villains who thwarted the party's (and simultaneously the people's) desires – in this case the 'revisionists' and 'bourgeois' experts – were sought out, identified, and overcome, no matter their culpability. While Mao's political vision and the leadership's ability to mobilize the masses may have contributed to an improved health care system and ultimately to overall better health, political factors had unintended yet truly negative consequences for the people's health. The political instability of the Mao era often meant that the public health policies and campaigns could not be sustained or carried out over time, and the result was radical fluctuations in the trajectory of any overall change.

Thus, the utopian goal of turning the Chinese countryside into a 'disease free socialist garden' through health improvements also had unplanned and lasting negative consequences on the environment and hence on the people's health. The application of molluscicides, as well as the use of radical engineering interventions such as land reclamation, to kill snails damaged the natural ecosystem. Such physical changes in the environment also conflicted with the system for water conservation, contributing to the severe flooding that is still haunting the population who live in the impacted regions along the Yangtze River and its flood plain. At the same time, human exploitation of the environment, as part of the agricultural expansion that was aimed at ending rural poverty and conquering diseases such as schistosomiasis, exposed the greater population to the disease and increased the number and geographic distribution of those becoming ill from it.

One further and important lesson that can be extrapolated from the Chinese experiences in dealing with the people's health during the first three decades of the PRC is that utopian solutions linking health to absolute political goals are bound to frustrate and disappoint those most directly affected. The reality of change, if not improvement, in people's health relies on multiple variables, which often shift from moment to moment in a kaleidoscope of causations and intended and unintended consequences. Utopian solutions, from the left and from the right, focus on specific relationships and causes – whether macroeconomic, 'racial', caste, geographic, or cultural – that are always shifting and indeed which are often invented and reinvented for purposes that have little or nothing to do with people's health. Who would have imagined that the radical success in combatting infectious diseases, beginning (at least in the West) with Edward Jenner and smallpox, continuing though the first age of biological thinking with Louis Pasteur (rabies) and Robert Koch (cholera), would have foundered in the twenty-first century, not because of war and poverty but on the economic success of a middle class oblivious to the horrors of infectious diseases and exposed to anti-vaccination claims through the new technology of the worldwide web?[27] Or that the promises of eradication of the vectors of other diseases – of snails, of mosquitos, of rats – would be shattered because of the vagaries of changes as radically different as cheap air travel and climate change? And that the powerful 'wonder cure' of antibiotics would lead to equally powerful drug resistance? If Mao's claims linking the people's health to the politics of his state were simultaneously supported and undermined by changes he attributed to the politics of the day, how much more can we claim that his utopian goals destroyed the lives of many more than it saved? In a speech to the Second Session of the Eighth Communist Party Congress on 8 May 1958, Mao announced that the PRC would make the superhuman breakthrough to achieve the Great Leap Forward by 'mak[ing] the high mountain bow its head; mak[ing] the river yield the way'. This goal ended with the worst famine in human history, claiming tens of millions of lives. Such destructive and often unintended consequences to people's health of such utopian goals remain today. The crisis of health care in the PRC today as seen in the response to the COVID-19 virus is, to a great extent, the result of this complex and contradictory history of the Maoist model to improve people's health. Through a nuanced understanding of different health systems' components, the contexts in which these systems exist, and the sequencing of actions, it can be seen how the claims to design better interventions to strengthen the health system, to increase health care coverage, and ultimately to improve people's health can have long-term consequences, intentional or unintended.

Notes

LIST OF ARCHIVES

Archives in China
BEIJING – Beijing Municipal Archive:
Beijing Municipal Bureau of Health and Hygiene (135)

GANSU – Gansu Provincial Archive:
Gansu Provincial Party Committee (91)

GUIZHOU – Chishui County Archive:
Chishui County Party Committee (1-A)

HUNAN – Hunan Provincial Archive:
Hunan Provincial Party Committee (140)
Hunan Province Bureau of Health and Hygiene (163)

HUNAN – Yueyang City Archive:
Yueyang Region Revolutionary Committee (100)

JIANGSU – Kunshan City Archive (Kunshan)

JIANGXI   Jiangxi Provincial Archive: Jiangxi Provincial Health Bureau
(X111)

SHANGHAI – Shanghai Municipal Archive:
Shanghai Municipal Party Committee Socialist Education Committee (A21)
Shanghai Municipal Party Committee Rural Work Department (A70)
Shanghai Municipal Party Committee Rural Work Committee (A72)
Shanghai Municipal Public Service Office (A59)

Shanghai Municipal Health Bureau (B242)
Shanghai Municipal Committee on Agricultural Work (B250)
Shanghai Association of Medical Workers (C3)
The Communist China Youth League Shanghai Branch (C21)
The United Front Shanghai Branch (C44)
Tongde Medical College (Q249)

SHANGHAI – Fudan University's School of Public Health Archive:
Professor Su Delong's Academic Papers (RM008-082)

SICHUAN – Sichuan Provincial Archive:
Sichuan Province Bureau of Health and Hygiene (JC133)
Western Sichuan Region Party Committee (JX1)
Xikang Province Health Department (JK32)
Xikang Province Party Committee (JK1)

SICHUAN – Xichang City Archive:
Xichang County Health Authority (62)

YUNNAN – Yunnan Provincial Archive:
Yunnan Province Bureau of Grain (120)
Yunnan – Dali Region Schistosomiasis Control Research Institute

ZHEJIANG – Zhejiang Provincial Archive:
Zhejiang Province Health and Disease Prevention Department (J166)

ZHEJIANG – Jiaxing City Archive:
Jiaxing Municipal Government (143)
Jiaxing County Authority (016)
Jiaxing Party History Research Office (191)
Jiaxing County Health Bureau (053)
Jiaxing Disease Prevention Station (078)
Jiaxing Schistosomiasis Control Office (008)
Jiaxing Agricultural Bureau (031)
Jiaxing Jingxiang Commune Schistosomiasis Control Work Team (102)

ZHEJIANG – Jiaxing City Library 'Schistosomiasis Control in Jiaxing
Oral History' Archive

Non-Chinese Archives
ROCKEFELLER FOUNDATION ARCHIVES
The Rockefeller Foundation Annual Reports
Projects (RG1.1)
General Correspondence (RG2)
China Medical Board (CMB)
Claude H. Barlow Papers, 1919–64

DIGITAL ARCHIVES FOR THE WHO AND THE LEAGUE OF
NATIONS DOCUMENTS:
Official Records of the World Health Organization at the WHO digital
library (IRIS: https://apps.who.int/iris/handle/10665/85537/
browse?type=dateissued)
Reports on the Work of the League at the Northwestern University
Library's digital collection of League of Nations Statistical and
Disarmament Documents (https://wayback.archive-it.org/6321/
20160901163206/http://digital.library.northwestern.edu/league/
search.html)

INTRODUCTION

1 I am using the term 'the people's health', *Volksgesundheit*, as an ideological construct of the latter half of the nineteenth century that encom-
passed the widest range of interventions from quarantine to vaccination,
to sewers to eugenics, to social hygiene. It also spawned multiple academic
subfields, from social medicine, to public health, to epidemiology tropical
medicine and beyond allopathic medicine into a wide range of arenas now
labelled as alternative and complementary medicine. It took various political forms, from Bismarck's anti-socialist interventions in 1884 to
Beveridge's idea of the nation's health in 1946. See, for example, Francis B.
Smith, *The People's Health* (New York: Holmes and Meier 1979); Robert
Proctor, *Racial Hygiene: Medicine under the Nazis* (Cambridge, MA:
Harvard University Press 1988); Jürgen Reulecke, Adelheid Gräfin zu
Castell Rüdenhausen, eds, *Stadt und Gesundheit: Zum Wandel von
'Volksgesundheit' und Kommunaler Gesundheitspolitik im 19. und frühen
20. Jahrhundert* (Stuttgart: Franz Steiner Verlag 1991); Steven Feierman
and John M. Janzen, eds, *The Social Bases of Health and Healing in Africa*
(Berkeley: University of California Press 1992); David Arnold, *Colonizing*

the Body: State Medicine and Epidemic Disease in Nineteenth-Century India (Berkeley, Los Angeles, and London: University of California Press 1992); Dorothy Porter, ed., The History of Public Health and the Modern State (Amsterdam: Rodopi 1994); Deborah Lupton, The Imperative of Health; Public Health and the Regulated Body (London: Sage 1995); Anne Harrington, Re-enchanted Science: Holism in German Culture from Wilhelm II to Hitler (Princeton: Princeton University Press 1996); Dorothy Porter, Health, Civilization and the State: A History of Public Health from Ancient to Modern Times (London: Routledge 1994); Milton J. Lewis, The People's Health: Public Health in Australia, 1788–1950 (Westport, CT, and London: Praeger 2003); Susan Bachrach, ed., Deadly Medicine. Creating the Master Race (Washington, DC: USHMM 2004); Brigitte Ruckstuhl and Elisabeth Ryter, Von der Seuchenpolizei zu Public Health: Öffentliche Gesundheit in der Schweiz seit 1750 (Zürich: Chronos Verlag 2017).

2 See Zhou Xun, ed., The Great Famine in China: A Documentary History, 1958–1961 (New Haven: Yale University Press 2012); Zhou Xun, Forgotten Voices of Mao's Great Famine: An Oral History (1958–1962) (New Haven: Yale University Press 2013); Gail Hershatter, The Gender of Memory: Rural Women and China's Collective Past (Stanford: Stanford University Press 2011).

3 Ruth Sidel and Victor W. Sidel, The Health of China: Current Conflicts in Medical and Human Services for One Billion People (Boston: Beacon Press 1982); John Z. Bowers, William J. Hess, and Nathan Sivin, eds, Science and Medicine in Twentieth-Century China. Research and Education (Ann Arbor: University of Michigan Center for Chinese Studies 1982); Nathan Sivin, Traditional Medicine in Contemporary China (Ann Arbor: University of Michigan Center for Chinese Studies 1987); Paul Unschuld, Medicine in China: A History of Ideas (Berkeley: University of California Press 1985, revised edition 2010); AnElissa Lucas, Chinese Medical Modernization: Comparative Policy Continuities, 1930s–1980s (New York: Praeger 1982); Sheila M. Hillier and J.A. Jewell, Health Care and Traditional Medicine in China, 1800–1982 (London: Routledge, Chapman & Hall 1983).

4 David M. Lampton, The Politics of Medicine in China: The Policy Process, 1949–1977 (Boulder, CO: Westview Press 1977); X. Feng, S. Tang, G. Bloom, M. Segall, and Y. Gu, 'Cooperative Medical Schemes in Contemporary Rural China', Social Science and Medicine 41 (1995): 1,111–18; G. Carrin, A. Ron, Y. Hui, et al., 'The Reform of the Rural Cooperative Medical System in the People's Republic of China: Interim

Experience in 14 Pilot Counties', *Social Science and Medicine* 48 (1999): 961–72.

5 Kim Taylor, *Chinese Medicine in Early Communist China, 1945–1963: A Medicine of Revolution* (London: Routledge Curzon 2005) remains undoubtedly an important contribution to the history of traditional Chinese medicine (TCM) in the Maoist period.

6 Fang Xiaoping, *Barefoot Doctors and Western Medicine in China* (Rochester, NY: University of Rochester Press 2012); Sydney D. White, 'From Barefoot Doctors to Village Doctor in Tiger Springs Village: A Case Study of Rural Health Care. Transformations in Socialist China', *Human Organization* 57 (1998): 480–90.

7 Miriam Gross, *Farewell to the God of Plague: Chairman Mao's Campaign to Deworm China* (Berkeley: University of California Press 2016).

8 J. Walsh and K. Warren, 'Selective PHC – An Interim Strategy for Disease Control in Developing Countries', *The New England Journal of Medicine* 30 (1979): 967–74.

9 K. Warren, Su Delong, et al., 'Morbidity in Schistosomiasis Japonica in Relation to Intensity of Infection: A Study of Two Rural Brigades in Anhui Province, China', *The New England Journal of Medicine* 25 (1982): 1533–9.

10 Rene Dubois, *Mirage of Health: Utopias, Progress, and Biological Change* (London: George Allen & Unwin 1960).

CHAPTER ONE

1 See Anthony Christie, *Chinese Mythology* (London: Paul Hamlyn 1968).

2 Yang Qiaoyun, '回忆渡江后的一次血防战斗 (Recall the Battle against Schistosomiasis after [the PLA] Crossed the River Yangtze)', 嘉兴文史资料通讯 *Bulletin of Jiaxing Historical Documents*, no. 41 (January 2005): 22–4.

3 Zhu Zhiwen, '缘 - 血防与寺庙 (My Fate Was Tied to Schistosomiasis Control and the Local Temple)', *Bulletin of Jiaxing Historical Documents*, no. 41 (January 2005): 27–35.

4 Yang Qiaoyun, 'Recall the Battle against Schistosomiasis', 22.

5 W. Wright, 'Bilharziasis as a Public Health Problem in the Pacific', *Bulletin of World Health Organization*, 2 no. 4 (1950): 581–95.

6 Jiaxing Archive 53-1-10嘉兴卫生局关于嘉兴县血防工作情况 (Jiaxing Health Bureau' Report on Schistosomiasis Control): 46.

7 Hsu Hsifan, '防治住血吸虫病 (Preventing Schistosomiasis)', 东南日报 *Dongnan Daily News*, Dec. 1948; Hsu Hsifan, '不可忽视之日本血吸虫

(We Mustn't Underestimate the Harm Caused by Schistosomiasis)', 大公报 *Ta Kun News*, 19 December 1948.

8 For further readings on this incident, see L. Frank Coxswain, *Yangtse River Incident 1949: The Diary of Coxswain Leslie Frank: HMS Amethyst–Yangtse River 19/4/49 to 31/7/49* (Uckfield: Navy & Military Press 2003).

9 See James Z. Gao, *The Communist Takeover of Hangzhou: The Transformation of City and Cadre, 1949–1954* (Honolulu: University of Hawaii Press 2004).

10 Ibid., 85–6.

11 See 资治通鉴全译 (Complete Translation of the Comprehensive Mirror in Aid of Governance), 283–84, Kun Shan University Open Access Resources, http://oa.lib.ksu.edu.tw/OA/retrieve/65815/%E8%B3%87%E6 %B2%BB%E9%80%9A%E9%91%91%E5%85%A8%E8%AD %AF%20A.pdf.

12 Li Yousong, '曹操兵败赤壁与血吸虫病关系的讨论 (The Defeat of Cao Cao at the Battle of Redcliff and Schistosomiasis)', *Chinese Journal of Medical History* 11 (1981): 87.

13 Liu Geng, '崔义田：为大上海 '清创'：新中国的第一场大清运动 (Cui Yitian Help to Clean up Shanghai's Wounded: The First Clean-up Campaign in New China)', 瞭望东方周刊, *Dongfang Liaowang Weekly*, no. 40 (2009): 18.

14 Li Yushan, 'A Schistosomiasis in North and East of Taihu Lake since the Early Ming Dynasty', 中医药杂志 *The Journal of Chinese Medicine*, Special Edition, no. 1 (2013): 133–7.

15 Ka-che Yip, *Health and National Reconstruction in Nationalist China: The Development of Modern Health Services, 1928–1937* (Ann Arbor: University of Michigan Press 1995): 50–3, 109.

16 J166-003-001 (1950–1) '一九四九年三月陈方之为浙江地方病防治所抄在 现阶段抢救血蛭病步骤之商酌 (Chen Fangzhi's Suggestion Regarding the Current Procedure for Emergency Treatment of Schistosomiasis)': 1–2, 12.

17 Shen Yubin, 'Malaria and Global Networks of Tropical Medicine in Modern China, 1919–1950', PhD dissertation (Washington, DC: Georgetown University April 2017): 77.

18 Hsu Hsifan, 'Preventing Schistosomiasis'; Hsu Hsifan, 'We Mustn't Underestimate the Harm Caused by Schistosomiasis'.

19 'Schistosomiasis', *Report on the Work of the League (1938)*, vol. 18: 45, the Northwestern University Library's Digital Collection of League of Nations Statistical and Disarmament Documents, https://wayback. archive-it.org/6321/20160902042901/http://digital.library.northwestern. edu/league/leoo248b.pdf.

20 R.T. Leiper and E.L. Atkinson, 'Observations on the Spread of Asiatic
    Schistosomiasis', *China Medical Journal* (CMJ), xxix, no. 3 (May 1915):
    141–9; R.T. Leiper, 'Reports on the Result of the Bilharzia Mission in
    Egypt', *Journal of Royal Army of Medical Corps*, xxv, no. 1 (July 1915): 3.
21 Leiper, 'Reports on the Result of the Bilharzia Mission in Egypt': 3.
22 Ibid., 24–48. See also John Farley, *Bilharzia: A History of Imperial
    Tropical Medicine* (Cambridge and New York: Cambridge University
    Press 1991): 67–71.
23 'Health Questions', *Report on the Work of the League* (1938), vol. 19: 86,
    the Northwestern University Library's Digital Collection of League of
    Nations Statistical and Disarmament Documents, https://wayback.
    archive-it.org/6321/20160902042931/http://digital.library.northwestern.
    edu/league/leoo251c.pdf.
24 For further readings, see Farley, *Bilharzia*, 158–70; P. Mason et al.,
    'Schistosomiasis Japonica: Diagnosis and Treatment in American Soldiers',
    Journal of Medicine, 235 no. 6 (August 1946): 179–82; Wright, Bilharziasis
    as a Public Health Problem in the Pacific', 581–2. See also 'Schistosomiasis
    Japonica', *War Department Technical Bulletin* 167 (June 1945): 1–10.
25 E. Faust and H.E. Meleney, *Studies on Schistosomiasis Japonica*, American
    Journal of Hygiene Monograph, Series no. 3 (Baltimore: American Journal
    of Hygiene 1924).
26 Norman Stoll, 'This Wormy World', *The Journal of Parasitology*, 33 no. 1
    (February 1947): 1–18.
27 'First World Health Assembly', *Official Records of the World Health
    Organization*, no. 13 (Geneva: WHO December 1948): 141–2.
28 'The State of Food and Agriculture, 1948: A Survey of World Conditions
    and Prospects', FAO, Washington, September 1948: 56–7, 61–2.
29 'First World Health Assembly': 142.
30 For further reading on this topic, see Richard Gardner, 'The Soviet Union
    and the United Nations', *Law and Contemporary Problems*, 29 no. 4 (Fall
    1964): 845–57.
31 As quoted in A-E. Birn and N. Krementsov, '"Socialising" Primary Care?
    The Soviet Union, WHO and the 1978 Alma-Ata Conference', *BMJ Global
    Health* 2018; 3:e000992, doi:10.1136/bmjgh-2018-000992:3.
32 'WHO: From Small Beginnings: Forum Interview with Sze Szeming', *World
    Health Forum*, 9 no. 1 (1988): 29–34.
33 'First World Health Assembly': 150.
34 Aly Tewfik Shousha, 'The Eradication of Anopheles Gambia from Upper
    Egypt 1942–1945', *Bulletin of the WHO*, 1 no. 2 (1948): 310–44; Fred
    Soper, 'Paris Green in the Eradication of Anopheles Gambiae: Brazil, 1940;

Egypt, 1945', *Mosquito News* 26, no. 4 (December 1966): 474–5. Also see Gordon Harrison, *Mosquitoes, Malaria and Man: A History of the Hostilities since 1880* (London: John Murray 1978); Nancy Elizabeth Gallagher, *Egypt's Other Wars: Epidemics and the Politics of Public Health* (Syracuse, NY: Syracuse University Press 1990): 77–96.

35 M.A. Barber and J.B. Hayne, 'Arsenic as a Larvicide for Anopheline Larvae', *Public Health Reports* 36 (1921): 3027–34, http://dx.doi. org/10.2307/4576211; Giancarlo Majori, 'Short History of Malaria and Its Eradication against the Infection in the Mediterranean Basin', *Mediterranean Journal of Hematology and Infectious Diseases*, 4 no. 1 (2012): e2012016, doi:10.4084/MJHID.2012.016.

36 Farley, *Bilharzia*, 191–2, 249–50.

37 *Official Records of the World Health Organization*, no. 18 (Geneva: WHO, April 1949): 72–3, 161.

38 *Official Records of the World Health Organization*, no. 21 (Geneva: WHO, June 1949): 182.

39 Shanghai C44-2-234-53 (16 May 1964) 从防治血吸虫病谈起 (Let's Talk about Controlling Schistosomiasis): 212–5.

40 Zhejiang J166-003-003(1950-1) 华东浙西血吸虫病防治所 一九五〇年度 工作总结报告 (Eastern China's Zhejiang West Schistosomiasis Control Institute's 1950 Work Report): 11–12.

41 Chen Chaochang, '中国人民的大敌-住血吸虫 (Schistosomiasis Is the Worst Enemy of the Chinese People)', *Kexue Xinwen* (*Science News*), 16 no. 2 (1950): 58.

42 Shanghai C3-1-10 (1950) 上海市郊区日本血吸虫病防治委员会委员名单 (The List of Committee Members of Shanghai Region Schistosomiasis Prevention and Treatment Committee): 52.

43 For further reading on the New Cultural Movement, see Chow Tse-tsung, *The May Fourth Movement: Intellectual Revolution in Modern China* (Cambridge, MA: Harvard University Press 1974).

44 Qian Yimin and Yann Zhiyuan, 颜福庆传 (*The Biography of Yan Fuqing*) (Shanghai: Fudan University Press 2004).

45 *The Rockefeller Foundation Annual Report 1919*: 74.

46 For further reading, see AnElissa Lucas, *Chinese Medical Modernization: Comparative Policy Continuities, 1930s–1980s* (New York: Praeger 1982): 48.

47 *The Rockefeller Foundation Annual Report 1919*: 128, 215; Qian Yimin and Yann Zhiyuan, *The Biography of Yan Fuqing*, ch. 2.

48 The most recent work on Mao and his colleagues' activities in Anyuan is

Elizabeth J. Perry, *Anyuan: Mining China's Revolutionary Tradition* (Berkeley and Los Angeles: University of California Press 2012).

49 The People's Government's Ministry of Health, ed., 卫生法令汇编 (第1 辑) (*Policies regarding Health Work*, vol. 1), published internally in 1951, 38; Mao Zedong, '必须重视卫生、防疫和医疗工作 (Must Pay Attention to Health, Disease Prevention and Medical Work)', in 毛泽东文集 (Collection of Mao Zedong's Writings), vol. 6 (Beijing: Renmin chubanshe 1997): 176.

50 For studies on the Anti-Germ Warfare Campaign, see Yang Nianqun, 'Disease Prevention, Social Mobilization and Spatial Politics: The Anti Germ-Warfare Incident of 1952 and the Patriotic Health Campaign', *Chinese Historical Review* 11, no. 2 (2004): 155–82; Ruth Ragaski, 'Nature, Annihilation, and Modernity: China's Korean War Germ-Warfare Experience Reconsidered', *Journal of Asian Studies* 61, no. 2 (2002): 381–415.

51 Zhejiang J166-003-015 (1954) 卫生部党组关于开展血吸虫病防治工作的报告 (The Ministry of Health's Party Committee's Report Regarding Carrying out Schistosomiasis Control Work): 1.

52 She County Local History Committee, ed., 安徽省歙县志 (*The Annals of She County in Anhui Province*) (Hefei: Huangshan shushe 2010): 802–8.

53 Ibid., 737.

54 'Article 48 of the Common Programme of the Chinese People's Political Consultative Conference', in *The Common Programme and Other Documents of the First Plenary Session of the Chinese People's Political Consultative Conference* (Peking: Foreign Language Press 1950): 18.

55 P. Manson-Bahr, *Patrick Manson: The Father of Tropical Medicine* (London and New York: T. Nelson 1962): 89. For a study on Patrick Manson's career in the Far East, see Douglas M. Haynes, *Imperial Medicine: Patrick Manson and the Conquest of Tropical Disease* (Philadelphia: University of Pennsylvania Press 2001).

56 Kong Benqu, '艰苦创业七十年 (Seventy Years of Hard Work to Create [Success])', in 上海医科大学七十年 (*Shanghai Medical University in the Past 70 Years*) (Shanghai: Shanghai Medical University Press 1997): 4; '医救人员关荣下乡为战士医治住血吸虫病 (Medical and Health Personnel Went to the Countryside to Treat Soldiers Suffering Schistosomiasis)', 科学新闻 (*Science News*), 16 no. 2 (1950): 105.

57 'Conversation between Stalin and Mao, Moscow, 16 December 1949', *Cold War International History Project Bulletin* 6–7 (Winter 1995–96): 5.

58 Shanghai C3-1-11-56 (1950) 中国人民解放军二十军政治部关于血吸虫病

防治工作情况的综合情况报告 (The Political Department of the PLA's Report on Schistosomiasis Control Work): 60–1.

59 Shanghai Q249-1-138 (1952) 防治通讯 (Schistosomiasis Prevention and Treatment Bulletin), no. 1: 12; Shanghai C3-1-10 (1950), 1949–1950 上海市医务工作者工会职工参加郊区驻军血吸虫病防治工作名单，功臣材料，统计表，慰问信，海报 (The Name List of Medical Personnel Assisted Schistosomiasis Treatment Work of the PLA, Their Achievements, Gratitude Letters, and Posters for Publicity): 50–2.

60 Shanghai C3-1-11-56 (1950) (The Political Department of the PLA's Report on Schistosomiasis Control Work): 58–61; '医护人员光荣下乡为战士医治住血吸虫 (Medical and Health Personnel Went to the Countryside to Treat Soldiers Suffering Schistosomiasis)', *Kexue Xinwen* (*Science News*) 16, no. 2 (1950): 105; Zhejiang J166-003-003 (1950–51) 一九五○年七月中旬在宁波协助部队防治血吸虫病工作总结报告 (Work Report of Assisting Schistosomiasis Treatment Work of the PLA): 4–8.

61 Interview with Madame Wu (Mao's sister) in Beijing, 2005. See also Sun Jiande, '毛守白 (1912–1992)' (Mao Shoubai), the website of the General Alumni Association of Southeast University in Nanjing, https://seuaa.seu.edu.cn/2008/0116/c1672a25994/pagem.htm.

62 For further readings on the problem of diagnosis, see J.V. Hamilton, M. Klinkert, and M.J. Doenhoff, 'Diagnosis of Schistosomiasis: Antibody Detection, with Notes on Parasitological and Antigen Detection Methods', in H.V. Smith et al., eds, *Infectious Diseases Diagnosis: Current Status and Future Trends, Supplement to Parasitology, vol. 117 (1998)*: S41-2.

63 C.G.K. Sharp, *Schistosomiasis vel Bilharziasis* (foreword by J.B. Christopherson) (London: J. Bale 1925). See also F.R. Sandbach, 'The History of Schistosomiasis Research and Policy for its Control', *Medical History*, 20 no. 3 (July 1976): 270; Ahmed Awad Adeel, 'When History Was Made in Khartoum Civil Hospital: First Introduction of Chemotherapy for Schistosomiasis', *Sudanese Journal of Pediatrics* 15, no. 2 (2015): 80–99; Farley, *Bilharzia*, 97–8.

64 C.S. Jang et al., 'Changshan, a Chinese Anti-Malaria Herb', *Science* 103, no. 2,663 (January 1946): 59, doi: 10.1126/science.103.2663.59-b.

65 Shanghai Q249-1-137 (1950) 上海市血吸虫病防治委员会简报 (*The Bulletin of Shanghai Region Schistosomiasis Prevention and Treatment Committee*), no. 18: 135–6.

66 Zhejiang J166-003-003 (1950–51) Eastern China's Zhejiang West Schistosomiasis Control Institute's 1950 Work Report: 8.

67 Zhejiang J166-003-001 (1950–51) Chen Fangzhi's Suggestion Regarding the Current Procedure for Emergency Treatment of Schistosomiasis: 2, 5–6.

68 Ibid., 5–7.

69 See, for example, L.S. Austin and K. Hustead, 'Cost-effectiveness of Television, Radio, and Print media Programs for Public Mental Health Education', *Psychiatric Services* 49 (1998): 808–11.

70 Zhejiang J166-003-002 (1950–51) 卫生部对住血吸虫病防治工作的指示 (20 April 1950) Weishengbu dui zhuxuexichongbing fangzhi gongzuo de zhishi (20 April 1950) (The Ministry of Health's Edict Regarding Control of Schistosomiasis, 20 April 1950).

71 For a study on Li Dequan, see Kate Merkel-Hess, 'A New Woman and Her Warlord: Li Dequan, Feng Yuxiang, and the Politics of Intimacy in Twentieth Century China', *Frontiers of History in China* 11, no. 3 (2016): 431–57.

72 For a study on the meanings of health, hygiene, and the culture of modernity in China in the first half the twentieth century, see Ruth Rogaski, *Hygienic Modernity: Meanings of Health and Disease in Treaty-Port China* (Berkeley and Los Angeles: University of California Press 2004).

73 Sichuan JC133-450 (4–25 December 1963) 陆定一同志的讲话 Liu Dingyi tongzhi de jianghua (Comrade Lu Dingyi's Speech): 85–110.

CHAPTER TWO

1 Shanghai C1-11-56 (1950) 中国人民解放军二十军政治部关于血吸虫病防治工作的综合情况报告 (The PLA's 20th Army's Comprehensive Report on Schistosomiasis Prevention and Treatment Work): 58–9.

2 E. Faust and H.E. Meleney, *Studies on Schistosomiasis Japonica*, American Journal of Hygiene Monograph, Series no. 3 (Baltimore: American Journal of Hygiene 1924), 171–2.

3 Meleney to Faust, 3 July 1923, Faust Papers Series II: Correspondence 1918–1966, Box 1 Folder 27–8, National Library of Medicine, Bethesda, MD.

4 Xu Fanxi and Li Shuyin, 'Schistosomiasis Control in the PRC', speech given at a meeting for American and Japanese parasitologists, held between 6 and 7 August 1973 at Pacific Grove, sponsored by the National Institute of Health (NIH).

5 Dong Guoqiang and Li Zhirong, eds, 南京通史— 中华人民共和国卷 (*History of Nanjing: The PRC Volume*) (Nanjing: Nanjing Chubanshe 2015), 135–6.

6 Ma Longrui, '把卫生宣传和爱国主义宣传结合起来 (Linking Health Propaganda with Patriotic Ideology Propaganda)', 上海卫生 (*Shanghai Health Journal*) 1 no. 8 (1 December 1951): 5; Shanghai C3-1-10 (1950)

The Name List of Medical Personnel Assisted Schistosomiasis Treatment Work of the PLA, their Achievements, Gratitude Letters, and Posters for Publicity: 50–2; Zhejiang J166-003-003 (1950) 一九五〇年七月中旬在宁波协助部队防治血吸虫病工作总结报告 (Work Report of Assisting Schistosomiasis Treatment Work of the PLA): 1–8.

7 Zhejiang J166-003-003 (1950) Eastern China's Zhejiang West Schistosomiasis Control Institute's 1950 Work Report: 1, 1–12; '华东军政委关于组织联合医院联合诊所的指示 (Eastern China Military Authority's Edict to Organize United Hospitals and Clinics)', *Shanghai Health Journal* 1, no. 8 (December 1951): 73.

8 Zhu Zhiwen, '缘 - 血防与寺庙 (My Fate Was Tied to Schistosomiasis Control and the Local Temple), *Bulletin of Jiaxing Historical Documents*, no. 41 (January 2005): 27–35.

9 See Carol Benedict, *Bubonic Plague in Nineteenth Century China* (Stanford: Stanford University Press 1996): 113–15. For further readings on the cult of Lord Guan, see Prasenjit Duara, 'Superscribing Symbols: The Myth of Guandi, Chinese God of War', *The Journal of Asian Studies*, 47 no. 4 (November 1988): 778–95; Barend J. ter Haar, *Guan Yu: The Religious Afterlife of a Failed Hero* (Oxford: Oxford University Press, 2017). See also Y.K. Leong and L.K. Tao, *Village and Town Life in China* (London: George Allen & Unwin 1915): 32–9.

10 'Article 41 of the Common Program of the Chinese People's Political Consultative Conference', 16–17. Also see Israel Epstein, 'Notes on the New Chinese Culture', *Science & Society* 15, no. 4 (1951): 334–40.

11 Zhejiang J166-003-89 (1959) 本厅关于十年来防治血吸虫病、丝虫病、钩虫病的伟大成就 (Zhejiang Provincial Health Bureau's Report Regarding Achievement in Controlling Schistosomiasis, Hookworm and Filariasis over the Past Ten Years): 18.

12 Shanghai Q249-1-138 (1952) 1952年1，2月间(医学院寒假)集体治疗血吸虫病工作总结 (Work Report of Schistosomiasis Mass Treatment Work between January and February 1952): 48.

13 Zhejiang 166-003-005 (1953) 浙江省一九五二年上半年度血吸虫防治工作总结 (A Summary Report of Zhejiang Province's Schistosomiasis Control in the First Half of 1952): 6; 浙江省血吸虫病防治工作三年总结报告 (Evaluation Report of Zhejiang Province's Schistosomiasis Control in the Past Three Years, 1950–1952): 4.

14 内部参考 (Internal Reference News), 21 November 1950: 96; 24 November 1950: 118–20; 7 September 1951: 22–4; 14 March 1952: 117; 18 March 1952: 153–8.

15 Huang Shuzhe and Lin Shixiao, eds, 当代中国的卫生事业 (*Health Services in Modern China*) (Beijing: Zhongguo shehui keixue chubanshe 1986): 3; Qian Xinzhong, '农村卫生建设的回顾和展望 (Reflection on Rural Health Construction in the Past and Future Prospect)', 健康报 (*Health News*), 25 September 1984: 1.

16 See Zhou Hong and Zhang Jun, *Towards a Society with Social Protection for All: A Concise History of Social Security Transformation in Modern China* (Beijing: China Social Science Press 2017): 6–11, 15–18.

17 Fu Qiyuan, '1949 年前后南京社会救济的变迁与重构 (The Change and Restructuring of the Social Welfare System in Nanjing prior to and after 1949)', *Journal of Jiangsu University* (Social Science Edition) 17, no. 5 (September 2015): 33–7; Dong Guoqiang and Li Zhirong, eds, *History of Nanjing: The PRC Volume* (Nanjing: Nanjing Chubanshe 2015): 142–4, 146–9.

18 Lu Jingxuan, '血防小记 (A Short Essay on Schistosomiasis Control)', in Hua Li, ed., 送瘟神: 嘉兴地区血防工作纪实 (*Send off the God of Plague: Schistosomiasis Control in Jiaxing*), Jiaxing Historical Sources vol. 4 (Beijing: Keji Chubanshe 1995): 128–9.

19 Sichuan JC133-2584 (1957), 我们于3月23日(57年)到 [绵阳]罗江了解中医治疗血吸虫 病的情况 (Our Field Trip to Longjiang in Mianyang to Investigate the Outcome of Treating Schistosomiasis with Chinese Medicine): 121–2.

20 Sichuan JX1-836 转发河南发现反动宣传的通报 (1951年5月21日) (Forward the Circular on Counter-revolutionary Propaganda in Henan): 46–7. For a recent study on the Patriotic Health Campaign, see Nianqun Yang, 'Disease Prevention, Social Mobilization and Spatial Politics: The Anti Germ-Warfare Incident of 1952 and the Patriotic Health Campaign', *The Chinese Historical Review* 11, no. 2 (2004): 155–82, doi:10.1080/154 7402X.2004.11827202.

21 He Cheng, '中西医团结与中医的进修问题 (The Issue of the Unification of Chinese and Western Medicines and the Further Improvement of Chinese Medical Practitioners)', *People's Daily* 13 June 1950: 5; 全国卫生会议在京开幕将制定卫生工作的总方针和任务 (The National Health Conference will be Held in Beijing to Draw up the Health Work's Guiding Principles and Tasks), *People's Daily* 8 August 1950: 1.

22 '央卫生部李德全部长 关于全国卫生会议的报告 (1950九月八日在中央人民政府政务院第四十九次政务会议上) (The Minister of Health Li Dequan's Report from the National Health Conference. Presented to the State Administration Council's 49th conference on 8 September 1950)', as appeared in the *People's Daily*, 23 October 1950: 1.

23 Xu Hui, 政府卫生支出问题研究 (*A Study of the Government Health Expenditure*) (Beijing: Zhongguo caizheng jinji chubanshe 2010), ch. 3, 59–60.

24 'China Medical Board – Hundred Years of Health Philanthropy for Health: 1914–2014', 1, China Medical Board, https://chinamedicalboard. org/sites/chinamedicalboard.org/files/cmb_100th_bangkok.pdf.

25 Claude H. Barlow, 'Life Cycle of Fasciolopsis Buski (Human)', *The China Medical Journal* 37, no. 6 (June 1923): 464, 471.

26 For a detailed account of Barlow's involvement in the IHB's Egyptian campaign, see J. Farley, *Bilharzia: A History of Imperial Tropical Medicine* (Cambridge and New York: Cambridge University Press 2003): 105–13, 189–93.

27 See Farley, *Bilharzia*, 189–93.

28 Bilharzia Work in China, Claude H. Barlow Papers, 1919–1964, Box 2, series 2, folder 18, Rockefeller Foundation Archive.

29 Farley, *Bilharzia*, 214–15.

30 Shanghai Q249-1-138 (1952) *Schistosomiasis Prevention and Treatment Bulletin* no. 12 (8 March 1952): 1–2; Shanghai B242-1-325 (1951) 全国医政工作会议上海卫生局准备之资料 (Data Prepared for the National Medical and Health Governance Work Conference): 13–14.

31 'Article 41 of the Common Program of the Chinese People's Political Consultative Conference'.

32 中央人民政府卫生部和教育部公布令关于发展卫生教育和培养各级卫生人员的决定 (The Ministry of Health and the Ministry of Education's Joint Edict to Develop Health Education and to Train Health Personnel), as printed in *Shanghai Health Journal* 1, no. 8 (1 December 1951): 70.

33 Zhejiang J166-003-005 (1953) A Summary Report of Zhejiang Province's Schistosomiasis Control in the First Half of 1952): 2.

34 Ren Jixian, '一个老血防战士的心愿 (A Former Schistosomiasis Control Soldier's Wish)', in Hua Li, ed., *Send off the God of Plague*, 139–42.

35 Interview with Ren Jixian in Jiaxing, Zhejiang province, April 2015.

36 Zhejiang J166-003-009 (1953) 浙江省卫生厅关于全省血吸虫病防治工作检查总结报告 (1953年3月6日) (Zhejiang Provincial Health Bureau's Investigative Report on Zhejiang's Schistosomiasis Control, 6 March 1953): 5.

37 Zhu Zhiwen, '在血防战线上的日日夜夜 (Day and Night in Fighting Schistosomiasis)', in Hua Li, ed., *Send off the God of Plague*, 144–6.

38 Ren Jixian, 'Former Schistosomiasis Control Soldier's Wish', 139.

39 Zhejiang J166-003-009 (1953) Zhejiang Provincial Health Bureau's Investigative Report on Zhejiang's Schistosomiasis Control (6 March 1953): 4.

40 Shanghai Q 249-1-138 (1952) Work Report of Schistosomiasis Mass Treatment Work between January and February 1952: 49–50.

41 Zhejiang J166-003-008 (1953) A Comprehensive Report of Zhejiang Province's Schistosomiasis Control Work in 1953 (6 March 1953): 3.

42 Zhejiang J166-003-009 (1953) Zhejiang Provincial Health Bureau's Investigative Report on Zhejiang's Schistosomiasis Control (6 March 1953): 5.

43 Ibid., 4.

44 Shanghai Q249-1-138 (1952) Work Report of Schistosomiasis Mass Treatment Work between January and February 1952: 49–50.

45 Ibid.

46 Zhejiang J166-003-005 (1953) Evaluation Report of Zhejiang Province's Schistosomiasis Control in the Past Three Years, 1950–1952: 3–4; Shanghai Q249-1-138 (1952) Work Report of Schistosomiasis Mass Treatment Work between January and February 1952: 48.

47 Shanghai Q249-1-138 (1952) 昆山血防大队工作总结 (The Kunshan Team's Work Report of Schistosomiasis Control): 87.

48 Zhejiang J166-003-003(1950) Eastern China's Zhejiang West Schistosomiasis Control Institute's 1950 Work Report: 12–13.

49 Zhejiang J166-003-010 (1952-3) 浙江省衢州地区血吸虫病防治所1952年工作总结 (Zhejiang Province Quzhou Regional Schistosomiasis Control Institute's Work Report for 1952): 3.

50 Zhejiang J166-003-008 (1953-54) 浙江省卫生厅关于全省血吸虫病防治工作检查总结报告 (March 1953) (A Comprehensive Report of Zhejiang Province's Schistosomiasis Control Work in 1953): 2–3; Yujiang Schistosomiasis Control Leadership Committee, ed., 江西省余江县血防志 Jiangxi sheng Yujiang xian xuefangzhi (Yujiang County Schistosomiasis Control Annals, Jiangxi Province) (Yujiang, 1984): 44.

51 Zhejiang J166-003-005 (1953) A Summary Report of Zhejiang Province's Schistosomiasis Control in the First Half of 1952): 3–4.

52 Zhejiang J166-003-001(1950-51) 浙江省1951年血吸虫病防治工作总结 (Evaluation of Zhejiang Province's Schistosomiasis Control Work in 1951).

53 Zhejiang J166-003-001 (1950-51) 浙江卫生实验院 三环畈血吸虫病防治实验区工作计划 (Zhejiang Health Laboratory's Work Plan for the Sanhuanfan Schistosomiasis Control Pilot District): 3–4.

54 Zhejiang J166-003-003 (1950–51) 嘉兴新丰步云乡捕捉钉螺蛳工作总结 (
一九五一年七月) (Evaluation Report of Xinfeng Township's Buyun Village
in Jiaxing, July 1951): 1–2.

55 Zheijiang J166-003-005 (1953) Evaluation Report of Zhejiang Province's
Schistosomiasis Control in the Past Three Years, 1950–1952: 1; Zhejiang
J166-003-008 (1953–54) A Comprehensive Report of Zhejiang Province's
Schistosomiasis Control Work in 1953.

56 Zheijiang J166-003-005 (1953) Evaluation Report of Zhejiang Province's
Schistosomiasis Control in the Past Three Years, 1950–1952): 4–5.

57 Ibid.

58 Zhejiang J166-003-008 (1953–54) A Comprehensive Report of Zhejiang
Province's Schistosomiasis Control Work in 1953; Zhejiang J166-003-009
(1953) 区干校关于血防工作人员学习总结报告 (District Cadre School's
Evaluation Report on Schistosomiasis Control Cadres' Political Training
Workshop): 1–4.

59 Zhang Ziwei, '嘉兴血防机构的变迁 (Jiaxing's Schistosomiasis Institutions
and Their Changes over the Past Decades)', in Hua Li, ed., *Send off the
God of Plague*, 117.

60 Ibid., 116.

61 Ibid., 116–17.

62 Zheijiang J166-003-008 (1953–54) A Comprehensive Report of Zhejiang
Province's Schistosomiasis Control Work in 1953. For further readings on
the New 'Three Antis'-Campaign, see Frederick Teiwes, *Revival: Politics
and Purges in China: Reification and Decline of Party Norms, 1950–65*
(Oxford and New York: Routledge 2015), ch. 4.

63 Wang Peixin and Liu Shixin, '土埋法杀灭日本血吸虫中间宿主钉螺蛳的实
验 (Pilot Study of Eliminating Snails by Earth Burial Method)', 中华医学
杂志 (*China Medical Journal* [Chinese Edition]) 39, no. 06 (1953):
401–12.

64 Zhejiang J166-003-009 (1953), 血吸虫病的防制工作 (Schistosomiasis
Control Work in Qu County's Jiang Village): 2.

65 O.T. Logan, '*A Case of Dysentery in Hunan Province*, Caused by the
Trematode, Schistosoma Japonicum', *The China Medical Missionary
Journal* 19 (1905): 243–5.

66 The South Dongting Lake Reconstruction Leadership Committee, '南洞庭湖
整修工程介绍 (An Overview of South Dongting Lake Reconstruction
Project)', 1952. An abridged version of this document is available online at
Hunan Provincial Archive Digital Library Hunan Historical Documents
Section, sdaj.hunan.gov.cn/wszt/xxsl/ztsl/200609/t20060928_1978096.html.

67 Chen Huxin, '洞庭湖区域自然环境的改造在消灭血吸虫病中的意义
(Eradicating Schistosomiasis by Controlling the Environment in the
Dongting Lake)', *Chinese Journal of Preventative Medicine* 5, no. 2
(1957): 69–74.

CHAPTER THREE

1 Li Fuchun, 'Report of the First Five-Year Plan for Development of the
National Economy of the People's Republic of China in 1953–1957', in
Communist China 1955–1959: Policy Documents with Analysis, with a
foreword by Robert R. Bowie and John K. Fairbank, prepared at Harvard
University under the joint auspices of the Centre for International Affairs
and East Asia Research Centre (Cambridge, MA: Harvard University Press
1965), 46.
2 Ibid., 65.
3 Ibid., 66–7.
4 Ibid., 67.
5 Mao Zedong, 'The Question of Agricultural Co-operatives', in *Communist
China 1955–1959: Policy Documents with Analysis* [document 2]: 100.
6 内部参考 (Internal Reference News), 8 November 1954.
7 Gao Wanglin, 中国农民反行为研究 (1950–1980) (A Study on Chinese
Peasants' 'Counter-actions', 1950–1980) (Hong Kong: Chinese University
of Hong Kong Press 2013), 32.
8 内部参考 (Internal Reference News), 28 May 1955.
9 Bo Yibo, 若干重大决策和事件的回顾 (*Reflections on Certain Major
Decisions and Events*), vol. 1 (Beijing: Zhonggong zhongyang dangxiao
chubanshe 1991): 373.
10 Shen Tong, '回忆主席的一次调研 (Reminiscing a Study Trip with the
Chairman)', 人民网领袖人物资料库 (digital resources of the CCP leaders
at the people.cn), http://www.people.com.cn/GB/shizheng/8198/
30446/30450/2265661.html.
11 Xi Zhongxun, '在纪念沈钧儒先生诞辰一百一十周年座谈会上的讲话
(Speech at the Meeting in Memory of Shen Junru)', *People's Daily* (3
January 1985): 4; Mao Zedong, 建国以来毛泽东文稿 (*Selected Works of
Mao Since 1949*), vol. 4 (Beijing: Zhongyang wenxian chubanshe 1990):
373.
12 Tricia Starks, *The Body Soviet: Propaganda, Hygiene, and the
Revolutionary State* (Madison: University of Wisconsin Press 2008), 3.
13 Mao Zedong, 'Be Concerned with Well-Being of the Masses', in *Selected

Works of Mao Tsetung, vol. 1 (Peking: Foreign Language Press 1965): 147–52; Mao Zedong, 'The Investigation of Changgang Township', in Stuart Schram, ed., *Mao's Road to Power: Revolutionary Writings, 1912–49*, vol. 4 (London and New York: Routledge 1997): 613–14.

14 Li Men, 毛澤東重整舊河山: 1949–1960 (*Mao Zedong Transformed the Landscape Old China, 1949–1960*) (Hong Kong: Zhonghe chubanshe 2013): 211–15.

15 Shen Tong, 'Reminiscing a Study Trip with the Chairman'; Xu Yunbai, '毛主席指挥送瘟神 (Chairman Mao Led Us to Send off the Plague God)', in 缅怀毛泽东 (*Reminiscing Mao Zedong*), vol. 1 (Beijing: Zhongyang wenxian chubanshe 1993): 340.

16 'Circular Requesting on the Seventeen Articles on Agricultural Work', in Michael Kau and John Leung, eds, *The Writings of Mao Zedong, 1949–1976*, vol. 1 (New York and London: Sharpe 1986): 689–92.

17 Shen Tong, '回忆毛主席调查研究拾零 (Anecdotes from Chairman Mao's Research Trips)', in *Reminiscing Mao Zedong*, vol. 2 (Beijing: Zhongyang wenxian chubanshe 1993): 541; Sichuan JC 133-450 (4–25 December 1963) 徐运北同志在第九次血吸虫病防治工作会议上的总结报告 (Comrade Xu Yunbai's Summary Speech at the Ninth National Conference on Schistosomiasis Control): 66–8.

18 Zhejiang J166-003-019 (1955) 中共中央血防九人小组关于第一次全国血防会议文件 (The Nine-Man Subcommittee's Documents of the First National Schistosomiasis Control Conference): 1–3.

19 Ibid., 1; Jiangsu 3119-[Short-term file]-631, 魏文伯同志在防治血吸虫病会议上的总结发言 (25 November 1955) (Comrade Wei Wenbo's Summary Speech at the Schistosomiasis Control Conference).

20 Zhejiang J166-003-025 (1955) 浙江省卫生厅关于中药腹水草治疗血吸虫病研究工作的总结报告 (Zhejiang Provincial Health Bureau's Evaluation Report on Using Folk Remedy Veronicastrum Axillare to Treat Schistosomiasis): 1; '初步小结 "腹水草" 治疗血吸虫疗效 (A Preliminary Report of Using Veronicastrum Axillare to Treat Schistosomiasis)', *Zhejiang Daily News* 17 September 1955: 3.

21 Kunshan 416-3-10 (July 1956) 昆山县篆葭区公所检查辅导组血吸虫病防治工作总结 (The Summary Report of Kundshan County's Lujia District Schistosomasis Control Work): 1, 3.

22 Sichuan JC133-2684 (January–October 1959) 除害灭病工作情况简报 (Summary Report of Disease Prevention and Eradication) vol. 6 (21 April 1959): 3–4.

23 For further reading on the changing power in schistosomiasis control, see David Lampton, 'Policy Change and China's Anti-Schistosomiasis

Programme: An Evaluation', *American Journal of Tropical Medicine and Hygiene* 23, no. 8 (1977): 458–62.

24 Zhejiang J166-3-089 (1959) 本厅关于十年来防治血吸虫病、丝虫病、钩虫病的伟大成就 (Zhejiang Provincial Health Bureau's Report Regarding Achievement in Controlling Schistosomiasis, Hookworm and Filariasis over the Past Ten Years): 11.

25 Li Honghe, 'Historic Study on Scientization of Traditional Chinese Medical Science in the Early Days of New China', *Contemporary China History Studies* 18, no. 4 (July 2011): 70–6; Chien-Jung Lin et al., 'Bai-Hu-Tang, Ancient Chinese Medicine Formula, May Provide a New Complementary Treatment Option for Sepsis', in *Evidence-Based Complementary and Alternative Medicine* 7 (May 2013), article ID: 193084, http://dx.doi.org/10.1155/2013/193084.

26 Guo Jisheng, 温病大家郭可明治疗乙脑实录 (*Biographic Account of Master Guo Keming's Therapy for Japanese Encephalitis*) (Beijing: Renming weisheng chubanshe 2017).

27 Li Honghe, 'Historic Study on Scientization, 73–6.

28 Zhejiang J166-003-022 (21 December) 宁波专区卫生工作调查情况综合汇报 (A Comprehensive Investigative Report of Ningbo Region's Health Work): 1–3.

29 Zhejiang J166-003-020 (1950–56) 浙江省血吸虫病防治工作资料汇编初稿第一号 (Jan. 1956) (Data Collected on Zhejiang Province's Schistosomasis Control Work, vol. 1, 1956): 57–9.

30 Zhejiang J166-003-016 (1954) 浙江省衢州血吸虫病防治所1954年1至6月份工作总结 (Zhejiang Province Quzhou Schistosomiasis Control Institute's Work Report for the Period of January to June 1956); Kunshan archive 416-3-10 (July 1956) The Summary Report of Kundshan County's Lujia District Schistosomasis Control Work: 31–2.

31 Shanghai B59-2-89 (1956) 事由: [中国电影公司上海分公司] 为配合防治血吸虫病害的运动发行有关短片的通知, 1956年1月16日 (Shanghai Film Studio Regarding the Notice to Support Schistosomiasis Control to Produce Short Educational Films): 17.

32 Zhejiang J166-003-020 (1950–56) Data collected on Zhejiang Province's Schistosomiasis Control Work, vol. 1, 1956: 22; Zhejiang J166-003-026 (1955) 嘉兴专署 报送本区一九五五年血吸虫病防治工作总结 (Jiaxing Authority's Submitted Report of the Local Schistosomiasis Control Work in 1955): 9–11.

33 Luo Lanying, '建国初期四川的禁毒运动 (1950–1952) (Anti-Narcotic Campaign in Sichuan in the Early PRC Period)', MA dissertation (Chengdu: Sichuan University 2002): 23.

34 For a further study on opium eradication in southwestern China, see Qing Heping, 西南民族地区的毒品危害及其对策 (*The Harm of Narcotics in the Ethnic Regions in the Southwest and Anti-Narcotic Measures*) (Chengdu: Sichuan Minzu chubanshe 2005).

35 Sichuan JK1-2441 (21 May–21 Nov. 1952) 西昌地委对盐边县种烟问题的三点意见报区党委并复盐边县委(1952年11月3日) (Xichang Region Party Committee's Opinion and Report for the Regional Party Committee on the Problem of Opium Growing in Yanbian as Well as Its Reply to the Yanbian County Party Committee): 19.

36 Luo Lanying, 'Anti-Narcotic Campaign in Sichuan, 23.

37 Xichang Schistosomiasis Control Station, ed., 西昌血吸虫防治志 (Xichang Schistosomiasis Control Annals) (Xichang: Xichang Archive June 1988): 33–4.

38 Dorothy Borg, 'Chinese Health Work Progressing Despite War', *Far Eastern Survey* 9, no. 11 (22 May 1940): 134.

39 R.C. Robertson, '*Schistosomiasis* in the Tali-fu Region of Yunnan Province', *Chinese Medical Journal* 57 (1940): 358–63.

40 Zhang Xianqing, ed., 云南血吸虫病防治史志 (Yunnan Province Schistosomiasis Control Annals) (Kunming: Yunnan keji chubanshe 1992), 12.

41 Sichuan JK32-158 (March–December 1951) 为请按中央规定处理泸定磨西麻疯院并将处理经过报卫生部由(8月22日) (The Reason to Report to the Ministry of Health Regarding the Central Government's Instruction to Deal with the Problem at Luding Moxi Leprosy Centre, 22 August): 1–2.

42 Dali Region Schistosomiasis Control Research Institute 385-1-2 (1954) [Region Schistosomiasis Control Research Institute file], Annual Report by Yunnan Schistosomiasis Prevention Centre: 11–17.

43 Xichang County Authority Health Department 62-1-17 (1953) 西康省爱卫会关于爱国卫生运动的总结，计划，通知 (Xikang Provincial Patriotic Health Campaign Committee's Report, Plan and Edict Regarding the Local Patriotic Health Campaign): 6

44 Xichang County Authority Health Department 62-1-6 (1953) 西康省人民政府函复 (Xikang People's Government Health Authority's Reply): 26.

45 Shanghai C44-2-234-53 (16 May 1964), Let's Talk about Controlling Schistosomiasis: 213.

46 Shanghai Medical University Department of Epidemiology and Shanghai Medical University Archive, eds, 苏德隆教授论文选集 Su Delong Jiaoshou Lunwen Xuanji (Selected Academic Essays of Professor Su Delong) (Tianjin: Tianjin Science and Technology Press 1995): 1.

47 '必须在五年内消灭血吸虫 (Zhejiang Province Determined to Eradicate Schistosomiasis within Five Years)', 浙江日报 (*Zhejiang Daily News*) 20 December 1955: 1.

48 Jiaxing 078-001-106 (1956) 嘉兴市防疫站关于简要汇报1956年血防工作情况及1957年血防工作打算的报告 (Jiaxing Municipal Disease Prevention Centre's Summary Report of Schistosomiasis Control Work in 1956 and Plan for 1957).

49 Li Dequan, 'The New Tasks of Protection of Public Health', *China News Agency* (16 June 1956), in *China Background* no. 405: 12.

50 The CCP Central Committee's Nine-Man Schistosomiasis Control Committee, 'Comrade Ke Qingshi's Summarised Speech at the Second National Meeting on Schistosomiasis Control' (printed in April 1956), Conference Document no. 1 [internal publication].

51 Farley, *Bilharzia*, 300.

52 Y. Komiya, 'A Recommendatory Note for the Control Problem of Schistosomiasis', *Japanese Journal of Medical Science and Biology* 10 (1957): 468.

53 Frank Dikötter, *Mao's Great Famine: The History of China's Most Devastating Catastrophe, 1958–62* (London: Bloomsbury 2010): 20

54 Li Ping and Ma Zhisun, eds, 周恩来年谱 (1898–1976) (*Chronological Biography of Zhou Enlai, 1898–1976*) (Beijing: Zhongyang wenxian chubanshe 1998): 665.

55 Ibid., 668.

56 'Report on Proposals for the Second Five-Year Plan for Development of the National Economy', delivered by Zhou Enlai on 16 September 1956 to the Eighth Party Congress, in *Communist China 1955–1959: Policy Documents with Analysis*, Document 11: 239–40.

57 Y. Komiya, 'A Recommendatory Note for the Control Problem of Schistosomiasis': 461–71. For a detailed study on the Komiya Mission, see Iijima Wataru, '"Farewell to the God of Plague": Anti–Shistosoma Japonicum Campaign in China and Japanese Colonial Medicine', *The Memoirs of the Toyo Bunko* 66 (2008).

58 Sichuan JC133-450 (4–25 December 1963) 国务院关于消灭血吸虫病的指示 (1957) (The State Council's Edict to Eradicate Schistosomiasis, April 1957): 7–12.

59 Ibid.

60 Jiaxing 016-001-204 (1957) 嘉兴县专署关于嘉兴血防医院和调整嘉兴市县医院的安排设置问题 (Jiaxing County Authority's Notice Regarding Jiaxing Schistosomiasis Control Hospital's Restructuring): 112; Jiaxing

191-002-164 专题 '大跃进时期血防工作, 精简干部职工, 压缩城镇人口' (Special Report on 'Schistosomiasis Control, Staff Cuts as Well as De-urbanization during the Great Leap Forward Period'): 9, 13–14.

61 Sichuan JC133-2684 (January–October 1959) 当前除害灭病质量需提高 (The Need to Improve the Quality of Disease Control Work): 2–3; Interview with ZM at Xichang, October 2014.

62 'Report on Proposals for the Second Five-Year Plan for Development of the National Economy', delivered by Zhou Enlai on 16 September 1956 to the Eighth Party Congress, in *Communist China 1955–1959: Policy Documents with Analysis* [Document 11]: 238–40.

63 Sichuan JC133-2624 (September 1957–December 1958) 四川省卫生厅钩防办公室西昌眉山等县血吸虫病调查经验总结 (Sichuan Provincial Health Bureau's Office of Hookworm Control's Evaluation Report of Schistosomiasis Epidemiological Survey in Xichang, Meishan, and Other Counties): 8–9.

64 Yueyang 100-1-2 (1958–59) 关于宁乡岳阳对专职血防干部的配备使用问题 (Problem Regarding the Supply and Management of Schistosomiasis Control Cadres in Ningxiang and Yueyang): 52.

65 Jiaxing 053-002-137 关于1959年2到5月血防工作总结 (Evaluation of Schistosomiasis Control Work between February and May in 1959): 28.

66 Sichuan JC133-2666 (1958) 防治工作情况 (58年1月18日) (Reports on Preventative Work, 18 January 1958): 2–4.

67 Chen Huxin, '洞庭湖区域自然环境的改造在消灭血吸虫病中的意义 (Eradicating Schistosomiasis by Controlling the Environment in the Dongting Lake)', *Chinese Journal of Preventative Medicine* 5, no. 2 (1957): 73–4.

68 Hunan 141-1-1051 (1958) 陈毅副总理接见波中友协代表团谈话记录 [1958.11.5] (Transcript of Vice Primer Chen Yi's Talk When He Met with the Poland-China Friendship Delegation, 5 November 1958): 124.

69 Sichuan JC133-2684 (January–October 1959) 除害灭病工作情况简报 (Summary Report of Disease Prevention and Eradication) no. 5 (8 April): 3–4; no. 14 (30 June): 5–6; no. 20 (20 September): 6.

70 Shanghai A70-2-42-84 (1958) 湖南省方用在第四次全国防治血吸虫病会议上的发言 (Hunan Province's Fang Yong's Talk at the Fourth National Schistosomiasis Control Conference): 85–7.

71 Sichuan JC133-450 (4–25 Dec. 1963) 几年来各地国营农场职工发生血吸虫病急性感染的一些情况 (Reports about Acute Schistosomiasis in State Farms around the Country in Recent Years): 59; Sichuan JC133-2684 (January–October 1959), Summary Report of Disease Prevention and Eradication no. 5 (8 April): 3–4; no. 14 (30 June): 5–6.

72　Yang Xiaokai, 牛鬼蛇神录 (*The Captive Spirits*) (Hong Kong: Hong Kong University Press 1988): 34, 88.

73　Sichuan JC133-450 (4–25 December 1963) Reports about Acute Schistosomiasis in State Farms around the Country in Recent Years): 59–60; Shanghai A70-2-42-84 (1958) Hunan Province's Fang Yong's Talk at the Fourth National Schistosomiasis Control Conference: 85–7.

74　Hunan 141-1-1292 (March–December 1959), 省防汛防旱指挥部关于汨罗围垦区溃决向中央的报告 (1959, 6.4) (Hunan Provincial Flood and Drought Control Leadership Committee's Report to the Central Committee of the CCP Regarding the Dyke Burst in Reclaimed Areas of Miluo River): 81–2; Deng Qiaonian, 无法无天' 时代的冤魂(组图) (Pictorial Memorial to the Spirits of Those who Died of Injustice), 往事微痕 (Wounds from the Past), https://www.flickr.com/photos/booknews/16099849380/in/photostream/.

CHAPTER FOUR

1　Wu Zhuim, '"Agriculture Developing and Fishery Shrinking": Historical Connotation of Economy, Ecology and Social Change in Poyang Lake District since the Ming and Qing Dynasties', *Journal of Jiangxi Normal University* (Social Sciences) 46, no. 3 (April 2013): 122–5.

2　Mao Huiren and Li Guifa, 余江县志 (*Yujian County Gazette*) (Nanchang: Jiangxi renmin chubanshe, 1993): 30–2; Yujiang Schistosomiasis Control Leadership Committee, ed., 江西省余江县血防志 (Yujiang County Schistosomiasis Control Annals, Jiangxi Province) (Yujiang 1984): 17–25; Xiao Jianwen, '江西的血吸虫病与地方社会—以民国时期及1950 年代为考察时限' (Local Society and Schistosomiasis in Jiangxi, from the Republican Period to 1959)', PhD dissertation (Nanchang: Jiangxi Normal University, 2006).

3　Zuo Yihua, 跨越死亡地带 (*Walking across the Death Zone*) (Beijing: Zuojia chubanshe 2012), 48–51.

4　'Report on the Proposal for the Second Five-Year Plan for Development of the National Economy', delivered by Zhou Enlai to the Eighth Party Congress on 16 September 1956. The English text of the report can be found in *Eighth National Congress of the Communist Party of China*, vol. 1 (Beijing: Foreign Language Press 1956): 261–328.

5　Yujiang Schistosomiasis Control Leadership Committee, ed., *Yujiang County Schistosomiasis Control Annals, Jiangxi Province*, 57–9; Jiangxi Zhengxie Wenshi Ziliao Yanjiuhui, et al., eds, 江西文史资料 –送瘟神纪实

(*Jiangxi Local Historical Sources: Send off the Plague God*) vol. 43 (Jiangxi Zhexie wenshi ziliao chubanshe 1992), 6, 10; Interview with Zou at Yujiang, 13 April 2018.

6 Shanghai A70-2-42 (February 1958) 安徽省赵一鸣同志在第四次全国防治血吸虫病会议上的发言 (Comrade Zhao Yiming's Conversation at the 4th National Schistosomiasis Control Conference): 28–9; Mao Shoubai, ed., 血吸虫生物学与血吸虫病的防治 (*Biology and Pathology Schistosomiasis and Its Prevention*) (Beijing: Renmin weisheng chubanshe 1990): 704.

7 Yujiang Schistosomiasis Control Leadership Committee, ed., *Yujiang County Schistosomiasis Control Annals*, 58–9.

8 Sichuan JC133-457 (1965) 四川省钉螺分布概况, 特点及血吸虫病流行的关系 (Relationship between Snail Habitat Area and the Spread of Schistosomiasis in Sichuan Province): 116–17; Sichuan JC133-450 (4–25 December 1963) 山丘型地区防治血吸虫病工作的调查报告 (Investigative Report on Schistosomiasis Control in Hilly Regions): 36–7.

9 Sichuan JC 133-2611 (November 1956–May 1957) 流行病学调查 (Epidemiology Report): 5.

10 Juan Qiu et al., 'Identifying Determinants of Oncomelania Hupensis Habitats and Assessing the Effects of Environmental Control Strategies in the Plain Regions with the Waterway Network of China at the Microscale', *International Journal of Environmental Research and Public Health* 11, no. 6 (June 2014): 6571–85.

11 Zhejiang J166-003-009 (1953) 浙江省卫生厅关于全省血吸虫病防治工作检查总结报告, 一九五三年三月六日 (Zhejiang Provincial Health Bureau's Investigative Report of the Provincial Schistosomiasis Control Work, 6 March 1953): 2–4; Report of Quzhou District's Grassroots Schistosomiasis Control (1953): 2, 9

12 Jiangxi Zhengxie Wenshi Ziliao Yanjiuhui et al., eds, *Jiangxi Local Historical Sources*, 8.

13 Deng Tuo, 'A Speech Given at the CCP National Propaganda Conference [May 1954]', published as '怎样改进报纸工作 (How to Advance Newspaper Work)', 中国共产党新闻工作文件汇编 (Collection of Documents on CCP Journalism Work) (Beijing: Xinhua chubanshe 1980), vol. 2, 323–44.

14 Jiangxi Zhengxie Wenshi Ziliao Yanjiuhui et al., eds, *Jiangxi Local Historical Sources*, 8.

15 Ibid., 116; Zuo Yihua, *Walking across the Death Zone*, 83–5.

16 Interview with Zuo at Yujiang, 13 April 2018.

17 Zuo Yihua, *Walking across the Death Zone*, 96–7.

18 Jiangxi Zhengxie Wenshi Ziliao Yanjiuhui, et al, eds, *Jiangxi Local Historical Sources*, 116, 191–3.

19 Zuo Yihua, *Walking across the Death Zone*, 86–91.

20 'Schistosomiasis Control in Yujiang', exhibition at China Schistosomiasis Control Memorial Hall, Yuiang County, Jiangxi province.

21 Yujiang Schistosomiasis Control Leadership Committee, ed., *Yujiang County Schistosomiasis Control Annals, Jiangxi Province*, 53.

22 The CCP Jiangxi Provincial Party Committee's Historical Sources Search Committee, ed., 江西党史资料 - 江西血吸虫病防治: 第37 辑 (Jiangxi Party History Sources, vol. 37, *Schistosomiasis Control in Jiangxi*) (Beijing: Zhongyang wenxian chubanshe 1996), 59.

23 Yujiang Schistosomiasis Control Leadership Committee, ed., *Yujiang County Schistosomiasis Control Annals, Jiangxi Province*, 55–6, 64–78; Zuo Yihua, *Walking across the Death Zone*, 102–6, 134–43; Wan Xin and Wang Zhenfan, 'The Historical Experiences of the Schistosomiasis Control in Yu Jiang County under the Leadership of the CPC in 1950s', *Journal of Jiangxi Normal University* (Social Sciences) 46 no. 1 (February 2013): 109–16.

24 Sichuan JC133-2666 (1958) 防治工作情况 (58年1月18日, 2月1日) (Reports on Preventative Work, 18 January and 1 February 1958); Sichuan JC133-2666 (1958) 血吸虫病防治工作情况简报 (58年4月17日) (Report on Schistosomiasis Control Work, 17 April 1958).

25 Interview with Zou in Yujiang, 13 April 2018.

26 Chen Rinong, 中国对外传播史 (*A Brief History of China's International Communication*) (Beijing: Waiwen chubanshe 2010), ch. 8.

27 See Frank Dikötter, *Mao's Great Famine: The History of China's Most Devastating Catastrophe, 1958–62* (London: Bloomsbury 2010), ch. 7.

28 See Shang Yiying, '他写的那篇报道让毛主席 '夜不能寐' (He Wrote the Report that made Chairman Mao Sleepless)', Xinhuanews, http://www.xinhuanet.com/mrdx/2016-10/31/c_135792572.htm.

29 Timothy Cheek, *Propaganda and Culture in Mao's China: Deng Tuo and the Intelligentsia* (Oxford: Oxford University Press 1997), 145.

30 Chen Bingyan and Liu Guanghui, '第一面红旗—记江西余江县根本消灭血吸虫病的经过 (The First Red Flag: Jiangxi Province's Yujiang County's Experience in Eradicating Schistosomiasis)', *People's Daily* (30 June 1958): 7.

31 Mao Zedong, '在成都会议上的讲话提纲 (1958年三月) (Summary of Mao's Speech at the Chengdu Conference, March 1958)', in 建国以来毛泽东文稿 Jianguo yilai Mao Zedong wenxuan (*Selected Writings of Mao Zedong since 1949*), vol. 7 (Beijing: Zhongyang wenxian chubanshe 1992), 110, 115–17, 121–2.

32 Chou Yang [Zhou Yang], 'The Path of Socialist Literature and Art in China', in *Report Delivered to the Third Congress of Chinese Literary and Art Workers on July 22, 1960* (Peking: Foreign Languages Press 1960): 5

33 Chen Bingyan and Liu Guanghui, 'The First Red Flag: Jiangxi Province's Yujiang County's Experience in Eradicating Schistosomiasis'.

34 Mao Zedong '介绍一个合作社 (Introducing an Agricultural Cooperative)', in Mao Zedong, *Selected Writings of Mao Zedong since 1949*, vol. 7, 177–8.

35 Feng Xianzhi, ed., 毛泽东年谱 (*Chronological Biography of Mao Zedong*) vol. 3 (Beijing: Zhongyang wenxian chubanshe 2013), 377–8.

36 Ibid.

37 Gansu 91-18-495 毛主席在八大二次会议上的讲话 (1958年5月8日) (Mao's Speech at the Second Session of the 8th National Party Congress, 8 May 1958): 255–9. I am grateful to Frank Dikötter for sharing this document with me while we collaborated on the social history of the Great Famine project.

38 Feng Xianzhi, ed., *Chronological Biography of Mao Zedong*, vol. 3, 381–2.

39 Gong Zizhen, 己亥杂诗注 (Cycle Poem with Commentary) (Beijing: Zhonghua shuju 1999): 125.

40 Mao Zedong, '送瘟神 (Send off the Plague God)', in Mao Zedong, *Selected Writings of Mao Zedong since 1949*, vol. 7, 298–9.

41 Feng Xianzhi, ed., *Chronological Biography of Mao Zedong*, vol. 3, 381.

42 Mao Zedong, 'Send off the Plague God', 298–9.

43 For further readings on the Plague God Festival, see Carol Benedict, *Bubonic Plague in Nineteenth-Century China*, 115–16.

44 Feng Xianzhi, ed., *Chronological Biography of Mao Zedong*, vol. 3, 381.

45 'Resolution of the Central Committee of the Chinese Communist Party on the Establishment of People's Communes in the Rural Areas', 29 August 1958, in *Communist China 1955–1959: Policy Documents with Analysis*, 456.

46 Lin Yang, 'Here's to Better Health', *Peking Review* no. 3 (20 January 1959): 12–14.

47 Zhang Jianzhong, Huang Yujin, and Chen Dai, '20 世纪50 年代万县地区献方运动述要 (Wanxian Region's Folk Remedy Collection Campaign in the 1950s)', *Culture Kaleidoscope* no. 3 (2017): 49–51, doi:10.1630 7/j.1673-6281.2017.03.009 (accessed 20 March 2019).

48 Sichuan JC133-2685 (1959) 卫生部血吸虫病防治局为检送土方防治钩虫病，丝虫病，疟疾等有关资料通知' (1959年6月29日) (The Ministry of

Health's Schistosomiasis Control Department's Notice Regarding Collecting Folk Remedies for Preventing and Treating Parasitic Diseases); Zhou Zaoxi, 'Malaria Eradication in County Rong, Sichuan', in A.J. Knell, ed., *Malaria*, A Publication of the Tropical Programme of the Wellcome Trust (Oxford: Oxford University Press 1991): 80.

49 Ke Qingshi, '劳动人民一定要做文化的主人 (The Labour Mass Must Become the Master of Culture)', *Red Flag Magazine*, no. 1 (1958): 28–32.

50 Elizabeth J. Perry, 'Moving the Masses: Emotion Work in the Chinese Revolution', *Mobilization* 7, no. 2 (2002): 111–28.

51 Chang-tai Hung, 'The Dance of Revolution: Yangge in Beijing in the 1950s', *China Quarterly* 181 (March 2005): 82–99.

52 James Z. Gao, *The Communist Takeover of Hangzhou: The Transformation of City and Cadre, 1949–1954* (Honolulu: University of Hawaii Press 2004): 231–6.

53 " Zhu Anping, '枯木逢春' 翻新枝 (How *Spring Comes to the Withered Tree* Grew New Branches)', *Popular Film*, no. 3 (2008): 24.

54 Zhang Yingjin, *Chinese National Cinema* (London and New York: Routledge 2004): 209.

55 Sichuan JC133-450 (4–25 December 1963) Comrade Lu Dingyi's Speech, 85–92.

56 JC 133-454 (January–December 1964) 防治血吸虫工作情况反映' (第一期) (Reports on Schistosomiasis Control Work, no. 1): 167.

57 Sichuan JC133-450 (4–25 December 1963), Comrade Lu Dingyi's Speech, 85–92.

58 For a detailed study on Zheng Junli, see Paul G. Pickowicz, *China on Film: A Century of Exploration, Confrontation, and Controversy* (Lanham: Rowman & Littlefield 2012), ch. 7, 189–210.

59 See Li Zhen, ed., 郑君里全传 (*The Complete Biography of Zheng Junli*), vol. 7 (Shanghai: Shanghai wenhua chubanshe 2016): 237–40, 288–326.

60 Sichuan JC133-2837 (20 February 1965) 1964 年的血防宣教工作 (The Anti- Schistosomiasis Campaign Propaganda Work in 1964): 5.

61 Wang Xuede et al., eds, 南京血防志 (Nanjing Schistosomiasis Control Annals) (Nanjing: Jiangsu Kexue jishu chubanshe 1995): 152–3.

62 Shanghai B242-1-1392-7 魏文伯同志在防治血吸虫工作会议上讲话记录稿 (Transcript of Comrade Wei Wenbo's Speech at the Schistosomiasis Control Work Conference): 9.

63 Li Zhen, ed., *The Complete Biography of Zheng Junli*, vol. 7, 344–6.

64 Gerard Lemos, *The End of the Chinese Dream: Why Chinese People Fear the Future* (New Haven and London: Yale University Press 2012).

CHAPTER FIVE

1 'Report on Government Work', speech delivered by Zhou Enlai to the First Session of the Second National People's Congress, 18 April 1959, in *Communist China 1955–1959: Policy Documents with Analysis*, Document 37, 511.

2 Günter Grass, *From the Diary of a Snail* (London: Vintage 1972): 12.

3 Sichuan JC133-2684 (January–October 1959) 除害灭病工作情况简报 (Summary Report of Disease Prevention and Eradication) no. 3 (23 March 1959).

4 Sichuan JC133-2684 (January–October 1959) 血吸虫病防治工作情况简报 (Schistosomiasis Control Summary Report) no. 35 (14 January 1959).

5 Shanghai B242-1-1351 (1961) 各县防治干部反映的思想情况 (County Level Schistosomiasis Control Cadres Reporting on Local Opinions): 126–7.

6 Y. Komiya, 'A Recommendatory Note for the Control Problem of Schistosomiasis', *Japanese Journal of Medical Science and Biology* 10 (1957): 466–7.

7 E. Paulini, 'Bilharziasis Control by Application of Molluscicides: A Review of Its Present Status', *Bulletin of the World Health Organization* 18 (1958): 975–88.

8 Mao Shoubai, ed., 血吸虫生物学与血吸虫病的防治 (*Biology and Pathology Schistosomiasis and Its Prevention*) (Beijing: Renmin weisheng chubanshe 1990): 716–17. For further readings on the topic of the damage to human health resulting from the overuse of pesticides in this period, see Rachel Carson, *Silent Spring*, First Mariner Books edition (New York: Mariner Books 2002 [1962]).

9 Su Delong, 'How to Eliminate Snails with Calcium Arsenate', in Professor Su Delong's Lecture Notes (10 July 1958) at Fudan University's School of Public Health archive, file number RM008-082. Also see Paulini, 'Bilharziasis Control by Application of Molluscicides: A Review of Its Present Status'.

10 Sichuan JC 133-2788 (1960) 关于冬季灭螺工作中的几个问题和意见 (Problem and Suggestion Regarding Carrying out Snail Elimination in Winter): 1–3.

11 Shanghai B242-1-1351 (1961) County Level Schistosomiasis Control Cadres Reporting on Local Opinions: 128.

12 Jiaxing 102-001-031 (1963) 嘉兴县净湘公社血防试点工作简报 (News Bulletin of Schistosomiasis Control Experiment Work in Jiaxing County's Jingxiang Commune): 102–3.

13 Sichuan JC133-2811 (January–November 1962) 绵阳县血防干部思想情况 (Some Ideological Issues among Schistosomiasis Control Cadres in Mianyang County): 14–18.

14 Mao Shoubai, *Biology and Pathology Schistosomiasis and Its Prevention*, 709.

15 Sichuan JC 133-2811 (January–November 1962) Some Ideological Issues among Schistosomiasis Control Cadres in Mianyang County: 14–18.

16 N. Levine, 'Integrated Control of Snails', *American Zoologist* 10 (1970): 579–82; P.A. Roger, 'Blue-Green Algae in Rice Fields, Their Ecology and Their Use as Inoculant', Proc. Consultants Meeting, FAO/IAEA Joint Project (Vienna, 11–15 October 1982).

17 Shanghai B242-1-1351 (1961) County Level Schistosomiasis Control Cadres Reporting on Local Opinions: 128.

18 Sichuan JC133-2788 (1960) 关于冬季灭螺工作中的几个问题和意见 (Problems of Snail Control Work in Winter and Some Suggestions): 1–3; Shanghai B242-1-1351, County Level Schistosomiasis Control Cadres Reporting on Local Opinions: 128.

19 Sichuan JC133-2684 (January–October 1959) Summary Report of Disease Prevention and Eradication, no. 16 (31 July 1959): 5–6.

20 For the prevalence of train robberies during the Great Leap famine, see Frank Dikötter, *Mao's Great Famine: The History of China's Most Devastating Catastrophe, 1958–62* (London: Bloomsbury 2010), 3, ch. 19; Zhou Xun, ed., *The Great Famine in China, 1958–1962: A Documentary History* (New Haven and London: Yale University Press 2012), 127–30.

21 Sichuan JC133-2684 (January–October 1959) Summary Report of Disease Prevention and Eradication, no. 16 (31 July 1959): 5–6.

22 Ibid., no. 20 (20 September 1959): 16; Sichuan JC133-2666 (1958) 防治工作情况 (58年1月18日) Fangzhi gongzuo qingkuang (Prevention Report, 18 January 1958).

23 B. Maegraith, 'Schistosomiasis in China', *The Lancet* 1, no. 7,013 (25 January 1958): 208–14; Mao Shoubai, ed., *Biology and Pathology Schistosomiasis and Its Prevention*, 721; Zhejiang J166-003-026 (1956) 嘉兴县血防站 一九五五年年度工作总结 (12 January 1956) (Jiaxing County Schistosomiasis Control Station's Report of 1955 Schistosomiasis Control Work): 6.

24 Gansu 91-18-177 (1960) 省委批转省科委关于贯彻全国工业废水处理和污水综合利用现场会议精神及我省开展这项科学研究工作的安排意见 (Gansu Provincial Party Committee Approve Gansu Province Science Committee's Plan to Implement the National Campaign to Utilise Industrial Waste Water): 16. I am grateful to Frank Dikötter for sharing

this file with me when we collaborated on the social history of the Great Famine project.

25 Sichuan JC133-259 (27 February–26 November 1963) 宜宾市区长江河流水质卫生调查报告 (Water Safety and Quality in the Section of Yangtze in Yibin): 29; Gansu 91-18-154 (1960) 中央批转工程部党委关于工业废水危害情况和加强处理利用的报告 (The CCP Central Committee Approve the Department of Industrial Construction's Report Regarding the Harms Caused by Industrial Waste Water as Well as to Make Every Effort to Utilise It): 252–5; Sichuan JC133-2666 (1958) 爱国卫生运动情况简报'(1958年6月12日) (Report on the Patriotic Hygiene Campaign, 22 June 1958): 4–5.

26 Li Ping and Ma Zhisun, *Chronological Biography of Zhou Enlai*, 803, 844; Gu Ming, '周总理是我国环保事业的奠基人 (Premier Zhou Founded the Environmental Protection in the PRC)', in Li Qi, ed., *Memoirs of Officials Who Worked alongside of Zhou Enlai* (Beijing: Zhongyang wenxian chubanshe 1998): 332.

27 Gansu 91-18-154 (1960): 252–3.

28 Mao Shoubai, ed., *Biology and Pathology Schistosomiasis and Its Prevention*, 717.

29 Ibid., 726; interview with Su in Xichang, May 2015.

30 Chen Jianmin et al., 'A Review of Biomass Burning: Emissions and Impacts on Air Quality, Health and Climate in China', *Science of the Total Environment* 579 (1 February 2017): 1,000–34.

31 Sichuan JC133-450 (4–25 December 1963) 几年来各地国营农场职工发生血吸虫病急性感染的一些情况 (An Evaluation of Acute Schistosomiasis Infections amongst Workers at State Farms in the Recent Years): 59–60.

32 Min Qian, 'Study on the Floods on the Poyang Lake in the 1990s', *Journal of Lake Science* 14, no. 4 (December 2002): 323–30; Li Jingbao and Deng Luojing, '洞庭湖滩地围垦及其对生态环境的影响 (Land Reclamation and Its Effects on the Eco-environment of the Dongting Lake)', *Resources and Environment in the Yangtze Valley* 2, no. 4 (1993): 340–6; Zeng T et al., 'Dongting Lake Floods and Its Future', 水利水电科技进展, *Advances in Science and Technology of Water Resources*) 24, no. 1 (February 2004): 7–10.

33 Interview with SM in Yueyang, 2 November 2014.

34 Li Jingbao and Deng Luojing, 'Land Reclamation and Its Effects on the Eco-environment of the Dongting Lake, 342–3.

35 Mao Shoubai, ed., *Biology and Pathology Schistosomiasis and Its Prevention*, 703–4.

36 Sichuan JC133-450 (4–25 December 1963) An Evaluation of Acute

Schistosomiasis Infections amongst Workers at State Farms in the Recent Years: 59–60.

37 Yueyang 100-1-5 (1964) 岳阳地区1964年血防工作总结 (The Evaluation of Schistosomiasis Control in Yueyang Region, 1964): 64–6; Zhou Xun, *Forgotten Voices of Mao's Great Famine: An Oral History* (New Haven and London: Yale University Press 2013), 28–9.

38 Yueyang 100-1-3 (1960–1962) 关于进一步做好湖沼地区血吸虫防护工作的建议 (Recommendation Regarding Enforcing Preventive Measures against Schistosomiasis Infection in Lake and Marsh Regions): 161–2.

39 For studies on the Great Famine in Mao's China, see Frank Dikötter, *Mao's Great Famine*; Yang Jisheng, *Tombstone: The Untold Story of Mao's Great Famine* (London and New York: Penguin Books 2013). For the long-term effect on the environment of the Great Leap Forward's agricultural practices, see Judith Shapiro, *Mao's War against Nature: Politics and the Environment in Revolutionary China* (New York: Cambridge University Press 2001); Zhou Xun, ed., *The Great Famine in China*, ch. 5; Zhou Xun, *Forgotten Voices of Mao's Great Famine: An Oral History*, ch. 3; Zhou Xun, 'Deforestation to Blame for Beijing's Pollution', *South China Morning Post* (1 April 2013), https://www.scmp.com/comment/insight-opinion/article/1204076/deforestation-blame-beijings-pollution.

40 Zhou Xun, *Forgotten Voices of Mao's Great Famine*, 28–9.

41 Sichuan JC133-447 (April–December 1962) 魏文伯同志在防治血吸虫病工作会议上讲话记录稿 (Transcript of Comrade Wei Wenbo's Speech at the Schistosomiasis Control Work Meeting): 2–3; Sichuan JC133-447 (April–December 1962) 关于防治血吸虫病工作的报告 (Report on Schistosomiasis Control Work): 7–8.

42 Sichuan JC133-450 (4–25 December 1963) 江西省余江县孙永久同志的发言 (Comrade Sun Yongjiu's Speech at the Ninth National Conference on Schistosomiasis Control): 165–7.

43 Sichuan JC133-2811 (January–November 1962) 邛崃县血防工作情况 (Schistosomiasis Control Work in Qionglai): 51.

44 Sichuan JC133-454 (January–December 1964) 防治血吸虫工作情况反映 (第10期) (Report on Schistosomiasis Control Work, no. 10): 101.

45 Sichuan JC133-447 (April–December 1962) Transcript of Comrade Wei Wenbo's Speech at the Schistosomiasis Control Work Meeting): 2–3; Sichuan JC133-447 (April–December 1962) 关于防治血吸虫病工作的报告 (Report on Schistosomiasis Control Work): 7–8.

46 Zhang Youguang, '反'五风'亲历记 (My Eyewitness Account of the Campaign Attacking the "Five-Winds")', 炎黄春秋 (China Through the Ages), no. 3 (2001), 民间历史 (Folk History), Universities Service Centre

for China Studies at the Chinese University of Hong Kong, http://mjlsh.
usc.cuhk.edu.hk/Book.aspx?cid=4&tid=1238.

47 Mao Shoubai, ed., *Biology and Pathology Schistosomiasis and Its
    Prevention*, 585–6; Sherif M. Abaza, 'Treatment of Schistosomiasis: From
    Praziquantel to Development of New Drug Targets', *Parasitologists United
    Journal 6*, no. 2 (2013): 128; Zhou Xuzhang, 'Clinic Evaluation of F30066
    in Long Course Treatment of Schistosomiasis Japonica', *CMJ*, no. 84
    (1965): 591–8

48 Sichuan JC133-2788 (1960) 关于血吸虫病粪检工作中存在的几个问题和
    今后工作意见 (Problems Regarding Schistosomiasis Diagnosis and
    Suggestion for Future Work).

49 Shanghai B242-1-1315-60 (1961) 上海市血吸虫病防治所关于当前农村形
    势与四病防治任务要 (Shanghai Schistosomiasis Control Institute's Report
    on Current Situation in the Countryside and the Edict to Control Four
    Parasitic Diseases).

50 人民保健 (*People's Health*) 2, no. 7 (May 1960): 278–80.

51 Yueyang 100-1-2 (1958–59) 临湘定湖防治组收药费工作的作法
    (Lingxiang County's Dinghu Township Impose a Fee for the
    Schistosomiasis Prevention and Treatment Drugs): 203–5.

52 Interview with Barber Feng in Jincheng Township, Langzhong County,
    Sichuan province, October 2006. Part of this interview was published in
    Zhou Xun, *Forgotten Voices of Mao's Great Famine*, 56–8.

53 Zhou Xun, *Forgotten Voices of Mao's Great Famine*.

54 Sichuan JC133-2819 (January–December 1963) 万县地区疟疾座谈会简况
    (63年3月12日) (A Summary Report of Malaria Control Conference for
    Wan County and Its Surrounding Region, 12 March 1963): 145–8.

55 Sichuan JC133-2666 (1958) Prevention Report (18 January 1958): 2–4;
    Sichuan JC133-2666 (1958) Prevention Report (11 January 1958): 2–3.

56 Sichuan JC133-447 (April–December 1962) Transcript of Comrade Wei
    Wenbo's Speech at the Schistosomiasis Control Work Meeting): 2–3.

57 Zhou Xuezhang, '四十年春秋话血防 (Forty Years of Schistosomiasis
    Control)', in Hua Li, ed., *Send off the God of Plague: Schistosomiasis Control
    in Jiaxing*, 45–7; Shi Youquan, '四战 "瘟神" 南湖旁 (Four Battles Attacking
    the Plague God in Jiaxing)', in *Memoire of Shi Youquan* (private publication,
    2012): 121; interview with Shi Youquan in Jiaxing, 13 March 2011.

58 'Report of the American Schistosomiasis Delegation to the PRC', *American
    Journal of Tropical Medicine and Hygiene 26*, no. 3 (1977): 429.

59 Sichuan JC133-2684 (January–October 1959) 除害灭病工作情况简报
    (Summary Report of Disease Prevention and Eradication), no. 24 (30
    November 1959): 2.

60 Shi Youquan, 'Four Battles Attacking the Plague God in Jiaxing', 121.

61 Sichuan JC133-2666 (1958) Prevention Report (29 January 1958), 2–4.

62 Shanghai B242-1315-49 (1961) 上海市长宁区卫生局关于长宁区部分地区，工厂，居民及职工到郊区摸蚌引起血吸虫病急性感染的情况报告（1961年7月1日）(Changning District Health Bureau's Report Regarding the Acute Schistosomiasis Infection amongst Factory Workers and Local Residents as a Result of Them Fishing for Shellfishes in the Suburbs): 1–2.

63 Sichuan JC133-450 (4–25 December 1963) 关于[江苏省]今年发生大量血吸虫病集体急性感染情况的报告 (Regarding a Huge Number of Acute Schistosomiasis Infections This Year in Jiangsu Province): 31–3; Sichuan JC133-449 (February–December 1962) 转发中央防治血吸虫病九人小组关于防治血吸虫病急性感染和疟疾流行的电文 (Forward the Telegraph from the Nine-Man Subcommittee Regarding Preventing and Treating Schistosomiasis Acute Infection as Well as the Malaria Epidemic): 73, 95; Shanghai B242-1-1392-7 (December 1962) 魏文伯同志在防治血吸虫病工作会议上讲话记录稿 (Transcript of Comrade Wei Wenbo's Speech at the Schistosomiasis Control Conference): 7.

64 Sichuan JC133-450 (4–25 December 1963) 关于加强对血吸虫病防治工作的报告 (Report on Putting More Effort on Schistosomiasis Control Work): 34.

65 Sichuan JC133-450 (4–25 December 1963) 关于绵竹县遵道公社进行血防工作试点经验的报告 (Report on Mianzhu County's Zundao Commune's Schistosomiasis Control Experiment): 2.

66 Hunan 163-1-1126 (March 1962) 关于当前疾病防治工作的情况和问题 (The Current Situation and Problems on Disease Control): 54–5.

67 Interview with WYH in Hubei province, October 2003.

68 Interview with Professor Yin in Shanghai, April 2015.

69 For a general reading, see Berry-Cabán CS, 'Return of the God of Plague: Schistosomiasis in China', *Journal of Rural and Tropical Public Health* 6 (2007): 45–53. For a case study, see Song Liang et al., 'Re-emerging Schistosomiasis in Hilly and Mountainous Areas of Sichuan, China', *Bulletin of the World Health Organization* 84, no. 2 (February 2006): 139–43.

CHAPTER SIX

1 Hunan 163-1-1126 (March 1962) 关于当前疾病防治工作的情况和问题 (The Current Situation and Problems on Disease Control): 54–5.

2 Sichuan JC133-449 (February–December 1962) 省委除害灭病办公室关于防病治病工作的计划，总结，报告，指示 (Sichuan Provincial Party

Committee Disease Eradication Office's Plan, Evaluation, Report and Edict on Disease Prevention and Treatment): 111.

3 For further readings on the links between malaria transmission and irrigation expansion and deforestation, see J. Ysuoka and R. Levins, 'Impact of Deforestation and Agricultural Development on Anopheline Ecology and Malaria Epidemiology', *The American Journal of Tropical Hygiene and Medicine* 76 no. 3 (2007): 450–60; Chung, 'Impact of Irrigation Extension on Malaria Transmission in Simret, Tigray, Ethiopia', *Korean Journal of Parasitology* 54, no. 4 (2016): 399–405; S.L. Zuo et al., 'Analysis of the Factors Causing Malaria Local Outbreak in An. Sinensis Area, Zaoyang City, Hubei Province', *Public Health and Preventive Medicine* 13 (2000): 6–7. For further reading on their long-term damage on the environment, see Zhou Xun, ed., *The Great Famine in China*: 73–4, 77–9, 86–90; Zhang Yaoqi, 'Deforestation and Forest Transition: Theory and Evidence in China', in M. Palo and H. Vanhanen, eds, *World Forests from Deforestation to Transition?* (Dordrecht: Kluwer Academic Publishers 2000): 41–62.

4 Oscar Felsenfeld, 'Some Observation of Cholera Epidemic in 1961–2', *Bulletin of the World Health Organization*, no. 28 (1963): 289–96; Shanghai Medical University Department of Epidemiology and Shanghai Medical University Archive, eds, 苏德隆教授论文选集 (*Selected Academic Essays of Professor Su Delong*) (Tianjin: Tianjin kexuejishu chubanshe 1995): 3, 280–4; Shanghai B242-1-1392-7 (December 1962) 魏文伯同志在防治血吸虫病工作会议上讲话记录稿 (Transcript of Comrade Wei Wenbo's Speech at the Schistosomiasis Control Conference): 7.

5 Sichuan JC133-449 (February–December 1962) Sichuan Provincial Party Committee Disease Eradication Office's Plan, Evaluation, Report and Edict on Disease Prevention and Treatment, 111; Sichuan JC133-453 (December 1963–January 1964) 魏文伯同志在第九次防治血吸虫病工作会议上的讲话 (1963年12月23日) (Comrade Wei Wenbo's Speech on 23 December 1963 at the Ninth National Conference on Schistosomiasis Control).

6 Hunan 163-1-1126 (March 1962) The Current Situation and Problems in Disease Control, 54–5.

7 Yunnan 120-1-224 (January–December 1964) 楚雄县三街八个公社医药卫生情况的调查 (Report on Medicine and Health Conditions in the Eight Communes in Chuxiong County's Sanjie Township): 61–2.

8 Sichuan JC133-449 (February–December 1962) 四川省1962年防病治病工作简况 (General Situation in Disease Prevention and Treatment in Sichuan Province, 1962): 111; Beijing 135-1-1368 (10 January–28 August 1963) 中华人民共和国卫生部关于进一步整顿和加强农村基层卫生问题的通知 (The Circular of the PRC's Ministry of Health Regarding Further Reifying

and Strengthening Rural Grassroots Health Work): 3; 农村医生集体办的医疗机构和开业医生暂行管理办法 (Temporary Measures to Manage Collective Medical Setups and Individual Medical Practitioners): 7-3.

9 Beijing 135-1-1368 (10 January–28 August 1963) 关于恢复农村基层医务人员吃商品粮的请示 (Request to Resume Food Ration for Grassroots Medical Employees in the Countryside): 37.

10 Sichuan JC133-123 (1963) 内江专区县医院工作情况调查报告 (1963年6月17日) (Investigative Report on Neijiang Region County-Level Hospitals, 17 June 1963): 16.

11 Sichuan JC133-174 (15 January–2 February 1964) 关于医院政治工作的几个问题 (Question on Hospital Governance): 33-4.

12 Sichuan JC133-2819 (January–December 1963) 万县地区疟疾座谈会简况 (63年3月12日 (A Summary Report of Malaria Control Conference for Wan County and Its Surrounding Region, 12 March 1963): 145-8.

13 For further readings on cannibalism during the Great Leap famine, see Zhou Xun, ed., *The Great Famine in China*, ch. 4.

14 Sichuan JC133-2819 (January–December 1963) A Summary Report of Malaria Control Conference for Wan County and Its Surrounding Region, 12 March 1963): 145-8.

15 Sichuan JX1-865 (1950-1952) 对少数民族政策及方针计划报告和李井泉的指示 (1952年8月24日) (Report on Planning Minority Policy and Edict by Li Jinquan, 24 August 1952): 77, 80; Sichuan JX1-851 (1950–1952) 转发玉树地委对各县工委的指示' 1951年3月5日)(Forward the Edict from Yushu Reginal Party Committee to County-Level CCP Work Committees, 5 March 1951): 6-8; Sichuan JX1-879 (1949–52) 转青海尖扎工委在昂拉地区工作经验(1952年7月4日) (Forward the Report of Qinghai Jianza CCP Work Committee's Work Experience in Angla Region): 23-4.

16 Sichuan JK1-1423 (1 January–31 December 1954) 西康省卫生宣传工作存在的主要问题 (Major Problems Regarding Health Propaganda Work in Xikang): 35-9.

17 Sichuan JC133-173 (23 January–28 December 1963) 四川省民族卫生工作情况报告 (Report on Health Work among Ethnic Groups in Sichuan Province): 37.

18 For further readings on how vernacular healing rituals strive to facilitate a convergence of visions and programs in time of illness and disease outbreak, see Ivette Vargas-O'Bryan and Zhou Xun, *Disease, Religion and Healing in Asia* (London: Routledge 2014), ch. 1 and 3.

19 See Erik Mueggler, *Age of Wild Ghosts: Memory, Violence, and Place in Southwest China* (Berkeley: University of California Press 2001), ch. 6.

20 Yunnan 120-1-60 (1957) 省委楚雄工作组关于姚安县解决闹粮食问题的报告 (March 1957) (Yunnan Provincial Party Committee Chuxiong Work Team's Report on Handling Yaoan County's Food Riots): 2–3.

21 Yunnan 120-1-224120-1-224 (January–December 1964) Report on Medicine and Health Conditions in the Eight Communes of Chuxiong County's Sanjie Township, 61–6. For an English translation of this document, see Zhou Xun, ed., *The Great Famine in China*, 111. See also Mueggler, *Age of Wild Ghosts*, ch. 7.

22 Qian Xiangli, '历史的变局: 从挽救危机到返修防修 (Historical Turn: Responding to Crisis and Combating Revisionism, 1962–1965)', *The History of PRC Series*, vol. 5 (1962–65) (Hong Kong: The Chinese University of Hong Kong Press 2008), 294.

23 Qian Xiangli, *Historical Turn*, 294.

24 Chishui 1-A14-15 (1963) 关于农村四清运动开展对敌斗争意见的报告 (Report on Fighting Enemies in the Rural Countryside [Zunyi region, Guizhou province]): 38. For an English translation of a part of this document, see Zhou Xun, ed., *The Great Famine in China*, 112–13. For violence during the Great Leap famine, see Zhou Xun, 'Violence during the Great Leap Forward', *Cambridge History of World Violence*, vol. 4 (forthcoming).

25 Gao Wanglin's book is a pioneer study on how unofficial practices on the ground and government policies converged to bring about change after the Great Leap famine; see 中国农民反行为研究Zhongguo Nonmin fanxingwei yanjiu (A Study on Chinese Peasants' 'Counter-actions') (Hong Kong: The Chinese University of Hong Kong Press 2013).

26 Chishui 1-A12-2 (1961) 遵义地委关于当前农村生活和今后工作情况的报告 (Zunyi Regional Party Committee's Report on Current Condition and Future Work): 141–3; Shandong A1-2-1157 (1963): 11–14.

27 Sichuan JC133-2797 (January–December 1961) 四川省卫生厅省委除害灭病办公室工作组关于血吸虫病，疟疾，钩虫病的防治工作和爱国卫生运动的调查材料 (Sichuan Provincial Health Bureau and Sichuan Provincial Party Committee Disease Eradication Office's Investigative Reports Regarding the Control of Schistosomiasis, Malaria and Hookworm as Well as the Implementation of the Patriotic Health Campaign): 215–16, 233–4.

28 For an English translation of Mao Huachu's conversation with villagers in Shaoshan, see Zhou Xun, ed., *The Great Famine in China*, 81–2.

29 As quoted in Gao Wanglin, *A Study on Chinese Peasants' 'Counter-actions'*, 184.

30 Jin Chongji, *The Biography of Mao Zedong (1949–1976)*, vol. 2 (Beijing: Zhongyang wenxian chubanshe 2003): 1,449.

31 Shanghai B242-1-1351 (1961) 关于灭螺工作若干政策问题规定的说明 (The Clarification on Several Matters Regarding the Policy of Snail Elimination): 40–4.

32 Zhejiang J166-003-005 (1953) 本厅浙江省一九五二年上半年度血吸虫病防治工作总计及下半年计划 (Zhejiang Provincial Health Bureau's Evaluation of Schistosomiasis Control Work in the First Half of 1952 and the Plan for the Second Half of the Year): 3–4.

33 Shanghai B242-1315-81 (1961) 上海市血吸虫病防治所关于上海市1961年防治四大寄生虫病的几点意见 (Shanghai Municipal Schistosomiasis Control Institute's Opinions regarding the Control of Four Major Parasitic Diseases in 1961).

34 Shanghai A72-2-936-65 (18 February 1962) 上海市1962–1967防治血吸虫工作的规划 (草案) (A Draft Five-Year Plan for Schistosomiasis Control in Shanghai Region): 3–5.

35 Zhejiang J166-003-010 (1953) 浙江省嘉兴地区血吸虫病防治所一九五二年工作总结, 血防重点地区(嘉兴、绍兴、衢州血防所)工作总结 (Zhejiang Province's Jiaxing Regional Schistosomiasis Control Institute's Report of 1952 Control Work as Well as Report of Control Work in Four Schistosomiasis Model Counties): 2–3; Zhejiang J166-003-026 (1956) 嘉兴县血防站一九五五年年度工作总结 (12 January 1956) (Jiaxing County Schistosomiasis Control Station's Report of 1955 Schistosomiasis Control Work): 24.

36 Sichuan JC133-450 (4–25 December 1963) 浙江省嘉兴县赵景常同志的发言 (Talk by Comrade Zhao Jingchang from Jiaxing County in Zhejiang Province): 195.

CHAPTER SEVEN

1 Zhang Letian, 告别理想: 人民公社制度研究 (Farewell to Ideal – Study on People's Commune) (Shanghai: Dongfang chubanshe 1998): 424–6.

2 Hunan 141-1-1914 (April–December 1961) 中央书记处电话会议记录 (11.6) (The Minutes of the Secretariat of the CCP's Telephone Conference on 6 November 1961); Hunan 141-2-138 (April–December 1961) 邓小平同志在中央书记处会议上讨论1962年计划时的发言 (12.10) (Comrade's Deng Xiaoping's Speech at the Secretariat of the CCP's meeting on 10 December 2016)

3 See Zhou Xun, Forgotten Voices of Mao's Great Famine, 199–200.

4 Qian Yangli, Historical Turn, 1–2; Gao Wanglin, A Study on Chinese Peasants' 'Counter-actions', 188–91; Sichuan JC133-174 (15 January–2 February 1964) 关于医院政治工作的几个问题 (Question on Hospital Governance): 32–4.

5 Feng Xianzhi, ed., 毛泽东年谱 (*Chronological Biography of Mao Zedong*), vol. 5 (Beijing: Zhongyang wenxian chubanshe 2013): 108–9; 'Zhou Enlai's Speech at the Tenth Plenum of the Eighth Central Committee, 26 September 1962', as cited in Feng Xianzhi and Jin Chongji, eds., 毛泽东传 Mao Zedong zhuan (*Mao's Biography: 1949–1976*) (Beijing: Zhongyang wenxian chubanshe 2003): 1222.

6 Hunan Provincial Archive, ed., 彭德怀元帅回故乡档案史料 (Archival Documents on Marshall Peng Dehuai's Trip to Hunan Xiangtan) (Changsha: Hunan Provincial Archive 1998).

7 Gao Wanglin's study on peasant resistance or resilience provides a rounded view of why the Great Leap famine did not result in a bloody civil war as it did in Ukraine in the 1930s; see Gao Wanglin, *A Study on Chinese Peasants' 'Counter-actions'*.

8 'Mao Zedong's Conversation with Provincial Leaders in Zhejiang Province and Zhejiang Work Team on Feb. 2, 1961', in Feng Xianzhi, ed., *Chronological Biography of Mao Zedong*, vol. 4, 539.

9 Feng Xianzhi and Jin Chongji, eds, *Mao's Biography: 1949–1976*, 1592.

10 Qian Xiangli, *Historical Turn*, 205–6, 268–88; Feng Xianzhi, ed., *Chronological Biography of Mao Zedong*, 124–51.

11 Mao Zedong, '论人民民主专政 (On People's Democratic Dictatorship)', 30 June 1949; for an English translation, see 'On People's Democratic Dictatorship', in *Selected Works of Mao Tse-tung*, vol. 4, Marxist Internet Archive Reference Section, www.marxists.org/reference/archive/mao/selected-works/volume-4/mswv4_65.htm.

12 '关于向全体农村人口进行一次较大规模社会主义教育的指示 (Edict to Carry out a Massive Socialist Education Campaign in the Countryside)', as in *People's Daily*, 10 August 1957. For further readings, see Sun Dongfang, '对1957年农村社会主义教育运动的历史考察 (A Historical Analysis of the Socialist Education Campaign in 1957)', 北京党史 (*Beijing Party History Journal*), no. 1 (2006): 8–11.

13 Hunan 141-1-1914 (April–December 1961) The Minutes of the Secretariat of the CCP's Telephone Conference on 6 November 1961.

14 Hunan 141-2-138 (April–December 1961) Comrade's Deng Xiaoping's Speech at the Secretariat of the CCP's Meeting on 10 December 2016.

15 Qian Xiangli, *Historical Turn*, 292–3.

16 Ibid., 293.

17 Feng Xianzhi, ed., *Chronological Biography of Mao Zedong*, vol. 5, 213.

18 Sichuan JC133-453 (December 1963–January 1964) 魏文伯同志在第九次防治血吸虫病工作会议上的讲话(1963年12月23) (Comrade Wei Wenbo's Speech on 23 December 1963 at the Ninth National Conference on

Schistosomiasis Control); Sichuan JC133-450 (4–25 December 1963) Comrade Xu Yunbai's Summary Speech at the Ninth National Conference on Schistosomiasis Control, 62.

19 Sichuan JC133-2837 (20 February 1965) 1964 年的血防宣教工作 (The Anti-Schistosomiasis Campaign Propaganda Work in 1964): 5.

20 Interview with Yuxiang, Sichuan province, 11 November 2014.

21 Sichuan JC133-450 (4–25 December 1963) Comrade Xu Yunbai's Summary Speech at the Ninth National Conference on Schistosomiasis Control, January 1964, 62.

22 Sichuan JC133-453 (December 1963–January 1964) 廖鲁言部长在全国第九次血防工作会议上的讲话' (1964年1月 (Minster Liao Luyan's Speech at the Ninth National Conference on Schistosomiasis Control, January 1964): 61–2.

23 Sichuan JC133-450 (4–25 December 1963) 柯庆施同志在第九次防治血吸虫工作会议上的讲话 (3 January 1964) (Comrade Ke Qingshi's Speech at the Ninth National Conference on Schistosomiasis Control, 3 January 1964).

24 Ibid., 62.

25 '乘胜前进' 为消灭血吸虫而斗争 (Seize the Victory and Go Forward to Eradicate Schistosomiasis)', *People's Daily*, 24 January 1964: 2.

26 Sichuan JC133-450 (4–25 December 1963) Comrade Xu Yunbai's Summary Speech at the Ninth National Conference on Schistosomiasis Control, January 1964, 62.

27 Song Renqiong, 宋仁穷回忆录 (*Song Renqiong's Memoirs*) (Beijing: Jiefangjun chubashe 1994): 291–317.

28 Sichuan JK1-2995 (30 May–6 June 1955) 中央批转宋任穷同志关于贵州农业合作，粮食，镇反等问题的报告(1955年6月6日) (The CCP Central Committee Endorse Comrade Song Renqion's Report on Agricultural Co-operation, Procuring Grain and Suppression of Counter-revolutionaries in Guizhou, 6 June 1955).

29 Hunan 141-2-138 (April–December 1961) 周恩来同志在全国计划，财贸工作，农业会议上的报告 (12.4) (Comrade Zhou Enlai's Speech at the National Planning Conference for Commerce and Agriculture on 4 December 1961).

30 *Song Renqiong's Memoirs*, 377.

31 Ibid, 385–6.

32 Ibid., 406.

33 '毛主席的好战士雷锋 (Lei Feng: Chairman Mao's Good Soldier)', '伟大的普通一兵 (The Great yet Ordinary Soldier)', *People's Daily*, 7 February 1963: 2; '雷锋日记摘抄 (Excerpts of Lei Feng's Diaries)', *People's Daily*, 7 February 1963: 5.

34 For a biography of Norman Bethune, see Roderick Stewart and Sharon Stewart, *Phoenix: The Life of Norman Bethune* (Montreal: McGill-Queen's University Press 2011).

35 Mao Zedong, 'In Memory of Norman Bethune (21 December 1939)', in *Selected Works of Mao Zedong*, vol. 2 (Beijing: Foreign Language Press 1965): 337–8.

36 Fu Lianzhang [Fu Lien-Chang], 'What We Should Learn from Dr Norman Bethune's Revolutionary Humanitarianism', *CMJ* 7, no. 13 (May–June 1953): 163.

37 Ibid., 163–5.

38 Sichuan JC133-174 (15 January–2 February 1964) 全国医院工作会议报告提纲' (中华人民共和国卫生部付部长钱信忠) (The Summary Report of the National Conference on Hospital Governance by the Deputy Minister of the PRC Ministry of Health Qian Xinzhong).

39 Zhang Zhikuan, 'Hospital Service in China', *CMJ* 84 (June 1965): 416

40 Ibid.; Sichuan JC133-130 (1965) 本厅有关卫生工作的调查报告及在人代会的发言稿 (Sichuan Provincial Health Bureau's Report on Health Work and Prepared Speech to Be Delivered at the People's Congress): 103–4.

41 '《草原曼巴》: 从一部戏看民族之情和医改之路 ("The Manba of Grass Land": From a Play to Talk about National Sentiment and the Health Reform', 齐鲁网 (Qilu.com), http://pinglun.iqilu.com/weipinglun/wenyu/2011/0811/529369.shtml.

42 Zhang Zhikuan, 'Hospital Service in China', 413.

43 Ibid.

44 Adam Yuet Chau, *Miraculous Response: Doing Popular Religion in Contemporary China* (Stanford: Stanford University Press 2006), 47.

45 Feng Xianzhi, ed., *Chronological Biography of Mao Zedong*, vol. 5, 422. For a most recent study about the Third Front project, see Covell F. Meyskens, *Mao's Third Front: The Militarization of Cold War China* (Cambridge: Cambridge University Press 2020).

46 Ibid., vol. 5, 382; Xichang Schistosomiasis Control Station, ed., 西昌血吸虫防治志 (Xichang Schistosomiasis Control Annals) (Xichang: Xichang Archive June 1988): 12.

47 Sichuan JC133-130 (1965) Sichuan Provincial Health Bureau's Report on Health Work and Prepared Speech to Be Delivered at the People's Congress: 44–5.

48 See Yi Jiamin, ed., 红墙知情录（一）新中国的风雨历程 (*Inside the Red Wall: Stormy Years of the PRC*) vol. 1 (Beijing: Dangdai Zhongguo chubanshe 2010), ch. 3.

49 Sichuan JC133-226 (1961) 四川省防疫站，万县，西昌，绵阳专区，阿坝州等
自然疫源地调查工作的通知，报告，简报 (Edict to and Report from Sichuan
Provincial Disease Control Station Regarding Conducting Epidemiological
Survey in Natural Foci Regions Including Wan County, Xichang,
Mianyang, and Aba regions): 34–5, 86–7, 244–51.

50 Sichuan JC133-282 (1965) 疫情简报 (Reports on Disease Prevention and
Control) vol. 9 (October 1965): 61.

51 Sichuan JC13-2336 (1965) 市，专关于工地卫生的总结，报告 (Reports on
Health Conditions at Industrial Construction Sites): 3.

52 Ibid., 34–5.

53 Sichuan JC133-282 (1965) 省卫生厅，省防疫站1965年疫情简报和疫情预
报 (Sichuan Provincial Health Bureau and Sichuan Province Disease
Prevention Centre 1965 Epidemic Report and Forecast).

54 Sichuan JC133-171 (1963) 四川省农村基层卫生组织调整精简中的一些问
题 (Some Problems Regarding Consolidating and Restructuring Rural
Health Organization in Sichuan Province).

55 Sichuan JC133-130 (1965) Sichuan Provincial Health Bureau's Report on
Health Work and Prepared Speech to Be Delivered at the People's
Congress, 41–2.

56 Wumeng Ruomu, '军工军工枯死的青藤 (The Dying Tree: Military
Industry)', digital essay (Shanghai Huawen Innovative Writing Centre
2015), Green Apple Data Centre, https://books.google.co.uk/
books?id=VyMcCgAAQBAJ&pg=PT1&lpg=PT1&dq=%E5%90%B4%E
5%AD%9F%E8%8B%A5%E6%9C%A8&source=bl&ots=_1N8qVBIr8
&sig=fG3TV1a7Vje4UFGteujoxC9nkbY&hl=en&sa=X&ved=2ahUKEw-
jNj7LIstPdAhXJIcAKHWnFC-A4ChD0ATAAegQIARAB#v=onepage&q=
%E5%90%B4%E5%AD%9F%E8%8B%A5%E6%9C%A8&f=false.

57 Sichuan JC133-130 (1965) Sichuan Provincial Health Bureau's Report on
Health Work and Prepared Speech to Be Delivered at the People's
Congress: 41–2.

58 Sichuan JC133-2332 (1965) 三线建设卫生工作会议报告 (The Third Front
Construction Health Conference Report); Wumeng Ruomu, The Dying
Tree.

59 Sichuan JC133-2335 (1965) 自贡市，万县，南充专区，隆昌，营昌县关于防
尘，矽肺的总结报告及河流，水库卫生调查报告 (Investigative Report
Regarding the Problem of Pneumoconiosis and Water Pollution in Rivers
and Reservoirs in Zigong City, Wan County, Nanchong Region,
Longchang and Yin County; Sichuan JC133-2332 (1965) The Third Front
Construction Health Conference Report; Sichuan JC133-130 (1965))

Sichuan Provincial Health Bureau's Report on Health Work and Prepared Speech to Be Delivered at the People's Congress, 41–2.

60 Sichuan JC133-2823 (March–August 1964) 泸州气矿学习大庆经验结合生产大搞矿容卫生情况 (Report on Luzhou Gas Mine Field Launching Mass Cleaning-up Campaign by Learning from Daqing).

61 Feng Xianzhi, ed., *Chronological Biography of Mao Zedong*, vol. 5, 367.

62 Ibid., vol. 5, 383; Hunan 140-2-62 (March–November 1958) 毛主席十月中旬来天津视察的谈话纪要 (Summary of Chairman Mao's Conversation during His Visit to Tianjin in October 1958): 27.

63 Huang Jiasi, 'Our Medical Team in the Countryside', CMJ 84 (December 1965): 802.

64 Sichuan JC133-130 (1965) Sichuan Provincial Health Bureau's Report on Health Work and Prepared Speech to Be Delivered at the People's Congress, 34–5.

65 Sichuan JC133-457 (1965) 关于调整血吸虫病专业人员口粮标准的意见 (Opinion on Adjusting Food Ration for Schistosomiasis Control [Personnel]): 124.

66 C.C. Chen, *Medicine in Rural China: A Personal Account* (Los Angeles: University of California Press 1989): 129.

67 Sichuan JC133-2823 (March–August 1964) 关于了解17个县的夏季血防工作的情况 (Investigative Report on Schistosomiasis Control in Seventeen Counties): 98–9; 154.

68 C.C. Chen, *Medicine in Rural China*, 129.

69 Sichuan JC133-450 (4–25 December 1963) Comrade Ke Qingshi's Speech at the Ninth National Schistosomiasis Control Conference.

70 Sichuan JC133-457 (1965) 中央血防九人小组办公室郑岗同志在绵竹座谈会上的讲话' (Comrade Zheng Gang's Speech at the Mianzu Meeting): 178.

71 C.C. Chen, *Medicine in Rural China*, 129.

72 Sichuan JC133-133 (January 1965) 关于举办半农半读中医学校的意见 (Regarding Open Part-Time Chinese Medicine Training Schools): 90.

73 Sichuan JC133-1771 (1965) 培训卫生员参考资料之三 (Reports on Training Health Auxiliaries, vol. 3): 36–7.

74 Sichuan JC133-130 (1965) Sichuan Provincial Health Bureau's Report on Health Work and Prepared Speech to Be Delivered at the People's Congress, 35.

75 Sichuan JC133-1771(1965) 关于建设农村地区医院中若干问题的调查汇报 (Investigative Report Regarding Building Hospitals in Rural Regions): 92–3; Sichuan JC133-130 (1965) Sichuan Provincial Health Bureau's Report on Health Work and Prepared Speech to Be Delivered at the People's Congress, 67–9.

76 Sichuan JC133-130 (1965) Sichuan Provincial Health Bureau's Report on Health Work and Prepared Speech to Be Delivered at the People's Congress, 61–2.

77 Li Haihong, *A Research on the Barefoot Doctors and Chinese Rural Society: Taking Henan Province as an Example* (Beijing: Social Science Academy Press 2015): 174–5, 179–180.

78 Huang Jiasi, 'Our Medical Team in the Countryside', CMJ 84 (December 1965): 802.

79 关于继续加强农村不脱离生产的卫生员，接生员训练工作 (April 1965) (Regarding Training Part-Time Health Worker and Midwife in the Countryside), as quoted in Zhang Kaining, Wen Yiqun, and Liang Ping, eds., *From Barefoot Doctors to Village Doctors* (Kunming: Yunnan Renmin chubanshe 2002): 17.

80 For a study in English on Mao and Liu's political rivalry in the aftermath of the Great Leap Forward famine, see Lowell Dittmer, *Liu Shaoqi and the Chinese Cultural Revolution* (New York: M.E. Sharp 1998): 32–48. For a study in Chinese, see Qian Xiangli, *Historical Turn*, 295–403.

81 Feng Xianzhi, ed., *Chronological Biography of Mao Zedong*, vol. 5, 505–6.

82 Li Zhishui, *The Private Life of Chairman Mao* (London: Arrow Books 1996): 419–21.

83 Feng Xianzhi, ed., *Chronological Biography of Mao Zedong*, vol. 5, 501–2.

84 Mao Zedong, '为印发张鲁传写的批语 (Remarks on the Publication of Biography of Zhang Lu)', in Mao Zedong, *Selected Works of Mao Zedong since 1949*, vol. 7 (Beijing: Zhongyang wenxian chubanshe 1992): 627–8.

85 Paul Michaud, 'The Yellow Turbans', *Monumenta Serica* (1958): 76–94.

86 Mao Zedong, 'Be Concerned with the Well-Being of the Masses' (27 January 1934), in *Selected Works of Mao Tsetung*, vol. 1 (Peking: Foreign Language Press 1965): 147–8.

87 '毛泽东在听取钱信忠、张凯汇报卫生工作时的谈话 (Mao's Interlude When Listening to Qian Xinzhong and Zhang Kai Reporting on Health Work)', 2 August 1965, Cultural Revolution Data Base, https://ccradb.appspot.com/post/1062.

88 Feng Xianzhi, ed., *Chronological Biography of Mao Zedong*, vol. 5, 521–2.

89 '中共中央批转卫生部党委 '关于把卫生工作重点放到农村'的报告 (The CCP Central Committee Endorse the Ministry of Health's Report Regarding Health Work Puts Stress on the Countryside, 21 September 1965)', in 建国以来重要文献选编 (Selection of Important Party

Documents in the PRC since 1949), vol. 20 (Beijing: Zhongyang wenxian chubanshe 1998): 527.

90 C.C. Chen, *Medicine in Rural China*, 130–1.

91 Sichuan JC133-130 (1965) Sichuan Provincial Health Bureau's Report on Health Work and Prepared Speech to Be Delivered at the People's Congress, 35.

92 'Pioneer Midwife', in Zhang Kaining, Wen Yiqun, and Liang Ping, eds., *From Barefoot Doctors to Village Doctors*, 150.

93 There are a number of studies on the Great Proletarian Cultural Revolution. For a detailed account, see Roderick MacFarquhar and Michael Schoenhals, *Mao's Last Revolution* (Cambridge, MA: Harvard University Press 2006). For a more recent account, see Frank Dikötter, *The Cultural Revolution: A People's History, 1962–1976* (London: Bloomsbury 2016).

94 Feng Xianzhi, ed., *Chronological Biography of Mao Zedong*, vol. 6, 185–7; Mao Zedong, 建国以来毛泽东文稿 (Selected Works of Mao since 1949), vol. 12 (Beijing: Zhongyang wenxian chubanshe 1998): 526–34; 560.

95 '关于知识分子再教育问题 (On the Re-education of Intellectuals)', *Red Flag Magazine* no. 3 (10 September 1968): 2–4.

96 '从 '赤脚医生' 的成长看医学教育革命的方向 (The Orientation of the Revolution in Medical Education as Seen in the Growth of "Barefoot Doctors")', *Red Flag Magazine*, no. 3 (10 September 1968): 20–6.

97 Shanghai B242-3-143 (1969) 华东血防工作目前处于无人领导状态 (There Is Currently No One to Lead Schistosomiasis Control Work in Eastern China): 1.

98 'The Orientation of the Revolution in Medical Education as Seen in the Growth of the "Barefoot Doctors"' *Peking Review* no. 38 (20 September 1968): 18–22.

CHAPTER EIGHT

1 This is discussed in Frank Dikötter, *The Cultural Revolution: A People's History, 1962–1976* (London: Bloomsbury 2016): 220–31. For Mao's economic ideas, see Jack Gray, 'Mao and the Chinese Rural Economy', *World Development* 6, no. 5 (May 1978): 567–81.

2 Sichuan JC133-130 (8 July 1965) Sichuan Provincial Health Bureau's Report on Health Work and Prepared Speech to Be Delivered at the People's Congress, 67–9.

3 农村卫生工作简报 (Rural Health Work Briefing) no. 1 (December 1965): 4–5, 7.

4 'Comrade Mao's Conversation with the Polish Communist Party Delegation on October 14, 1959', in Feng Xianzhi and Jin Chongji, eds., *Mao Zedong's Biography*, 1283.

5 Hua Sheng and Hsiang Jung, 'Kwangxi: Revolution in Health Work (II)', *Peking Review*, no. 9 (25 February 1977): 19–23.

6 'Lower and Middle Peasants Welcomed the Co-operative Medicine Service', *People's Daily*, 5 December 1968: 1.

7 For an overview and key features of the RCMS, see David M. Lampton, *The Politics of Medicine in China: The Policy Process, 1949–1977* (Boulder, CO: Westview Press 1977): ch. 10; G. Carrin et al., 'The Reform of the Rural Co-operative Medical System in the People's Republic of China: Interim Experience in 14 Pilot Counties', *Social Science and Medicine* 48 (1999): 961–72.

8 'Happy to See Patients Recover', in Zhang Kaining, Wen Yiqun, and Liang Ping, eds., *From Barefoot Doctors to Village Doctors*, 81.

9 See David A. Lampton, *The Politics of Medicine in China*; G. Carrin et al., 'The Reform of the Rural Co-operative Medical System in the People's Republic of China', 961–72.

10 For an in-depth study on peasants resisting collectivization, see Gao Wanglin, *Study on Chinese Peasants' 'Counter-actions', 1950–1980*.

11 'Happy to See Patient Recover', 78–81.

12 'A Barefoot Doctor with Traditional Skills', in Zhang Kaining, Wen Yiqun, and Liang Ping, eds, *From Barefoot Doctors to Village Doctors*, 82.

13 'I was Born to Be a Doctor', in Zhang Kaining, Wen Yiqun, and Liang Ping, eds, *From Barefoot Doctors to Village Doctors*, 96.

14 'Let's Talk about Barefoot Doctors', in Zhang Kaining, Wen Yiqun, and Liang Ping, eds, *From Barefoot Doctors to Village Doctors*, 191–3.

15 'Swallow from the Tianjia Mountain', in Zhang Kaining, Wen Yiqun, and Liang Ping, eds, *From Barefoot Doctors to Village Doctors*, 299.

16 Li Haihong, *A Research on 'the Barefoot Doctors', and Chinese Rural Society: Taking Henan Province as an Example* (Beijing: Social Science Academy Press 2015): 116.

17 Ibid., 116–26.

18 Ibid., 151.

19 'I Never Regretted Being a Barefoot Doctor', in Zhang Kaining, Wen Yiqun, and Liang Ping, eds, *From Barefoot Doctors to Village Doctors*, 75.

20 Jiangxi Provincial Archive X111-1973 (1973) 关于巩固和发展农村合作医疗的意见 (Opinions Regarding Developing RCMS): 2.

21 Jiangxi Provincial Archive X111-1971 (1971) 关于全省农村实行合作医疗的报告 (Report on Implementing RCMS in Jiangxi Province): 5.

22 'The Female Barefoot Doctor in D'ian Lake Community', in Zhang Kaining, Wen Yiqun, and Liang Ping, eds, *From Barefoot Doctors to Village Doctors*, 114.

23 Shanghai B250-1-471 (1973) 在前进道路上的江镇赤脚医生情况简报 (A Brief Report of the Ever-Advancing Barefoot Doctors in Jiangzhen County); Shanghai B242-2-312 (August 1974) 上海市郊区文教组召开的市郊县农村赤脚医生工作经验交流会的通知与上海市卫生局的请示报告 (Edict to hold Barefoot Doctors Working Experience Meeting and Shanghai Health Bureau's Proposal).

24 Shanghai B250-5-71 (1980) 关于加强本市郊外赤脚医生管理的若干意见 (Opinion Regarding How to Manage Barefoot Doctors in Suburban Shanghai).

25 Shanghai B250-1-471 (1973) A Brief Report of the Ever-Advancing Barefoot Doctors in Jianzhen County; Shanghai B250-5-71 (1980) 关于加强本市郊外赤脚医生管理的若干意见 (Opinion Regarding How to Manage Barefoot Doctors in Suburban Shanghai).

26 Shanghai B242-2-312 (August 1974) Edict to Hold Barefoot Doctors Working Experience Meeting and Shanghai Health Bureau's Proposal.

27 'Let's Talk about Barefoot Doctors', 192.

28 Shanghai B242-2-136-35 (1971) 上海市卫生工作会议简报 (Bulletin of Shanghai Health Work Conference).

29 '赤脚医生不能兼职过多 (The Barefoot Doctor Should Not be Multitasking)', *People's Daily*, 10 November 1972: 2.

30 Li Haihong, *A Research on 'the Barefoot Doctors', and Chinese Rural Society*, 153–68.

31 Fang Xiaoping, *Barefoot Doctor and Western Medicine in China*, 53.

32 Shanghai B250-1-471 (1973) A Brief Report of the Ever-Advancing Barefoot Doctors in Jianzhen County.

33 Norma Dimond, 'Collectivization, Kinship, and the Status of Women in Rural China', *Bulletin of Concerned Asian Scholars* 7 (1975): 25–32.

34 'A Village Doctor Who Practised Medicine Passed Down from His Family Tradition', in Zhang Kaining, Wen Yiqun, and Liang Ping, eds, *From Barefoot Doctors to Village Doctors*, 62.

35 Interview with Ling in London, 9 August 2013.

36 Ibid.

37 There are many accounts of Sun Lize from different perspectives. Many of them were collected in a recent edited volume by Jin Zilin, *Memories of a Barefoot Doctor* (Beijing: Zhongyi chubanshe 2016).

38 Fang Xiaoping, *Barefoot Doctors and Western Medicine in China*, 37.

39 Interviews with Doctor Xu, Fuyang County in Zhejiang province, 28 April 2015.

40 'I Never Regretted Being a Barefoot Doctor', 72.

41 'A Barefoot Doctor and a Witch Doctor', in Zhang Kaining, Wen Yiqun, and Liang Ping, eds, *From Barefoot Doctors to Village Doctors*, 257–9.

42 S.M. Hillier and J.A. Jewell, *Health Care and Traditional Medicine in China, 1800–1982*, 320–1.

43 'I see the Barefoot Doctor as Different', in Zhang Kaining, Wen Yiqun, and Liang Ping, eds, *From Barefoot Doctors to Village Doctors*, 112.

44 Francis Hsu, *Exorcising the Trouble Makers: Magic, Science, and Culture* (Westpoint: Greenwood Press 1983): 35–72.

45 Ibid., 68.

46 'A Barefoot Doctor and a Witch Doctor', 257–9.

47 For a detailed study of modernization of childbirth in republican China, see Tina Johnson, *Childbirth in Republican China: Delivering Modernity* (Lanham, MD: Lexington Books 2011).

48 'Article 48 of the Common Program of the Chinese People's Political Consultative Conference', in *The Common Programme and Other Documents of the First Plenary Session of the Chinese People's Political Consultative Conference* (Peking: Foreign Language Press 1950), 18.

49 'Pioneer Midwife', in Zhang Kaining, Wen Yiqun, and Liang Ping, eds, *From Barefoot Doctors to Village Doctors*, 151–3.

50 'The Turning Point in my Life', in Zhang Kaining, Wen Yiqun, and Liang Ping, eds, *From Barefoot Doctors to Village Doctors*, 131.

51 Gail Hershatter, *The Gender of Memory: Rural Women and China's Collective Past* (Berkeley and Los Angeles: University of California Press 2011): 163–70.

52 Mary Douglass, *Purity and Danger, an Analysis of Concepts of Pollution and Taboo* (New York: Frederick A. Praeger 1966).

53 Interview with Zhenan in Chengdu, April 1996.

54 Ibid.

55 'Barefoot Doctor Actives in Rural Child Health', CMJ 1 no. 2 (March 1975): 95–8.

56 Interview with Yang in Tianzhu, Guizhou, 2 July 2015.

57 Ibid.

58 For an excellent study on the question of 'safety' in global health practice, see Paul Kadetz, 'Problematising the "Global" in Global Health: an Assessment of the Global Discourse of Safety', *Fudan Journal of Humanities and Social Sciences* 9, no. 1 (March 2016): 25–40.

59 Interview with Muchu in Danbo village in Barkam on 5 June 2016; interview with Yang in Tianzhu, Guizhou, 2 July 2015.

60 For an account of this rural health experiment, see C.C. Chen, *Medicine in Rural China: A Personal Account* (Berkeley and Los Angeles: University of California Press 1989): 57–99.

61 H.Y. Yao, 'The First Year of Rural Health Experiment in Ting Hsien', *The Milbank Memorial Fund Quarterly Bulletin* 9, no. 3 (1931): 62.

62 C.C. Chen, *Medicine in Rural China*, 78.

63 Interview with Muchu in Danbo village in Barkam, 5 June 2016.

64 'I Never Regretted Being a Barefoot Doctor', 73–4.

65 See, for example, N. Guerrero, C.F. Mendes de Leon, D.A. Evans, and E.A. Jacobs, 'Determinants of Trust in Health Care in an Older Population', *Journal of the American Geriatric Society* 63, no. 3 (2015): 553–7.

66 'Being the Daddy of 40 Children', in Zhang Kaining, Wen Yiqun, and Liang Ping, eds, *From Barefoot Doctors to Village Doctors*, 143.

67 'Being a Barefoot Doctor Made My Dream Come True', in Zhang Kaining, Wen Yiqun, and Liang Ping, eds, *From Barefoot Doctors to Village Doctors*, 229.

68 Ibid., 226–31.

69 'I Was Born to Be a Doctor'.

70 'Let's Talk about Barefoot Doctors'.

71 Li Haihong, *A Research on 'the Barefoot Doctors', and Chinese Rural Society*, 242.

72 For further reading, see Fang Xiaoping's detailed study on how Barefoot Doctors were trained: Fang Xiaoping, *Barefoot Doctors and Western Medicine in China*, 55–66.

73 Li Haihong, *A Research on 'the Barefoot Doctors', and Chinese Rural Society*, 228–33

74 Hsu, Robert, 'The Barefoot Doctors of the People's Republic of China: Some Problems', *New England Journal of Medicine* 291 no. 3 (18 July 1974): 125–6; interview with Chen Fujun in Chengdu, 29 May 2015.

75 See Lawrence K. Altman, *Who Goes First? The Story of Self-Experimentation in Medicine* (New York: Random House 1986).

76 Fang Xiaoping, *Barefoot Doctors and Western Medicine in China*, 105–23.

77 Interview with Muchu in Danbo village in Barkam, 5 June 2016.

78 Interview with Chen Fujun in Chengdu, 29 May 2015.

79 Shanghai B242-4-222 (1979) 上海市卫生局关于转发卫生部卫生革命简报
    1978年第五期有关材料的通知 (Shanghai Health Bureau's Edict to
    Disseminate Ministry of Health's Health Revolution News Bulletin – issue
    no. 5, 1978): 3.

80 Interview with Chen Fujun in Chengdu, 29 May 2015.

81 See 'China Needs Many More Primary-Care Doctors', *Economist*, 11 May
    2017, https://www.economist.com/china/2017/05/11/
    china-needs-many-more-primary-care-doctors?frsc=dg%7Ca.

82 Interview with Chen Fujun in Chengdu, 29 May 2015; also see C.C. Chen,
    Medicine in Rural China, 130.

83 Xiuyun Li et al., 'Revisiting Current "Barefoot Doctors" in Border Areas
    of China: System of Services, Financial Issue and Clinical Practice Prior to
    Introducing Integrated Management of Childhood Illness (IMCI)', *BMC
    Public Health* 2012, 12: 620, https://doi.org/10.1186/1471-2458-12-620.

84 Shanghai B242-3-688-45 (1975) 上海市卫生局革命委员会关于印发 '上海
    市崇明县新民公社卫生院实行赤脚医生和转职医务人员轮换制', 有力推动
    了医院斗批改' 一文的通知 (Shanghai Municipal Health Bureau
    Revolutionary Committee's Notice Regarding Chonming County's Xinmin
    Commune Introducing Mandatory Job Sharing between Commune
    Medical Staffs and Barefoot Doctors): 2.

85 See Fang Xiaoping, *Barefoot Doctors and Western Medicine in China*, 78.

86 *People's Daily*, 25 September 1969: 1.

87 C.C. Chen, *Medicine in Rural China*, 150.

88 Frank Diköter, Lars Laamann, and Zhou Xun, *Narcotic Culture: A
    History of Drugs in China* (London: Hurst & Co. 2004): 74–92.

89 Fang Xiaoping, *Barefoot Doctors and Western Medicine in China*,
    105–23.

90 Gao Wangling, *Study on Chinese Peasants' 'Counter-action', 1950–1980*,
    191–4, 226–34.

91 Yang Dali, *Calamity and Reform in China: State, Rural Society, and
    Institutional Change since the Great Leap Famine* (Stanford: Stanford
    University Press 1996): 157; also see William Hinton, *Great Reversal: The
    Privatization of China, 1978–1989* (New York. Monthly Review Press
    1990).

92 Kate Xiao Zhou, *How the Farmers Changed China: Power of the People*
    (Boulder, CO: Westview Press 1996).

93 Shanghai B242-4-555 (1980) 卫生部与上海市卫生局关于公社卫生院管
    理, 赤脚医生补助及农场医疗卫生问题的意见, 通知, 通报 (The Ministry of
    Health and Shanghai Health Bureau's Opinion and Edict on Issues of the

Management of Commune Clinics, the Subsidies for Barefoot Doctors and Medical and Health Care in State Farms): 1–4.

94 Dong et al., 'Drug Policy in China: Pharmaceutical Distribution in Rural Areas', *Social Science & Medicine* 48 (1999): 784.

95 C.C. Chen, *Medicine in Rural China*, 149–50; interview with Chen Fujun in Chengdu, 29 May 2015. For antibiotic overuse in rural China, see Ding et al., 'Antibiotic Use in Rural China: A Cross-Sectional Survey of Knowledge, Attitudes and Self-Reported Practices among Caregivers in Shandong Province', BMF *Infectious Disease* 15 (2015): 576

96 Dong et al., 'Drug Policy in China', 784.

97 Ibid.

98 David Blumenthal, MD, MPP, and William Hsiao, 'Privatization and Its Discontents – The Evolving Chinese Health Care System', *The New England Journal of Medicine* 353 (15 September 2005): 1165–70.

99 Interview with Muchu in Danbo village in Barkam, 5 June 2016. This problem is discussed in Xiulan Zhang et al., 'Advancing the Application of Systems Thinking in Health: Managing Rural China Health System Development in Complex and Dynamic Contexts', *Health Research Policy and Systems* 2014, 12/44 http://www.health-policy-systems.com/content/12/1/44.

CHAPTER NINE

1 In a report titled 'International Trends in Health Care' based on the preliminary survey of health system and health care developments in twelve countries in the developed West as well as in South Africa, undertaken for the Rockefeller Foundation's International Health Division (IHD). See John B. Grant, 'International Trends in Health Care', *American Journal of Public Health* 38, no. 3 (March 1948): 381.

2 John B. Grant, 'International Trends in Health Care', 381–97; John Farley also wrote about Grant's idea of social medicine (see John Farley, *Bilharzia: A History of Imperial Tropical Medicine* [Cambridge and New York: Cambridge University Press 1991]: 184–7).

3 As quoted in Farley, *Bilharzia*, 200.

4 'Article 48 of the Common Program of the Chinese People's Political Consultative Conference'.

5 Adam Fifield, *A Mighty Purpose: How Jim Grant Sold the World on Saving Its Children* (New York: Other Press 2015): ch. 3.

6 John Farley, 'John Black Grant: The Rockefeller Bolshevik', *Acadia Bulletin* 74, no. 3 (1990): 12–14. For a history of PUMC in the early

twentieth century, see Mary Brown Bullock, *An American Transplant: The Rockefeller Foundation and the Peking Union Medical College* (Berkeley: University of California Press 1980).

7 Arthur Newsholme, *Medicine and the State* (London: George Allen and Unwin 1932); Arthur Newsholme, 'The Historical Development of Public Health Work in England', *American Journal of Public Health* IX no. 12 (December 1919): 907–18. For a biography of Newsholme, see John M. Eyler, *Sir Arthur Newsholme and State Medicine, 1885–1935* (Cambridge: Cambridge University Press 1997).

8 Arthur Newsholme and John Adams Kingsbury, *Red Medicine: Socialised Health in the Soviet Union* (London: William Heinemann Medical Books 1934): vii.

9 For Kingsbury, see Arnold S. Rosenberg, 'The Rise of John Adams Kingsbury', *The Pacific Northwest Quarterly* 63, no. 2 (April 1972): 55–62.

10 Newsholme and Kingsbury, *Red Medicine: Socialised Health in the Soviet Union*, vii.

11 There are number of studies on John B. Grant's public health work in China. See Bu Liping, 'From Public Health to State Medicine: John B. Grant and China's Health Profession', *Harvard Asia Quarterly* no. 4 (December 2012): 26–34; Socrates Litsios, 'John Black Grant: A 20th-Century Public Health Giant', *Perspectives in Biology and Medicine* 54, no. 4 (2011): 532–49.

12 *The American Bureau for Medical Aid to China Bulletin* November–December 1960: 2.

13 'Medical Conditions in China', J.B. Grant to Captain Parker Tenney (29 December 1931), RG1.1 Series 601 Box 4 Folder 46.

14 R. Lim and C.C. Chen, 'State Medicine', *China Medical Journal* 51 (June 1937): 784.

15 This was discussed in detail by Socrates Litsios in Socrates Litsios, 'John Black Grant: A 20th-Century Public Health Giant', 536.

16 *The American Bureau for Medical Aid to China Bulletin* (November–December 1960): 2–4.

17 Frank Ninkovich, 'The Rockefeller Foundation, China and Cultural Change', *The Journal of American History* 74, no. 4 (March 1984): 810. Socrates Litsios has also written extensively on Grant and Gunn's collaboration and their social experiment in rural China. See Socrates Litsios, 'Selskar Gunn and China: The Rockefeller Foundation's "Other" Approach to Public Health', *Bulletin of the History of Medicine* 79, no. 2 (Summer 2005): 295–318.

18 For eugenic discourse in republican China, see Frank Dikötter, *Discourse of Race in Modern China* (Oxford and New York: Oxford University Press 2015 [1992]): ch. 6, 'Race as Seed'. For the New Life Movement and race improvement, see Frank Dikötter, *Imperfect Conceptions: Medical Knowledge, Birth Defects, and Eugenics in China* (London: Hurst and Company 1998) 104–18; Zhou Xun, 'Discourse of Disability in Modern China', *Pattern and Prejudice* 36, no. 1 (2002): 109–10.

19 Chen, *Medicine in Rural China*, 119.

20 As quoted in S.M. Hillier and J.A. Jewell, *Health Care and Traditional Medicine in China, 1800–1982*, 66.

21 As quoted in Anne-Emanuelle Birn and T.M. Brwon, eds, *Comrades in Health: U.S. Health Internationalists, Abroad and at Home* (New Brunswick, NJ: Rutgers University Press 2012): 33.

22 This is explored by Sara Silverstein in S. Silverstein, 'Man of Impossible Mission: Andrija Štampar's Separation of Politics and Health Care in Yugoslavia and the World Health Organization' (unpublished paper, 2013), 10–12.

23 Randall Packard, *The Making of a Tropical Disease: A Short History of Malaria* (Baltimore, MD: The Johns Hopkins University Press 2007): 134–49. For the Bandoeng Conference on Rural Hygiene, see T. Brown and E. Fee, 'The Bandoeng Conference of 1937: A Milestone in Health and Development', *American Journal of Public Health* 98, no. 1 (January 2008): 42–3; Socrates Litsios, 'Revisiting Bandoeng', *Social Medicine* 8, no. 3 (November 2014): 113–28.

24 R.M. Packard and F. Cooper, *International Development and the Social Sciences: Essays on the History and Politics of Knowledge* (Berkeley: University of California Press 1997): 109–11.

25 Sichuan JC133-431 (August 1959) 魏文伯书记在中央九人小组第六次扩大会议上作的总结报告 (Wei Wenbo's Summary Report at the Nine-Man Subcommittee's Ninth Meeting).

26 B. Maegraith, 'The Chinese Are "Liquidating" Their Disease Problems', *New Scientist* 3, no. 55 (5 December 1957): 19.

27 T.F. Fox, 'The New China: Some Medical Impressions (Part Two)', *The Lancet* 270, no. 7,004 (16 November 1957): 995.

28 T.F. Fox, 'Russia Revisited: Impressions of Soviet Medicine', *The Lancet* 264, no. 6,841 (9 October 1954): 748.

29 Theodore Fox, 'Purposes of Medicine', *The Lancet* 286, no. 7,417 (23 October 1965): 801–5

30 T.F. Fox, 'Russia Revisited, 48–53, 805–6.

31 T.F. Fox, 'The New China: Some Medical Impressions', *The Lancet* 270, no. 7,002 (9 November 1957): 935.

32 Ibid.

33 Ibid., 939.

34 F. Avery Jones, 'A Visit to China', *British Medical Journal* 2, no. 5,053 (9 November 1957): 1107.

35 For Brian Gilmore Maegraith, see Helen J. Power, *Tropical Medicine in the Twentieth Century: A History of the Liverpool School of Tropical Medicine, 1898–1990* (London and New York: Kegan Paul International 1999): 113–14, 134; H.M. Giles, 'Brian Maegraith', *Transactions of the Royal Society of Tropical Medicine and Hygiene* 83, no. 4 (1 July 1989): 576; Gregory T. Kennedy (2011), 'The "Golden Rule" of Tropical Medicine: Brian Maegraith and the Early Emergence of Community-Based Medicine in Thailand', Allen Institute for Artificial Intelligence Semantics Scholar Project, https://www.semanticscholar.org/paper/The-%E2%80%9CGolden-Rule%E2%80%9D-of-Tropical-Medicine%3A-Brian-and-Kennedy-Adviser/6a19d96ef5d1b284b51cecf3f91e3e5e4bdc28de?.

36 B. Maegraith, 'Tropical Medicine Today', *Transactions of the Royal Society of Tropical Medicine and Hygiene* 63, no. 6 (22 October 1969): 689.

37 Ibid., 689–92; B. Maegraith, 'Tropical Medicine: What It Is Not, What It Is', *Bulletin of the New York Academy of Medicine* 48, no. 10 (November 1972): 1210–30.

38 Maegraith, 'Tropical Medicine: What It Is Not, What It Is', 1228.

39 As quoted in Kennedy, 'The "Golden Rule" of Tropical Medicine', 25.

40 B. Maegraith, 'History of the Liverpool School of Tropical Medicine', *Medical History*, no. 16 (1972): 365.

41 B. Maegraith, 'Schistosomiasis in China', *The Lancet* 1, no. 7,013 (25 January 1958): 213.

42 Ibid., 209.

43 The focus in the post-war era remained, as it had in the nineteenth century, on rural China and elsewhere because the pressure of urbanization after the war was imagined to be a reflex of the displacement of peoples by the fighting rather than a prefiguration of what would come to be a parallel mass movement of peoples into urban areas. Saskia Sassen, 'The Global City: Introducing a Concept', *Brown Journal of World Affairs* 9 (2005): 27–43.

44 B. Maegraith, 'The Chinese Are "Liquidating" Their Disease Problems', 19–21.

45 B. Maegraith, 'Schistosomiasis in China', 208.

46 Ibid., 208–14.

47 Ibid., 209, 214.

48 Felix Greene, 'Foreword', in *What's Really Happening in China?* (San Francisco: City Lights Books 1959).

49 B. Maegraith, 'Tropical Medicine Today', 691.

50 For further readings on the Great Leap famine, see Frank Dikötter, *Mao's Great Famine: The History of China's Most Devastating Catastrophe, 1958–62* (London: Bloomsbury 2010); Yang Jisheng, *Tombstone: The Great Chinese Famine* (London: Allen Lane 2012); Zhou Xun, ed., *The Great Famine in China, 1958–1962: A Documentary History* (New Haven, Yale University Press 2012).

51 See Zhou Xun, *Forgotten Voices of Mao's Great Famine, 1958–1962: An Oral History* (New Haven: Yale University Press 2013), 28.

52 'Communist China's Domestic Crisis: The Road to 1964', 81–5, CIA Open-Source Library, https://www.cia.gov/library/readingroom/docs/polo-10.pdf.

53 John S. Service, 'Edgar Snow: Some Personal Reminiscences', *The China Quarterly*, no. 50 (April–June 1972): 217.

54 Edgar Snow, *The Other Side of the River: Red China Today* (London: Victor Gollancz 1963): 627.

55 B. Lown, *Prescription for Survival: A Doctor's Journey to End Nuclear Madness* (San Francisco: Berrett–Koehler 2008): 335–6.

56 For more on George Hatem, see Edgar Porter, *The People's Doctor: George Hatem and China's Revolution* (Honolulu: University of Hawaii Press 1997). For Hatem's trip to Yan'an with Edgar Snow, see Snow, *The Other Side of the River: Red China Today*, 261–5.

57 Edgar Snow, *The Other Side of the River: Red China Today*, 274–5.

58 Joshua Horn, *Away with All Pests: An English Surgeon in People's China* (London and New York: Monthly Review Press, first paperback edition 1971 [1969]): 89–93.

59 Ibid., 94.

60 'Dr Joshua Horn on Red China' (recorded on 21 April 1971 in New York), Pacific Radio Archive, PRA BB4272. An edited version of the lecture was published as Joshua Horn, 'The Mass Line', *Health Care in China*, a pamphlet published by the Anglo-Chinese Educational Institute (1976): 11.

61 Joshua Horn, '我在新中国十五年 (My Fifteen Years in New China)', a lecture given at the University of Hong Kong in 1970, published by 香港文汇报 (*Wenwei News*, Hong Kong), 7 November 1974.

62 Anne-Emanuelle Birn and T.M. Brwon, eds, *Comrades in Health: U.S. Health Internationalists, Abroad and at Home*, 10.

63 Edgar Snow, 'Mao Tse-tung Thought Guide a Revolution in Medicine', *L'Epoca* (25 April 1971); 'China Is a Mass Military Camp with 7 Million Soldiers', *L'Epoca* (9 May 1971).

64 See the obituary for Dimond, 'E.G. Dimond – Obituary', in *The New York Times*, 17 November 2013.

65 For a more detailed study of how this visit came about, see Zhou Xun, 'From China's "Barefoot Doctor" to Alma Ata: The Primary Health Care Movement in the Long 1970s', in P. Roberts and O.A. Westad, eds, *China, Hong Kong, and the Long 1970s: Global Perspectives* (London: Palgrave Macmillan 2017): 135–40.

66 E. Grey Dimond, 'More Than Herbs and Acupuncture', *Saturday Review* 18 December 1971, 17–19, 71.

67 William Hinton, *Fanshen: A Documentary of Revolution in a Chinese Village* (New York: Monthly Review Press 1966).

68 Victor Sidel and Ruth Sidel, 'Barefoot in China, the Bronx, and Beyond', in Anne-Emanuelle Birn and T.M. Brwon, eds, *Comrades in Health*, 121.

69 Ibid., 126.

70 Ivan Illich, *Medical Nemesis: The Expropriation of Health* (New York: Pantheon Books 1976): 5.

71 Richard Smith, 'Limits to Medicine. Medical Nemesis: The Expropriation of Health', *British Medical Journal* 324 (2002), article ID: 923, http://dx.doi.org/10.1136/jech.57.12.928.

72 Robin Stott, 'Foreword' for *Health Care in China*, a pamphlet published by the Anglo-Chinese Educational Institute, i.

73 See Alan M. Kraut, *Goldberger's War: The Life and Work of a Public Health Crusader* (New York: Hill and Wang 2004).

74 Michael H. Alderman, 'Summary Report of White House Conference on Health, November 3–4, 1965, Washington, D.C.', *Public Health Reports* 81, no. 2 (February 1966): 118.

75 P.R. Lee, 'Medicine and Public Health in the People's Republic of China: Observations and Reflections of a Recent Visitor', *Western Journal of Medicine* 120 (May 1974): 430–7.

76 V. Sidel and R. Sidel, 'Barefoot in China, the Bronx, and Beyond', 128.

77 For further readings on postcolonial healing in Africa, see Stacey A. Langwick, *The Matter of Maladies: Ontological Politics in Postcolonial Healing in Tanzania* (Bloomington: Indiana University Press 2011).

78 John Iliffe, *East African Doctors: A History of the Modern Profession* (Cambridge: University of Cambridge Press 1998), 202.

79 Stacey Langwick, 'From Non-aligned Medicines to Market-Based Herbals: China's Relationship to the Shifting Politics of Traditional Medicine in Tanzania', *Medical Anthropology* 29, no. 1 (10 February 2010): 20.

80 Interview with WCQ in December 2013 in Chengdu; George T. Yu, 'China and the Third World', *Asian Survey* 17, no. 11 (November 1977): 1,036–48. For further readings on the PRC's health diplomacy in Africa, see George T. Yu, 'China's Role in Africa', *The Annals of the American Academy of Political and Social Science* 432 (July 1997): 96–109; Jeremy Youde, 'China's Health Diplomacy in Africa', *China: An International Journal* 8, no. 1 (March 2010): 151–63.

81 Feng Xianzhi, ed., *Chronological History of Mao Zedong*, vol. 6, 476.

82 Li Ping and Ma Zhisun, eds., *Chronological History of Zhou Enlai*, 1,427.

83 For further readings, see David Shinn, 'Africa, China, and Health Care', *Inside AISA* 3/4 (2006): 15; Drew Thompson, 'China's Soft Power in Africa: From the "Beijing Consensus" to Health Diplomacy', *China Brief* 5 (13 October 2005): 4; Li Anshan, *Chinese Medical Cooperation in Africa: With Special Emphasis on the Medical Teams and Anti-Malaria Campaign* (Uppsala: Nordiska Afrikainstitutet 2011).

84 Stacey Langwick, 'From Non-aligned Medicines to Market-Based Herbals, 15–43.

85 Interview with Luo Laoshi in Chengdu, 2 January 2014.

86 See Alan Hutchison, *China's African Revolution* (Boulder, CO: Westview Press 1975), 220–1.

87 Shanghai B242-3-256 (1971) 中国赴索马里血吸虫病防治考察组的考察报告，工作简报 (The Study Report of the PRC Schistosomiasis Delegation's Study Trip to Somalia): 22–4, 35, 39, 209.

88 George T. Yu, 'Africa in Chinese Foreign Policy', *Asian Survey* 28, no. 8 (August 1988): 855; Li Anshan, *Chinese Medical Cooperation in Africa*, 9.

89 Richard Hottelet, 'What New Role for the People's Republic of China', *Saturday Review*, 18 September 1971, 29.

90 Ibid., 30.

91 For further reading on the politics behind China's rejoining the World Health Assembly, see Javed Siddiqi, *World Health and World Politics: The World Health Organization and the UN System* (London: Hurst & Co. 1995), 110–12.

92 Shanghai B250-1-471-32 (1974) 上海市川沙县江镇公社赤脚医生王桂珍关于参加联合国在瑞士日内瓦召开的第27界世界卫生组织大会的情况汇报 (Barefoot Doctor Wang Guizhen's Report of the 27th World Health Assembly): 23–8, 52–64.

93 J.H. Bryant, *Health and the Developing World* (Ithaca, NY: Cornell University Press 1967), ix–x.

94 See G. Paterson, 'The CMC Story, 1968–1998', *Contact* 161–2 (1998): 3–18; Socrates Litsios, 'The Christian Medical Mission and the Development of World Health Organization's Primary Health Care Approach', *American Journal of Public Health* 94, no. 11 (November 2004): 1887–8; Marcos Cueto, 'Origins of Primary Health Care and Selective Primary Health Care', *American Journal of Public Health* 94, no. 11 (November 2004): 1864–5.

95 K.W. Newell, 'The Investigation and Control of Salmonellosis', *Bulletin of the World Health Organization* 21 (1959): 295.

96 V. Djukanovic and E.P. Mach, eds, *Alternative Approaches to Meeting Basic Health Needs in Developing Countries: A Joint UNICEF/WHO Study* (Geneva: World Health Organization 1975), 8, http://www.who.int/iris/handle/10665/40076.

97 V. Sidel and R. Sidel, 'Barefoot in China, the Bronx, and Beyond', 125; Kenneth Newell, *Health by the People* (Geneva: World Health Organization 1975).

98 V. Djukanovic and E.P. Mach, *Alternative Approach to Meeting Basic Health Needs in Developing Countries*, 104.

99 'Address by the President of the Twenty-Eighth World Health Assembly', The Official Records of the WHO, no. 227 (Geneva: WHO 1975): 47.

100 Socrates Litsios, 'The Long and Difficult Road to Alma-Ata: A Personal Reflection', *International Journal of Health Services* 32, no. 4 (2002): 710.

101 H.T. Mahler, 'Review of the Annual Report of the Director-General on the Work of WHO in 1975', *The Official Records of the WHO*, no. 234 (Geneva: WHO 1976): 52.

102 David A. Tejada de Rivero, 'Alma Ata Revisited', *Perspectives in Health* 8, no. 2 (2003), http://www.medint.at/fileadmin/bilder/bildung_und_lehre/Literatur/Literatur_pdf/tejeda2003.pdf.

103 M. Cueto, 'The Origins of Primary Health Care and Selective Primary Health Care, 1886–7'. A recent account by Birn and Krementsov gives the Soviet perspective of the conference; see A-F. Birn and N. Krementsov, '"Socialising" Primary Care?'

104 Fiona Fleck, 'Consensus during the Cold War: Back to Alma Ata', *Bulletin of the World Health Organization* 86, no. 10 (October 2008): 745. Also see David A. Tejada de Rivero, 'Alma Ata Revisited'.

105 Fiona Fleck, 'Consensus during the Cold War: Back to Alma Ata', 746. Also see David A. Tejada de Rivero, 'Alma Ata Revisited'.

106   Paula A. Michaels, 'Medical Propaganda and Cultural Revolution in Soviet Kazakhstan, 1928–41', *Russian Review* 59 no. 2 (April 2000): 160.

107   On famine in Kazakhstan, see Niccolò Pianciola, 'The Collectivization Famine in Kazakhstan, 1931–1933', *Harvard Ukrainian Studies* 25, no. 3/4 (Fall 2001): 237–51.

108   David A. Tejada de Rivero, 'Alma Ata Revisited'.

109   'Primary Health Care Comes Full Circle. An Interview with Dr Halfdan Mahler', *Bulletin of the World Health Organization*, http://www.who.int/bulletin/volumes/86/10/08-041008/en.

110   David A. Tejada de Rivero, 'Alma Ata Revisited'.

111   'Primary Health Care Comes Full Circle'.

112   'Declaration', *Report of the International Conference on Primary Health Care* (Geneva: WHO 1978): 2–3.

113   'Primary Health Care Comes Full Circle'.

114   Clare Griffiths and Anita Brock, 'Twenty-Century Mortality Rates in England and Wales', *Health Statistics Quarterly* 18 (2003): 5–17.

115   K.S. Babiarz, K. Eggleston, G. Miller, and Q. Zhang, 'An Exploration of China's Mortality Decline under Mao: A Provincial Analysis, 1950–80', *Population Studies* 69, no. 1 (2015): 39–56.

AFTERWORD

1   J. Walsh and K. Warren, 'Selective Primary Health Care: An Interim Strategy for Disease Control in Developing Countries', *New England Journal of Medicine* 301, no. 18 (1979): 967–74.

2   Conrad Keating, *Kenneth Warren and the Great Neglected Diseases of Mankind Programme* (Springer International 2017), xvi.

3   B. Lown, *Prescription for Survival: A Doctor's Journey to End Nuclear Madness* (San Francisco: Berrett-Koehler 2008), 333.

4   For Warren and the GND, see Conrad Keating, 'Ken Warren and the Rockefeller Foundation's Great Neglected Diseases Network, 1978–1988: The Transformation of Tropical and Global Medicine', *Molecular Medicine* online, http://www.molmed.org (doi: 10.2119/molmed.2014.00221).

5   'Primary Health Care Comes Full Circle. An interview with Dr Halfdan Mahler', *Bulletin of the World Health Organization*, http://www.who.int/bulletin/volumes/86/10/08-041008/en.

6   David A. Tejada de Rivero, 'Alma Ata Revisited', *Perspectives in Health* 8, no. 2 (2003), http://www.medint.at/fileadmin/bilder/bildung_und_lehre/Literatur/Literatur_pdf/tejeda2003.pdf.

7　See A. Wagstaff, W. Yip, M. Lindelow, and W.C. Hsiao, 'China's Health System and Its Reform: A Review of Recent Studies', *Health Economics* 18, issue S2 (2009): S7–S23, doi: 10.1002/hec.1518, accessed on 31 March 2019; Xiulan Zhang et al., 'Advancing the Application of Systems Thinking in Health: Managing Rural China Health System Development in Complex and Dynamic Context', *Health Research Policy and Systems* 12, no. 1 (2014): 44, doi: 10.1186/1478-4505-12-44, accessed on 20 February 2019.

8　Interview with villager Xu in Fuyang County, Zhejiang province, 28 April 2015.

9　Kenneth S. Warren, 'Farewell to the Plague Spirit: Chairman Mao's Crusade against Schistosomiasis', in John Bowers, J. Hess, and Nathan Sivin, eds, *Science and Medicine in Twentieth-Century China*, vol. 3 (Ann Abor: University of Michigan Press 1988), 132–40; K. Warren, Su Delong, et al., 'Morbidity in Schistosomiasis Japonica in Relation to Intensity of Infection: A Study of Two Rural Brigades in Anhui Province, China', *The New England Journal of Medicine* 309, no. 25 (December 1982): 1,533–9.

10　Interview with Professor Yuan Hongchang in Shanghai, 5 April 2015.

11　'The Control of Schistosomiasis: Report of a WHO Expert Committee' (meeting held in Geneva from 8 to 13 November 1984) (Geneva: World Health Organization 1984): 82.

12　Zhou Xiaolong et al., '我国血吸虫病防治历程与监测 (Schistosomiasis Control and Surveillance in the PRC)', in Wang Delong, ed., 中国血吸虫病防历程与展望 (*The PRC's Schistosomiasis Control and Prospect*) (Beijing: Renmin weisheng chubanshe 2006), 61–2.

13　Chen Xianyi et al., 'Schistosomiasis Control in China: The Impact of a 10-Year World Bank Loan Project (1992–2001)', *Bulletin of the World Health Organization* 83, no. 1 (2005): 43–8; X.H. Wu, M.G. Chen, and J. Zheng, 'Surveillance of Schistosomiasis in Five Provinces of China Which Have Reached the National Criteria for Elimination of the Disease', *Acta Tropica* 96, nos. 2–3 (2005): 276–81.

14　J. Xu et al., 'Evolution of the National Schistosomiasis Control Programmes in the People's Republic of China', *Advances in Parasitology* 92, no. 1 (2016): 11–12.

15　Interview with Professor Gu Xueguang in Chengdu, Sichuan province, 11 September 2014; interview with Tang in Danlin, Sichuan province, 14 October 2014.

16　Jin Chen et al., '"Farewell to the God of Plague": The Importance of Political Commitment towards the Elimination of Schistosomiasis', *Tropical Medicine and Infectious Disease* 3, no. 108 (2018): 2.

17 Tom Williamson, 'The Disappearance of Malaria from the East Anglian Fens', *International Journal of Regional and Local Studies* 2, no. 2 (2006): 109–123; interview with Tang in Danling, Sichuan province, 14 October 2014.

18 '云南山地血吸虫疫情调查 (Report on Yunnan's Schistosomiasis)', CCTV Economic Channel's Economy Half Hour programme, broadcast at 21:30 on 5 July 2004; interview with Feng in Dali, Yunnan province, 13 November 2014.

19 Interview with Dr Wu in Jiaxing, Zhejiang province, May 2012; Jiaxing 143-005-477 (1995) 杜云昌市长在嘉兴第19次血防工作会议上的讲话 (Mayor Du Yunchang's speech at the 19th Jiaxing Schistosomiasis Control Meeting): 93.

20 Jiaxing 143-005-477 (1995) Mayor Du Yunchang's Speech at the 19th Jiaxing Schistosomiasis Control Meeting, 93; Q. Wang et al., 'Analysis of Endemic Changes of Schistosomiasis in China from 2002 to 2010', 中国血吸虫病防治杂志 (*China Journal of Schistosomiasis Control*) 27, no. 3 (June 2015): 229–34.

21 R. Zhu and J. Xu, 'Epidemic Situation of Overseas Imported Schistosomiasis in China and Thinking about Its Prevention and Control', 中国血吸虫病防治杂志 (*China Journal of Schistosomiasis Control*) 26, no. 2 (April 2014): 111–14.

22 J. Xu et al., 'Evolution of the National Schistosomiasis Control Programmes, 21.

23 Sui-Lee Wee, 'Lines, Bribes and Violence: A Health Care Crisis', *The New York Times*, 1 October 2018, A1.

24 Ibid.; also see 'Chinese Doctors Are under Threat', *The Lancet* (28 August 2010).

25 *Dying to Survive*, dir. Wen Muye (China, 2018), 115 mins.

26 Yanzhong Huang, 'If a Government Can't Deliver Safe Vaccines for Children, Is It Fit to Rule', *The New York Times*, 30 January 2019, https://www.nytimes.com/2019/01/30/opinion/china-vaccine-scandal-legitimacy.html.

27 Gabrielle M. Bryden et al., 'Anti-vaccination and Pro-CAM Attitudes Both Reflect Magical Beliefs about Health', *Vaccine* 36, no. 9 (2018): 1,227–34; Beth L. Hoffman et al., 'It's Not All about Autism: The Emerging Landscape of Anti-vaccination Sentiment on Facebook', *Vaccine* 37, no. 16 (2019): 2216–23.

Index